LIBRARY OF HEBREW BIBLE/
OLD TESTAMENT STUDIES

702

Formerly Journal for the Study of the Old Testament Supplement Series

Editors
Laura Quick, Oxford University, UK
Jacqueline Vayntrub, Yale University, USA

Founding Editors
David J. A. Clines, Philip R. Davies and David M. Gunn

Editorial Board
Sonja Ammann, Alan Cooper, Steed Davidson, Susan Gillingham,
Rachelle Gilmour, John Goldingay, Rhiannon Graybill, Anne Katrine Gudme,
Norman K. Gottwald, James E. Harding, John Jarick, Tracy Lemos,
Carol Meyers, Eva Mroczek, Daniel L. Smith-Christopher,
Francesca Stavrakopoulou, James W. Watts

NEW PERSPECTIVES ON RITUAL IN THE BIBLICAL WORLD

Edited by
Laura Quick and Melissa Ramos

LONDON • NEW YORK • OXFORD • NEW DELHI • SYDNEY

T&T CLARK
Bloomsbury Publishing Plc
50 Bedford Square, London, WC1B 3DP, UK
1385 Broadway, New York, NY 10018, USA
29 Earlsfort Terrace, Dublin 2, Ireland

BLOOMSBURY, T&T CLARK and the T&T Clark logo are trademarks of
Bloomsbury Publishing Plc

First published in Great Britain 2022
Paperback edition published 2024

Copyright © Laura Quick, Melissa Ramos and contributors, 2022

Laura Quick and Melissa Ramos have asserted their rights under the Copyright,
Designs and Patents Act, 1988, to be identified as Editors of this work.

For legal purposes the Acknowledgments on p. viii constitute an
extension of this copyright page.

All rights reserved. No part of this publication may be reproduced or transmitted in
any form or by any means, electronic or mechanical, including photocopying,
recording, or any information storage or retrieval system, without prior
permission in writing from the publishers.

Bloomsbury Publishing Plc does not have any control over, or responsibility for, any
third-party websites referred to or in this book. All internet addresses given in this
book were correct at the time of going to press. The author and publisher regret any
inconvenience caused if addresses have changed or sites have ceased to exist,
but can accept no responsibility for any such changes.

A catalogue record for this book is available from the British Library.

Library of Congress Control Number: 2022933747

ISBN: HB: 978-0-5676-9337-2
PB: 978-0-5677-0776-5
ePDF: 978-0-5676-9338-9

Series: Library of Hebrew Bible/Old Testament Studies, volume 702
ISSN 2513-8758

Typeset by Newgen KnowledgeWorks Pvt. Ltd., Chennai, India

To find out more about our authors and books visit www.bloomsbury.com
and sign up for our newsletters.

CONTENTS

List of Figures   vii
Acknowledgments   viii
List of Abbreviations   ix

INTRODUCTION   1

Part I
BODIES, GENDER, AND RITUAL

Chapter 1
AN INDECENT PROPOSAL OR A RITUALIZED QUEST FOR SURVIVAL?
THE THRESHING FLOOR EPISODE IN RUTH 3 RECONSIDERED
   Ekaterina E. Kozlova   13

Chapter 2
RITUAL, GENDER, AND HISTORY IN 1–2 KINGS
   Cat Quine   29

Chapter 3
MILK, MEAT, AND MOTHERS: THE PROBLEM OF MOTHERHOOD IN SOME RITUAL FOOD LAWS
   Nicole J. Ruane   51

Chapter 4
DRINKING THE GOLDEN CALF: CONSUMPTION AND TRANSFORMATION IN EXODUS 32
   Laura Quick   71

Part II
MAGIC AND RITUAL

Chapter 5
SATAN AND THE HIGH PRIEST: ZECHARIAH 3 AS EXORCISM
   Isabel Cranz   89

Chapter 6
CONTESTED DIVINATION: BIBLICAL NECROMANCY AND COMPETITION AMONG RITUAL SPECIALISTS IN ANCIENT ISRAEL
   Kerry M. Sonia   103

Chapter 7
BINDING ASMODEUS: A LEXICAL ANALYSIS OF THE RITUAL AND MEDICAL USE OF FISH IN TOBIT
Lindsey A. Askin — 117

Chapter 8
ENCHANT THE SABBATH DAY TO MAKE IT HOLY: CONJURATION AND PERFORMATIVITY IN EXODUS 20:8–11
Timothy Hogue — 139

Part III
TEXTUALIZATION AND RITUAL

Chapter 9
AARON'S BODY AS A RITUAL VESSEL IN THE EXODUS TABERNACLE BUILDING NARRATIVE
Alice Mandell — 159

Chapter 10
THE LITERARY REPRESENTATION OF SACRIFICE IN BIBLICAL NARRATIVE
Liane M. Feldman — 183

Chapter 11
THE OFFERINGS OF THE TRIBAL LEADERS, THE PURIFICATION OF THE LEVITES, AND THE HERMENEUTICS OF RITUAL INNOVATION
Nathan MacDonald — 199

Chapter 12
MONUMENTALIZING SLAUGHTER: "CUTTING A COVENANT" IN THE HEBREW BIBLE AND LEVANTINE INSCRIPTIONS
Melissa Ramos — 213

Chapter 13
SILVER SCRIPTS: THE RITUAL FUNCTION OF PURIFIED METAL IN ANCIENT JUDAH
Jeremy D. Smoak — 237

List of Contributors — 255
Index of Scripture — 257
Author Index — 267

FIGURES

1 Rosette Stamp Seal Impressions on a Storage Jar (Site of Khirbet el-Garra)   173
2 Inscribed Rim of a Stone Bowl, Šmʿyw son of ʿzr (ninth–eighth century BCE)   176
3 Kuntillet ʿAjrud Inscribed Stone Bowl (ninth–eighth century BCE)   177
4 Rim Inscription   178
5 Chart of Vessels Inscribed with QDŠ   179
6 Shoulder Inscription on a Krater, Beersheba   179

ACKNOWLEDGMENTS

One of the nicest things about finishing any project is the opportunity to thank those who helped us along the way. We would like to thank Claudia V. Camp and Andrew Mein for accepting our volume to LHBOTS, and Lucy Carroll, Lily McMahon, and Dominic Mattos for shepherding us through the process so smoothly at Bloomsbury. We also wish to thank Noah Dale for his work compiling the Scriptural Index for this volume. Melissa Ramos would like to thank George Fox University's Faculty Development Grant Committee for the research leave that supported in part the completion of this project (GFU2019-20L1). Finally, we wish to express our thanks to each of the contributors to this volume whose original scholarship and exciting ideas added momentum to our own and whose good humor and perseverance to write in the midst of a global pandemic made this collection of essays an especially rewarding project.

ABBREVIATIONS

AB	Anchor Bible
ABD	Freedman, David Noel et al. 1992. *Anchor Yale Bible Dictionary*, 6 vols. (Garden City, NY: Doubleday)
AfO	*Archiv für Orientforschung*
AHSNM	Acta historica scientiarum naturalium et medicinalium
AHw	von Soden, Wolfram. 1868–1947. *Akkadisches Handwörterbuch: unter Benutzung des lexikalischen Nachlasses von Bruno Meissner* (Wiesbaden: Harrassowitz)
Akk.	Akkadian
AMT	Thompson, R. C. 1923. *Assyrian Medical Texts* (Oxford: Clarendon)
ANEM	Ancient Near East Monographs
Ant.	Josephus, *Antiquitates judaicae*
Anthol.	Vettius Valens, *Anthology*
AOAT	Alter Orient und Altes Testament
AramSt	*Aramaic Studies*
ARM	Archives royales de Mari
AT	Arslan Tash
b. Ber.	Babylonian Talmud Berakhot
b. Ḥul.	Babylonian Talmud Ḥullin
b. Qidd.	Babylonian Talmud Qiddushin
b. Zar.	Babylonian Talmud Avodah Zarah
BaF	Baghdader Forschungen
BAM	Köcher, F. 1963–. *Die babylonisch-assyrische Medizin in Texten und Untersuchungen* (Berlin: de Gruyter)
BAR	*Biblical Archaeology Review*
BASOR	*Bulletin of the American School of Oriental Research*
BDB	Brown, Francis, S. R. Driver, and Charles A. Briggs. 2005. *Brown-Driver-Briggs Hebrew and English Lexicon: With an Appendix Containing the Biblical Aramaic* (repr.; Peabody, MA: Hendrickson)
BETL	Bibliotheca Ephemeridum Theologicarum Lovaniensium
BGU	*Ägyptische Urkunden aus den königlichen Museen zu Berlin: Griechische Urkunden* (Berlin, 1863–)
Bib	*Biblica*
BibInt	*Biblical Interpretation*
BibOr	*Bibliotheca Orientalis*
BibTr	*The Bible Translator*
BINS	Biblical Interpretation Series
BJS	Brown Judaic Studies
BKAT	Biblischer Kommentar, Altes Testament

BR	*Bible Review*
BZABR	Beihefte zur Zeitschrift für Altorientalische und Biblische Rechtsgeschichte
BZAW	Beihefte zur Zeitschrift für die alttestamentliche Wissenschaft
c.	circa
CAD	Roth, Martha T. 1956–2010. *The Assyrian Dictionary*. 21 vols. (Chicago: Oriental Institute of the University of Chicago)
CBC	Cambridge Bible Commentaries
CBQ	*Catholic Biblical Quarterly*
CBQMS	Catholic Biblical Quarterly Monograph Series
CBS	Museum siglum of the University Museum in Philadelphia (Catalogue of the Babylonian Section)
CEJL	Commentaries on Early Jewish Literature
CHANE	Culture and History of the Ancient Near East
CSHB	Critical Studies in the Hebrew Bible
CTH	*Catalogue of Hittite Texts*
Cyr.	Xenophon, *Cyropaedia*
D	Deuteronomy
DCH	Clines, David J. A., ed. 1993. *The Dictionary of Classical Hebrew*. 8 vols. (Sheffield: Sheffield Academic Press)
DCLS	Deuterocanonical and Cognate Literature Studies
DDD	van der Toorn, Karel, Bob Becking, and Pieter W. van der Horst, eds. 1999. *Dictionary of Deities and Demons in the Bible* (2nd ed.; Leiden: Brill).
De morbis Mul.	Hippocrates, *De morbis Mulierum*
De natura animal.	Claudius Aelianus, *De natura animalium*
DJD	Discoveries in the Judean Desert
DSD	*Dead Sea Discoveries*
DtrH	Deuteronomistic History
EBR	Helmer, Christine et al. eds. 2009–19. *Encyclopedia of the Bible and Its Reception*, 17 vols. (Leiden: Brill)
EI	*Eretz-Israel*
FAT	Forschungen zum Alten Testament
fol.	folio
FSBP	Fontes et subsidia ad Bibliam pertinentes
G^I	Short Recension of Greek Tobit
G^{II}	Long Recension of Greek Tobit
G^{III}	Intermediary Recension of Greek Tobit
Haem.	Hippocrates, *Haemorrhoids*
HALOT	Koehler, Ludwig and Walter Baumgartner. 2001. *The Hebrew and Aramaic Lexicon of the Old Testament* (Leiden: Brill)
HAR	*Hebrew Annual Review*
HBM	Hebrew Bible Monographs
HBS	Herders biblische Studien
HCANE	Studies in the History and Culture of the Ancient Near East
HdO	Handbuch der Orientalistik

Abbreviations

HeBAI	*Hebrew Bible and Ancient Israel*
Hier.	Xenophon, *Hiero*
HS	*Hebrew Studies*
HSM	Harvard Semitic Monographs
HTKzAT	Herders Theologischer Kommentar zum Alten Testament
HTR	*Harvard Theological Review*
HUCA	*Hebrew Union College Annual*
HzAT	Handbuch zum Alten Testament
ICC	International Critical Commentary
IEJ	*Israel Exploration Journal*
IG	*Inscriptiones Graecae, consilio et auctoritate Academiae Scientiarum Berolinensis et Brandenburgensis editaei* (Berlin, 1873–)
Int	*Interpretation: A Journal of Bible and Theology*
IosPE I^2	Latyshev, V. 1916. *Inscriptiones Antiquae Orae Septentrionalis Pontis Euxini Graecae et Latinae*. Vol. 1: *Inscriptiones Tyriae, Olbiae, Chersonesi Taurice* (2nd ed.; St. Petersburg)
JANER	*Journal of Ancient Near Eastern Religions*
JANES	*Journal of Ancient Near Eastern Studies*
JAOS	*Journal of the American Oriental Society*
Jastrow	Jastrow, Marcus. 1903. *A Dictionary of the Targumim, the Talmud Babli and Yerushalmi, and the Midrashic Literature* (New York: Shalom)
JBL	*Journal of Biblical Literature*
JCS	*Journal of Cuneiform Studies*
JEA	*Journal of Egyptian Archaeology*
JHS	*Journal of Hebrew Scriptures*
JJS	*Journal of Jewish Studies*
JNES	*Journal of Near Eastern Studies*
JNSL	*Journal of Northwest Semitic Languages*
JPC	*The Journal of Popular Culture*
JPS	Jewish Publication Society
JQR	*Jewish Quarterly Review*
JSJ	*Journal for the Study of Judaism*
JSJSup	Journal for the Study of Judaism Supplements
JSOT	*Journal for the Study of the Old Testament*
JSOTS	Journal for the Study of the Old Testament Supplement Series
JSP	*Journal for the Study of the Pseudepigrapha*
JSQ	*Jewish Studies Quarterly*
JSSS	Journal of Semitic Studies Supplement Series
JTS	*Journal of Theological Studies*
KAI	Donner, Herbert and Wolfgang Röllig. 2002. *Kanaanäische und aramäische Inschriften 1* (Wiesbaden: Harrassowitz)
KTU^3	Dietrich, Manfred, Oswald Loretz, and Joaquín Sanmartín. 2013. *Die keilalphabetischen Texte aus Ugarit, Ras Ibn Hani und anderen Orten* (3rd ed.; Münster: Ugarit-Verlag)
LAB	Pseudo-Philo, *Liber antiquitatum biblicarum*
LBH	Late Biblical Hebrew

LCL	Loeb Classical Library
LEH	Lust, Johan, Erik Eynikel, and Katrin Hauspie, eds. 2015. *Greek-English Lexicon of the Septuagint* (3rd ed. Stuttgart: Deutsche Bibelgesellschaft)
LHBOTS	Library of Hebrew Bible/Old Testament Studies
Louw-Nida	Louw, J. P. and Eugene A. Nida, eds. 1989. *Greek-English Lexicon of the New Testament: Based on Semantic Domains*. 2 vols. (2nd ed.; New York: United Bible Societies)
LSJ	Liddell, H., et al. 1940. *A Greek-English Lexicon* (9th ed.; Oxford: Clarendon)
LSTS	Library of Second Temple Studies
LXX	Septuagint
m. Ḥul.	Mishnah Ḥullin
m. Qid.	Mishnah Qiddushin
m. Soṭah	Mishnah Soṭah
MH	Mishnaic Hebrew
MM	Pedanius Dioscorides, *De materia medica*
MRLA	Magical and Religious Literature of Late Antiquity
MS(S)	manuscript(s)
MT	Masoretic Text
NCBC	New Century Bible Commentary
NEA	*Near Eastern Archaeology*
NET	New English Translation
NETS	New English Translation of the Septuagint
NH	Pliny the Elder, *Natural History*
Nich.	Aristotle, *Nicomachean Ethics*
NICOT	New International Commentary on the Old Testament
NJPS	New Jewish Publication Society
NRSV	New Revised Standard Version
NT	New Testament
NTOA	Novum Testamentum et orbis antiquus
OBO	Orbis biblicus et orientalis
Or	*Orientalia*
OTL	Old Testament Library
OtSt	Oudtestamentische Studiën
P.Ebers	Papyrus Ebers
P.Grenf.	Grenfell, B. P., ed. 1896. *An Alexandrian Erotic Fragment and Other Greek Papyri Chiefly Ptolemaic* (Oxford: Clarendon)
P.Mag.Leid.	Dieterich, A., ed. 1891. *Leiden Magical Papyrus W. Abraxas: Studien zur Religionsgeschichte des spätern Altertums* (Leipzig: Societas Philologa)
P.Mich.	Michigan Papyri. 19 vols. (1931–99)
P.Oxy.	*The Oxyrhynchus Papyri* (London, 1898–)
PGM	Preisendanz, Karl. 1973. *Papyri Graecae Magicae*, ed. Albert Henrichs (Stuttgart: Teubner)
Prog.	Hippocrates, *Prognostics*
Prorrh.	Hippocrates, *Prorrhetic*
QH	Qumran Hebrew
r.	recto
RevBib	*Revue Biblique*

RevQ	*Revue de Qumrân*
SAA	State Archives of Assyria
SAA 20	Parpola, Simo. 2017. *Assyrian Royal Rituals and Cultic Texts* (SAA 20; Helsinki: Neo-Assyrian Text Corpus Project)
SAAS	State Archives of Assyria Studies
SBL	Society of Biblical Literature
SBLANEM	Society of Biblical Literature Ancient Near East Monographs
SBLDS	Society of Biblical Literature Dissertation Series
SBLSCS	Society of Biblical Literature Septuagint and Cognate Studies
SBLWAW	Society of Biblical Literature Writings from the Ancient World
SBS	Stuttgarter Bibelstudien
SCS	Septuagint and Cognate Studies
SJOT	*Scandinavian Journal of the Old Testament*
SJSHRZ	Studien zu den Jüdischen Schriften aus hellenistisch-römischer Zeit
STE	Esarhaddon's Succession Treaties
TA	*Tel Aviv*
Targ. Neof.	Targum Neofiti
Targ. Onq	Targum Onqelos
TDOT	Botterweck, G. Johannes, Helmer Ringgren, and Heinz-Josef Fabry, eds. 1977–2012. *Theological Dictionary of the Old Testament*, 15 vols. (Winona Lake, IN: Eerdmans)
TOTC	Tyndale Old Testament Commentaries
UDB	*Ugaritic Data Bank*
UF	*Ugarit-Forschungen*
Virt.	Philo, *de Virtutibus*
VL	Vetus Latina
Vlg	Vulgate
VT	*Vetus Testamentum*
VTSup	Vetus Testamentum Supplements
War	Josephus, *Jewish War*
WBC	Word Biblical Commentary
WO	*Die Welt des Orients*
ZAR	*Zeitschrift für altorientalische und biblische Rechtsgeschichte*
ZAW	*Zeitschrift für die alttestamentliche Wissenschaft*
ZDPV	*Zeitschrift des Deutschen Palästina-Vereins*
[ ]	reconstruction
...	uncertain reading or lost
°	uncertain letter

INTRODUCTION

Laura Quick and Melissa Ramos

This collection of thirteen previously unpublished essays explores the ritual background of the Hebrew Bible. Each essay takes a narrow focus, grappling with a particular ritual phenomenon or text from biblical literature. But taken together, these essays present a broad overview of ritual action encompassing subjects that have habitually been the focus of ritual studies, such as sacrifice, as well as a diverse range of other ritual phenomena and practices of personal piety that, to date, have not been given as much attention in scholarship. This collection makes a unique contribution to the field of ritual studies in Hebrew Bible research in three ways: (1) Texts that have traditionally been understudied in the context of the ritual canon, such as the books of Kings or Ruth, are mined for their ritual content. (2) Alongside the traditional tools of biblical scholarship such as historical criticism and comparative methods, these essays bring new methodological approaches and questions to bear on current discourse around texts traditionally included in the ritual canon, such as gender and food studies, the elision of the categories of magic and ritual, and the interplay between ritual action and materiality. (3) Several of the essays in this collection take advantage of the recent increase in the publication of ancient Near Eastern ritual texts and supply fresh data or make hitherto unacknowledged connections between that corpus and the ritual corpus in biblical literature.

In particular, this collection of essays emphasizes materiality and embodiment in the study of religious practices, highlighting three broad areas that are essential for reconstructing the ritual world of the Hebrew Bible: Part I explores the intersection of ritual with gender and the body; Part II problematizes the boundaries of ritual practice into official and nonofficial spheres; while Part III explores the nature of biblical ritual as a textualized phenomenon. In so doing, these essays provide a reorientation of discourse on ritual in biblical literature and shift it beyond the centralized cult of state religion that is constructed and endorsed by the Hebrew Bible to encompass the religious lives of more marginalized socioreligious groups. As such, this volume provides a fuller perspective on the religious world that shaped the Hebrew Bible.

The number of recently published essays and books focused on ritual phenomena from the world of ancient Israel and Judah demonstrates an uptick in interest among scholars of the Hebrew Bible with ritual and religious practice. Since ritual studies is more of a field than a methodology,[1] work in the area of ritual tends to be interdisciplinary and is open to a variety of commingled approaches.[2] However, the relative openness of the field of ritual studies has also led to methodological obstacles and has created a lack of coherence around the study of ritual phenomena in biblical literature. For example, biblical scholars must rely upon overly technical specialized literature from the fields of anthropology and sociology for the theoretical underpinnings of ritual studies. Moreover, there is a significant difficulty in applying methods originally drawn from modern ethnographic study to ancient texts and phenomena: the descriptions of ritual found in the Hebrew Bible do not provide a precise textual account of the ritual process in the way that modern ethnographic studies do, and instead present a narration of that process that may or may not significantly deviate from actual practice.[3]

The challenges inherent to a ritual studies approach require intentionality and a deliberate reflection on theoretical underpinnings. The methodological complexity of ritual studies has led to a number of studies that focus on a narrow concept or a single corpus in the biblical literature,[4] while fewer attempt a broader

---

1. Ronald Grimes, "Ritual Studies," *Encyclopedia of Religion* 12 (2012): 422; *The Craft of Ritual Studies* (Oxford Scholarship Online, 2014), 4 (doi:10.1093/acprof:oso/9780195301427.001.0001).

2. For an overview of the origins of ritual studies, see Paul Post, "*Ritual Studies*" (Oxford Research Encyclopedia of Religion, 2015), 1–33 (doi:10.1093/acrefore/9780199340378.013.21).

3. This phenomenological dilemma has led some scholars to significantly criticize the application of ritual theory to understanding ritual phenomena in the Hebrew Bible. Specifically countering the application of Victor Turner's description of the ritual process to the book of Leviticus, for example, Rolf Knierim described the problem thus: "The prescription of a ritual in a text is not identical with the description of an observed ritual, let alone with a performed ritual itself." See Rolf Knierim, *Text and Concept in Leviticus 1:1–9* (FAT 2; Tübingen: Mohr Siebeck, 1992), 19–20.

4. Several edited volumes focus on a single topic such as Christian A. Eberhart, ed., *Ritual and Metaphor: Sacrifice in the Bible* (Resources for Biblical Study 68; Atlanta, GA: SBL Press, 2011); Brad E. Kelle, Frank Ritchel Ames, and Jacob L. Wright, eds., *Warfare, Ritual, and Symbol in Biblical and Modern Contexts* (Ancient Israel and Its Literature 18; Atlanta, GA: SBL Press, 2014); Nathan MacDonald, ed., *Ritual Innovation in the Hebrew Bible and Early Judaism* (BZAW 468; Berlin: de Gruyter, 2016); Naphtali S. Meshel, David P. Wright, Jeffrey Stackert and Baruch J. Schwartz, eds., *Perspectives on Purity and Purification in the Bible* (LHBOTS 128; London: T&T Clark, 2008); Saul M. Olyan, ed., *Ritual Violence in the Hebrew Bible: New Perspectives* (Oxford: Oxford University Press, 2015). A number of monographs also focus on a single topic, a methodological approach to ritual, or a single textual corpus such William K. Gilders, *Blood Ritual in the Hebrew Bible: Meaning and*

overview.⁵ This volume aims to address the openness of ritual studies as a field by presenting a set of articles that employ a broad range of interdisciplinary approaches but that are focused around common themes. Thus, the volume emphasizes the interdisciplinary nature of ritual studies as a field and seeks both to capitalize on its multifaceted epistemology and to focus discussion around three major methodological approaches: gender studies, history and comparative religion approaches, and anthropological studies of the social meanings of textualized representations of ritual action.

Part I: Bodies, Gender, and Ritual

Part I of this volume examines the intersection of ritual and embodiment in biblical texts outside of the priestly literature. With its vast and varied descriptions and prescriptions of and for ritual procedures, the priestly literature has been a key focus of studies concerned with ritual practice in the biblical world.⁶ In the

---

Power (Baltimore, MD: Johns Hopkins University Press, 2004); David Janzen, *The Social Meaning of Sacrifice in the Hebrew Bible: A Study of Four Writings* (BZAW 344; Berlin: de Gruyter, 2004); Jonathan David Lawrence, *Washing in Water: Trajectories of Ritual Bathing in the Hebrew Bible and Second Temple Literature* (Academia Biblical 23; Atlanta, GA: SBL Press, 2006); Saul M. Olyan, *Violent Rituals of the Hebrew Bible* (Oxford: Oxford University Press, 2019); Melissa Ramos, *Ritual in Deuteronomy: The Performance of Doom* (The Ancient Word; London: Routledge, 2021); Jaime L. Waters, *Threshing Floors in Ancient Israel: Their Ritual and Symbolic Significance* (Minneapolis, MN: Fortress Press, 2015).

5. A classic work that attempts a more sweeping overview of ritual in the Hebrew Bible from an anthropological perspective is Ithamar Gruenwald's *Rituals and Ritual Theory in Ancient Israel* (The Brill Reference Library of Judaism 10; Atlanta, GA: SBL Press, 2003). An introductory textbook that provides an overview of ritual theory from the perspective of social sciences is Gerald A. Klingbeil, *Bridging the Gap: Ritual and Ritual Texts in the Bible* (Winona Lake, IN: Eisenbrauns, 2007). A reference work that provides a broad overview of ritual practices in the Hebrew Bible is Samuel E. Balentine's *The Oxford Handbook of Ritual and Worship in the Hebrew Bible* (Oxford: Oxford University Press, 2020).

6. The priestly source in general and the book of Leviticus in particular are well represented in treatments of biblical rituals. For example, James W. Watts, *Ritual and Rhetoric in Leviticus: From Sacrifice to Scripture* (Cambridge: Cambridge University Press, 2007), uses rhetorical analysis to focus on the persuasive intentions of the biblical book. Wesley J. Bergen, *Reading Ritual: Leviticus in Postmodern Culture* (LHBOTS 417; London: T&T Clark, 2005), focuses on Leviticus 1–7. Bryan D. Bibb, *Ritual Words and Narrative Worlds in the Book of Leviticus* (LHBOTS 192; London: T&T Clark, 2009), looks at both legal prescriptions and narrative descriptions of ritual in the book of Leviticus. Leigh M. Trevaskis, *Holiness, Ethics and Ritual in Leviticus* (Sheffield: Sheffield Phoenix Press, 2011), focuses on Leviticus 1–16, arguing that holiness in these chapters has both an ethical and a ritual dimension.

main, these procedures concern a system of practice concentrated upon the Jerusalem Temple—and, as such, the religious lives of only a very small subsection of society, the male priesthood. The essays in this segment provide an important corrective by focusing on ritual in biblical literature (1) in texts outside of the typical ritual studies canon such as the books of Ruth and Kings; and (2) using the interpretational frameworks of materiality, corporeality, and especially gendered bodies. Women ritual practitioners are prominently featured in this segment, whether as ritual leaders, initiators of oaths, mothers, or performers of ritual actions. Embodiment more generally provides a lens through which to reinterpret and reconfigure existing perspectives on well-known texts. In so doing, these essays reorient discussion of biblical ritual to include diverse practices encompassing women's religion, personal piety, and other practices that were unendorsed by the centralized cult, such as rituals of inversion.

Ekaterina E. Kozlova's "An Indecent Proposal or a Ritualized Quest for Survival? The Threshing Floor Episode in Ruth 3 Reconsidered" examines a seemingly scandalous episode from the book of Ruth involving the uncovering and touching of a man's genitals by a young woman late at night in a secluded location. But utilizing an interpretational framework of embodiment and materiality, Kozlova recontextualizes the episode in light of the role of the reproductive organs in biblical and ancient Near Eastern oath-making rituals, in which the genitals function as sensory organs that participate in the construction of meaning. According to Kozlova, the uncovering of the body of Boaz by Ruth constitutes a ritual act in which she initiates a marriage oath by touching Boaz's body. This represents a reversal of traditional expectations in biblical and Near Eastern literature that typically feature male characters as ritual initiators and practitioners. Kozlova argues that Ruth's actions at the threshing floor should be understood as a ritualized marriage proposal that would ensure economic stability for herself and Naomi.

Like Kozlova's essay, Cat Quine's "Ritual, Gender, and History in 1–2 Kings" also explores female characters as ritual practitioners. Quine's essay explores the role of textual authority in narratives of women ritual practitioners, observing that religious narratives create socially constructed versions of history that especially empower anonymous authors of accepted texts and their presentations of events. Quine argues that women such as Athaliah, Maacah, Jezebel, and Huldah are portrayed in biblical literature playing powerful roles in politics and the cult; however, their roles as ritual practitioners are deliberately omitted from their narratives. Quine's essay explores how ritual communicates power and how this is gendered. According to Quine, the textualization of ritual in biblical narratives serves a rhetorical purpose of creating consensus around ritual legitimacy by constructing for the reader a positive view of male ritual practitioners while problematizing female practitioners. Since the text is the arbiter of ritual authority, argues Quine, its canonization bolsters these perspectives of ritual authority as gendered that are embedded within the text.

Gender and ritual performance are also the focus of Nicole J. Ruane's "Milk, Meat, and Mothers: The Problem of Motherhood in Some Ritual Food Laws." According to Ruane, the biology of motherhood is problematized in the ritual laws of the Pentateuch by the exclusion of mothers from sacred foods and other ritual activities. This prohibition of sacrifices associated with motherhood includes both human mothers and animal mothers. According to Pentateuchal law, human mothers are regarded as impure after giving birth and during menstruation; thus, they are prevented from participating in sacrificial ritual worship during these states. Ruane argues convincingly that the exclusion of milk and eggs from the sacrificial system is also due to its association with motherhood and femininity. Furthermore, certain laws also prohibit eating animal mothers as sacrificial victims. However, Ruane also observes that the exclusion of mothers and food products derived from motherhood does not imply that motherhood is viewed negatively in the Pentateuch; rather that symbols of maternity express one of the social functions of cultic practice in the Hebrew Bible, which was to enact separation between offspring and mothers.

Laura Quick's "Drinking the Golden Calf: Consumption and Transformation in Exodus 32" also explores materiality, corporeality, and consumption, in this case in the narrative of the destruction of the Golden Calf. After burning the calf with fire, grinding it into powder, and mixing it with water, Moses forces the Israelites to drink the resultant mixture. Like the other essays in this section, Quick emphasizes the role of bodies as agents of cultic action and especially ingestion as a ritual act. Quick's essay compares the Golden Calf episode with other narratives of cultic destruction of illicit ritual objects and practices in the Hebrew Bible and Ugaritic religious literature. In this comparative analysis, Quick's essay also features an exploration of women's reproductive organs as the locus of ritual action in Numbers 5 and the role of a female ritual practitioner in Anat's destruction of Mot in the Ugaritic Baal Cycle. In these narratives, unsanctioned cultic innovations are reversed by performative actions of burning, grinding, and scattering. But the Golden Calf narrative takes this further in its depiction of forced consumption. Here, Quick contends, the act of consumption is one of "ritual inversion": eating the object transforms it from a dangerous and illicit substance into an ordinary and benign one in a ritual of desacralization. Thus, just as the calf was ritually formed by melting objects taken from bodies, namely jewelry, it is destroyed by ingesting the object within bodies. The danger of the calf is mitigated as its divinity is denied and the calf incorporated back into the mundane realm.

Part II: Magic and Ritual

The essays in Part II of this volume explore the boundaries between ritual practices that are presented in the Hebrew Bible as legitimate versus ambiguous or exoticized,[7]

---

7. For these terms and relative juxtapositions, see David Frankfurter, "Ancient Magic in a New Key: Refining an Exotic Discipline in the History of Religions," in *Guide to the Study of Ancient Magic*, ed. David Frankfurter (Religions in the Graeco-Roman World 128; Leiden: Brill, 2019), 3–7.

such as exorcism, necromancy, and the conjuring of deities or persons. These essays challenge the traditional bifurcation between sanctioned ritual actions and magic or illicit ritual practices by exploring the elision of expiation with exorcism, necromancy with prophecy, and remembering with conjuring. The essays in this segment bring fresh comparative data to bear on the biblical texts that center on ritual activity by engaging with previously unexamined texts from the ancient Near East including Namburbi incantation texts, as well as necromantic and exorcistic texts. The comparative analyses in these essays demonstrate conceptual overlap, parallel terminology, and imagery between biblical texts and extra-biblical literature typically categorized as magical. This segment of the volume brings a methodology of ritual studies to discussions about ritual and alterity, and about ritual practitioners whom biblical literature portrays as either mainstream or marginalized.[8]

Isabel Cranz's "Satan and the High Priest: Zechariah 3 as Exorcism" explores commonalities between ritual actions whose aim is to attain divine expiation, or forgiveness, and those that aim to perform an exorcism. Cranz compares the visionary account of Joshua's installation as high priest in Zechariah 3 with Namburbi incantation texts and observes several parallels. According to Cranz, Zechariah 3 and the Namburbi ritual texts share the following features: a literary setting of a messenger before a divine council, a common theme of the messenger receiving an omen of doom, and proscribed ritual actions intended to avert the prophesied doom that include changing clothing as a symbol of purification. Cranz also observes that, while the Namburbi texts center on seeking forgiveness, the Zechariah 3 vision communicates that forgiveness has already been granted. Both the Namburbi texts and Zechariah 3 focus on the banishment of evil with shared imagery, especially of the clothing change. The parallel imagery and ritual systems presented by Cranz suggest conceptual overlap between exorcism in Mesopotamian incantation texts and expiation in biblical prophetic literature.

Like Cranz, Kerry M. Sonia also explores the boundaries between ritual practices that are considered legitimate by the authors of biblical literature and practices that are problematized or viewed as unorthodox. In "Contested Divination: Biblical Necromancy and Competition among Ritual Specialists in Ancient Israel," Sonia examines the episode in 1 Samuel 28 of Saul consulting the necromancer of Endor in order to consult with the ghost of Samuel. According to Sonia, necromancy has overlap with divination and prophecy since both are accomplished by consulting with ritual specialists whose field involves furnishing specialized or otherwise inaccessible information. One might conclude that necromancy should be regarded as a subset of prophecy, given the overlap between these roles. Sonia proposes that the necromancer of Endor should be understood as a ritual specialist in competition with other ritual specialists for social power, privilege, or material gain. According to Sonia's framework, rhetoric against

---

8. See Frankfurter, "Ancient Magic in a New Key," for a more thorough discussion of magic and alterity.

necromancy in biblical literature can be interpreted as propaganda by authors seeking to undermine certain classes of ritual specialists by exoticizing them while bolstering the authority of others by presenting them as orthodox practitioners.

Lindsay A. Askin's "Binding Asmodeus: A Lexical Analysis of the Ritual and Medical Use of Fish in Tobit" examines the elision between ritual practices traditionally categorized as medical versus magic. Utilizing a comparative and lexicographical approach, Askin explores the ritual use of fish products in Tobit in light of exorcistic rituals in Mesopotamian ritual incantation texts such as *Maqlû* and *Šurpu*. Askin argues that while exorcism is commonly associated with artifacts traditionally associated with magic, such as Aramaic bowls, it was part of ancient Jewish religious practice and medical knowledge. Askin concludes that the ritual fumigation practices in Tobit have an exorcistic function and employ lexicography typically associated with exorcistic practices. Like Cranz, Askin posits an overlap between exorcistic practices, concepts, and terminology in ritual texts outside of the Bible with those found in the book of Tobit.

In "Enchant the Sabbath Day to Make It Holy: Conjuration and Performativity in Exodus 20:8–11," Timothy Hogue interprets the command to "remember" (זכר) the commandments in Exodus 20 as a ritual performance enacted to imbue the day with the divine. Hogue's comparative study of the ancient Near Eastern uses of the term זכר ("remember") demonstrates that the implication of this term is a ritual action taken in order to invoke the presence of a deity. Hogue argues convincingly that ancient Near Eastern ritual conceptual frameworks view ontological categories such as cause and effect per ritual agent and recipient as blended and overlapping rather than as divergent or distinct. According to Hogue, the ritual term זכר represents both a cognitive category and a materialized form of the idea; thus, to זכר something is a performative act that conjures it, or brings it into material being. Hogue posits ritual as a participatory act and as a form of being and זכר as an act of participating in the being of God. Hogue's essay also challenges the boundaries between native and sanctioned ritual practice and other forms of ritual enactment typically viewed as magical or exoticized practice. According to Hogue, one of the most commonly mentioned ritual practices in the Hebrew Bible, observing the Sabbath, has overlap with practices that might be considered as magical in extra-biblical literature.

Part III: Textualization and Ritual

Part III explores the interplay between ritual and text. Any account of ritual in the biblical world is necessarily based in the main upon a written product, namely the Hebrew Bible. Instead of observing actual ritual practice, the object of study is instead the biblical texts that purport to describe these practices—or, more likely, to *prescribe* them: to establish and normalize various behaviors within an idealized system, which reflects the ideologies and preferences of the Yehud literati. At the same time, and because of the location of literacy largely within the domain of this elite group, writing itself becomes numinous, employed with ritual efficacy. Utilizing a comparative approach, the essays in this section bring together a diverse set of texts including not only biblical literature but also epigraphic remains such as ancient Near Eastern treaty texts, seal impressions, and the Ketef Hinnom amulets. While the focus of the individual essays is diverse, unpacking various ritualized behaviors including not only sacrifice but also ritual dress and performance, all of the essays reflect upon the interplay of writing and ritual in the world of the Hebrew Bible.

Alice Mandell explores "Aaron's Body as a Ritual Vessel" by focusing upon the inscribed gemstones and headdress that were affixed to the shoulders, chest, and forehead of the High Priest. In particular, Mandell addresses two important and hitherto underexplored aspects of these inscriptions: namely, their execution in the manner of "seal engravings" (פתוחי חתם) that suggests an analogy to seals and sealing practices; as well as their location and layout on Aaron's body, analogous to the inscribed pottery vessels that were ubiquitous in the southern Levant and used in cultic contexts. By utilizing a methodologically innovative approach, Mandell emphasizes the multimodality of these inscriptions as both linguistic objects and also material things that communicate not only through their words but also through their design, context, and spatial layout. Through these inscriptions, the body of the High Priest is remade: Aaron is marked as a "dedicated" thing, an authorized ritual vessel dedicated to the cult of YHWH.

Liane M. Feldman also focuses upon the priestly cult in "The Literary Representation of Sacrifice in Biblical Narrative," making an important observation: scholarship focused upon sacrificial practice in the Hebrew Bible has primarily been studied through the lens of ritual theory as representative of a version of actual historical practice. But we must also recall, Feldman argues, that these texts are pieces of *literature*, and descriptions of sacrifice within the Hebrew Bible are nearly always embedded within larger narrative contexts. By approaching two sacrificial texts through a literary perspective, Feldman shifts the discussion from attempts at historical reconstruction to instead unpack these texts through literary analysis. In so doing, she uncovers the ways in which the description of sacrifice in 1 Kings 18 functions to create satire and humor in the Elijah cycle. Sacrifice in the book of Leviticus, on the other hand, constructs as well as subverts boundaries within the tent of meeting and the Israelite encampment. Ultimately, Feldman's intervention demonstrates the interpretative possibilities raised by the nature of biblical sacrificial texts as textualized objects and therefore pieces of literature.

A similar concern for biblical ritual as literature is found in Nathan MacDonald's "The Offerings of the Tribal Leaders, the Purification of the Levites, and the Hermeneutics of Ritual Innovation." MacDonald explores two rituals from the book of Numbers: Num 7:1–88, in which the leaders of the secular tribes bring offerings to the Tabernacle; and Num 8:5–22, in which Moses and the Israelites are purified in order to be made ready for service in the sanctuary. The former is apparently devised by the tribal leaders on their own initiative, while the latter is enjoined upon Moses and the Israelites by the Lord—but both rituals essentially function to provide a role for the secular tribes and the Levites in the inauguration of the Temple. Employing a methodologically plural approach encompassing historical criticism, narrative criticism, literary theory, ritual theory, and inner-biblical interpretation, MacDonald explores the ways in which these two texts develop subtle intertextual connections with other existing ritual texts. As such, MacDonald uncovers a literary strategy in which ritual innovation is authorized by means of a sophisticated bricolage. These textualized rituals do not therefore reflect actual ritual practice but were instead constructed to make a larger theological point about the respective status of priests and Levites, a larger literary concern of the book of Numbers.

The interplay of actual ritual practice with the textualized language through which it is described in the Hebrew Bible is also a starting point of Melissa Ramos's "Monumentalizing Slaughter: 'Cutting a Covenant' in the Hebrew Bible and Levantine Inscriptions." Ramos considers the technical linguistic terminology for oath-making found throughout the Hebrew Bible in light of the ritual performances inherent to the ratification of treaties and covenants. Thus, the expression "to cut a covenant" (לכרות ברית) directly encapsulates the ritual practice of slaughtering animals that accompanied the ratification of treaties and oaths in the ancient Levant. Through her comparative analysis drawing upon a range of epigraphic remains, Ramos demonstrates that animal sacrifice was a particularly West Semitic feature of treaty enactment. But beyond animal sacrifice, Ramos shifts the discussion by highlighting an important diachronic development in the ritual practice of Iron Age treaty formulation, in which the emphasis upon ritual slaughter is replaced with a concern for enacting covenant via monumentality and textualization. The expression "to cut a covenant" thus reflects not only sacrificial action but also the process of cutting, inscribing, and erecting stone monuments as a symbol of the covenant.

Symbolic writing is also a focus of the final essay of Part III, Jeremy D. Smoak's "Silver Scripts: The Ritual Function of Purified Metal in Ancient Judah." Smoak begins with an important observation: the Ketef Hinnom amulets have been primarily explored in light of their relation to the priestly blessing of Num 6:24–26, but Smoak emphasizes that the inscriptions, incised upon thin silver sheets rolled over to give the appearance of scrolls, could not have been read by human eyes. Considering the materiality of the amulets, Smoak instead determines to explore the implications of the material composition of the amulets from purified silver and shaped into tiny scrolls. Adopting a material religion approach, Smoak moves the discussion beyond consideration of the economic implications of the silver to instead explore the ritual logic of the metal, where silver is bound up with notions of the divine presence, the decoration of the temple, and rituals of purification. The shaping of the amulets as tiny scrolls, on the other hand, creates an analogy to the tradition of Egyptian, Phoenician, and Punic *lamellae* (gold and silver sheet-metal) that were inscribed with incantations to be worn upon the body. As such, these amulets have associations beyond protection or blessing, and could also reveal the presence of the divine for the wearer, with implications of purification and healing. These amulets thus take us beyond the limited confines of state-sponsored religion and the literate elite and into the realm of personal piety.

Taken together, the essays in this volume advance the discourse around the ritual world of the Hebrew Bible and expand the canon of texts traditionally considered as part of this corpus. A special focus of the essays in the volume is the socialized corporeality and materiality of ritual action in the Hebrew Bible. Catherine Bell observes that rituals are a "social act" and that "ritualization is a strategic way of acting in social situations."[9] The essays in this volume share a common exploratory theme of examining the social context of ritual actions, and each deliberately reflects on social strategies inherent within literary presentations of ritual performance. Whether one understands the Hebrew Bible as literature reflecting the social realities that gave impetus to its composition and shape, or as systems of power in their own right crafted as a means to influence the social reality of ancient audiences, or as both—these essays intentionally consider the embeddedness of ritual practitioners, actions, and objects within the constructed world of the Hebrew Bible. Finally, the collection also specifically explores the materiality of ritual action and performance, including the physical bodies of ritual practitioners, material substances manipulated in ritual processes, or objects crafted as symbols and monuments of ritual performances. Exploratory questions are raised around which ritual practitioners are presented in the Hebrew Bible as legitimate while others as illegitimate, which ritual actions are considered orthodox and which are prohibited or presented as ambiguous, and the role played by the texts and their presentation of ritual objects in creating or shaping systems of ritual authority.

9. Catherine Bell, *Ritual Theory, Ritual Practice* (Oxford: Oxford University Press, 1992), 67.

Part I

BODIES, GENDER, AND RITUAL

Chapter 1

AN INDECENT PROPOSAL OR A RITUALIZED QUEST FOR SURVIVAL? THE THRESHING FLOOR EPISODE IN RUTH 3 RECONSIDERED

Ekaterina E. Kozlova

1. Introduction

One of the recent foci in biblical scholarship has been the subject of *embodiment* or *embodied experience*, with academics writing on the body and a variety of topics and aspects adjacent to it—the divine body, royal body, heroic body, bodies in ritual, the sensorium, and so on.[1] In the study of religion in general and ritual in particular, the body and its materiality have also dominated scholarly discourse. Thus, for example, a somewhat recent volume of *Hebrew Bible and Ancient Israel* edited by Marti Nissinen and Francesca Stavrakopoulou addresses the subject by offering a corrective on the understanding commonly espoused in Western academic circles that "the body was merely a 'symbol' or passive marker of religious constructs."[2] To that end the volume discusses how "the very materiality and malleability of the body, its component parts and modifications, was considered an inherently powerful religious substance—within or without sacred space and its rituals."[3] From a variety of angles contributors to the volume argue that:

---

1. See, e.g., Benjamin Sommers, *The Bodies of God and the World of Ancient Israel* (Cambridge: Cambridge University Press, 2011); Andreas Wagner, *God's Body: The Anthropomorphic God in the Old Testament* (London: T&T Clark, 2019); Mark W. Hamilton, *The Body Royal: The Social Poetics of Kingship in Ancient Israel* (Leiden: Brill, 2005); Brian Doak, *Heroic Bodies in Ancient Israel* (Oxford: Oxford University Press, 2019); Joan E. Taylor, ed., *The Body in Biblical, Christian and Jewish Texts* (New York: Bloomsbury Press, 2014); Yael Avrahami, *The Senses of Scripture: Sensory Perception in the Hebrew Bible* (London: T&T Clark, 2012); Laura Quick, *Dress, Adornment, and the Body in the Hebrew Bible* (Oxford: Oxford University Press, 2021); Francesca Stavrakopoulou, *God: An Anatomy* (London: Picador, 2021); etc.

2. Francesca Stavrakopoulou and Martti Nissinen, "Introduction: New Perspectives on Body and Religion," *HeBAI* 2 (2013): 453–7, here 455.

3. Ibid., 455.

Within the context of religion, the body is not simply a canvas onto which certain ideals and preferences are projected and displayed; rather, as D. Morgan argues, "more than passively enabling it, the body shapes, colors, tunes, tastes, and performs belief." The performance of religion thus renders the material body an essential *site* of religion.[4]

Building on these and similar studies, this chapter aims to consider the place of the body in ritual contexts with special reference to the reproductive organs in biblical and ancient Near Eastern oaths.

The focal point for this discussion will be an episode in the book of Ruth that has been notoriously problematic for both ancient and modern scholarship. Characterized by some readers as "indecent" or "outrageous," this scene involves the uncovering of a man's genitals, that is, Boaz's, by a young woman, that is, Ruth, late at night in a secluded location on the threshing floor. Carolyn Sharp captures the general opinion on this episode well by saying, "Ruth uncovers Boaz's feet and lies down—the euphemism for a sexual overture is clear—and stays the night. She leaves surreptitiously at dawn with a payment of barley. These would seem to be the actions of a woman who has traded sex for economic security."[5] Against this and similar readings of Ruth 3, this essay will reconsider the "scandalous" scene by placing it in a broader context of oath-taking ceremonies in the ancient world. It will analyze the episode in Ruth 3 in light of the procedures that either include reproductive (and other) organs in their ritual elements or target them through the accompanying curses. Additionally, using studies on genitals as *sensory* organs, that is, organs that participate in *epistemological* processes of the body, it will be argued that by engaging these vital parts in an oath-making ceremony the ritual actors in Ruth 3 are able to make claims that would be impossible to communicate otherwise. Hence, it will be suggested that if modern (and at times ancient) sensitivities around the body are set aside, the episode in Ruth 3 can be viewed not as the Moabite widow's "sexual machinations with a man she barely knew"[6] but as a *ritualized* quest for economic security and thus survival, that is, a *ritualized* marriage proposal.

---

4. Francesca Stavrakopoulou, "Making Bodies: On Body Modification and Religious Materiality in the Hebrew Bible," *HeBAI* 2 (2013): 532–53, here 534 (citing David Morgan, "Materiality, Social Analysis, and the Study of Religion," in *Religion and Material Culture: The Matter of Belief*, ed. David Morgan [London: Routledge, 2010], 55–74, here 59).

5. Carolyn J. Sharp, *Irony and Meaning in the Hebrew Bible* (Bloomington: Indiana University Press, 2009), 117. For similar views see references in Edward F. Campbell, *Ruth: A New Translation with Introduction, Notes, and Commentary* (Garden City, NY: Doubleday, 1975), 7; Robert Hubbard, *Ruth* (Grand Rapids, MI: Eerdmans, 1988), 9–10.

6. Sharp, *Irony*, 120.

2. What Did Ruth Do on the Threshing Floor?

Regarding the exact nature of the events at the threshing floor in Ruth 3, both ancient and modern scholar are at a loss.[7] The uneasiness felt by the readership of this narrative can be seen in how, for example, the Syriac Peshitta of Ruth 3:4 does not mention the act of uncovering of Boaz's "feet" and simply states that Ruth should "draw near [Boaz] and lie down near his feet." Understanding the text as sexually charged, the Targum, too, seeks to censure it by adding an explanatory note in v. 8: "He [Boaz] saw a woman lying at his feet, but he restrained his desire and did not approach her, just as Joseph the Righteous did, who refused to approach the Egyptian woman, the wife of his master."[8] Similarly, many modern readers see the episode in question as inappropriate and even pornographic.[9] Among Hebrew Bible scholars, for example, Carolyn Sharp generally holds Ruth in high regard, yet analyses the events in Ruth 3 alongside irony-laden "prostitute narratives" stating that "Boaz has been used by Ruth just as Judah was used by Tamar [Genesis 38]. Survival gained through prostitute-like dissembling."[10] Other scholars acknowledge that Ruth's actions are of a sexual nature but believe that her behavior should be viewed positively, or at least it is presented as such within the story itself (Ruth 3:10–13).[11] Admittedly, a plethora of narrative details in the text—not the least of which are the ethnicity of Ruth, a Moabite (cf., Gen 19:30–38; Num 25:1-5), and the location of the episode, the threshing floor (cf., Hos 9:1)[12]—may warrant the reading of ch. 3 as Ruth's attempt at a sexual coercion of Boaz and thus as morally suspect. Yet, as will be demonstrated below, another reading of the story is possible.

To unravel some of the mysteries surrounding the midnight encounter between Ruth and Boaz, it is important to consider the following three Hebrew verbs: (1) "to know," ידע (v. 3); (2) "to uncover," גלה (vv. 4, 7); and (3) לפת, traditionally

---

7. John Kaltner, Joel Kilpatrick, and Steven L. McKenzie, *The Uncensored Bible: The Bawdy and Naughty Bits of the Good Book* (New York: Harper One, 2008), 178.

8. Derek R. G. Beattie, *The Targum of Ruth, Translated with Introduction, Apparatus, and Notes* (Edinburgh: T&T Clark, 1994), 26-7.

9. The Bible Society of India, e.g., thought that the book of Ruth was so inappropriate that it needed to be printed separately and made available only to an adult readership. See Jan de Waard and Norman A. Mundhenk, "Missing the Whole Point and What to Do about It—With Special Reference to the Book of Ruth," *BibTr* 26 (1975): 420-33, here 420-1.

10. Sharp, *Irony*, 118. For those who understand that Ruth slept with Boaz see, e.g., Calum M. Carmichael, "'Treading' in the Book of Ruth," *ZAW* 92 (1980): 248-66.

11. Carolyn Pressler, *Joshua, Judges, and Ruth* (Louisville, KY: Westminster John Knox, 2002), 290; Moshe J. Bernstein, "Two Multivalent Readings in the Ruth Narrative," *JSOT* 50 (1991): 15-26, here 17-20.

12. Campbell, *Ruth*, 131-2; André LaCocque, *Ruth: A Continental Commentary* (Minneapolis, MN: Fortress Press, 2004), 81-97; Kirsten Nielsen, *Ruth: A Commentary* (Louisville, KY: Westminster John Knox, 1997), 13-17.

rendered as "to turn, grope or twist about" (v. 8). Again, in ch. 3 Naomi sends Ruth, her daughter-in-law, to the threshing floor and gives her a set of instructions regarding their kinsman Boaz (vv. 3b–4). Given the formulation of v. 3b, it is not unlikely that Naomi indeed envisaged a scenario in which Ruth would have to sleep with Boaz. When she tells Ruth to wait for Boaz to finish eating and drinking, she says that it is only then that Ruth could be "[made] known" to or by him, אל־תודעי לאיש עד כלתו לאכל ולשתות. As the verb "to know" is used euphemistically in the Hebrew Bible to represent intercourse, Naomi could have indeed had an outright act of seduction in mind. However, since Ruth does not follow Naomi's instructions slavishly, and since later in the story Boaz wants to give another, closer relative an opportunity to redeem Ruth (vv. 12–13, cf., 4:13), it is unlikely that there was a "roll in the hay"[13] at the threshing floor after all.

Likewise, the verb "to uncover," גלה, carries sexual overtones as it often appears as part of the collocation "to uncover the nakedness of …," which connotes a sexual act (Leviticus 18). Yet whenever this phrase appears, its subject is usually a male and its object a female. Accordingly, since it is Ruth who is doing the "uncovering" and not Boaz and since the verb גלה does not appear in Ruth 3 as part of the full idiom, it is unlikely that the text has sexual intimacy in view. Additionally, puzzled by the significance of Boaz's uncovered "feet," some scholars, like Kirsten Nielsen, argue for the internal piel of גלה in Ruth 3 and believe that Ruth uncovers *herself* on the threshing floor, that is, she undresses before Boaz and then lies down next to him.[14] Yet given that the internal piel of גלה is at best hypothetical,[15] and since the reflexive nuance of גלה can be represented by hithpael (cf., Gen 9:22), Nielsen's theory remains conjectural. As will be demonstrated below, if v. 7 is taken to mean that Ruth uncovers Boaz's "feet," that is, his genitals,[16] the Moabite's act is not nonsensical but is, in fact, intentional and ritual in nature.

The final verb of significance for the discussion at hand is לפת. Following Naomi's instructions, Ruth indeed goes to Boaz at night, uncovers his "feet," and lies down next to him (v. 6b). But this is where her compliance with Naomi's plan ends. Then the text says, ויהי בחצי הלילה ויחרד האיש וילפת והנה אשה שכבת מרגלתיו, "At midnight the man was startled, and turned over, and there, lying at his feet, was a woman" (v. 8 [NRSV]). The verb חרד, which is usually rendered as "[he] was startled, troubled," may indicate fear or confusion, but the source of Boaz's fright is not clear.[17] The verb לפת has proven to be even more problematic. It appears three times in the Hebrew Bible—in niphal here and in Job 6:18; and in qal in Judg

---

13. Kaltner et al., *The Uncensored Bible*, 168.
14. Nielsen, *Ruth*, 69–70. Jeremy Schipper, *Ruth: A New Translation with Introduction and Commentary* (New Haven, CT: Yale University Press, 2016), 143–4.
15. For the refutation of Nielsen's view, however, see Kaltner et al., *The Uncensored Bible*, 174–8.
16. *HALOT*, 1185.
17. For a theory that Boaz's trembling resulted from the fear of Lilith, a female demon, see Jack M. Sasson, *Ruth: A New Translation with a Philological Commentary and a Formalist-Folklorist Interpretation* (Sheffield: JSOT Press, 1989), 78–80.

16:29. The versions seem to have understood לפת in Ruth 3:8 as synonymous with חרד—the LXX and Vulgate, for example, have "to be disturbed" (LXX: ἐξέστη ὁ ἀνὴρ καὶ ἐταράχθη; Vulg: *expavit homo et conturbatus est* …). The Targum links לפת with לפתא/לפת saying that Boaz "was afraid and his flesh became soft like turnip from fear."[18]

Among modern scholars, Oswald Loretz argued for the meaning of לפת "to touch, to grasp" in all three attestations of לפת (Judg 16:29; Ruth 3:8; and Job 6:18), and saw it as "to grope" in Ruth, that is, Boaz awoke in the middle of the night and groped for something to cover himself with and found Ruth next to him.[19] Frederic Bush in turn observes that there is nothing in the text to suggest it was a cold night, and so Boaz's "groping" about is difficult to explain. Using the Arabic *lafata*, "to turn, twist," he states, "Boaz awoke with a start or shudder (cause unknown), rolled over, and became aware that someone lay beside him. In our present state of knowledge, this seems the most plausible interpretation."[20] Interestingly enough, no one questions the meaning of לפת in qal in Judg 16:29, where Samson *grabs* (וילפת) the pillars of the Philistine temple with the intention of bringing it down. But if this verb in niphal is taken at face value in Ruth 3:8, that is, Boaz or rather his uncovered genitals were *grabbed/touched*, then the resultant image bears a striking resemblance to ritual gestures in ancient oath-swearing ceremonies and thus does make sense contextually (cf., Ruth 3:13).[21] In fact, the Akkadian verb *lapātu* appears in ritual contexts where individuals either hold or touch objects and/or body parts as part of a ritual and more specifically as part of an oath. Thus,

---

18. Beattie, *The Targum of Ruth*, 26.
19. Oswald Loretz, "Das Hebräische Verbum LPT," in *Studies Presented to A. Leo Oppenheim*, ed. Robert D. Biggs and John A. Brinkman (Chicago: Oriental Institute of the University of Chicago, 1964), 155–8. Followed by Hubbard, *Ruth*, 210; Campbell, *Ruth*, 114, 122; Sasson, *Ruth*, 78–80; John Gray, *Joshua, Judges, Ruth* (Basingstoke: Marshall, Morgan & Scott, 1986), 394; Paul Joüon, *Ruth. Commentaire philologique et exégétique* (Rome: Biblical Institute, 1993), 71–2.
20. Frederic Bush, *Ruth/Esther* (Dallas, TX: Word Books, 1996), 163.
21. Of interest here is that in Judges Samson grabs (לפת) two pillars (עמדים) of the Philistine temple. In Ruth, the Moabite widow grabs (לפת) Boaz (בעז), who incidentally shares his name with one of the two pillars (עמדים) of the Israelite temple (1 Kgs 7:21). Charles Halton links לפת with the Akkadian verb *lapātu* and understands it in sexual terms, that is, seduction, which according to him is part of the notion of *ḥesed*, that is, "being willing to take extreme measures for the sake of others." See "An Indecent Proposal: The Theological Core of the Book of Ruth," *SJOT* 26 (2012): 30–43, here 32, 39. Cf., Meir Malul, who sees Ruth as sexually aggressive (cf., Gen 39:12, Prov 7:13). See *Knowledge, Control and Sex; Studies in Biblical Thought, Culture and Worldview* (Tel Aviv: Archaeological Center, 2002), 239, 242. Cf., *Ruth Rabbah*, which says that "Ruth clung to him [Boaz] like an ivy" (cf., Rashi). Hayim Tawil in turn understands לפת as Boaz *grasping himself*, that is, "his two hands grasped themselves." See *An Akkadian Lexical Companion to Biblical Hebrew* (Jersey City: KTAV, 2009), 192.

for example, the phrase *tamû qaqqad ilišunu laptū*, "they have touched the head of their god," means they have sworn an oath[22] and the phrase *lipit napištim*, "touching the throat," indicates an act of treaty-making.[23] Given this the verb וילפת in Ruth 3 could be viewed in a similar light—subverting Naomi's plan of seduction and taking a higher moral road, Ruth steers the course of events at the threshing floor in a ritual, and hence more efficacious, direction. Given the order of the verbs in v. 8—Boaz shuddered first (ויחרד) and then he was grasped (וילפת)—it appears that Ruth waited for an opportune moment, and when Boaz was startled in his sleep and awoke (cf., והנה), she moved into action and touched his genitals. The next narrative detail—והנה אשה שכבת מרגלתיו—highlights the ritual actor, that is, אשה, a woman (Ruth); the target of her ritual gesture, that is, מרגלתיו, Boaz's reproductive organs; and her petitionary posture, that is, שכבת, lying on the ground.[24] Since the Moabite widow initiates a covenant agreement sealed by a loyalty oath earlier in the story (Ruth 1:17), the episode in Ruth 3, too, could be viewed not as indecorous machinations of a Moabite woman but as a marriage proposal ratified by a mutually binding oath of allegiance (vv. 9, 13).[25]

3. Reproductive Organs in Oaths in the Hebrew Bible: Gen 24:2-9 and 47:29

Of pertinence for the discussion at hand is that in the ancient world it was customary to make loyalty pacts by means of ritual manipulation of objects and/or body parts that were deemed to be of a heightened socioreligious value.[26] These objects were either physically present in ceremonial procedures or, if not easily accessible (even through rental arrangements[27]), were invoked verbally via a solemn proclamation. Of further significance here is that at times in oath-taking ceremonies the role of special objects was played by ritual participants' genitalia, organs that throughout

---

22. CAD_L, 84–5.

23. *ARM* 1 37, 19–20.

24. On prostration as a "gestural plea," that is, when the whole body is used to make a request (cf., 1 Sam 25:23–24; 2 Sam 12:16 [note the verb שכב]), see Pietro Bovati, *Re-Establishing Justice: Legal Terms, Concepts and Procedures in the Hebrew Bible* (Sheffield: Sheffield Academic Press, 1994), 133–35.

25. Admittedly, the text does not explicitly mention Ruth's oath, yet her ritual touch in v. 8 and her marriage offer in v. 9 should be viewed as an indication of another pledge of allegiance (cf., 1:17).

26. R. David Freedman, "'Put Your Hand Under My Thigh'—The Patriarchal Oath," *BAR* 2 (1976): 3–4; CAD_L, 84–5; CAD_S, 4, 18, 81; Yael Ziegler, *Promises to Keep: The Oath in Biblical Narrative* (Leiden: Brill, 2008), 43.

27. Rivka Harris, "The Journey of the Divine Weapon," in *Studies in Honor of Benno Landsberger on His Seventy-fifth Birthday*, ed. Hans G. Güterbock and Thorkild Jacobsen (Chicago: University of Chicago Press, 1965), 217–24.

human history have been thought to possess a degree of sacredness and/or special magic valency. Hence the apotropaic use of male or female privates, or of their iconographic representations, is richly attested in various parts of the world,[28] and in the Hebrew Bible is reflected, for example, in Exod 4:24-26. In this enigmatic episode Zipporah, Moses' wife, circumcises her son and throws his foreskin at Moses' feet (genitals?), or at the feet of YHWH, to prevent a deadly attack by the latter.[29] Additionally, in the Hebrew Bible male genitals attain a privileged, if not sacred, status through the rite of circumcision, "a modification practice by which the male body ... is materially marked and manifested as a site of Yhwh-religion."[30] Hence, socially and religiously privileged, these vital organs gain ritual potency as inferred by two texts in Genesis (24:2-9; 47:29), in which one covenanting party is required to place their hand under another party's "thigh"/genitalia to take an oath.[31]

Regarding the significance of the ritual gesture in Genesis 24 and 47, some scholars hypothesize that it is linked to ancient Near Eastern practices of making loyalty pacts either in the presence of gods or in the presence of artifacts closely associated with them. Thus R. David Freedman, for example, argues that in Genesis 24 by holding Abraham's circumcised private parts his servant secures God's involvement in the ceremony (cf., v. 3: ואשביעך ביהוה אלהי השמים ואלהי הארץ).[32] Thus invoked and mediated, God functions as a witness to the servant's promise and would have been expected to punish the violator of the pact. Others, however, view the "thighs" in question as ciphers for Abraham's and Jacob's procreative powers and thus their descendants, who in turn will seek redress.[33] For some, breaching the

28. Christa Sütterlin, "Universals in Apotropaic Symbolism: A Behavioral and Comparative Approach to Some Medieval Sculptures," *Leonardo* 22 (1989): 65-74; David N. Friedman, *A Mind of Its Own: A Cultural History of the Penis* (New York: Free Press, 2001); Alain Daniélou, *The Phallus: Sacred Symbol of Male Creative Power* (New York: Inner Traditions, 1995); Catherine Blackledge, *The Story of V: A Natural History of Female Sexuality* (New Brunswick: Rutgers University Press, 2004); Miriam R. Dexter and Victor H. Mair, *Sacred Display: Divine and Magical Female Figures of Eurasia* (Amherst, NY: Cambria Press, 2010).

29. Christopher Hays, "'Lest Ye Perish in the Way': Ritual and Kinship in Exodus 4:24-26," *HS* 48 (2007): 39-54. If Hays's reading is correct, that is, Zipporah marks her family as kin to the Lord by using her son's foreskin in an apotropaic fashion, then Exod 4:24-26 echoes Ruth 3 where another foreigner forges an alliance by touching circumcised genitals.

30. Stavrakopoulou, "Making Bodies," 535.

31. On "thigh" as a euphemism for procreative organs, see Gen 46:26; Exod 1:5; Judg 8:30; Num 5:21, 22, 27.

32. Freedman, "Put Your Hand," 3-4. The rabbis and medieval commentators understood this oath as involving the sign of circumcision. Ziegler, *Promises*, 43n. 89. Ephraim Speiser thinks that this was an oath accompanied with "the threat of sterility for the offender or the extinction of his offspring." See *Genesis: Introduction, Translation and Notes* (Garden City, NY: Doubleday, 1964), 178.

33. Nahum M. Sarna, *Genesis* (Jerusalem: Jewish Publication Society, 1989), 162; Claus Westermann, *Genesis 12-36: A Commentary* (Minneapolis, MN: Augsburg Publishing House, 1985), 384. Thomas K. Cheyne observed that the practice in Genesis 24 and 47 "grew

promises made by touching these patriarchs' genitals means to "arouse the wrath of the ancestral spirits" who witnessed these solemnized agreements.³⁴ Yet, as recent reassessments of the body across social sciences and biblical studies claim, the body is an indispensable vehicle for religious expression. Hence, dichotomizing the ritual tenor of the patriarchs' genitals (i.e., God vs. posterity) seems unnecessary, that is, in their *circumcised* state they are in fact multi-referential. However, if punishment was indeed presupposed in these ceremonies (cf., Gen 24:41), then in the light of the appeal to God in Gen 24:3 (ביהוה אלהי השמים ואלהי הארץ), any possible retribution would have been of divine origin.

4. Reproductive Organs in Oaths in the Ancient Near East

Of interest for the present discussion is that the potency of generative organs in oath-taking ceremonies is likewise showcased in a few cuneiform texts that deal with family-related issues. Featuring ritual actors of the opposite gender, these texts are of particular pertinence for the threshing floor episode in Ruth 3. Hence, in the *Enlil and Ninlil* myth the god Enlil in the guise of a gatekeeper is repeatedly made to swear an oath of allegiance to Ninlil, which involves the touching of Ninlil's private parts with his hand. Commenting on this text, T. Jacobsen explains, "what is involved, directly and by implication, is not easy to say with any degree of certainty except, perhaps, that the fact of the genitalia being the sacred power behind this type of oath suggests relation to generation and descent."³⁵ In fact, in the course of this procedure Ninlil mentions that she has a child in her womb, which according to Jacobsen can serve as "the ultimate object of the oath of allegiance."³⁶

---

out of the special sacredness attached to the generative organ." See Thomas K. Cheyne and J. Sutherland Black, eds, *Encyclopaedia Biblica: A Dictionary of the Bible* (London: Adam and Charles Black, 1899), 3:3453.

34. Meir Malul, "More on *Paḥad Yiṣḥāq* (Genesis 31:42, 53) and the Oath by the Thigh," *VT* 35 (1985): 192–200, here 198. Malul also understands the enigmatic פחד יצחק in Gen 31:42, 53 as "the thigh of Isaac" and hence sees v. 53 as another occurrence of an oath involving one's genitals. See "Touching the Sexual Organs as an Oath Ceremony in an Akkadian Letter," *VT* 37 (1987): 491–2. Victor Hamilton notes that a number of words related to "testimony" come from Latin *testes*, which may indicate that "Roman society had some kind of symbolic gesture of touching (some)one's genitals when an oath was taken." See *The Book of Genesis. Chapters 18–50* (Grand Rapids, MI: Eerdmans, 1995), 139n. 13; cf., Robert A. Barakat, "Arabic Gestures," *JPC* 6 (1973): 761, 784.

35. Thorkild Jacobsen, *The Harps That Once: Sumerian Poetry in Translation* (New Haven, CT: Yale University Press, 1987), 168; Marten Stol, *Women in the Ancient Near East* (Berlin: de Gruyter, 2016), 105.

36. Jacobsen, *Harps*, 168; Gwendolyn Leick, *Sex and Eroticism in Mesopotamian Literature* (London: Routledge, 2003), 44, 49. Cf., the myth of *Enki and Ninhursaga*, which contains an analogous practice. Leick, *Sex*, 282.

1. Threshing Floor Episode in Ruth 3 Reconsidered

Another text of relevance is the so-called Tavern Sketch, in which a young woman demands an oath from her lover who apparently has been away.[37] Yitschak Sefati understands this text to be about Inanna and Dumuzi and identifies the ceremony in question as an "oath of chastity," by which Dumuzi promises to his beloved not to have sex with other women.[38] Additionally, the *Epic of Gilgamesh* contains a comparable gesture that would have symbolized an acceptance of Ishtar's marriage proposal by Ishullānu, her father's gardener, "Oh my Ishullānu, ..., stretch out your hand to me, and touch our vulva," *qātka šūṣâm-ma luput ḫurdatni* (GE VI 69).[39] Incidentally the verb used for touching of Ishtar's genitals is *lapātu* (cf., Ruth 3:8).

Given the subject matter of these mythological texts, it appears that the symbolic act in them was initiated between persons of the opposite gender in romance- and marriage-related contexts. However, an old Babylonian letter in which a messenger, prior to his mission, is asked to take an oath in a comparable manner indicates that the practice was implemented in diverse settings and irrespective of the combination of genders of ritual actors.[40] Furthermore, it is noteworthy that in addition to reproductive organs, other body parts are featured in oath-making ceremonies as seen, for example, from the idiomatic expression *ṣibit tulê*, which represents an oath sworn by touching the breast of the covenantal partner (SAA II:35, 153–155).[41]

---

37. Jacobsen, *Harps*, 86, 97–8; Thorkild Jacobsen, "Two *BAL-BAL-E* Dialogues," in *Love & Death in the Ancient Near East: Essays in Honor of Marvin H. Pope*, ed. John H. Marks and Robert M. Good (Guilford: Four Quarters, 1987), 60–3.

38. Yitschak Sefati, "An Oath of Chastity in a Sumerian Love Song (*ŠRT* 31)," in *Bar-Ilan Studies in Assyriology Dedicated to Pinhas Artzi*, ed. Jacob Klein and Aaron Skaist (Ramat-Gan: Bar-Ilan University Press, 1990), 45–63; Yitschak Sefati, *Love Songs in Sumerian Literature* (Ramat-Gan: Bar-Ilan University Press, 1998), 128–31. Stol opines that this poem would have been used in the celebration of the Sacred marriage. Stol, *Women*, 105.

39. Jacobsen, *Harps*, 86; cf., Jacobsen, "Two *BAL-BAL-E* Dialogues," 61.

40. Burkhart Kienast, *Die altbabylonischen Briefe und Urkunden aus Kisurra* (Wiesbaden: Franz Steiner Verlag, 1978), 2: 157, no. 175A (cited in Malul, "Touching," 491–2n. 1).

41. $CAD_Ṣ$, 165–6; Simo Parpola and Kazuko Watanabe, *Neo-Assyrian Treaties and Loyalty Oaths* (Helsinki: Helsinki University Press, 1988), 35. Regarding this custom, Cynthia R. Chapman hypothesizes that it might be analogous to a "kind of symbolic breastfeeding or breast-milk-related allegiance" attested in Islamic cultures. See "'Oh That You Were like a Brother to Me, One Who Had Nursed at My Mother's Breasts': Breast Milk as a Kinship-Forging Substance," *JHS* 12 (2012): 1–41, here 7. Yet, the "breast" in SAA II:35, 153 and other texts featuring the phrase *ṣibit tulê* is not exclusively a nurturant organ ($CAD_Ṣ$, 165–6). However, of pertinence here is that in the ancient world breasts (or breastmilk) were also thought to possess apotropaic powers. E.g., in an omen text a man who encounters an unclean prostitute grabs her breast to ward off evil. Franz Köcher and A. Leo Oppenheim, "The Old Babylonian Omen Text VAT 7525," *AfO* 18 (1957–8): 62–80, here 76; Stol, *Women*, 400, 440. Cf., the use of "hands-on-breasts" figurines in the Late Bronze and Iron II Ages.

As pointed out by Meir Malul, reproductive organs can be viewed as "part and parcel of the human epistemic sensorial apparatus" alongside other senses.[42] He claims that since "the sex organs coming closer to the tactile sense in their operation in the process of carnal knowledge ... sexual activity would then be perceived as an epistemic activity as much as the activities of looking, hearing, and touching."[43] In light of the texts cited above, it could be argued that it is not only in the context of intimacy that reproductive organs participate in the knowledge creation/acquisition; when engaged ritually, they can likewise facilitate ritual communication. Furthermore, in regard to the sense of touch, which is key to the solemnized agreements listed above, he observes that "various terms and concepts from the field of tactile activities are very common as expressions of the epistemic process in biblical and ANE languages."[44] Additionally, in the realm of religious expression the traditional hierarchy of senses, which privileges sight and hearing, is often reordered. That is, in religious practices the haptic as well as other "lower" senses move to the forefront. Hence, Mark Smith contends that nowhere is "tactility more important than in elaborating religious beliefs."[45] Thus, it could be argued that the texts above contain instances of ritualized *epistemic* activity, that is, exchanges of information essential for constructing, shaping, and directing life beyond the ritual procedures themselves. By channeling claims and goals of ritual actors while boosting the influence of their oaths, the body in general, and generative organs in particular, enhance communication in crucial socioreligious and political pacts.

5. Adverse Manipulation of the Body in Ancient Near Eastern Rituals

In light of the foregoing discussion it is noteworthy that in the ancient world religious practices attest to both positive and negative engagement of individual parts of the body and/or of the body in its entirety.[46] In terms of adverse manipulation of the bodies of ritual participants or those closely associated with them, it could take place either immediately in the performance of a ritual or be implemented at a later time through the injury(ies) projected on them via curses and maledictions accompanying the ritual. In fact, of interest here is that in the aforementioned Genesis 24, some (corporeal?) harm was envisaged for Abraham's

---

Erin Darby, *Interpreting Judean Pillar Figurines: Gender and Empire in Judean Apotropaic Ritual* (Tübingen: Mohr Siebeck, 2014), 61–97, 328–38.
42. Malul, *Knowledge*, 313.
43. Ibid.
44. Malul, *Knowledge*, 154.
45. Mark Smith, *Sensing the Past: Seeing, Hearing, Smelling, Tasting, and Touching in History* (Berkeley: University of California Press, 2007), 93–116, here at 97.
46. Heath Dewrell, "Human Beings as Ritual Objects: A Reexamination of Sefire I A, 35B–42," *Maarav* 17 (2010): 45–55.

servant in case of his failure to keep the promise given to the patriarch. Thus in v. 3, Abraham uses the verb to swear (ואשביעך, "and I will make you swear") for an "oath." Later, however, when his servant explains his mission to Laban he uses the word אלה, "ban," which is linked to the verb "to curse" (v. 41), signifying that a curse-oath may have been involved in the initial agreement with his master.[47]

Of further pertinence here is that in the book of Ruth the Moabite widow takes an oath of loyalty in 1:17, which contains a clause of punitive, albeit unspecified, action—כה יעשה יהוה לי וכה יסיף, "*May the Lord do thus and so to me, and more as well*" (NRSV).[48] As Ruth subjects herself to (bodily?) harm as an outcome of her breach of promise in 1:17,[49] it is not unlikely that her ritual act in ch. 3 may have likewise been a curse-oath with some penal retribution for its infringement. Additionally, given that the loyalty pact she seeks at the threshing floor is matrimonial in nature, it is worthy of note that ancient Israel had a clearly prescribed course of action in cases of female marital infidelity, that is, the test for an unfaithful wife in Num 5:11–31.[50] As a formal oath ritual,[51] the *Soṭah* procedure investigated (in)fidelity by subjecting the suspected culprit's body, more specifically her reproductive organs (ירך, בטן), to a set of thoroughgoing curses (vv. 20–22, 27). According to AnneMarie Kitz, the outcome of the curse(s) on the woman is "distended stomach and closure of the womb," that is, a punishment of sterility attested in curse materials across many ancient Near Eastern cultures.[52] Incidentally, corporeal penalty entailing frustrated fertility and failed nurturance was habitually invoked in ancient covenantal curses and maledictions irrespective of the nature of agreements they accompanied and reinforced, that is, personal, political, or religious. In the Hebrew Bible, for example, in the book of Hosea, when Israel breaks her covenant with God (9:1), a covenant that is (in)famously metaphorized as a marital arrangement, the people are first threatened with "no birth, no pregnancy, no conception" (Hos 9:11; cf., vv. 12–13) and then are promised

47. Hamilton, *Genesis*, 141–2, 153.
48. Mark S. Smith, "'Your People Shall Be My People': Family and Covenant in Ruth 1:16-17," *CBQ* 69 (2007): 242–58, here 255.
49. This could be indicated by the lexeme לי, "to me." Some scholars see the phrase כה יעשה יהוה לי וכה יסיף as a merely formulaic element in a conventional oath. However, given Naomi's take on the origin of losses in the family (Ruth 1:13, 19–20), Ruth could have understood YHWH as a deity with a malevolent side and thus could have envisaged real harm from him if she broke the promise to Naomi. Cf., Hubbard, *Ruth*, 119.
50. Incidentally Numbers 5 shares a few key lexemes with Genesis 24, that is, an "oath," שבעה a "curse," אלה, a "thigh," ירך.
51. AnneMarie Kitz, "Effective Simile and Effective Act: Psalm 109, Numbers 5, and KUB 26," *CBQ* 69 (2007): 440–56, here 453.
52. Kitz, "Effective Simile," 451n. 33, 453-4. For an analysis of this harm predicted in other ancient cultures, see Norbert Oettinger, *Die militärischen Eide der Hethiter* (Wiesbaden: Harrassowitz, 1976), 71–3. For harm envisaged in cases of female marital infidelity in the ancient Near East, see Stol, *Women*, 234–53.

"wombs that miscarry and breasts that are dry" (v. 14). Similar motifs are found in both West and East Semitic materials, where the vital capacities for reproduction and postnatal sustenance of offspring are targeted ritually in human and animal females (e.g., KAI 222:A 21–22; Sefire IA, 21b; Fekheriye 21b; Šurpu III 98).[53] These and similar traditions once again highlight the significant weight held by the body, and more specifically by reproductive organs, in ancient socioreligious ceremonies and explain the efficacy of oath practices that featured these vital organs.

Admittedly, not all oaths in the ancient world were formulated as conditional self-curses, and the encounter at the threshing floor in Ruth 3 contains no explicit curse element. Yet, given that vital procreative capacities were regularly targeted in pacts of alliance and other types of agreements and given that ancient marriage contracts could include curses and maledictions,[54] it is not unlikely that the ritualized oath of allegiance in Ruth 3 could have likewise presupposed some corporeal penalty, at least for one ritual actor, that is, Ruth, in case of its transgression (Numbers 5; cf., Ruth 1:17). In light of the ubiquitous, sterility-focused curses cited above, the presence of the ritualized marriage proposal in Ruth 3 makes the nuptial blessings of *fertility* at Ruth and Boaz's wedding in ch. 4 all the more poignant (vv. 11–12).

6. A Loyalty Oath at the Threshing Floor in Ruth 3

Having surveyed the texts that attest to ritual potency of the body, this discussion is now better placed to revisit the threshing floor episode in Ruth 3. Given the aforementioned rituals in Genesis 24 and 47, it is important to note that the book of Ruth has a high concentration of motifs that echo Genesis in general, and the Abraham cycle in particular, so much so that the book of Ruth has been called a microcosm of Genesis. In fact, it has been noted that through a number of narrative details the young Moabite widow is cast as Abraham *redivivus*.[55] Hence, the usage of a ritual gesture twice attested in Genesis is not implausible in a comparable context in the book of Ruth. Additionally, and as indicated above, the Moabite woman appears to be well-versed in the Israelite oath practices and initiates

---

53. Melissa Ramos, "A Northwest Semitic Curse Formula: The Sefire Treaty and Deuteronomy 28," *ZAW* 128 (2016): 205–20; Laura Quick, *Deuteronomy 28 and the Aramaic Curse Tradition* (Oxford: Oxford University Press, 2017), 68–106.

54. For curses included in Babylonian marriage contracts see Martha Roth, *Babylonian Marriage Agreements: 7th-3rd Centuries B.C.* (Neukirchen-Vluyn: Neukirchener Verlag, 1989), 19; Kathleen Abraham, "West Semitic and Judean Brides in Cuneiform Sources from the Sixth Century BCE: New Evidence from a Marriage Contract from Āl-Yāhūdū," *AfO* 51 (2005/2006): 201–6.

55. Phyllis Trible, *God and the Rhetoric of Sexuality* (Philadelphia, PA: Fortress Press, 1978), 166–99; Hubbard, *Ruth*, 120–1.

a covenant agreement sealed by a *loyalty* oath earlier in the story (Ruth 1:17).[56] Furthermore, as ch. 4 contains a *ritualized* transaction ratified by a symbolic gesture (Ruth 4:7, 8),[57] it is not unreasonable to assume that the negotiations that precipitate the transaction (Ruth 3:9–13) could likewise involve a ritual act. Thus, the presence of these elements in the story strengthens the premise of the ritual reading of Ruth 3 as proposed here. However, more needs to be said about the immediate and broader contexts of the threshing floor account.

Of further pertinence for the discussion at hand are the themes and language which the book of Ruth, and ch. 3 in particular, shares with the aforementioned scenes in Genesis 24 and 47. As pointed out by many, Ruth 3 and Genesis 24 contain a number of thematic links, the most prominent of which is a quest for marriage, that is, for Isaac and Ruth respectively. Likewise, Genesis 47 holds a cluster of terms and formulations that appear in the book of Ruth, especially in the threshing floor episode. Thus, both Jacob and Ruth extend their requests based on the favor (חן) they found, or hope to have found, in the eyes of Joseph and Boaz respectively (Gen 47:29, cf., Ruth 2:10, 13). Additionally, indicating resolve to grant the request of their petitioners, both Joseph and Boaz respond with the so-called formula of agreement[58]—"I will do as you say," אנכי אעשה כדברך (Gen 47:30) and "I will do everything you request," כל אשר־תאמרי אעשה־לך (Ruth 3:11, cf., 3:5–6). Finally, the two texts in question are linked through the concept of חסד centered around intergenerational cohesion within a family. Thus, in Genesis 47 Jacob, an aging patriarch, is seeking a חסד of having his remains buried with the ancestors in Canaan; and in Ruth, through her combined efforts, the Moabite is promoting a חסד for the living and the dead in Naomi's family (cf., Ruth 2:20). Regarding the oath ceremonies in Genesis 24 and 47, Meir Malul observes that "it is the purity and continuity of the family conceived as an entity existing and significant throughout time, both within and beyond the confines of life on earth, which are at stake in these last requests [of Abraham and Jacob]."[59] Merging concerns from Genesis 24 and 47, and ensuring the continuity of Naomi's clan, the Moabite woman, too, resorts to a ritual act comparable to those found in the patriarchal narratives. If חסד, as defined by some, is a risky abandonment of the self for the sake of others, and if the ceremony in Ruth 3 indeed contained a curse element of bodily harm, then Ruth's ritual on Naomi's behalf was yet another act of self-endangerment (cf., 1:17; 2) and as such embodies the real essence of חסד.[60]

In addition to the intertextual links with Genesis, a few other elements in the book of Ruth support the ritual reading of ch. 3 as proposed here. Having

---

56. Smith, "Your People," 242–58.

57. Bob Becking, Anne-Mareike Wetter, "Boaz in the Gate (Ruth 4, 1–12): Legal Transaction or Religious Ritual," *ZAR* 19 (2013): 283–97, here 265; cf., Carmichael, "Treading," 248–66.

58. Hubbard, *Ruth*, 216n. 47.

59. Malul, "More on *Paḥad Yiṣḥāq*," 197–8.

60. Halton, "An Indecent Proposal," 36–9.

ascertained Boaz's benevolence toward her (Ruth 2) and having taken a ritual initiative herself (Ruth 3:7, 8), Ruth now invites Boaz to do the same. Indicating her eligibility for marriage (Ruth 3:9),[61] she articulates her request, "Spread your *skirt/wing* over your servant, for you are a kinsman redeemer," ופרשת כנפך על־אמתך כי גאל אתה (cf., Ezek 16:8). Echoing Boaz's earlier speech regarding YHWH's "wings" as a place of refuge (Ruth 2:12), the Moabite woman asks Boaz to act on his redemptive duty by marrying her (Ruth 3:9). As "the religious substance of the body was not restricted to the biological bounds of the physical form, but comprised even its non-fleshy modifications such as vestments, adornments, and attachments,"[62] having engaged Boaz's body in vv. 7–8, Ruth now appeals to its "non-fleshy," extrasomatic extension, that is, the hem of his garment, his "wing."[63] Bringing Boaz's "wing" (3:9) and YHWH's "wings" (2:12) into a critical dialogue, Ruth suggests that in YHWH-ism theology and social action must coalesce. The religion hosted in Boaz's circumcised body, she claims, cannot be reduced to empty platitudes and disembodied claims. Thus, it could be argued that Ruth's initiative at the threshing floor is not only a case of ritualized *communication* (a marriage request with a pledge of allegiance) but a case of ritualized *education* as well.[64] Impressed with (or convicted by) her integrity (vv. 10–11), Boaz agrees to marry Ruth and seals his promise with *an oath* (v. 13), bringing the Moabite's ritual goal to completion.[65]

7. Conclusion

Admittedly, the language used to represent a ritual touch in the Genesis and Ruth texts is not identical: שים־נא ידך תחת ירכי in Gen 24:2–9 (cf., Gen 47:29) and וגלית מרגלתיו and וילפת in Ruth 3:4, 7, 8 respectively. Yet, the *direction* of the ritual gesture

---

61. Note the use of אמה, "servant" here. Hubbard, *Ruth*, 211.

62. Nissinen and Stavrakopoulou, "Introduction," 455.

63. Paul A. Kruger, "The Hem of the Garment in Marriage: the Meaning of the Symbolic Gesture in Ruth 3:9 and Ezek 16:8," *JNSL* 12 (1984): 79–86. Also, Ruth's use of cosmetics in ch. 3 signals her eligibility for marriage. See Laura Quick, "Decorated Women: A Sociological Approach to the Function of Cosmetics in the Books of Esther and Ruth," *BibInt* 27 (2019): 366–70.

64. On ritual communication see, e.g., Catherine Bell, *Ritual Theory, Ritual Practice* (Oxford: Oxford University Press, 1992), 110–14. On Ruth as a teacher of YHWH-ism, see Anthony Curtis, "'My God Will Be Your God': Divine Agency and the Role of the Outsider in the Hebrew Bible" (PhD dissertation, University of Durham, 2019), 97–134.

65. Cf., Ezek 16:8, where having covered his "wife" with his hem, YHWH takes an oath (ואשבע לך) to enter into a covenant with her (ואבוא בברית אתך). Note also that later Boaz gives Ruth barley, which indicates that he promises to provide for her. To provide "food, cosmetics (oil) and clothes" was a husband's duty in the ancient Near East. See Kruger, "The Hem," 81n. 14.

in these stories is quite consistent—Abraham's servant touches *Abraham*, Joseph touches *Jacob*, and Ruth touches *Boaz*. Hence, regardless of the roles of ritual participants in these texts (oath-initiators, oath-takers, and oath-beneficiaries), it is the bodies of those who hold, or appear to hold, socioreligious superiority that serve as the ritual focus in the three ceremonies in question. Arguably, as their circumcised genitals point to God's covenant with Israel, the bodies of the three patriarchs are imbued with greater ritual potency. Again, as Morgan put it, each body exhibits its own "'topography' of religious reality" and so it "does more than signify belief: it hosts belief."[66] Hence, in the book of Ruth the uncovered body of Boaz becomes a ritual site upon which the terms of new social realities are negotiated. As a multireferential symbol, Boaz's "feet," through circumcision, point to a national covenant with God and portend marriage and posterity. For Ruth, a widowed outsider, both of these referents carry hope for inclusion, integration, and survival. Touching Boaz's body is Ruth's tactile version of her previous (now iconic) verbal declaration: "*Your people shall be my people, and your God my God*" (cf., Ruth 1:17). As mentioned earlier, some scholars see Ruth as Abraham *redivivus*. The foregoing discussion indicates that the story of this Moabite woman is styled in a way that resonates with a broader set of traditions from Boaz's ancestral history, a history marked by constant forced relocations, and thus by constant foreign assistance, in and out of the Promised land. Thus, by using this archaic ritual with Boaz, a patriarch of Israel, Ruth hints at his own *migrant*-filled lineage, while simultaneously putting a positive spin on her own ethnic background. In the words of Carolyn Sharp, "Ruth as hermeneut brilliantly rereads Israel's own traditions regarding her acceptability in the community and regarding her right to press a legal claim."[67] Forgoing Naomi's plan of coercion by sex in favor of yet another loyalty oath, this time fortified by a ritual act, Ruth emerges from the threshing floor as a real אשת חיל, "a woman of integrity" (Ruth 3:11).

66. Morgan, "Materiality," 59.
67. Sharp, *Irony*, 118.

Chapter 2

RITUAL, GENDER, AND HISTORY IN 1-2 KINGS

Cat Quine

1. Introduction

Ritual is the measure for authorial assessment in 1-2 Kings and stands at the heart of the history portrayed therein. Kings, queens, and non-royal characters are presented as good or bad on the basis of their engagement in what the author deems to be "correct" or "incorrect" ritual practices. Coronation rituals are used to reassure readers of the legitimacy of Solomon, Jehu, and Joash when they are challenging for the throne; the presence of the temple vessels and high places is in constant flux; and the temple reforms of Hezekiah and Josiah are undoubtedly high points in the text. Yet the concept and terminology of ritual rarely appear in studies on 1-2 Kings, and 1-2 Kings is usually absent from broader works on ritual in general.[1] Rather, the terminology of "cult," "temple/religious/cultic reforms," and "deuteronomistic" dominates discussions of religious phenomena in Kings; ritual and ritual theory rarely enter the frame.[2] If, however, we used

---

1. For notable exceptions, see Lauren A. S. Monroe, *Josiah's Reform and the Dynamics of Defilement: Israelite Rites of Violence and the Making of a Biblical Text* (Oxford: Oxford University Press, 2011); David Janzen, *The Social Meanings of Sacrifice in the Hebrew Bible: A Study of Four Writings* (BZAW 344; Berlin: de Gruyter, 2004); Cat Quine, *Casting Down the Host of Heaven: The Rhetoric of Ritual Failure in the Polemic against the Host of Heaven* (OtSt 78; Leiden: Brill, 2020). Wright also offers a useful appendix on impurity and idol pollution in Kings and Chronicles. See David P. Wright, *The Disposal of Impurity: Elimination Rites in the Bible and in Hittite and Mesopotamian Literature* (SBLDS 101; Atlanta, GA: Scholars Press, 1987), 279–90.

2. Compare the terminology and focus in, for example, James W. Watts, *Ritual and Rhetoric in Leviticus: From Sacrifice to Scripture* (Cambridge: Cambridge University Press, 2007); William K. Gilders, *Blood Ritual in the Hebrew Bible: Meaning and Power* (Baltimore, MD: Johns Hopkins University Press, 2004); Wesley J. Bergen, *Reading Ritual: Leviticus in Postmodern Culture* (JSOTS 417; PTT 7; London: T&T Clark, 2005); Frank H. Gorman Jr., *The Ideology of Ritual: Space, Time and Status in the Priestly Theology* (JSOTS 91; Sheffield: JSOT Press, 1990); Philip P. Jenson, *Graded Holiness: A Key to the*

"ritual" in some of these conversations, we could talk about "ritual reforms," "ritual innovations," or "ritual vessels and locations," as themes in the narratives. Such terminological changes could open Kings up to wider discussions about ritual that take place elsewhere in biblical studies.[3] There are likely multiple reasons underlying the ritual vs. cult divide, including increasing specialization of subdisciplines within biblical studies, possible bias against ritual in certain circles,[4] and the dominance of Deuteronomistic debates in Kings' studies.[5] The increase in

Priestly Conception of the World (JSOTS 106; Sheffield: JSOT Press, 1992); Ronald S. Hendel, "Prophets, Priests, and the Efficacy of Ritual," in *Pomegranates and Golden Bells: Studies in Biblical, Jewish, and Near Eastern Ritual, Law, and Literature in Honor of Jacob Milgrom*, ed. David P. Wright, David Noel Freedman, and Avi Hurvitz (Winona Lake, IN: Eisenbrauns, 1995), 185–98; Bryan D. Bibb, "The Prophetic Critique of Ritual in Old Testament Theology," in *The Priests in the Prophets: The Portrayal of Priests, Prophets and Other Religious Specialists in the Latter Prophets*, ed. Lester L. Grabbe and Alice Ogden Bellis (LHBOTS 408; London: T&T Clark, 2004), 31–43; Erich Zenger, "Ritual and Criticism of Ritual in the Old Testament," in *Liturgy and Human Passage*, ed. David Power and Luis Maldonado (Concilium; New York: Seabury, 1979), 39–49; with the language and focus found in works focusing on 1–2 Kings: e.g., Erik Eynikel, *The Reform of King Josiah and the Composition of the Deuteronomistic History* (OtSt 33; Leiden: Brill, 1996); Rich Lowry, *The Reforming Kings: Cult and Society in First Temple Judah* (JSOTS 120; Sheffield: JSOT Press, 1991); Juha Pakkala, "Why the Cult Reforms in Judah Probably Did Not Happen," in *One God—One Cult—One Nation: Archaeological and Biblical Perspectives*, ed. Reinhard G. Kratz and Hermann Spieckermann (BZAW 405; Berlin: de Gruyter, 2010), 221–35; Victor Avigdor Hurowitz, "Solomon's Golden Vessels (1 Kings 7:48-50) and the Cult of the First Temple," in Wright, Freedman, and Hurvitz, *Pomegranates and Golden Bells*, 151–64; John McKay, *Religion in Judah under the Assyrians 732–609 BC* (London: SCM Press, 1973). There are exceptions, of course (see n.1 above), and some works utilize a thematic approach or language that avoids such categorizations: e.g., Saul Olyan, *Rites and Rank: Hierarchy in Biblical Representations of Cult* (Princeton, NJ: Princeton University Press, 2000; Andrew C. Smith, "Furthering Prostration in the Hebrew Bible: A Non-Denotative Analysis of hištaḥăwah," *JSOT* 41 (2017): 263–85; Peter R. Ackroyd, "The Temple Vessels: A Continuity Theme," in *Studies in the Religion of Ancient Israel*, ed. G. W. Anderson et al. (VTSup 23; Leiden: Brill, 1972), 166–81. But on the whole, there is a noticeable absence of explicit studies of and reference to "ritual" in works on 1–2 Kings.

3. The essays in MacDonald's volume on *Ritual Innovation*, in particular, demonstrate the breadth of discussions available with a more thematic approach to ritual. See Nathan MacDonald (ed.), *Ritual Innovation in the Hebrew Bible and Early Judaism* (BZAW 466; Berlin: de Gruyter, 2016).

4. For comments on Christian—especially Protestant—bias see Frank H. Gorman Jr., "Ritual Studies and Biblical Studies: Assessment of the Past, Prospects for the Future," *Semeia* 67 (1994): 13–36, 14–20; and Bibb, "Prophetic Critique," 31–43.

5. See, for example, the detailed overview in Thomas Römer and Albert De Pury, "Deuteronomistic Historiography (DH): History of Research and Debated Issues," in *Israel Constructs its History: Deuteronomistic Historiography in Recent Research*, ed. Albert De

discovery and publication of ancient Near Eastern ritual texts has also created a wider corpus for scholars of ritual to work with, and comparative approaches with extra-biblical texts may have drawn attention away from inner-biblical texts that do not immediately look similar.[6] The aim in this chapter, therefore, is to explore the ritualizing dynamics and literary strategies of selected passages in 1-2 Kings.[7] I have chosen to focus here on passages pertaining to women because 1-2 Kings' portrayals of ritual often come at the expense of women, whether explicitly or implicitly. The historical narratives of Kings are both ritualized and ritualizing; they seek to persuade the reader of their perception of ritual and history via appealing to and creating worldviews about the efficacy of certain rituals. As these texts retain importance for our understanding of Israelite and Judahite history, scribal compositions and ritual, it seems important to interrogate their use of ritual with a view to gender.[8] The first section of what follows thus focuses on Queen Athaliah in 2 Kings 11, as this chapter offers one of the most detailed glimpses of coronation

Pury, Thomas Römer and Jean-Daniel Macchi (JSOTS 306; Sheffield: Sheffield Academic Press, 2000), 24-144; and further discussion in Eynikel, *King Josiah*; P. S. F. van Keulen, *Manasseh through the Eyes of the Deuteronomists: The Manasseh Account* (OtSt 38; Leiden: Brill, 1996); Christoph Levin, "Joschija im deuteronomistischen Geschichtswerk," *ZAW* 96 (1984): 351-71; G. E. Gerbrandt, *Kingship According to the Deuteronomistic History* (SBLDS 87; Atlanta, GA: Scholars Press, 1986); Bernd Gieselmann, "Die sogennnte josianische Reform in der gegenwärtigen Forschung," *ZAW* 106 (1994): 223-42; Frank Moore Cross, "The Themes of the Book of Kings and the Structure of the Deuteronomistic History," in *Reconsidering Israel and Judah: Recent Studies on the Deuteronomistic History*, ed. G. N. Knoppers and J. G. McConville (Winona Lake, IN: Eisenbrauns, 2000), 79-94; and Helga Weippert, "'Histories' and 'History': Promise and Fulfilment in the Deuteronomistic Historical Work," in Knoppers and McConville, *Reconsidering Israel and Judah*, 47-62.

6. Klingbeil notes that the rise of comparative biblical approaches may be partly due to the increase in discovery and publication of ancient Near Eastern ritual texts and partly due to the temptation to focus on a new cuneiform tablet rather than wading through generations of "text-layer-oriented research that is not concerned with the meaning and communicative function of the ritual." See Gerald A. Klingbeil, *Bridging the Gap: Ritual and Ritual Texts in the Bible* (Winona Lake, IN: Eisenbrauns, 2007), 51. With a view to 1-2 Kings, this seems especially pertinent.

7. This is, in part, an attempt to take up Frank Gorman Jr.'s call to reassess the relationship of narrative and ritual texts. See Gorman, "Ritual Studies," 23, 29. See also the contribution of Liane M. Feldman in this volume.

8. Other areas for potential discussion might include, for example, Josiah's scroll as a ritual text and its implications vis-à-vis 1-2 Kings; Josiah's ritualistic destruction of various cultic objects (see the contribution of Laura Quick in this volume); the interconnections between history, memory, and ritual; the emphasis on prophecy and royal (narrative) control over ritual and 1-2 Kings' relation to the priesthood; discussions of scribal culture and literary ritual; and 1-2 Kings' emphasis on organization of ritual space in relation to the destruction of the temple.

rituals in the Hebrew Bible and clearly uses ritual as a literary strategy: through ritual, men overcome a woman. The second section then turns to Maacah in 1 Kings 15 and Jezebel in various passages in 1–2 Kings, observing the connection between female cultic involvement and criticism. The final section then discusses Huldah's role as prophetess in relation to the Book of the Law in 2 Kings 22.

2. Ritual and the Right to Rule in 2 Kings 11

The death of a monarch opens the door for crisis; the political situation may become unstable, and ideologies of social representation, continuity, and legitimacy may be called into question. Ritual is usually the medium through which this crisis is resolved. Appropriate and elaborate burial and mourning rituals lay the dead monarch to rest, while symbols of office are bestowed on the successor and ritual processes are enacted emphasizing continuity and legitimacy.[9] Coronation rituals are especially important in reassuring the people of the legitimacy of the royal office, the choice of successor, and the maintenance of the social order.[10] In the Hebrew Bible, we only see glimpses of coronation rituals in narratives concerning five figures: Saul, David, Solomon, Jehu, and Joash. With the exception of Saul, all of the coronation rituals appear during times of monarchic upheaval, where the rituals serve to mark the individual out as the "legitimate" challenger for the throne despite the previous monarch still being alive.[11] 2 Kings

---

9. Theo P. J. van den Hout, "Death as a Privilege: The Hittite Royal Funerary Ritual," in *Hidden Futures: Death and Immortality in Ancient Egypt, Anatolia, the Classical, Biblical and Arabic-Islamic World*, ed. J. M. Bremer, Th. P. J. van den Hout, and R. Peters (Amsterdam: Amsterdam University Press, 1994), 37–75, here 37–40.

10. The role of ritual as crisis-solver is well known; ritual performances of all kinds seek to keep chaos at bay and maintain order, whether the underlying threats are openly acknowledged in the ritual performance or not; e.g., David I. Kertzer, *Ritual, Politics, and Power* (New Haven, CT: Yale University Press, 1988), 134; Klingbeil, *Bridging the Gap*, 140–2; Gorman, *Ideology of Ritual*, 18, 26–9; Ithamar Gruenwald, *Rituals and Ritual Theory in Ancient Israel* (Leiden: Brill, 2003), 16–17.

11. 1 Sam 16:13; 1 Kgs 1:32–48; 2 Kgs 9:6, 12–13; 11:12. All four accounts involve anointing by a religious figure and public acclamation of kingship. In addition, Solomon rides a mule, Jehu's men spread their garments on the ground for him, and Joash is crowned and presented with the עדות . The 1–2 Kings accounts (Solomon, Jehu, Joash) also feature trumpets (all) and processions (Solomon and Joash only). Due to lack of evidence, it is unclear whether these accounts were an accurate representation of ancient Israelite/Judahite coronation rituals, but the length and detail of the Neo-Assyrian coronation ritual preserved in SAA 20 7 suggests that the biblical texts are only offering a glimpse of basic royal symbolism. See Simo Parpola, *Assyrian Royal Rituals and Cultic Texts* (SAA 20; Helsinki: Neo-Assyrian Text Corpus Project, 2017), 14–18. The rest of the material in that volume also highlights the paucity of royal inscriptions from ancient Israel and the lack of attention to royal rituals in the Hebrew Bible.

11 states that Athaliah ruled Judah after apparently seizing the throne following her assassination of "the royal seed of Judah." No accession notice or coronation rituals are recorded for her and she is presenting as acting alone—no cultic or prophetic figure or public acclamation gives her legitimacy. In contrast, Joash is crowned by the priest Jehoiada and given the עדות in 11:12.[12] He is then presented to the guards and people, who anoint him, blow trumpets, clap their hands, and proclaim him king (11:12–14).[13] Following Athaliah's execution (11:15–16), Jehoiada mediates two covenants, one between YHWH–king–people and one between the king–people (11:17), before the people of the land destroy the temple of Baal and kill the priest Mattan (11:18). Jehoiada then leads a procession that escorts the king from the temple to the palace where "he took his seat on the throne of the kings" (11:19). In this short passage, the ritual transcript conspires to underscore Joash's legitimacy at the expense of Athaliah. The male characters are associated with rituals, symbols, and power, while Athaliah is disassociated from all of this.[14] Throughout 2 Kings 11, the twin spheres of (male) political/royal and (male) cultic/priestly stand alongside each other[15] and combine into ultimate power: prince and priest, crown and עדות,

12. עדות elsewhere in Kings appears in reference to Solomon and Josiah keeping YHWH's testimony (along with his statutes and commandments): לשמר חקתיו מצותיו משפטיו ועדותיו ...ככתוב בתורת משה (1 Kgs 2:3b); לשמר מצותיו ואת־עדותיו ואת־חקותיו (2 Kgs 23:3b), but nowhere else is a king said to be "given" (ויתן) "the עדות," which renders its interpretation unclear in 2 Kgs 11:12. Evidently, however, it was intended to serve as a symbol of legitimacy and perhaps priestly approval. For Sweeney, it was a "tangible expression of YHWH's commandments"; Marvin A. Sweeney, I&II Kings: A Commentary (OTL; Louisville, KY: Westminster John Knox, 2007), 346.

13. Bench argues that the terms גזר, עדות, עמוד, as well as the proclamation of the people were "part of the traditional way of understanding kingship, coronation, and succession". See Clayton Bench, *The Coup of Jehoiada and the Fall of Athaliah: The Discourses and Textual Production of 2 Kings 11* (Gorgias Dissertations 65; Piscataway: Gorgias, 2016), 59. Patricia Dutcher-Walls previously termed it an "associational cluster," wherein the parallels between Joash, Solomon, and other royal investitures in the Deuteronomistic History serve to present the scene as "an illustration of a legitimate royal investiture." See Patricia Dutcher-Walls, *Narrative Art, Political Rhetoric: The Case of Athaliah and Joash* (JSOTS 209; Sheffield: Sheffield Academic Press, 1996), 77–80, 78. On other methods by which Solomon is legitimized see Isaac Kalimi, "Love of God and *Apologia* for a King: Solomon as the Lord's Beloved in Biblical and Ancient Near Eastern Contexts," *JANER* 17 (2017): 28–63.

14. Patricia Dutcher-Walls, "Athaliah: The Queen Who Was Not," in *Characters and Characterization in the Book of Kings*, ed. Keith Bodner and Benjamin J. M. Johnson (LHBOTS 670; London: Bloomsbury, 2020), 182–98, 192.

15. On the contrast between Athaliah (palace) and Joash (temple) see Dutcher-Walls, *Narrative Art*, 69–83. Whereas they were separate under Athaliah, the two spheres combine in the coronation of Joash.

royal covenant and divine–human covenant, enthronement, and foreign temple destruction.[16]

As noted above, all other coronation rituals in the Hebrew Bible involve cultic and/or prophetic figures. Samuel selects and anoints both Saul and David (1 Sam 10:1; 16:13); Solomon is supported by Nathan and anointed by Zadok at the Gihon (1 Kgs 1:13, 39); and Jehu is anointed by an anonymous prophet sent by Elisha (2 Kgs 9:6). In these passages, the ritual actions of the religious figures are vital in reflecting YHWH's choice of king but in 2 Kings 11, Jehoiada's ritual performance of king-making is on another level.[17] This may be due, in part, to Joash's young age, which opened the door for Jehoiada and others to seize political influence.[18] It is also likely due to the authorial agenda, wherein the author sought to overemphasize priestly ritual performance and legitimacy in order to literarily overcome the chaos caused by the divestiture and assassination of Athaliah. Here we must note the depth of this chaos: although her son Ahaziah had been killed in a conflict outside Judah (2 Kgs 9:27–28), Athaliah was the first monarch of Judah to be assassinated. She also had Israelite royal heritage and probable political links with parts of the northern kingdom. Moreover, in order to rule as a woman during a monarchic crisis, she must have had a high level of ritual, political, and symbolic legitimacy; higher even, perhaps, than a male king would have had.[19] Finally, she was also Joash's grandmother (2 Kgs 11:2). Bloodlines, political alliances, and Judah's own royal ritual complexes were at stake in her assassination.

The depth of this potential for crisis helps explain the uniqueness of the emphasis on ritual in 2 kings 11. This was not a simple male king–male challenger transfer of power, such as we see in all other instances of coronation rituals. This

---

16. The power relationship between Joash and Jehoiada is somewhat paradoxical; the ritual power lies with Jehoiada, who enacts the rituals to make Joash king, but Jehoiada also needs Joash to be king—and thus of a higher office than him—in order to overthrow the queen. See comments on coronation and power paradoxes in Kertzer, *Ritual, Politics*, 27.

17. On the innovations of 2 Kings 11 vis-à-vis other coup d'états in the Hebrew Bible see Bench, *Coup of Jehoiada*, 40–4. In particular, the role of priest instead of the usual prophet sets 2 Kings 11 apart from many other biblical coups.

18. Perhaps reflected in 2 Kgs 12:2 replacing Joash's father Ahaziah with the notice that Jehoiada "instructed him all his days."

19. It is widely recognized that Athaliah could not have ruled without internal support within Judahite royal circles, but I think it is useful to be more explicit about what we mean by this. Although Athaliah would have needed the support of various actors (including priests, the military, and political advisors) to rule, she must also have had some level of ritual and divine/cultic legitimacy. It is also possible that her ritual legitimacy was overemphasized by her supporters to allay concerns from critics about a woman holding the role of monarch.

was a uniquely gendered transfer of power in ancient Judah[20] and the only explicit example of intrafamilial assassination in monarchic coups in the Davidic dynasty. Both elements are noteworthy. First, the intrafamilial bloodshed involved in assassinating Athaliah may have threatened to fundamentally undermine the legitimacy of Joash and of the royal office more broadly.[21] According to the Hebrew Bible, no other Judahite monarch was killed by a Davidic descendant: Joash was killed by two servants, Jozacar and Jehozabad (2 Kgs 12:20–21 [or Jozabad and Jozabad; 2 Kgs 12:23 MT]); Amaziah was assassinated by a vague "they"— seemingly a group in Jerusalem (2 Kgs 14:19); and Amon was assassinated by unnamed servants (2 Kgs 21:23). Earlier in Israelite history, the text is very clear

---

20. I do not wish to say it was a specifically female–male transfer of power as recent studies indicate the masculinity of female royal power and the complexity and fluidity of gender and power more broadly. That said, the authors do seem to react against Athaliah's gender in some way, whether viewing her as illegitimately masculine or as illegitimately feminine for a role they believed should be masculine. See especially Stuart Macwilliam, "Athaliah: A Case of Illicit Masculinity," in *Biblical Masculinities Foregrounded*, ed. Ovidiu Creangă and Peter Ben-Smit (HBM 62; Sheffield: Sheffield Phoenix Press, 2017), 69–85; and more broadly Cat Quine, "Bereaved Mothers and Masculine Queens: The Political Use of Maternal Grief in 1–2 Kings," *Open Theology* 6 (2020): 407–22; Hilary Lipka, "Queen Jezebel's Masculinity," in *Biblical Masculinities Anew*, ed. Ovidiu Creangă (HBM 79; Sheffield: Sheffield Phoenix Press, 2019), 125–50.

21. This, I suspect, is why Athaliah herself is accused of bloodshed in 2 Kgs 11:1. For a number of reasons, scholars do not believe that the accusations of her slaughtering the royal seed of Judah are historically accurate. Firstly, if she wanted to rule as regent, she would have needed at least one child alive. Secondly, such slaughter would have limited her internal support and she clearly was well-supported internally to rule for so long. Thirdly, the bloodshed somewhat parallels Jezebel's bloodshed in the Northern Kingdom and may work polemically via association. Fourthly, the idea of a woman murdering children may be intended to undermine her and present her ideologically as an anti-mother. See, for example, Wabayanga Robert Kuloba, "Athaliah of Judah (2 Kings 11): A Political Anomaly or an Ideological Victim?" in *Looking through a Glass Bible: Postdisciplinary Biblical Interpretations from the Glasgow School*, ed. A. K. M. Adam and Samuel Tongue (BibInt 125; Leiden: Brill, 2014), 139–52, 143–4; Song-Mi Suzie Park, *2 Kings* (Wisdom Commentary 12; Collegeville, MN: Liturgical Press, 2019), 145–51; Ginny Brewer-Boydston, *Good Queen Mothers, Bad Queen Mothers: The Theological Presentation of the Queen Mother in 1 and 2 Kings* (CBQMS 54; Washington, DC: Catholic Biblical Association of America, 2016), 116 n. 90; Omer Sergi, "Queenship in Judah Revisited: Athaliah and the Davidic Dynasty in Historical Perspective," in *Tabou et transgressions: Actes du colloque organisé par le Collège de France, Paris, les 11–12 avril 2012*, ed. J.-M. Durand, M. Guichard, and T. Römer (OBO 274; Göttingen: Vandenhoeck & Ruprecht, 2015), 99–111, 105–10; and L. S. Schearing, "Models, Monarchs, and Misconceptions: Athaliah and Joash of Judah," (PhD dissertation, Emory University, 1992), 123–37. If Athaliah could be accused of intrafamilial bloodshed, however, then her execution has connotations of justice rather than illegitimacy.

that Saul and his descendants did not die at the hands of David (1 Samuel 31–2 Samuel 1) and David was clear that Joab should not kill Absalom, despite his attempted coup (2 Samuel 18–19). Solomon also does not immediately have Adonijah killed when he is proclaimed king; Absalom is only executed later after making inappropriate advances for Abishag (1 Kgs 1:50–53; cf., 1 Kgs 2:13–25). There thus needed to be a good reason why Joash—or those acting on his behalf—could have Athaliah executed. Her portrayal as foreign (and thus not Davidic) goes some way toward this, but I also suspect the accusation that Athaliah shed Judahite royal blood created permission—even if only literarily—for Joash and his supporters to shed the blood of this Judahite royal. The bloodshed creates a sense of talionic justice that is not found in any other assassinations of Judahite monarchs and without this, Athaliah's execution would look significantly more suspect.[22] Second, the fact that Judah's own ritual complexes had permitted a woman to rule may have required their redefinition or reorientation for those of a more conservative perspective. In this light, it is unsurprising that Jehoiada's coup is very male oriented.[23] Jehosheba gets a passing mention in 11:1, but thereafter Joash is surrounded by men while Athaliah appears alone—one woman against a nation.[24] Furthermore, at the climax of the narrative, the ritual procession ends in Joash taking his seat on the throne *of kings* (כסא המלכים). No mention is made of the fact that a woman previously sat on this throne; the seat of royal power is simply (re-)defined as male. In addition, no mention is made of ritual failure or ritual dysfunction. While in other texts, the kings that David, Solomon, and Jehu replaced are deemed too ritually incompetent to continue their reign, in 2 Kings 11 Athaliah is not directly connected with any form of ritual failure or incompetence.[25] Although the Baal temple is destroyed, its construction and patronage are not directly associated with her and she is not said to have been a Baal worshipper.[26] It thus seems that the author(s) did not wish to raise the specter

---

22. Barré notes that, in contrast to Jehu's extermination of the Omrides, the execution of Athaliah is orderly and swift: despite Jehoiada's precautions, only her blood is shed. See Lloyd M. Barré, *The Rhetoric of Political Persuasion: The Narrative Artistry and Political Intentions of 2 Kings 9–11* (CBQMS 20; Washington, DC: Catholic Biblical Association of America, 1988), 93–5.

23. Dutcher-Walls, "Athaliah," 196, notes that Athaliah is surrounded by male elites, though Macwilliam, "Athaliah," 73–4, also highlights her unfavorable comparison with Jehosheba.

24. As Dutcher-Walls observes, the fact that Athaliah appears alone is an important part of her characterization; while Joash apparently has the support of the army, people, and the priests, Athaliah has lost all support. See Dutcher-Walls, "Athaliah," 190–1.

25. Saul is presented as ritually incompetent in 1 Sam 13:8–14; 14:24–45; 15:2–34; 28:3–19; while David is impotent and unable to participate in the rituals of kingship himself in 1 Kings 1. Joram, meanwhile, is presented as sinful and associated with "incorrect" ritual practices (2 Kgs 3:2–3).

26. Though Josephus later blames her for its construction (*Antiquities* 9.154), the temple could have been built before her reign, or it may just be a literary creation inserted to link

of ritual at all with Athaliah. Rather than present her as ritually incompetent or inappropriate, the author(s) dealt with the challenge posed by her ritual status by simply omitting it from history and replacing it with an overemphasis on the ritual significance of Joash's coronation.[27] Athaliah is presented as a ritual void while Joash and Jehoiada are *the* ritual performers.

Yet, we must recall that these are textualized rituals created to achieve textual goals. They legitimize not only Joash in the eyes of the reader but also themselves—these royal rituals overcome chaos, restore order, and cause the people to rejoice. They inculcate in the reader a sense of their own necessity.[28] They also legitimize and bolster priestly authority, as the priest Jehoiada had both the political foresight to see Athaliah's "evil" and the ritual means to coronate a new king.[29] The passage is thus designed to persuade the reader to acquiesce to the authorial presentation of events.[30] To resist the authorial agenda means questioning a priest of YHWH, the legitimacy of YHWH's chosen king(s) as symbolized in the royal rituals, and also the will of the people of Judah who participated in and rejoiced at Joash's coronation.[31] In so doing, the reader has to align themselves with Athaliah, who

Jehoiada's coup with Jehu's overthrow of the Omrides: Barré, *Political Persuasion*, 120–2; Dutcher-Walls, "Athaliah," 194–5.

27. The lack of accusations of ritual failure is certainly interesting, particularly in light of ritual failures recorded for other monarchs or ritual competition between royal figures elsewhere. Thus, for example, Saul's ritual legitimacy gradually ebbs toward David and Solomon and Adonijah both have priests on their side, but Solomon eventually triumphs through a prophet. In these cases, the loser is acknowledged to have had some form of ritual competence or cultic support, but Athaliah simply has nothing. Given that accusations of ritual failure or ritual mistakes are effective strategies in the negotiation of power even in modern cultures (e.g., Brigitta Hauser-Schäublin, "Rivalling Rituals, Challenged Identities: Accusations of Ritual Mistakes as an Expression of Power Struggles in Bali," in *When Rituals Go Wrong: Mistakes, Failure and the Dynamics of Ritual*, ed. Ute Hüsken [Leiden: Brill, 2007], 245–71), the omission of such accusations raises questions. Do the authors isolate Athaliah from all forms of ritual because it would help more than harm her reputation? Or is it a matter of gender, and a belief that women should not be involved in religious rituals?

28. Klingbeil, *Bridging the Gap*, 225, calls this the "strategic dimension" of ritual.

29. Barré, *Political Persuasion*, 89, notes that Jehoiada's political and religious skills are directed toward the well-being of the nation and he is portrayed as a national hero. However, Schearing, "Models," 182–3, argues that the coup was more of a palace coup than a national one and Athaliah may have fallen victim to Jehoiada's ambition for himself and the Jerusalem temple.

30. Janzen argues that ritual is not open to negotiation; participants—for us, readers—must either accept the ritual or reject it. Ritual does not invite dialogue. See Janzen, *Social Meanings of Sacrifice*, 20–1.

31. The associational model of ritual also means that if the reader questions the ritual transcript proclaiming Joash's legitimacy here, then the other examples of biblical coronation rituals drawing from the same reservoir of textualized ritual are also open to question. While

was of foreign origin, blurred gender boundaries by ruling as monarch, apparently murdered the royal seed, and was connected to Baal. Aligning oneself this way is tantamount to a self-identification outside Judahite/Yahwistic identity. Although the literary trope of a young king fleeing and later claiming his throne was known in the ancient Near East, it is the use of ritual that proves persuasive here, as it forces the reader to either accept or deny Joash's legitimacy and face the consequences.³² Accepting Joash as legitimate comes at the price of declaring Athaliah and female royal power and ritual status as illegitimate.

3. Maacah and Jezebel: Women "Meddling" in Ritual

According to 1 Kings 15, Maacah, daughter of Abishalom, was the mother of King Abijam (15:2) and King Asa (15:10) and she made an image for Asherah.³³ 1 Kings 15:12 states that Asa sent away the קדשים from the land, removed all the idols his ancestors had made, removed Maacah from being גבירה because she made an image for Asherah (15:13), and cut down and burned the image at the Wadi Kidron (15:13).³⁴ 1 Kings 15:14 then notes that he did not remove the high places, but his

---

interrogating the legitimacy of a child hidden in the temple all his life may seem prudent, questioning the legitimacy of David and Solomon, in particular, is a weighty task. The associations of Joash's coronation ritual thus dissuade the reader from digging deeper.

32. See, e.g., the comparison between Joash and Idrimi in Mario Liverani, "The Story of Joash," in *Myth and Politics in Ancient Near Eastern Historiography*, ed. Zainab Bahrani and Marc Van De Mieroop (Ithaca, NY: Cornell University Press, 2004), 147–60.

33. Her exact relationship to Asa is slightly unclear because 1 Kgs 15:8 states that Asa was Abijam's son, which might imply that Maacah was his grandmother, but 2 Chr 15:16–17 names her only as Asa's mother; see discussion in Brewer-Boydston, *Good Queen Mothers*, 96–7.

34. Her removal from being גבירה has been the foundation for theories that the גבירה was a formal position in the Judahite court; see especially the cogent discussion of that theory in Nancy Bowen, "The Quest for the Historical *Gĕbîrâ*," *CBQ* 63 (2001): 597–618. For the moment, although I agree with other scholars that the queens and queen mothers held important positions in the Judahite royal court (contra Ben-Barak's argument that only a few exceptional women held high office; Zafira Ben-Barak, "The Status and Right of the *Gĕbîrâ*," *JBL* 110 [1991]: 23–34), I prefer to leave גבירה untranslated, as I am not sure we have an adequate English translation. Although often translated "queen mother," it is only used in reference to a few queen mothers (1 Kgs 15:13; 2 Kgs 10:13–14; Jer 13:18; 29:2; Isa 47:5, 7) and can be used for non-royal women as well (Gen 16:4–9; Ps 132:2; Prov 30:23; Isa 24:2). "Great lady" would be a possible reading (so Bowen, "The Quest," 598–9), though the root גבר has connotations of maleness and male strength. Given the frequency with which Neo-Assyrian royal women could be called "lord" (e.g., SAA 16 56; SAA 18 85), and the fluidity of gender and power highlighted in recent publications (e.g., Saana Svärd, *Women and Power in Neo-Assyrian Palaces* [SAAS XIII; Helsinki: Neo-Assyrian Corpus Text Project, 2015], 83–4,

heart was true to YHWH all his days and he brought into the temple the votive gifts of his father and his own votive gifts of silver, gold, and vessels. Although a brief—and often overlooked—account, this appears to be a fairly significant ritual reform; along with the removal of idolatrous people and items, the installation of votive gifts from Asa and his father (קדשי אביו) hints at wider ritual changes.[35] Most striking, of course, is the removal of Maacah, which stands at the heart of the reform.[36]

Maacah stands out as the only named person to be deposed in this or any other Judahite ritual reform in 1–2 Kings; elsewhere, only vague groups of people are targeted (e.g., קדשים 1 Kgs 15:12; כמרים 2 Kgs 23:5). Although her demotion is a consequence of the reform and thus somewhat logical, her inclusion among the items being reformed objectifies her. She could have been mentioned with the other people—the קדשים of 15:12—but instead she appears with the objects, sandwiched between the idols of the ancestors and her own image for Asherah. The verb used for her removal (סור) is the same as is used for the removal (סור) of the idols made by the ancestors and the author seems to draw a deliberate parallel between these two. The idols had been made by Asa's ancestors (הגללים אשר עשו אבתיו) much like Maacah made an image for Asherah. If "ancestors" is more literally translated as "fathers," then Asa *removed* **the idols** *his fathers had made* and also *removed* Maacah *his mother* from being גבירה *because she made* **an image for Asherah**. Here we can see clearly the similarities and the difference: Asa only removed his fathers' idols but removed his mother.[37] Although this could be explained if we assume that all of Asa's ancestors/male relatives were dead (so could not be demoted/punished) and Maacah was alive, the treatment of idolatrous items matches that of the figures who made them. The ancestors' idols—despite being explicitly called *idols*—are only removed (סור), while the mother's image for Asherah was cut down (כרת) and burned (שׂרף) in the Wadi Kidron. The mention of his father's votive gifts is also surprising because Abijam receives a negative evaluation: he was said to have followed the sins of his father Rehoboam and his heart was apparently not true to YHWH (1 Kgs 15:3). Under Rehoboam, Judah apparently engaged in non-Yahwistic ritual practices (1 Kgs 14:22–24), including making Asherahs (14:22), so quite what 1 Kgs 15:14 refers to is unclear. In addition, in Asa's reform there is a double identification of female players: the male ancestors who made the idols are unnamed and so are the deities for whom they were made, but Maacah and Asherah are named explicitly. Gender and ritual are intertwined.

87–143, 173), something like "strong one" might be a more literal reading, though here I leave it untranslated. See further Quine, "Masculine Queens," 414–15, ns. 62–5.

35. Not least because it raises questions about where these votive gifts were before Asa put them in the temple.

36. Brewer-Boydston, *Good Queen Mothers*, 99.

37. It then seems somewhat ironic that he *did not remove* the high places (והבמות לא סרו, 1 Kgs 15:14a).

That Asherah worship was normative throughout Judahite history should no longer be doubted.³⁸ Archaeological evidence, repeated references to Asherah in other biblical texts, and the number of times in which an object for Asherah/the Asherah was moved in or out of the Jerusalem temple in 1–2 Kings suggest that Asherah was an ever-present part of the Judahite cultic scene. Ackerman even argues that the Asherah cult was politically linked to the role of the queen mother.³⁹ 1 Kings 15 does not explicitly say where Maacah's image was located, but Asa's destruction of it at the Wadi Kidron has more than a few resonances with Josiah's destruction of cultic items from the temple, which included an Asherah (2 Kgs 23:4–8). As Lauren Monroe observes, Josiah's reform uses language of ritual destruction, wherein terminology of beating items to dust (דקק לעפר), burning (שׂרף), defiling (טמא), and casting (שׁלך Hiphil) suggests an origin other than Deuteronomistic.⁴⁰ Josiah destroyed the Asherah by burning it (שׂרף) and beating it to dust (דקק לעפר) and he cut down (כרת) the ones at the high places around Jerusalem. In 1 Kings 15, Asa also destroyed the image of Asherah via ritual actions of destruction: cutting it down (כרת) and burning it (שׂרף).⁴¹ Strikingly, in 1 Kings 15, only the image of Asherah is destroyed in this ritual manner; the *man*-made idols are simply removed.

The connections of the Asherah to the Jerusalem temple strongly implies that Maacah's image may have been there also.⁴² If so, then she was the only woman

---

38. See—among many examples—Susan Ackerman, "The Queen Mother and the Cult in Ancient Israel," *JBL* 112 (1993): 385–401, esp. 390–5; Judith M. Hadley, *The Cult of Asherah in Ancient Israel and Judah: Evidence for a Hebrew Goddess* (Cambridge: Cambridge University Press, 2000); Saul M. Olyan, *Asherah and the Cult of Yahweh in Israel* (SBLMS 34; Atlanta, GA: Scholars Press, 1988); Walter A. Maeir III, '*Ašerah*: Extrabiblical Evidence (HSM 37; Atlanta, GA: Scholars Press, 1986); Sung Jin Park, "The Cultic Identity of Asherah in Deuteronomistic Ideology of Israel," *ZAW* 123 (2011): 553–64; Tilde Binger, "Ashera in Israel," *SJOT* 9 (1995): 3–18; J. A. Emerton, "'Yahweh and His Asherah': The Goddess or Her Symbol?" *VT* 49 (1999): 315–37; Raphael Patai, "The Goddess Asherah," *JNES* 24 (1965): 37–52; and John Day, "Asherah in the Hebrew Bible and Northwest Semitic Literature," *JBL* 105 (1986): 385–408.

39. Ackerman, "Queen Mother."

40. Monroe, *Josiah's Reform*, 9–11, 24–76. For Monroe, the language suggests a core close to the circles that produced the Holiness code that later underwent (Deuteronomistic) redaction.

41. This was already reminiscent of Josiah, but 2 Chr 15:16 formalizes the parallel by adding דקק לעפר to Asa's list of destructive ritual actions. The other king to destroy an Asherah, Hezekiah, cuts it down but does not burn it (2 Kgs 18:4). As Hadley, (*Cult of Asherah*) notes, many of the references to Asherah belong to the Deuteronomistic redactional layers, and the similarities between Asa and Josiah's treatment of their respective Asherahs might suggest further explorations of Asa's reform in this light would be worthwhile.

42. Ackerman, "Queen Mother," 390–1.

named in 1-2 Kings as having made any material changes to the Jerusalem temple.[43] As the king's reaction is to destroy the image and demote Maacah, a number of interpretive possibilities arise. First, perhaps Maacah's crime was a ritual one; the biblical texts claim that Asherah worship was not permitted, though even if it was permitted, it is possible that something (or someone) in the process of making the Asherah was wrong and the image necessitated destruction to protect the people from the potential fallout of ritual dysfunction. In this interpretation, it might be possible to read Asa's votive gifts as something of an appeasement to YHWH. Second, it is possible that Maacah's crime was more gendered than ritual; perhaps the issue was that she overstepped the boundaries of what a woman was allowed to do more than the image itself. Third, perhaps it was gendered *and* ritually illegitimate; a woman creating an image for prohibited goddess worship. Fourth, Maacah's crime may have been more political or social, undermining the king and his own devotions and ritual performances. As a king could not afford to lose face, perhaps he had Maacah's image destroyed, demoted her, and set his own votive gifts up in the temple. In this interpretation, the votive gifts may have been an attempt to outdo Maacah or to replace her destroyed installation.

To be sure, all of these options are speculative, but reading with the lenses of both gender and ritual highlights a wider range of issues and interpretations than is usually given for this brief passage. Although we cannot know the exact motivations underlying Maacah's demotion, Nancy Bowen notes that the text does not say to what extent she is demoted from her role and privileges in the royal court. It is possible, therefore, that she was only demoted from the capability to "influence cultic activities not associated by the writer(s) with Yahwism."[44] In this regard, the King of Aram's removal (סור) of the kings loyal to him and their replacement with captains to raise a bigger army in 1 Kgs 20:24 may be noteworthy. The kings leave their military post in that chapter, but they are not said to have been demoted from the office of kingship.

While Maacah only features once with a view to ritual, Jezebel is strongly associated with non-Yahwistic ritual practices. Her first mention in 1 Kgs 16:31-32 names her as daughter of Ethbaal, king of Sidon, and is accompanied with a notice that her husband Ahab worshipped Baal, built a temple and altar for Baal, and also made an Asherah. She apparently tried to slaughter the Yahwistic prophets (1 Kgs 18:4) while providing for prophets of Baal and Asherah at her table (18:19).[45]

43. With the possible exception of the unnamed women who weave for Asherah in 2 Kgs 23:7.
44. Bowen, "The Quest," 609; Brewer-Boydston, *Good Queen Mothers*, 101.
45. Though BHS notes the prophets of Asherah may be a gloss and prophets of Asherah are not mentioned anywhere else in the biblical texts. Ackerman, "Queen Mother," 391-2, notes that although it is likely a gloss, this does not prove that Jezebel did not worship Asherah. Sweeney, *I&II Kings*, 227, notes that Jezebel's provision for the non-Yahwistic prophets parallels YHWH's provision for Elisha in 1 Kgs 17:1-7.

She threatened Elijah (1 Kgs 19:2-3)[46] and supposedly influenced her son, King Ahaziah, in worshipping Baal (1 Kgs 22:52-53).[47]

Yet, although Jezebel is often characterized as interfering in and trying to destroy Yahwism, her destructive actions are directed toward the prophets—at no point does she try to kill off the Yahwistic priests. Indeed, priests are conspicuously absent from the Jezebel narratives; the main competition is between factions of prophets following different deities (especially in 1 Kings 18).[48] The privileging of the prophetic word over the priesthood in these chapters is noteworthy, as the absence of priests—recognizable figures of ritual/cultic authority—bolsters Elijah's claims of authority and legitimacy.[49]

In addition, although the aura of Baalism is always associated with Jezebel, unlike Maacah, she is not accused of having set up any ritual images or altars for Baal herself; rather, her great sin seems to be her patronage of the Baal cult and her opposition to Elijah.[50] Athalya Brenner-Idan has proposed that Jezebel was a Baal priestess from a young age and her ritual skill combined with her father's economic and political connections aided in her marriage into Israel and her standing once married.[51] She argues that the biblical texts did not mention this due to the author(s) incredulity that a woman could act in a priestly capacity, but Jezebel's patronage of

---

46. Brenner-Idan notes that Elijah's flight indicates that he thought she was capable of carrying out her threat; Athalya Brenner-Idan, *The Israelite Woman: Social Role and Literary Type in Biblical Narrative* (2nd ed.; Cornerstones; London: T&T Clark, 2014), 21.

47. Her other son, King Jehoram, apparently did not follow her example though it states he removed *Ahab's* pillar for Baal (not Jezebel's; 2 Kgs 3:2). That said, if there were still plenty of Baal worshippers and a temple active for Jehu to destroy during his reign (2 Kgs 10:18-28) then he cannot have been ardently against Baal worship. Patai, "Asherah," 46, also notes that there is no mention of him removing the Asherah.

48. Priests appear, however, in the coup narratives of Jehu, who killed all of Ahab's priests and supporters (10:11) and there would presumably have been priests among the worshippers of Baal that Jehu slaughtered, as burnt offerings and sacrifices were offered prior to the slaughter (10:18-27, esp. 10:24).

49. Elijah emerges as an "oppositional figure" resisting (some of) the institutions of ancient Israel, but the reader never sees him competing with Yahwistic ritual authorities or performers. In the absence of alternatives, Elijah can claim to be *the* representative of YHWH's word. See discussion of the role of prophets in religious competition in Marilyn Robinson Waldman and Robert M. Baum, "Innovation as Renovation: The 'Prophet' as an Agent of Change," in *Innovation in Religious Traditions: Essays in the Interpretation of Religious Change*, ed. Michael A. Williams, Collett Cox, and Martin S. Jaffee (Religion and Society; Berlin: de Gruyter, 1992), 241-84.

50. Brewer-Boydston notes that the competition in 1 Kings 18 is not between Ahab and Elijah but between Jezebel and Elijah: her many prophets against a prophet of YHWH. See Brewer-Boydston, *Good Queen Mothers*, 105.

51. Brenner-Idan, *Israelite Woman*, 24-5. Followed by Brewer-Boydston, *Good Queen Mothers*, 107; slightly differently see Park, *2 Kings*, 125.

the cult (and apparent economic means to do so) indicates that she may have been a priestess and patroness.⁵² This is a tempting interpretive option, but it is primarily founded on later traditions and conclusive evidence is lacking.

In any case, when it comes to ritual performance or significance, Jezebel is noticeably only mentioned in passing, rather than as an active character. 1 Kings 16:31-32 mentions her in connection with Ahab building a temple and altar for Baal, but Jezebel does nothing herself. The text does not explicitly say that she was a Baal worshipper, or that she influenced Ahab to build the temple; it is only implied. The construction of a temple may, indeed, have been more of a political move by Ahab to help seal the alliance with the King of Sidon. In 1 Kgs 18:4, 13 Jezebel is only indirectly said to have been killing the prophets and the comment that the non-Yahwistic prophets sat at her table in 18:19 is also more associative than direct. The reference to her son Ahaziah following the ways of his parents is formulaic and Jehu's destruction of the Baal worshippers in 2 Kgs 10:18-28 is not directly linked to her, though it signifies the culmination of his extermination of the Omrides. Although the narratives conspire to shape the perception of her as (Yahwistic) prophet-killer and (Baalistic) prophet-patron, Jezebel is at her most active in narrative scenes that are more political than ritual or cultic (e.g., 1 Kings 21).⁵³ In this sense, she is almost an opposite of Maacah, whose only action is to be directly involved in ritual. This might suggest that Jezebel—like Athaliah—was narratively removed from ritual actions and denied a role or power in the ritual sphere. Seemingly these two women were too powerful to afford them ritual actions—decontextualizing them from ritual may have made the creation of polemic against them easier.

Finally, we might consider Jezebel's death to be of ritual significance. While Maacah was only removed from being גבירה and her image for Asherah was cut down and burned, Jezebel herself is destroyed beyond (full) burial (2 Kgs 9:30-37). The gruesome nature of her death is beyond that of any man killed by Jehu and the passage plays on a series of poetic ironies.⁵⁴ The one who shed the blood of prophets has her blood shed by a man anointed by a prophet;⁵⁵ the reference to

---

52. Brenner-Idan, *Israelite Woman*, 26.

53. Patricia Dutcher-Walls, *Jezebel: Portraits of a Queen* (Interfaces; Collegeville, MN: Liturgical Press, 2004), 32-3. Gane notes that to a non-believer, ritual can appear "impractical, absurd and wasteful." See Roy E. Gane, *Ritual Dynamic Structure* (Piscataway: Gorgias, 2004), 6. This certainly seems to happen with Jezebel—in the absence of any textual support for her Baalism, her loyalty to that cult seems absurd, especially after the failure of the Baal prophets in 1 Kings 18.

54. Dutcher-Walls notes that her death is drawn out as if to convey enough detail for closure; Dutcher-Walls, *Jezebel*, 77. Park suggests that the text is "an inverted literary exorcism," seeking to both expel Jezebel and consume her, see *2 Kings*, 132-3.

55. Sweeney also notes that her blood spattering against the wall may parallel the derogatory references to Omride men as "those who piss against a wall." See Sweeney, *I&II Kings*, 336.

burying her because "she is a king's daughter" serves to highlight her lack of corpse and dignity; her fall from a window may be a reversal of the woman in the window motif;[56] and while she is an active character in the scene, her rival Elijah is only mentioned in passing (2 Kgs 9:36), yet his words prove his power.[57] The lack of a corpse also denies Jezebel the chance of a normal burial and the rites that would usually be due to a dead queen.[58]

What have Maacah and Jezebel got in common? Well, they are both presented as meddling in male ritual and cultic affairs. The relatively unknown Maacah directly intervenes in the ritual life of Judah—perhaps that of the Jerusalem temple—by creating an image for Asherah. The infamous Jezebel, meanwhile, only indirectly intervenes in ritual affairs in the narrative but is presented as a powerful force behind the scenes, where even her arrival in Israel prompted the creation of a temple. Both are punished by men and judged by the male author. Whereas Maacah herself is demoted and her image destroyed, Jezebel seems to be presented as the image for destruction, carefully made up and falling in a picturesque scene to her violent death. It may, of course, be pure coincidence that both of these individuals are women, but the lack of other narratives about female ritual involvement in 1–2 Kings means that these two narratives draw the eye. Both women bring about ritual innovation, which is presented as an abomination, yet the narratives present much wider male-centered ritual innovations that are deemed correct.[59] Maacah's

---

56. For example, Park, *2 Kings*, 128–31; Don Seeman, "The Watcher at the Window: Cultural Poetics of a Biblical Motif," *Prooftexts* 24 (2004): 1–50; Tina Pippin, "Jezebel Re-Vamped," in *A Feminist Companion to Samuel and Kings*, ed. Athalya Brenner (Feminist Companion to the Bible 5; Sheffield: Sheffield Academic Press, 1994), 196–208; Nehama Aschkenasy, *Woman at the Window: Biblical Tales of Oppression and Escape* (Detroit, MI: Wayne State University Press, 1998), 13–18.

57. On the general fulfilment of prophecy with her death see, e.g., Volkmar Fritz, *1 & 2 Kings: A Continental Commentary* (Minneapolis, MN: Fortress Press, 2003), 287; Burke O. Long, *2 Kings* (FOTL X; Grand Rapids, MI: Eerdmans, 1991), 121; Dutcher-Walls, *Jezebel*, 78.

58. The Neo-Assyrian text SAA 30 24 (Parpola, *Royal Rituals*, 93–4) gives an example of a detailed ritual enacted for the burial of a queen. Presumably Israel and Judah would have had their own versions of laying a queen to rest, though none are preserved in the Hebrew Bible.

59. For a discussion of the unequal portrayals of ritual innovations in 1–2 Kings, albeit not with a gender lens, see Quine, *Casting Down the Host of Heaven*, 78–83. Note Williams, Cox, and Jaffee's important observation that religion is not inherently stable with rare occurrences of innovation (often resulting from crisis); rather, it is constantly innovating itself. See Michael A. Williams, Collett Cox and Martin S. Jaffee, "Religious Innovation: An Introductory Essay," in Williams, Cox and Jaffee, *Innovation in Religious Traditions*, 1–18. 1–2 Kings draws attention to certain ritual innovations that it deems to be acceptable or idolatrous (and even these may simply be scribal innovations, see discussion in Christian Frevel, "Practicing Rituals in a Textual World: Ritual *and* Innovation in the

innovative image for Asherah is unacceptable, but Asa's ritual reforms are fine. Similarly, Jezebel's support for the Baal cult is unacceptable, yet the Baal temple evidently existed without issue during Jehoram's reign. Only when Jehu came on the scene and turned the monarchy and cultic life of Israel violently on its head do we have a detailed narrative about its destruction, which conveniently distracts from the chaos Jehu caused and the smaller notice in 2 Kgs 10:11 that he killed other (Yahwistic?) priests. Essentially, in both Maacah and Jezebel's narratives, the female-led or female-associated ritual innovations are presented as sinful and deserving of punishment.

4. Women, Prophets, and a Scroll

In 2 Kings 22, after the discovery of the law scroll in the temple, the high priest Hilkiah gave it to Shaphan the scribe who read it to the king.[60] The king then sent five men— Hilkiah, Shaphan, Ahikam son of Shaphan, Achbor son of Micaiah, and the king's servant Asaiah—to inquire of YHWH about the book.[61] As Esther Hamori notes, it is these men who decide to consult Huldah, who is the only female prophet in 1-2 Kings and the only prophetess to give a traditional prophetic oracle in the Hebrew Bible.[62] Evidently, the priest, scribe, and king needed confirmation from a higher

---

Book of Numbers," in MacDonald, *Ritual Innovation*, 129–50), but in reality, innovation would have been continual. Levinson also observes the "inherent tension" in biblical laws between innovation and conservatism, wherein they develop a "rhetoric of concealment" that presents new law as not replacing older laws ascribed to the deity; Bernard M. Levinson, "The Human Voice in Divine Revelation: The Problem of Authority in Biblical Law," in Williams, Cox and Jaffee, *Innovation in Religious Traditions*, 35–71, 45. A similar thing happens in Kings, where the biggest ritual innovations (Asa, Hezekiah, Josiah) are presented as a "return" to the "traditional way" of doing things rather than presented as new innovations in Judahite religion.

60. I will return to the law scroll further on, but my interest in this chapter is not whether or not the scroll historically existed. For discussions on that topic see, for example, Katherine Stott, "Finding the Lost Book of the Law: Re-Reading the Story of 'The Book of the Law' (Deuteronomy–2 Kings) in Light of Classical Literature," *JSOT* 30 (2005): 153–69; Nadav Na'aman, "The 'Discovered Book' and the Legitimation of Josiah's Reform," *JBL* 130 (2011): 47–62.

61. Handy has clearly demonstrated that inquiring for an oracle or omen for confirmation of the divine word was common in Mesopotamia and Huldah is filling this role in Josiah's reform; Lowell K. Handy, "The Role of Huldah in Josiah's Cult Reform," *ZAW* 106 (1994): 40–53, esp. 40–6. And see comments in Jonathan Ben-Dov, "Writing as Oracle and Law: New Contexts for the Book Find of King Josiah," *JBL* 127 (2008): 223–39, here 232–5; Na'aman, "The 'Discovered Book,'" 53–62.

62. Esther J. Hamori, *Women's Divination in Biblical Literature: Prophecy, Necromancy, and Other Arts of Knowledge* (London: Yale University Press, 2015), 148, 151. Other

authority.[63] Tal Ilan notes that while priests' and kings' positions were hereditary and maintained a patriarchal monolith, prophets were a different story as they were chosen by the deity rather than born into their role.[64] Yet, Huldah is presented as "wife of Shallum, son of Tikvah, son of Harhas, keeper of the wardrobe," although her location is centered around her—"she lived in Jerusalem in the Mishneh."[65] The level of detail in her introduction seems designed to create a sense of authenticity as male prophets in 1–2 Kings do not have such detailed introductions; they are identified either by their patronym or their place of origin, not both.[66] The first part of Huldah's oracle is evidently Deuteronomistic, with phrases within it occurring in Jeremiah and 1 Kings 14 and 21.[67] The second part, praising Josiah, suggests links between Huldah and the royal court and is also incorrect in its prediction of Josiah's peaceful death, which implies it predated his death.[68]

Hamori argues that gender is a "non-issue" in this narrative.[69] I agree in part with this sentiment, as the existence of prophetesses elsewhere in the Hebrew Bible shows that they existed, were presumably consulted, and some seem to have reached high status. The consultation of Huldah—or prophetesses in general—may not have been that unusual. However, in the wider context of 1–2 Kings, I think Huldah's gender and role as a prophetess is significant, as she is the *only* woman in 1–2 Kings to have an active role in ritual or cultic practice and not be a target of polemic. Elsewhere, as we have seen, the intersections between royal women and ritual tend to end badly, while the wife of Jeroboam and non-royal women consult male prophets, but do not enact ritual or cultic practices themselves. For example, the wife of Jeroboam travels to Ahijah at Shiloh to enquire of her son's

---

prophetesses include Miriam, Deborah, Noadiah, Isaiah's wife, and the unnamed prophetesses mentioned in Ezekiel 13.

63. Hamori, *Women's Divination*, 152–3.

64. Tal Ilan, "Huldah, The Deuteronomic Prophetess of Kings," *lectio difficilior* 1 (2010): 1–16, here 4. Ilan's article also usefully offers discussion of Huldah in light of Rabbinic literature.

65. Hamori, *Women's Divination*, 149.

66. Compare, for example, "Ahijah the Shilonite" (1 Kgs 11:29); "the man of God came from Judah" (1 Kgs 13:1); "Elijah the Tishbite from Tishbe (in) Gilead" (1 Kgs 17:1); "Elisha son of Shaphat" (1 Kgs 19:19); "Micaiah son of Imlah" (1 Kgs 22:8); "Zedekiah son of Chenaanah" (1 Kgs 22:24); "Isaiah son of Amoz" (2 Kgs 19:2). Deborah, however, might be considered similar to Huldah in that readers are told the name of her husband, Lappidoth, and her location of judgment under a palm tree (Judg 4:4).

67. Ilan offers a nice visual comparison in "Huldah," 8.

68. Hamori, *Women's Divination*, 154–5, notes ways in which some scholars have tried to circumvent the incorrect prophecy but argues that these go against the plain meaning of the text. In another article she notes that the Deuteronomist seems to find this insignificant, to which we will return; Esther J. Hamori, "The Prophet and the Necromancer: Women's Divination for Kings," *JBL* 132 (2013): 827–43, here 838.

69. Hamori, *Women's Divination*, 159.

fate when he is ill (1 Kgs 14:1–18); the widow of Zarephath turns to Elijah when her son dies (1 Kgs 17:17–24); the widow of a member of the company of prophets asks Elisha for help so her children will not be sold into slavery (2 Kgs 4:1–7); and the great woman of Shunem travels to Elisha at Mount Carmel and provokes him into returning with her and healing her son (2 Kgs 4:8–38). With the exception of the wife of Jeroboam, all of these women receive what they ask for from the prophets—YHWH grants their children life.[70] These narratives ideologically uphold the power of the male prophets and the institution of prophecy. In 1–2 Kings, therefore, the usual pattern when a woman and prophet appear together is that a woman consults a male prophet about her child.[71]

In 2 Kings 22, however, a group of men consult a woman about the scroll. The significance of this, I suggest, is that the true authority is located in the scroll itself, rather than any of the characters. Priest, scribe, prophetess, and king all act in the service of the scroll; their status and gender do not harbor competition or polemic because there is a higher ritual authority present that transcends such categories.[72] In this light, Huldah may have been chosen by the author specifically because she was a prophetess. Given the incorrect prophecy concerning the king, the consultation of Huldah may have been historical, but her role may also have been emphasized and her words later augmented because the authors wanted to bring female prophecy—among other institutions—in line with recognition of, and subordination to, textual authority. Huldah thus demonstrates what a good female prophet should do: she confirms the authority of the Book of the Law and the views of the Deuteronomist. Through her, women are specifically included in the shift toward acknowledging scrolls as repositories of ritual authority, but the resulting ritual reform is carried out only by men (2 Kgs 23:4). Huldah confirms the scroll's authority, but in doing so, she also confirms male control of ritual practice.

5. Conclusion: Going Forward—History, Ritual, and Narrative

The preceding discussion has attempted to show that ritual can be an interesting avenue of research for 1–2 Kings. We need not abandon terminology of "cult/ cultic," "religious reforms," nor our discussions of composition, redaction, and the Deuteronomistic history, yet we need not be limited to them. As shown in section one, ritual is one of the primary literary strategies and concerns in 2 Kings 11. The author(s) remove Queen Athaliah from any notion of ritual legitimacy or authority and literarily transpose the symbols and ritual legitimacy of kingship to Joash. Such

---

70. On this theme, see Quine, "Masculine Queens."
71. With the exceptions of Bathsheba who listens to Nathan and Jezebel who threatened Elijah.
72. The ability of the scroll to transcend gender boundaries is also quite interesting, though in 1–2 Kings men control the enactment of its contents.

literary use of ritual becomes ritualizing: the reader must accept or reject the rituals and symbols presented to them in the text. Acceptance means acknowledging Joash as the rightful monarch, which requires rejection of Athaliah and female kingship. The ritual transcript of this passage is vital in understanding the assassination of Athaliah and the coronation of Joash. Without ritual, Joash would simply be an anonymous, speechless child who was hidden from public view for six of his seven years of age and Athaliah's assassination would have little merit. As shown in section two, the Maacah and Jezebel narratives have a strong gender bias in the reports of their ritual or cultic actions. While 1 Kings 15 presents Maacah as actively creating an image for Asherah, Jezebel is never said to have performed a ritual action herself; the vast majority of references to her cultic loyalties are indirect mentions of patronage. While the narrative uses of ritual are different, both women are presented as interfering with cultic matters and consequently are punished by men and judged by the author. Section three then focused on Huldah, who bears the distinction of being the only woman in Kings to be actively involved in ritual/cultic matters and not a target of polemic. Although prophetesses were known in ancient Israel, they are unknown in the previous chapters of Kings, wherein women exclusively seek out male prophets. With Huldah, gender may also be a point of subversion, because the real ritual authority in 2 Kings 22–23 is the scroll found in the temple. The scroll is beyond gender itself, though men control and enact the rituals resulting from it. Huldah's presence thus serves to connect female prophecy to the recognition of the ritual authority inherent in the scroll, and her absence from the subsequent reform is telling.

The three sections clearly show different literary uses of ritual to achieve their aims. I thus hope to have demonstrated narratives in Kings could be fruitfully discussed in terms of ritual and ritual theory. The latter, in particular, increasingly offers insights into the textualization of rituals, literary and reading strategies, and political uses of ritual.[73] The books of Kings also prompt us to consider how history and ritual intersect as the text purports to inform the reader about the relevant historical events in the preceding four centuries. Yet, its depiction of ritual failures leading to political destruction uses the experience and reality of *now* to create consensus about what happened *then*. The portrayal of ritual dysfunction leading to historical disaster supports broader worldviews about ritual's role in the cosmos while simultaneously persuading the reader that this view of ritual is correct. The persuasive aspects of ritual combined with knowledge of Israel and Judah's history and texts thus serve to support the author's implicit claim to authority.[74] As ritual

---

73. E.g., Janzen, *Social Meanings of Sacrifice*; Bergen, *Reading Ritual*; Gruenwald, *Ritual Theory*; Klingbeil, *Bridging the Gap*; Quine, *Casting Down the Host of Heaven*; Gorman, "Ritual Studies"; Watts, *Ritual and Rhetoric*; James W. Watts, "From the Ark of the Covenant to the Torah Scroll: Ritualizing Israel's Iconic Texts," in MacDonald, *Ritual Innovation*, 21–34; Ute Hüsken, "Ritual Dynamics and Ritual Failure," in Hüsken, *When Rituals Go Wrong*, 337–66.

74. This may be helped by the fact that the historicizing literature in 1–2 Kings, like ritual, is formal in its communication. The literal formulae help, as do the rhetorical references to

clarifies and creates social reality, the ritualization of history renders the history ritualizing in and of itself.[75] 1–2 Kings does not objectively narrate battles, events, dates, and burials—it has been constructed in such a way that it demands a moral response from the reader. The anonymity of the authors also furthers these aims because, like Josiah's scroll, the lack of a self-identified author lets the text "speak for itself." Like that scroll, the authority of 1–2 Kings is located in and of itself—the authors' actual status and roles are conveniently laid aside so that the content literarily creates its own authority. This anonymity also limits the reader's ability to debate and disagree with the authors while widening the authorial ability to critique others.[76] The criticism of the kings, who would have been the highest authorities in the kingdoms, standing at the heart of the social structure, should be striking to the reader but it is not because the author is not an oppositional figure whom we can evaluate.[77] Readers have no option but to accept or reject the textual portrayals. In the presentation of kings and history via ritual, the text thus becomes a source of ritual authority. The absence of female involvement in ritual therein requires acknowledgment as, over the centuries, these texts have become canonized, taking on a whole new form of ritual authority for their content.

other authoritative texts in Israel and Judah's histories; on the latter, see Mark Leuchter, "The Sociolinguistic and Rhetorical Functions of the Source Citations in Kings," in *Soundings in Kings: Perspectives and Methods in Contemporary Scholarship*, ed. M. Leuchter and K.-P. Adam (Minneapolis, MN: Fortress Press, 2010), 119–35.

75. Janzen, *Social Meanings of Sacrifice*, 20–1. On the power of textualization of rituals see especially Catherine Bell, "The Ritualization of Texts and Textualization of Ritual in the Codification of Taoist Literature," *History of Religions* 27 (1988): 366–92; Frevel, "Practicing Rituals in a Textual World"; D. P. Wright, "Ritual Theory, Ritual Texts, and the Priestly-Holiness Writings of the Pentateuch," in *Social Theory and the Study of Israelite Religion: Essays in Retrospect and Prospect*, ed. S. M. Olyan (Atlanta, GA: SBL Press, 2012), 195–216. On the dangers of accepting a text's portrayal of rituals and ritual performers at face value see Philippe Buc, *The Dangers of Ritual: Between Early Medieval Texts and Social Scientific Theory* (Princeton, NJ: Princeton University Press, 2001).

76. The ritual aspects also dissuade debate, as ritual's formal character leaves participants—and for us, readers—with no room for discussion. See Janzen, *Social Meanings of Sacrifice*, 11.

77. Gruenwald, *Ritual Theory*, 215.

Chapter 3

MILK, MEAT, AND MOTHERS: THE PROBLEM OF MOTHERHOOD IN SOME RITUAL FOOD LAWS

Nicole J. Ruane

1. Introduction

Gender analysis is not a new method of interpretation in biblical studies, yet I believe that gender critical approaches have many more results to offer. This is especially so for ritual and legal texts, which have had comparatively less gender analysis than narrative and poetry. In this chapter I will show that an awareness of gender, of the demands of a patrilineal culture, and especially of the ideological understanding of biological birth within that culture explain a number of enigmatic ritual laws in the Pentateuch. These laws are not about human gender but about regulating certain foods related to mother animals, such as their own meat, their newborn offspring, and the products of milk and eggs. The laws limit the consumption and offering of these foods in both sacrificial settings, such as pilgrimage feasts, and in general food rules. Taken together, they show a legal construction of motherhood, and that it is consistently restricted, especially from public ritual settings related to sacrifice. This gender-based interpretive focus illustrates that motherhood and birth pose an ideological problem for a patrilineal culture, which must necessarily deemphasize them in order to socially prioritize the bonds created through males over the biological power of female reproduction. Moreover, the exclusion of animal mothers and materials associated with them from ritual activity aligns with laws and narratives that exclude human mothers from sacrifice and other official ritual settings. This proposal does not mean that the Hebrew Bible in general attempts to minimize motherhood—mothers are important and highly valued in many biblical texts—but it does indicate that in some contexts the realities of birth and the nature of motherhood conflict with aspects of ritual and culture. Focusing on the ways in which these food laws engage the material problem of mother animals helps explain not only the rituals themselves but also general biblical concepts of gender.

In this analysis, I will rely on the work of Nancy Jay, whose 1992 study of animal sacrifice made the remarkable observation that a universal feature of all sacrificing cultures is the exclusion of childbirth and women who experience it.[1] She explained that women of childbearing age are usually prevented from officiating in sacrificial rituals (unless they are understood to be virgins), and that most sacrificial systems exclude women who have recently given birth from bringing offerings and eating offered meat. Jay's explanation for this exclusion is that the function of sacrificial systems is to forge social patrilineal lines that overcome the biological relations created through childbirth. Because paternity is never completely sure, and because such cultures depend upon these male ties, groups of men who sacrifice together form social bonds that supersede (though usually overlap with) the biological connections that are formed through women. Sacrifice is "birth done better"; it is a controlled way to create social ties and descent systems apart from women, sex, and birth. Part of this construction entails the exclusion of reproductively active women from rituals, especially by characterizing them as "impure" or ritually unfit during menstruation and after childbirth; this impurity prevents them from approaching sacred objects, including sacrificial offerings and the meat that comes from them. Using Jay's theory, I suggest that the same drive to exclude human mothers from sacrifice also underlies the need to exclude not only animal mothers but eggs and milk, the substances related to them. Though I am doubtful that Jay's theory fits all sacrificial circumstances, her focus on the inherent problem of biological childbirth for patrilineal cultures, and rituals whose aim is to minimize this problem, helps to explain several aspects of biblical ritual that are otherwise difficult to understand.

2. *The Exclusion of Human Mothers from Sacrificial Acts*

The exclusion of human motherhood from public ritual acts involving animal sacrifice and from other ritual regulations about food is most clearly apparent in Leviticus 12. This chapter indicates that a parturient (new mother) may not participate in sacrificial worship due to her impurity immediately after giving birth. If she has given birth to a son, for seven days she enters a state of ritual uncleanness (טמאה), as at menstruation (נדת דותה 12:2; cf., Lev 15:19–24), in which she easily transmits this uncleanness to other people and to objects, requiring them to be separated from sancta. After the seven days, she enters into a lesser state of impurity for thirty-three days, though she can still transmit impurity to others. If she bears a girl, she is more severely impure for fourteen days and then in the lesser state for sixty-six days. Since impure people are not allowed to participate in sacred gatherings, nor are they allowed to eat any meat or other food that has been ritually offered (Lev 7:19–21, 22:3), the laws of impurity specifically exclude these mothers from participating in those ritual activities. Similarly, the laws regarding the impurity of intercourse and menstruation in Leviticus 15 clarify that menstruants are also not

---

1. Nancy Jay, *"Throughout Your Generations Forever": Sacrifice, Religion and Paternity* (Chicago: University of Chicago Press, 1992).

allowed to participate in sacrificial worship or eat the food that comes from it, as they also are in a state of ritual impurity for seven days. Both men and women who have engaged in intercourse or who have pathological genital conditions are considered unclean, though for intercourse the period of uncleanness is less than a day. Thus, all people recently connected with reproduction are unclean and restricted from official rituals. Yet the repercussions of uncleanness fall disproportionately on women, and childbirth, especially of a girl, is the most extreme impurity, at least in terms of the length of time required to recover from impurity.

Another biblical text, though not a law, illustrates a juxtaposition between childbirth and sacrificial offerings for a different reason related to motherhood and for a different period of time. Hannah refrains from participating in sacrifice for three years until she has finished nursing her son. 1 Samuel 1:20–25 reads,

> When the days were completed, Hannah conceived and bore a son. ... Then the man Elkanah went up, with all of his house, to sacrifice to Yahweh the yearly sacrifice as well as his votive offering. But Hannah did not go up, for she said to her husband, "When the boy is weaned, I will bring him so that he will appear before Yahweh and stay there forever." Elkanah her husband said to her, "Do what seems good to you. Stay until you wean him, but let Yahweh fulfill his word." So the woman stayed and nursed her son until she weaned him. When she weaned him, she took him up with her, along with a three-year old bull,[2] an ephah of flour, and a skin of wine and she brought him to the house of Yahweh at Shiloh, though the boy was very young. They slaughtered the bull and they brought the boy to Eli.

Although in this instance Hannah's exclusion from sacrifice appears self-imposed and not an official requirement of a cultic system, the passage exhibits a structural separation of a woman from sacrifice related to her motherly act of nursing.[3] Hannah is not required to participate at the yearly offering as she takes on this maternal work.[4] So whereas the parturient of Leviticus 12 is explicitly

---

2. This reading follows the LXX and Syriac. The MT has בפרים שלשה meaning "with three bulls," a variant that is probably due to a misreading of the *mem* at the end of בפרים; it should go with the following word (yielding מ'שלש). See P. Kyle McCarter Jr., *I Samuel: A New Translation and Commentary* (AB 8; New Haven, CT: Yale University Press, 1980), 56–7.

3. Mayer Gruber suggests that Hannah's breastfeeding prevents her from worshipping until Samuel is weaned. See "Breastfeeding Practices in Biblical Israel and in Old Babylonian Mesopotamia," *JANES* 19 (1989): 61–83, here 67.

4. It is unclear whether the yearly sacrifice discussed in 1 Samuel 1 is one of the three official pilgrimage feasts, or a different pilgrimage ceremony, or a private family sacrifice that is not necessarily required on a set day each year. Carol Meyers argues that it should be understood as a family event. See "Hannah and Her Sacrifice: Reclaiming Female Agency," in *A Feminist Companion to Samuel and Kings*, ed. Athaliah Brenner (Sheffield: Sheffield University Press, 1994), 93–104, here 101.

barred from sacrificial activity by her impurity from childbirth, Hannah's work of nursing and being the mother of a young child sets her in opposition to sacrificial worship, though in a much less formal way. In both cases, activities related to motherhood interfere with participation in sacrificial ritual activity.[5] In the case of Hannah, the exemption of a nursing mother may be solely a matter of convenience; indeed ancient and modern interpretations of the text have questioned whether women were required to participate in time-bound ritual activities, especially sacrificial pilgrimages, because their roles as mothers prevented them from participating at set times.[6] This rationale is often given for the omission of women in the three pilgrimage feasts of Matsot, Shevuoth, and Sukkoth depicted in Exodus 23 and 34.[7] If reproductive activity is the reason that women are not required at these rites, or are possibly barred from them, the very structure of pilgrimage excludes mothers of very young children and their maternal work.

In both the story of Hannah and Leviticus 12, the women are not kept away from sacred events forever but only for a limited period of time related to birth. It is the fact that they have participated in childbirth that causes them to be restricted. Therefore, both texts construct the ritual character of the new mother and indicate that both she and childbirth itself are problematic for ritual practice that includes sacrifice.

3. "Feminized Protein" and the Sacrificial Cult(s)

Although the primary image of a religious offering is an animal, in fact many different kinds of food are important sacrificial offerings in the Hebrew Bible. According to Num 15:1–16, for example, every sacrificial animal must be accompanied by offerings of grain, oil, and wine. One of the "most holy" priestly offerings is the מנחה, the cereal offering mixed with incense that is burnt upon the altar (Leviticus 2), and grain can also be offered in place of an animal for the חטאת sacrifice if the offerer cannot afford an animal (Lev 5:11–12). Similarly, first fruits

---

5. Gen 21:8 shows a similar juxtaposition between nursing and meat-eating when Abraham makes a feast for Isaac on the day he is weaned.

6. See, e.g., Ismar J. Peritz, "Woman in the Ancient Hebrew Cult," *JBL* 17 (1898): 111–48, here 133; and Carol Meyers, *Exodus* (NCBC; New York: Cambridge University Press, 2005), 202. The Mishnah states that women are not required at the pilgrimages (m. Qid. 1:8).

7. In contrast, Deuteronomy specifically includes women, at least at the feasts that accompany the sacrificial offerings (Deut 12:12, 18; 16:11, 14), though these women are never said to be mothers (cf., 29:11). For discussion see Caroline M. Breyfogle, "The Religious Status of Women in the Old Testament," *Biblical World* 5 (1910): 405–19, here 414; and Mayer Gruber, "Women in the Cult According to the Priestly Code," in *Judaic Perspectives on Ancient Israel*, ed. Jacob Neusner, Baruch A. Levine and Ernest S. Frerichs (Philadelphia, PA: Fortress Press, 1989), 35–48, here 36, 41n. 5.

3. Milk, Meat, and Mothers

of the harvest must either be handed over to priests or Levites in the form of an offering, or consumed in the ritual manner of Sukkot.[8]

Although many different kinds of food are offered in biblical texts, nowhere in the Hebrew Bible are milk products presented as offerings or included as part of any sacrificial system.[9] This omission is especially significant since the only land animals permitted for sacrifice in the legal texts—cows, goats, and sheep—produce milk fit for human consumption and were raised largely for their milk. As W. Robertson Smith noted, "Milk ... though one of the commonest articles of food among the Israelites, has no place in Hebrew sacrifice."[10] Indeed, it is surprising that in biblical ritual law there are no offerings of milk, or curds, cheese, yogurt, butter or any other dairy items. They do not accompany meat offerings, nor are they ever mentioned as tithes to priests, nor any kind of first fruit. Milk is never even discussed in the legal texts except for the prohibition against boiling a kid in its mother's milk (Exod 23:19b; 34:26b; Deut 14:21b; discussed below) where it is specifically excluded from a cultic context.

Several interpretations have been offered for milk's exclusion from the sacrificial system. For example, Robertson Smith suggested that it was excluded because milk ferments quickly in hot climates and so would violate the prohibitions on leavening (Exod 23:18; Lev 2:11).[11] However, wine, which appears in numerous sacrificial texts, would have to be excluded on the same basis.[12] Bodenheimer argued that some modern-day nomads consider milk to be too lowly and common to sell and therefore it would have been perceived as an inadequate gift for deities.[13] However, the Israelites offered grain, fruits, and bread, which are cheap and lowly foodstuffs themselves, and multiple biblical texts indicate that cheese was expensive or extravagant (Judg 4:19; 5:25; Isa 55:1); 1 Sam 17:17–18 illustrates that milk was more valuable than bread and was food for a person with a high status.[14] David Daube suggested that milk was originally part of the sacrificial system but was excluded following the prohibition on boiling a kid in its mother's milk.[15] According to Daube, this law is an intentional exclusion of milk products

---

8. Exod 23:16, 19; 34:22, 26; Lev 2:14–16; 23:10–14, 17, 20; Num 18:13; 28:26; Deut 18:4–5.

9. However, in Gen 18:8, when Abraham prepares a meal for the three "men" who come to announce the birth of his child, he gives them curds (חמאה), milk (חלב), and meat. Perhaps this detail indicates that the combination of meat and milk is food fit only for divine beings, or is one connected with female fertility, as the men are about to bestow upon Sarah.

10. W. Robertson Smith, *The Religion of the Semites: The Fundamental Institutions* (New York: Meridian Books, 1956), 220.

11. Smith, *The Religion of the Semites*, 220–1. See also Caquot's citation of M. J. Lagrange and F. Blome, who hold the same perspective (André Caquot, "*ḥālāb*," TDOT IV, 386).

12. F. S. Bodenheimer, *Animal and Man in Bible Lands* (Leiden: Brill, 1960), 209.

13. Ibid.

14. George Cansdale, *Animals of Bible Lands* (Exeter: Paternoster Press, 1970), 60.

15. David Daube, "A Note on a Jewish Dietary Law," JTS 37 (1936): 289–91.

from sacrifice and "the rejection of a class of offerings."[16] Similarly, André Caquot refers to milk as "a purely secular foodstuff."[17]

Numerous biblical passages indicate that milk was a primary, important, and desired substance, especially the repeated characterization of the land of Israel as a "land flowing with milk and honey." However, the omission of milk from sacrificial offerings indicates a certain understanding of milk that is unique to the Hebrew Bible since other ancient Semitic peoples made milk offerings.[18] There is one obvious fact about milk that makes it different from all other offerings mentioned in the Bible: it only comes from mother animals. Whereas meat may come from animals of either sex, milk is a specifically female product, and beyond that, it is a product that comes only from animals that have recently given birth.[19] The objection might be raised that there are all kinds of foodstuffs that never appear as biblical offerings. However, since all the primary sacrificial animals are milk producers, and since milk is otherwise repeatedly mentioned as an ideal food in the Hebrew Bible, milk's omission from sacrificial practice is significant.[20]

16. Ibid., 290.

17. André Caquot, "ḥālāb," TDOT IV, 386.

18. E.g., Bodenheimer, *Animal and Man in Bible Lands*, 209; Smith, *The Religion of the Semites*, 220; Jacob Milgrom, "Sacrifices and Offerings, OT," *ABD* 4: 156; Marten Stol, "Milk, Butter and Cheese," *Bulletin on Sumerian Agriculture* 7 (1993): 99–113, here 100; Caquot, "ḥālāb," 386.

19. Thus Carol Adams states with regard to modern animals, "Female animals become oppressed by their femaleness, and become essentially surrogate wet-nurses. These ... animals are oppressed as *Mother* animals" (her italics). See *The Sexual Politics of Meat: A Feminist-Vegetarian Critical Theory* (New York: Continuum, 1990), 91.

20. Other foodstuffs are problematic for the Israelite cult. Leaven is forbidden from the Passover sacrifice, the Feast of Matsot, the cereal offering (Lev 2:11), and the bread that accompanies sacrificial meat (Lev 6:17 [Heb 6:10]), but it is required in cakes during the Feast of Weeks (Lev 23:17) and in loaves that accompany שלמים offerings (Lev 7:13). Wine must accompany some offerings (e.g., Exod 29:40–41; Lev 23:13; Num 15:5, 7, 10; 28:14) though it must be avoided by nazirites (Num 6:3–4, 20) and also by priests performing cultic service (Lev 10:9). While these products are restricted in some ways by cultic practice, they still have a place there, whereas dairy products never do. The only other animal product legislated by biblical law is honey (דבש), if in fact actual bee's honey is meant by this term (it could refer to dates or a substance made from them, see, e.g., Jacob Milgrom, *Leviticus 1-16* [AB 3; Garden City, NY: Doubleday, 1991], 189–90). Honey, like leaven, must never be burned on an altar (Lev 2:11), and therefore is a somewhat unacceptable ritual food. Milk and honey are both characterized as children's food (Isa 7:15–16; antithetically in Job 20:16–17; see William Propp, "Milk and Honey: Biblical Comfort Food," *BR* 15 [1999], 16, 54, here 16). Propp suggests that honey might be related to maternal imagery because some people encourage nursing by putting honey on a mother's breasts ("Milk and Honey," 54n. 2). It may be that honey's ability to induce fermentation (like leaven and wine) is its cultically objectionable aspect (Milgrom, *Leviticus 1-16*, 190; William Propp, *Exodus 1-18* [AB 2; Garden City, NY: Doubleday, 1999], 433), or it might be honey's ambiguous quality as a

A number of interpreters have recognized that cross-culturally milk can stand for relationships formed through mothers. The anthropologist Victor Turner argued that milk can be a "natural symbol" for the relationship between a mother and child.[21] Robertson Smith also reported that among some Semitic peoples the sharing of milk can be a way of fostering ties with adopted or foster children when bringing them into the family. In these situations, the drinking of milk creates socially constructed consanguinity.[22] This idea is apparent in some biblical ideology, such as in the Song 8:1 which states, "O that you were like a brother to me, who nursed at my mother's breast!" (NRSV).[23] However, biblical ritual law does not utilize milk as a ritual means of positively constructing familial bonds. Furthermore, milk is obviously related to children and immaturity. Both human and animal milk are portrayed biblically as children's food (Isa 28:9 [as curds, Isa 7:15]; 1 Cor 3:2). Thus, milk is aligned with femininity, maternity, offspring, and immaturity. For these reasons it might be an appropriate ritual material for creating private familial bonds but not the social public bonds with which sacrifice is often concerned.

Similarly, eggs are never mentioned as a sacrificial food or offering: there are no egg offerings in the Hebrew Bible nor any sort of egg tithe, yet the only permissible sacrificial victims that do not produce milk are doves and pigeons, both of which lay eggs fit for human consumption. Like milk, eggs only come from female animals and are intrinsically related to birthing. Laying eggs is a means of giving birth and eggs themselves are an embodiment of gestation and birth. Whether milk and eggs are not offered because they come from mother animals, or because they have some other significance, the effect is the same: these particularly maternal substances are excluded from the cult. The omission matches the exclusion of human mothers from cultic activity. Moreover, the exclusion of milk and eggs—the material Carol Adams calls "feminized protein"[24]—illustrates that meat, the other animal product, is the cultically preferred foodstuff. The sacrificial systems of the Hebrew Bible not only exclude mothers but also foods related to them.

---

secondary animal product, like milk and eggs, that makes it objectionable for the sacrificial system (Caquot, "ḥālāb," 386, makes this point regarding milk). Honey, milk, and eggs are the only food products that animals make while they are alive (Adams, *The Sexual Politics of Meat*, 91).

21. Victor Turner, *The Forest of Symbols: Aspects of Ndembu Ritual* (Ithaca, NY: Cornell University Press, 1967), 19–47; cited in Howard Eilberg-Schwartz, *The Savage in Judaism: An Anthropology of Israelite Religion and Ancient Judaism* (Bloomington: University of Indiana Press, 1990), 132.

22. Smith, *The Religion of the Semites*, 284.

23. For other examples, see also Cynthia Chapman, "Oh That You Were like a Brother to Me, One Who Had Nursed at My Mother's Breasts: Breast Milk as a Kinship-Forging Substance," *JHS* 12 (2012): 1–42. Note that her examples emphasize relationships through women, whereas the legal texts do not.

24. Adams, *The Sexual Politics of Meat*, 91.

4. Mothers and Meat

The ritual exclusion of motherly substances from food offerings goes even further in four laws that disallow eating mother animals or offering them as sacrificial victims. These laws discuss the circumstances in which infant animals can be taken away from their mothers and used for food or as sacrificial victims. In the process these statutes define and characterize animal mothers as legal entities, and then exclude them from ritual or other consumption. The four laws that mention female animals as mothers are: (1) Deut 22:6-7, a prohibition on consuming a mother bird along with her eggs or newborn offspring; (2) the thrice-repeated prohibition on boiling a baby goat in its mother's milk (Exod 23:19b; Exod 34:26b; Deut 14:21b); (3) Exod 22:28-29, which states that firstborn males must be sacrificed after spending seven days with their mother; and (4) Lev 22:27-28, which includes two statutes, the first being that a baby animal must remain with its mother for seven days before being sacrificed, and then a ban on slaughtering a parent animal and its offspring on the same day.

These stipulations have often been interpreted together as though they are various manifestations of one single phenomenon, but interpreters have given quite different explanations of that phenomenon. For example, Menachem Haran, following lines of interpretation that go at least as far back as Philo, understands the laws to exemplify a humane disgust at harming an infant and its parent together.[25] Jacob Milgrom finds the basis for these to lie less in ethical concerns than a violation of the principle of separating life and death. By harming offspring in or along with the source of its life, the separation between life and death that is foundational to cultic thought has been destroyed.[26] Based on ancient Near Eastern images of suckling animals, Othmar Keel suggests that the laws have to do with a common belief that the bond between mother and child is an indication of the divine/numinous sanctity of life that is sustained by the divine order of the universe.[27] The suckling mother with her child is the symbol of that power of life; the cultic taboo shows that the Israelite deity has "traits of maternal warmth" and the love and tenderness of a mother.

These interpretations are not necessarily mutually exclusive. Surely to kill a mother along with her child could be problematic on many ethical or ideological grounds. But all of these interpretations fail to notice that each of the laws focuses on the child as the eventual proper victim for slaughter while dismissing the mother as such. Each law constructs a situation that characterizes an animal in

---

25. Menachem Haran, "Seething a Kid in Its Mother's Milk," *JJS* 30 (1979): 23-35.

26. See especially Jacob Milgrom, "Milk and Meat: Unlikely Bedfellows," in *By Study and also by Faith*, vol. 1: *Essays in Honor of Hugh W. Nibley on the Occasion of His Eightieth Birthday*, ed. John M. Lundquist and Stephen D. Ricks (Salt Lake City: Deseret Book, 1990), 144-54.

27. Othmar Keel, *Das Böcklein in der Milch Seiner Mutter und Verwandtes: Im Lichte eines altorientalischen Bildmotivs* (Göttingen: Vandenhoeck und Ruprecht, 1980).

relation to its mother and then prescribes how it may properly be taken from her. Each law also clarifies that the offspring is the proper cultic food, and thus the sacred object, while proscribing the mother or her milk from the sacred realm. Motherhood is the problematic element in these stipulations, not cruelty. In fact, the only context in which the Hebrew Bible remotely discusses any "ethical" slaughtering of animals is in this situation of the relationship of the animal to its mother. There are no laws on humane methods of cutting or burning animals in the Hebrew Bible as there are in Rabbinic commentary or in Greek descriptions of sacrifice.[28] While the prevention of cruelty to animals does not seem to be the primary purpose of these laws, it may add to their effect. Importantly, these laws call attention to the relationship between mother and child; they do not *invoke* that relationship by specifically using it in the cult of the divine but *exclude* it as objectionable to this particular deity.

4.1 *Deuteronomy 22:6-7*

Deut 22:6-7 is not a sacrificial law. It does not describe any sacrificial or festal act, and unlike the other laws, it concerns wild animals, not domesticated animals under human control. Nevertheless, it merits discussion here not only because interpreters have grouped it together with the other laws but also because it parallels the other laws on the relationship of animals used for food and their mothers. It is also the only mention of eggs in biblical law. The passage reads,

> If a bird's nest should appear before you on the road, in any tree or on the ground, with fledglings or eggs and with the mother sitting on the fledglings or on the eggs, do not take the mother who is over her offspring. You will send the mother away but the offspring you can take for yourself, so that it will go well for you and you can have a long life.

Like other laws concerning animal mothers, this law stipulates that the mother bird is not to be taken as food herself. One would assume that if she were found alone she could be captured,[29] but when she is characterized as a mother, by sitting over her offspring, she is off-limits and not allowed to be a food herself. The eggs also cannot be exchanged for the mother; one can only take the offspring. Though the prescription may have other functions or purposes, there is no "humane" reason that it is better to kill or capture multiple infant birds instead of one adult bird; arguably it is more unethical to kill the infant birds.[30] However, to protect

---

28. E.g., b. Ḥul. 1-2; *Shulchan Arukh*—Yoreh Deah 1-28; *Mishneh Torah*, Kedushah, Shechitah (5.3). On Greek slaughter, see, e.g., Gunnel Ekroth, "Animal Sacrifice in Antiquity," in *The Oxford Handbook of Animals in Classical Thought and Life*, ed. Gordon Lindsey Campbell (Oxford: Oxford University Press, 2014).

29. Milgrom, "Milk and Meat," 148.

30. This has been proposed by several interpreters, e.g., Gerhard von Rad, *Deuteronomy: A Commentary*, trans. Dorothea Barton (OTL; Philadelphia, PA: Westminster, 1966), 141.

the mother is a wise choice as a potential food source since she is a proven nubile source of eggs.³¹ But regardless of the motivation, mothers are protected and excluded as food, while their offspring are not.

This law also clarifies the nature of the "feminized protein" of eggs in this context. It indicates that eggs, which might be an ambiguous substance, are to be treated like the fledglings and thus, like meat, may be eaten.³² Yet while the consumption of eggs is permissible here, they are a clean but apparently secular food; the law does not apply to specifically ritual contexts, and there is no other biblical mention of the ritual status of eggs. This law accords with the others by prohibiting the consumption of an animal recognized as a mother, while allowing her offspring to be legitimately consumed, though not in a ritual context.

4.2 Exodus 23:19b; Exodus 34:26b; Deuteronomy 14:21b

The statement "you shall not boil a kid in its mother's milk" (לא־תבשל גדי בחלב אמו) occurs three times in the Pentateuch: twice in Exodus, in 23:19b and 34:26b; and a third time in Deut 14:21b. This sole legalistic mention of milk is a restriction on its use in ritual, not a prescription for it. Both times in Exodus it appears as part of a larger instruction on the three pilgrimage festivals of Matzot, Shevuot, and Sukkot, when all Israelite males (כל־זכורך; Exod 23:17; 34:23) must attend the sanctuary with offerings. In Deuteronomy the phrase does not appear in connection with a specific cultic event but rather in the context of other general restrictions on eating animals. It follows the list of animals forbidden as food (14:3–20) and a prohibition on eating carcasses of animals that have died on their own (14:21a).

This enigmatic statement has merited a great deal of discussion, in part not only because its purpose is cryptic but especially because it is the foundation of the Jewish practice of separating meat products from milk products. Early Judaism expanded the prohibition to apply to the commingling of all meat (but not fish) with the milk of any animal, not just its own mother.³³ It is possible that the law inherently applied to multiple species. The Septuagint translated the term "kid" (גדי) as ἄρνα, a term that applies mainly to sheep but may also include goats. It is possible that the Hebrew term for "kid" (גדי) refers to lambs as well.³⁴ However, it

---

31. Peter C. Craigie, *The Book of Deuteronomy* (NICOT; Grand Rapids, MI: Eerdmans, 1976), 288–9; Jack M. Sasson, "Ritual Wisdom?: On 'Seething a Kid in its Mother's Milk,'" in *Kein Land für sich allein: Studien zum Kulturkontakt in Kanaan, Israel/Palästina und Ebirnari für Manfred Weippert zum 65. Geburtstag*, ed. Ulrich Hübner and Ernst Axel Knauf (Freiburg: Universitätsverlag, 2002), 294–308, here 305.

32. Though this case discusses eggs and birds in the wild, it is possible that domesticated birds were treated differently. See the debate over the law's application to domestic and wild animals in b. Ḥul. 78b.

33. m. Ḥul. 8:4; b. Ḥul. 113a–16a; b. Qidd. 57b (as cited in Propp, *Exodus 19-40*, 285). See also Philo, *Virt.* 144 and Targ. Onq.

34. b. Ḥul. 113a–b, cited, along with other sources, by Propp, *Exodus 19-40*, 284.

is likely that a goat is the intended subject of the Hebrew term since goats were the main source of milk in ancient Israel.[35]

Interpretations of the biblical law have varied. One of the most important theories, propounded especially by Maimonides, is that boiling a baby goat in its mother's milk was a Canaanite cultic practice.[36] To do so, then, would be to enact a pagan rite. The literary placement of the stipulation in Deut 14:21, where it immediately follows a statement associating banned food with foreigners, would seem to strengthen the association of the practice with non-Israelites. As Propp notes, the stipulation, like many dietary restrictions in general, acts as an ethnic marker that distinguishes social groups.[37] However, there is no evidence that intentionally boiling a kid in its own mother's milk was a specific ritual practice in foreign cults, a point that Maimonides himself conceded. At one point some modern scholars argued that the Ugaritic text "The Gods Fair and Beautiful" (KTU 1.23) prescribed the practice of boiling a kid in milk, but that interpretation of the text has been disproven.[38] However, even if boiling a kid in its mother's milk were a Canaanite rite, there must be some other underlying aspect of this practice that was significant to the Hebrew Bible's understanding of it as a non-Yahwistic practice. There are many rituals, such as sacrifice, that are performed in non-Yahwistic religions but that are also important and legitimate aspects of biblical religion. Boiling a kid in mother's milk must have its own problematic significance.

Another interpretation with a long history is that cooking a baby animal in its mother's milk is an inhumane and morally abhorrent practice.[39] Yet while such an act can certainly be perceived as inhumane, cruelty cannot be the sole reason for this proscription. The writers of the Hebrew Bible could have found many practices related to the killing of animals to be abhorrent, yet they focused on this

---

35. Edwin Firmage, "Zoology," *ABD* IV, 1128.

36. *The Guide for the Perplexed* III, 28. See also Martin Noth, *Exodus: A Commentary*, trans. J. S. Bowden (OTL; Philadelphia, PA: Westminster, 1962), 192; Brevard S. Childs, *The Book of Exodus: A Critical, Theological Commentary* (OTL; Louisville, KY: Westminster, 1974), 486.

37. Propp, *Exodus 19-40*, 286.

38. This position was especially championed by Charles Virolleaud in his translation, "La Naissance des Dieux Gracieux et Beaux," *Syria* 14 (1933): 128-51, here 140. However, more recent translations assume that the proper reading concerns an herb and not a milk product. See discussion and critiques in Haran "Seething a Kid in Its Mother's Milk," 25-7; Robert Ratner and Bruce Zuckerman, "'A Kid in Milk?' New Photographs of KTU 1.23, Line 14," *HUCA* 57 (1986): 15-60.

39. See especially Haran, "Seething a Kid in Its Mother's Milk." Note also Nahum Sarna who, following Rashbam, suggests that to boil a kid in its mother's milk would be "insensitivity to the animal's feelings" (*Exodus* [JPS Torah Commentary; Philadelphia, PA: Jewish Publication Society, 1991], 147), a concern that is not iterated anywhere else in the Torah save the possible context of the slaughter of animals with their mothers.

cultic practice, in a law repeated three times, twice in cultic contexts. Additionally, if a concern for cruelty were at issue, one would expect a restriction related to slaughtering the offspring, not boiling it, so that the text would focus on the details of the killing rather than the cooking.[40] The objectionable aspect of this ritual act is not that the kid is cooked, or even that it is boiled, but that it is boiled in its mother's milk; the mother's milk remains the problematic element. So, while there may be a concern for animal cruelty entwined in such a ban, there again must be some larger idea that the practice would violate.

As mentioned above, Milgrom suggests that the problem with boiling a kid in its mother's milk is that the practice is contrary to the ideology of biblical religion, which separates out life from death and promotes life. To kill an animal in the very substance meant to feed it and promote its life is contrary to the worship of the living God, which makes clear divisions between life and death. If he is correct, it is difficult to understand why in this instance the substance symbolic of life (milk) is problematic for the worship of life, while the substance related to death (meat) is its primary material.[41] By Milgrom's reasoning, life (milk) is excluded from the worship of life (the deity) in this circumstance, which does not make sense; one would think milk would be included in ritual if it were emblematic of life. Moreover, although it is easy to understand why one might perceive milk as related to life, it is never characterized that way in the Hebrew Bible, in contrast to blood (Gen 9:4; Lev 17:11–14; Deut 12:23–27).[42] Milk is treated less like sacred animal blood and more like female reproductive blood, which is also excluded from sacrificial practice and which, like milk, is connected to female reproduction.[43]

---

40. C. J. Labuschagne, "'You Shall Not Boil a Kid in Its Mother's Milk': A New Proposal for the Origin of the Prohibition," in *The Scriptures and the Scrolls: Studies in Honor of A.S. van der Woude on the Occasion of His 65th Birthday*, ed. F. García Martínez, A. Hilhorst, and C. J. Labuschagne (Leiden: Brill, 1992), 6–17, here 8.

41. Similarly, Calum Carmichael suggests that this and the other laws separate God's life-giving from God's life-taking roles ("On Separating Life and Death: An Explanation of Some Biblical Laws," *HTR* 69 [1976]: 1–7). If this is the case, we must conclude that sacrifice is theologically promoting God as life-taker in these contexts.

42. According to Labuschagne ("'You Shall Not Boil a Kid in Its Mother's Milk'"), the prohibition is based on blood: he suggests that the law alludes to a mother animal's first milk of colostrum (or "beestings"), which appears to contain blood because it has an intense amount of proteins that turn the milk a deep yellow color. It would be forbidden to consume this first milk at Sukkot as a violation on eating blood.

43. Note also the theory of Jean Soler ("The Semiotics of Food in the Bible," in *Food and Drink in History: Selections from the Annales, Economies, Societes, Economies, Societes, Civilisations Vol. 5*, ed. Robert Forster and Orest A. Ranum [Baltimore, MD: Johns Hopkins University Press, 1979], 126–38) and Eilberg-Schwartz (*The Savage in Judaism*, 129), who argue that the prohibition relates to incest, and indicates that "you shall not put a mother and her son into the same pot, any more than into the same bed" (Soler, "The Semiotics of Food in the Bible," 136). They believe that the maternal/child bond, which could become

The literary contexts in which the law appears to speak to its function. Whatever its purpose, the ban appears in Exodus twice as the concluding remark of two parallel pericopes about pilgrimage festivals. This placement demonstrates that in Exodus the ban was understood to be a sacrificial law, important to public and official worship. It appears first in Exod 23:14–19:

> Three times a year you will make a pilgrimage for me ... Three times a year all your males will appear before the lord Yahweh. You will not sacrifice the blood of my sacrifice with leaven; and you will not leave overnight the fat of my pilgrimage offering until morning. The best first fruits of your ground you will bring to the house of Yahweh your god. You will not boil a kid in its mother's milk.

Though the law appears in the context of the pilgrimage feasts, scholars debate whether it applies only to offerings made at Sukkot;[44] to firstlings offered at both Sukkot and Shevuot;[45] to the Passover offering;[46] to all three pilgrimage festivals; to all sacrifice in general;[47] or only to firstling offerings.[48] Alternatively, some have argued that the law is not connected to sacrifice at all but to secular feasts that accompany all three festivals.[49] But regardless of whether the stipulation regarding milk applies only to one pilgrimage or in all sacrificial circumstances, the passages regard it as related to pilgrimage.

Importantly, the text emphasizes that at the three pilgrimage feasts "all your males" (כל־זכורך) must attend. The feasts therefore become occasions for defining, creating, and binding together the community of males who attend them. Banning the practice of boiling a kid in its mother's milk, as an image of mothers and

too close, is in need of regulation. This interpretation seems far-fetched, though it has the benefit of showing that the prohibition addresses motherhood and illustrates that a bond between mothers and their children could become problematically close. However, I believe the problem is a genealogical/matrilineal one rather than a sexual one.

44. Haran, "Seething a Kid in Its Mother's Milk," 34–5; Sarna, following Rashbam (*Exodus*, 147).

45. Suggested by Labuchange, "'You Shall Not Boil a Kid in Its Mother's Milk,'" 14.

46. Bernard R. Goldstein and Alan M. Cooper, "The Festivals of Israel and Judah and the Literary History of the Pentateuch," *JAOS* 110 (1990): 19–31, here 29. However, they suggest that it was originally a northern requirement for general sacrifice that R[JE] combined with other Passover legislation in this context. The general law for festal sacrifices, in their opinion, leads to the later priestly restriction against boiling the Passover sacrifice in Exod 12:8.

47. Milgrom suggests that either all three pilgrimages or all sacrifice in general is a possibility. See "Milk and Meat," 148.

48. Labuschange, "'You Shall Not Boil a Kid in Its Mother's Milk,'" 15.

49. Axel Knauf, "Zur Herkunft und Sozialgeschichte Israels: 'Das Böckchen in der Milch seiner Mutter,'" *Bib* 69 (1988): 153–69.

motherhood, reinforces the masculine character of these rites that create patrilineal social bonds. The law appears to be a means of rejecting a maternal "natural symbol" of milk in order to emphasize the masculine nature of the proceedings and the bonds among men. To boil a kid in its mother's milk in this ritual context might embrace the relationship between mother and offspring, while prohibiting it shuns that relationship. While the prohibition does not necessarily entail restricting the relationship between mothers and offspring at all times, and perhaps even only once a year, its appearance here in the ritual context of one or all sacrificial pilgrimage feasts adds to the focus on masculinity, patrilineality, and the prioritization of the male line on those occasions.

In Deuteronomy the injunction against boiling a kid in milk appears at the end of ch. 14, which begins with restrictions against foreign mourning practices (vv. 1–2), and then recites a list of animals forbidden as food (vv. 3–20; cf., Leviticus 11). The stipulation immediately follows a ban on eating the meat of an animal that has died of natural causes. Deuteronomy 14:21 states, "You will not eat a carcass; give it to the resident alien in your gates so that he will eat it or sell it to a foreigner. For you are a holy people to Yahweh your god. You will not boil a kid in its mother's milk." Although the phrase appears to be something of a non-sequitur here, it suggests that eating a kid boiled in its mother's milk is like eating something that is diseased or impure and non-Israelite.[50] Thus here the idea of milk, which again might be associated with life, becomes related to death and impurity. In this context, boiling meat with milk also associates it with foreignness so that the image of the maternal bond is distinctly outside the lineage and identity of Israel. Since again there is no restriction on boiling a kid in some other substance, we must assume here that the mother's milk itself is the problematic element.[51]

In Deuteronomy the law against boiling a kid in milk is detached from the sacrificial context of the three pilgrimage feasts. These are mentioned elsewhere, in Deut 16:16, which reiterates the same phrase regarding the requirement that all males (כל־זכורך) must attend. So, in Exodus these two aspects of pilgrimage feasts, the gathering of males and the exclusion of boiling milk, are related to each other, but in Deuteronomy they are separated and speak to different contexts. While males are still required to attend the feasts, the prohibition against boiling in mother's milk here applies to every context of eating young animals. It is not just a sacrificial law but a general food law. But the restriction, whose aim was to solidify

---

50. Note that the Codex Freer Manuscript of Deut 14:21b adds, "whoever does so, is doing as if offering a mole, an impurity (evoking the wrath) of the God of Jacob." Cited in Sasson, "Ritual Wisdom?" 296.

51. It should be noted that Stefan Schorch has argued that the law should be interpreted to mean that one should not eat a suckling kid (i.e., "who is with the milk of its mother"). If that is the case, the interpretation would in some ways cause this law to align even more strongly with its parallels, as it would imply that when the kid is still being suckled, and thus is in its mother's domain, it is not permissible for this form of ritual setting. "'A Young Goat in Its Mother's Milk'?: Understanding an Ancient Prohibition," VT 60 [2010]: 116–30.

the members of the sacrificing community of the pilgrimage feast(s), now aims to help unify the community of all people in Israel. Unlike the priestly laws, Deuteronomy secularizes meat-eating away from the centralized shrine, yet it retains this sacrificial law to help create a more national community of practitioners on a larger ideological kinship level. The law encourages the communal/kinship connection of all Israelites, including women (Deut 12:12, 18; 16:11, 14), who are nevertheless organized along patrilineal kinship lines.

Implicitly, this law about boiling a kid, like the others, excludes not only a symbol of the mother but the mother herself as a ritual substance. Though the mother goat is not explicitly discussed in this stipulation, the formulation seems not to see her as a source of meat herself since she must be alive to be producing milk.[52] If the mother has milk to feed the infant, it would make little sense to slaughter her at that time, since this milk could be used for human food. Thus, as in the bird law of Deuteronomy, the mother is treated as a source of potential food and is therefore left alone and not offered herself. As in the bird law, there is also no problem with viewing the offspring as food; the only issue is in how it may be cooked. Again, this is not a humane concern but one of practicality for animal husbandry and of the ideology of motherhood.

4.3 Exodus 22:29–30 and Leviticus 22:27–28

The assumptions that a mother should not be slaughtered or consumed and that her offspring instead is the suitable food or offering lie behind another law. Exodus 22:29–30 [Heb 28–29] also discusses a sacrificial animal in relation to its mother: "You will not be late with your produce and what you have pressed. The firstborn of your sons you will give to me. So you will do with your oxen and your flock: seven days it will be with its mother; on the eighth day you will give it to me."

This decree does not necessarily specify the sex of firstborn children or offspring, because the term "sons" (בנים) can at times mean "children,"[53] yet the parallels stipulate that it must be male (but cf. Exod 13:2). In its treatment of animals, this law is similar to another, Lev 22:27, which reads, "Any ox or sheep or

---

52. Jack M. Sasson offers the interpretation that it is not the mother's milk (חָלָב) that is the problem but the mother's fat (חֵלֶב). The two words have the same consonants and thus appear as the same word in unpointed Hebrew texts ("Ritual Wisdom," 294–308). In that case, the law bans the killing and cooking of the mother along with the child, as in Deuteronomy 22 and Leviticus 22. I find Sasson's argument doubtful because: (1) there is already a parallel law about the cultic use of fat in both Exodus 23 and 34; (2) other passages forbid the consumption of fat in any sense (e.g., Lev 3:17; 7:23–25); (3) there is no textual witness or interpretive tradition that supports the reading of "fat" instead of "milk"; and (4) the wording is perfectly clear and does not require emendation. A Karaite interpretation is that the law means one should not delay the offering of a firstling so that it ripens (בשל) on its mother's milk (Haran, "Seething a Kid," 28; Propp, *Exodus 1-18*, 432).

53. E.g., Gen 3:14; 21:7; Exod 21:5; 22:23. See BDB "בֵּן" §3, 4.

goat that is born shall stay seven days with its mother, but from the eighth day onwards it will be acceptable as an offering by fire to Yahweh." Like the others, the verse in Exodus understands the offspring as the primary commodity to be taken as an offering but shows there must be some qualification on this use. It also portrays the mother as living, and thus not as a victim, at least during the seven days that her offspring is alive. However, while the law in Exodus demands the sacrifice or possible donation to the sanctuary on the eighth day of the animal's life, Leviticus mentions only the animal's acceptability for sacrifice from the eighth day forward. Also, the law in Exodus discusses firstlings while Lev 22:27 concerns any domesticated animal used for sacrifice. Nevertheless, here too the mother is juxtaposed to the cult and its deity since for the first week of its life, while it is with its mother, the infant is decidedly not acceptable as a sacrifice, but afterward it may be taken from her and given to the deity and the priests.

As in Exod 22:30, the seven-day ritual period in Lev 22:27 calls attention to the relationship between the mother and her young and highlights how the offspring belongs to the mother or is otherwise safe with her during this time. Yet after the seven days, the infant does or can belong to the deity and is thereby separated from the mother by ritual and sacrifice. This ideology also appears for human sons who are offered (and redeemed) on the eighth day of their lives or are circumcised on the eighth day (Gen 17:12; 21:4; Lev 12:3). In both cases the cultic acceptability of male offspring after their first week of life differentiates and separates them from their mothers, bringing them from the maternal and private domain into the patrilineal/paternal and public ritual domain. Taken together, all these stipulations create an opposition between the mother and the sacred, and their competing realms to which children belong. It also highlights that this relationship is strongest during the week following birth but can then be undone.

Interpreters have proposed several symbolic theories to understand Exod 22:30 and Lev 22:27, such as respect for the life of the infant; respect for the mother's feelings; or respect for the bond of the relationship between mother and offspring.[54] It is possible that the laws have the functional purpose of keeping the infant with the mother for seven days so that the infant will help her establish her milk production, which can then be taken over for milking once the infant is removed.[55] Some interpreters have suggested similar explanations for the

---

54. In his commentary on Leviticus, Milgrom gives the five usual rationales for this law: (1) it is modeled on circumcision; (2) after seven days the infant is considered "born"; (3) after seven days any disqualifying blemishes appear and one can tell if it was an aborted fetus; (4) the seven days is a purificatory period for the infant from its mother's impurity; and (5) the law is humanitarian in nature (*Leviticus 17-22*, 1883). Alternatively, Francis Gorman suggests that the seven days act as a buffer zone between the infant's life and its death, thus keeping these two forces separate. See *Leviticus: Divine Presence and Community* (Grand Rapids, MI: Eerdmans, 1997), 126.

55. Hans Goedicke suggests a similar interpretation, following Philo (*Virt.*, 128-9), that the law was meant to provide relief for the mother whose udders would be painful at this

prohibition on boiling a kid in its mother's milk.[56] If these more practical functions are the reason behind the seven-day waiting period for the sacrifice of animals, the process nevertheless becomes a means of ritually expressing the ideological contrast between the maternal and the sacred as a part of the sacrificial system.

Immediately following the Holiness writer's seven-day restriction on sacrificing infants is a law relating the death of an animal to that of its parents. The verses in Lev 22:27–28 state, "Any ox or sheep or goat that is born will stay seven days with its mother, but from the eighth day onwards it will be acceptable as a fire offering to Yahweh. However, you will not slaughter an ox or sheep on the same day together with its child." This second restriction regarding animals in relation to their parents resembles the law on birds in Deuteronomy 22 by prohibiting the simultaneous killing of offspring and mother. There are very good economic reasons for not slaughtering a mother animal on the eighth day after birth; at that time she is making a great deal of milk (and is also a proven source of offspring). Yet perhaps the reason Leviticus contains this prescription while Exodus does not is that Leviticus discusses any animal at any age along with its parent. Exodus 22 was concerned only with the firstling on the eighth day, when it is highly unlikely one would want to slaughter the mother. Since the prescription in Leviticus could extend for years, the possibility of offering a mother with her young is more likely; she could, for example, grow past her reproductive life and be slaughtered together with the offspring on some special occasion. Thus, these stipulations may reflect some immediate practical purpose, but ultimately they extend far beyond practicality. They imply that the relationship between mother and offspring that appears so strong in the first week after birth would also be found in their simultaneous death. Killing them together is a prohibited expression of their connection. Their mutual death somehow brings about the same kind of closeness as birth. According to these stipulations, either the child or the parent may be slaughtered at any time after the eighth day. After that point, killing either alone would be fine since their relationship would not be recognized.[57]

The law of the birds in Deuteronomy similarly expresses that the death, or the possession, of both at the same time is the forbidden state. The eggs or fledglings can be taken at any point, and the female bird may be taken if she is found on her own; but when she is sitting over her eggs or infants, and thus acting in a motherly way, taking her is forbidden. Restricting the simultaneous killing of mother and child at any time calls attention to their relationship yet does not glorify it. On the

---

early stage (See "Review of *Das Böcklein in der Milch Seiner Mutter und Verwandtes*, by Othamar Keel," *JNES* 42 [1983]: 302–3). Goedicke argues that the prohibition, like those in Exod 22:29–30 and Lev 22:27–28, is against killing an infant who is solely dependent upon its mother's milk.

56. Most notably J. G. Frazer, *Folk-Lore in the Old Testament III* (London: Macmillan, 1919), 111–64. Following him are T. H. Gaster, *Myth, Legend and Custom in the Old Testament Vol. I* (New York: Harper & Row, 1969), 250–63.

57. Milgrom, "Milk and Meat," 148.

other hand, offering them intentionally at the same time would seemingly have the ritual effect of highlighting their bond and embracing it, just as intentionally boiling a kid in its mother's milk might do. Instead, these laws highlight the bonds between mothers and their offspring, but explicitly forbid the sanctification of that relationship by ritual.

It is possible that the stipulation in Lev 22:28 proscribes the killing of an animal simultaneously not only with its mother but its father as well. Although the law is generally understood to apply to the infant and its mother, especially since it follows and is connected to a law concerning the mother, the grammar of the verse in Hebrew more properly reflects the possibility that it could be either parent.[58] It literally states, "and ox or sheep/goat, he/it and his/its son you shall not slaughter in one day" (ושור או־שה אתו ואת־בנו לא תשחטו ביום אחד). The entire verse contains only masculine or neutral nouns and pronouns. Although the grammatically masculine forms שור (cattle) and שה (sheep/goat) have generic meanings, had they indicated only female animals this could have been made clear by using a feminine pronoun (i.e., "she and her son"), if not the feminine names of the animals (פרה, כשבה). Moreover, it is possible that one might indeed be tempted to sacrifice a father animal and his offspring on the same day since large numbers of male animals, both young and old, were often slaughtered during important cultic events. For example, the returnees from exile during the time of Ezra offered as burnt offerings "twelve bulls on behalf of all Israel, ninety-six rams, seventy-seven lambs and twelve he-goats as a purification offering" (Ezra 8:35). This tremendous group does not seem to include any females and is made up of males of varying ages. There is therefore a real possibility of slaughtering the sire and his offspring on the same day; the law then would limit a practical situation.

If this is the meaning of the law, it would be the only stipulation regarding animals and their fathers. It would also be a variation on those that exclude the relationship between mother and offspring from sacred activity. Such a law would cause the person who bred the animals, as well as its seller and its slaughterer, to be aware of the animal's lineage, lest the father and kid be killed on the same day.[59] Yet, just as with its mother, it would place the animal's biological paternity at odds with its cultic purpose by discouraging that biological relationship between

---

58. Scholarship and the versions are divided as to which parent the prescription intends. b. Ḥul. 79b (in the argument of Hananiah), the Ramban, and 11QT 52:5-7 suggest that it refers to both the mother and the father (see Milgrom, *Leviticus 17-23*, 1884). Levine also hints at this interpretation (*Leviticus*, 152). However, the targumim (Targ. Onq., Targ. Neof.), the LXX, the Rabbis in b. Chul. 78b, and Erhard S. Gerstenberger (*Leviticus: A Commentary* [OTL; Louisville, KY: Westminster John Knox, 1993], 331) suggest that this prescription pertains only to the mother (for others holding this position see Milgrom, *Leviticus 17-23*, 1884). Milgrom argues that it is ambiguous because it is continuing the previous verse.

59. Jonathan Klawans, *Purity, Sacrifice, and the Temple: Symbolism and Supercessionism in the Study of Ancient Judaism* (New York: Oxford University Press, 2006), 60, 63.

males and their offspring. This reading of the stipulation supports Jay's thought that sacrificial activity, while intimately related to concepts of lineage, is one that supersedes biological reproduction. The biological relationship between parents and their offspring cannot be highlighted in sacrificial ritual; instead, the ritual forms bonds over biology. Moreover, if the intent of Lev 22:28 is to portray male reproduction in a cultically negative light, the stipulation then fulfills a function similar to Lev 15:16–18 (and parallels in Lev 22:4; Deut 23:10–11 [Heb. 11–12]; 1 Sam 21:4–5; cf., Exod 19:15), which characterizes male biological reproduction (i.e., ejaculation and intercourse) as impure and thereby also excluded from sacral activity. The human impurities of childbirth and ejaculation distance human reproduction from the sacred, while the proscriptions against the slaughter of animal parents distance their biological reproduction from it. Ritual bonds supersede physical bonds in both the human and animal worlds.

5. Conclusion

As mentioned above, Othmar Keel offers an opposing interpretation to that argued here: the origins of the milk law and on parent/child slaughter have to do with a common ancient belief that the bond between mother and child, as seen in images of a suckling mother animal with her offspring, is a manifestation of the divine sanctity of life, sustained by the order of the universe. The Israelite variations show that the biblical God has a mother's love and "traits of maternal warmth." Keel's interpretation has much to commend it, especially its focus on the mother. But the biblical ritual laws do not *embrace* this numinous power but instead specifically *reject* the power of the mother and separate it from the divine by desacralizing it. These laws contrast with many polytheistic sacrificial cults that offered not only milk and eggs but also pregnant (mother) animals, such as in the Roman rite of Fordicidia, where thirty-one pregnant cows were sacrificed to the earth goddess Tellus every year to promulgate the fertility of the earth.[60] Milk, eggs, and mother animals are emphatically not a part of the official sacrificial worship of the God of Israel. If the point were to embrace the mother-like features of the

---

60. See Ovid, *Fasti* IV. 629–72, 731–40. For other rituals of pregnant animals see Varro, *Res Rusticae* II. 5, 6–7; *De Lingua Latina* VI. 15; Lydus, *De Mensibus* IV. 49 and 72; F. T. Van Straten, *Hiera Kala: Images of Animal Sacrifice in Archaic and Classical Greece* (Religions in the Graeco-Roman World, 127; Leiden: Brill, 1995), 26, 77, 170, 180. Biblical law never addresses pregnant animals (or women). However, Philo (*Virt.* 26: 137) and the Temple Scroll (11QT52:5–7) both state that pregnant animals are forbidden as sacrificial victims, the latter because they are considered to be blemished (Joseph M. Baumgarten, "A Fragment on Fetal Life and Pregnancy in 4Q270," in *Pomegranates and Golden Bells: Studies in Biblical, Jewish and Near Eastern Ritual, Law and Literature in Honor of Jacob Milgrom*, ed. David P. Wright, David Noel Freedman and Avi Hurvitz [Winona Lake, IN: Eisenbrauns, 1995], 445–8, here 445).

deity, these substances might be included in the cult and ritually harnessed for their power. Such invocation of maternal fertility might be the case in Gen 18:8, where Abraham offers a meal of a calf and milk products to his divine visitors, who then announce Sarah's pregnancy. The symbolic highlighting of the motherly care for offspring might also be more properly found in the story of the two milk cows who carry the ark back to Israelite territory in 1 Samuel 6. The slaughter of these mother animals, who cried for their newborns as they left them, highlights their maternal love. But this is not the case in the official and codified versions of ritual practice where the cult is instead defined in opposition to maternal power. There, mother animals are decidedly not slaughtered and thus not characterized as sacred. However much the biblical deity is thought to have maternal aspects (e.g., Gen 49:25; Deut 32:18; Isa 66:13) the symbols of motherhood are not incorporated into the Bible's codified ritual practice.

Part of the effect of the rites addressed in this study is to break the bond between mother and child so that the offspring can be taken from her. These passages assume that killing offspring is always acceptable, just not when it includes anything having to do with the mother: one *should* slaughter a firstborn animal on the eighth day (just not the mother as well); one *should* cook a kid at pilgrimage feasts (just not in mother's milk); it *will* go well for you if you take wild fledglings (but not if you take the mother too). The ritual negotiation of this separation from the mother is parallel in laws for humans in patrilineal contexts, where offspring are taken over from the mother as the genealogical possessions of the father. Circumcision and the devotion of the firstborn son also negotiate means by which offspring, especially male offspring, become differentiated from their mothers. If we agree with Jay that a purpose of sacrificial rites is to establish patrilineal bonds that supersede maternal biological bonds, the separation between child and mother must be understood as one of the main purposes of the sacrificial cult.

Again, the secularization of mothers or their milk does not mean that they are understood negatively in larger biblical thought. The Hebrew Bible very often celebrates mothers, and Israel's utopian moniker is a "land flowing with milk and honey." Milk is a religiously valued food; however, milk (and honey) is incompatible with the *sacrificial cult* with its construction of kinship ties and by extension the negotiation of property. The omission of mothers and their substances in these circumstances does not entail their rejection from all things Israelite but only from the sacrificial contexts of the laws.

Chapter 4

DRINKING THE GOLDEN CALF: CONSUMPTION AND TRANSFORMATION IN EXODUS 32

Laura Quick

1. Introduction

In Exodus 32, with Moses delayed upon Mount Sinai, the Israelites gather around Aaron and ask him to make them an idol to worship. In v. 1 they declare,

> Get up, make us gods that will go before us. As for this fellow Moses, the man who brought us up from the land of Egypt, we do not know what has become of him![1]

Aaron responds in v. 2 with a command of his own:

> Break off the gold earrings that are on the ears of your wives, your sons, and your daughters, and bring them to me.

The people do as Aaron commands, removing their golden earrings and giving them to Aaron, who uses an engraving tool to fashion the jewelry into a molten golden calf. The calf is thus composed from items taken directly from the bodies of the Israelite people. Mundane items of bodily adornment are transformed through Aaron's craftsmanship to become an idol appropriate for worship.[2] Aaron therefore builds an altar before the golden calf and declares a feast. The Israelites celebrate, offering burnt offerings and peace offerings, eating, drinking, and playing (v. 6).

---

1. English Bible translations are based on the New English Translation (NET), with alterations where necessary. Verse enumeration follows the Hebrew Bible.
2. The verb used to describe the process of making the calf, צוּר, means "to cast out of metal," e.g., in 1 Kgs 7:15, where it refers to the production of two bronze pillars for the decoration of the tabernacle. Though this calf is described as a מסכה, "molten image," this need not imply that the calf was solid gold; the same term is used in Isa 30:22 for gold plating. Here in Exod 32:4, Aaron uses a חרט, "stylus," to engrave the gold: it is explicitly a crafted and worked image.

God quickly sends Moses back from the mountain to chastise his fellow Israelites. Furious, Moses breaks the tablets inscribed with the commandments of God. As for the calf,

> He took the calf they had made and burned it in the fire, ground it to powder, poured it out on the water, and made the Israelites drink it. (v. 20)

As one of the most evocative descriptions of the sins of the people of Israel in the Hebrew Bible, the story of the golden calf has been the subject of numerous treatments by subsequent commentators. Scholars have connected the story of the golden calf to the sins of Jeroboam described in the books of Kings, as well as considered the ritualistic nature of the destruction of the religious object. Typically, this has been understood in one of two ways: either (1) as a "trial by ordeal"; or (2) as the utilization of a literary trope known elsewhere from ancient Near Eastern literature to depict total annihilation. In this essay, I will consider these suggestions. Without disputing the connections between the story of the golden calf either with the books of Kings or the ancient Near Eastern material, I argue that approaches in this direction fail to account for one important aspect of the golden calf account: the forced consumption of the destroyed calf by the Israelites. At the same time, the interpretation of this consumption as a "trial by ordeal" does not make good sense of the narrative either. Instead, by considering the ritual potential of consumption as a transformative act, I argue for an additional implication to Moses' destruction of the calf: as a ritual inversion aimed at transforming the object from sacred to mundane. This has implications for both ancient Israelite religious ritual and practice, as well as the treatment of the golden calf episode in subsequent biblical retellings.

2. The Destruction of the Golden Calf and the Cultic Reforms of the Books of Kings

As noted, a number of scholars have argued for a connection between the narrative of the golden calf in Exodus 32 with the story of Jeroboam's cultic innovations in 1 Kings 12. Both narratives describe the production of a calf or calves for worship, and additionally we find parallels in the phrase "These are your gods, O Israel, that brought you up out of Egypt"; the construction of altars; and the proclamation of a feast.[3] Consequently, it has been argued that the Exodus narrative was created as a polemic against Jeroboam's cultic "reform," which according to the books of

---

3. Exod 32:4; cf., 1 Kgs 12:28; Exod 32:5; cf., 1 Kgs 12:32-33. Nathan MacDonald has explained the use of the plural "gods" in Exod 32:4, 8, although the calf is singular, in light of the Jeroboam account. See "Recasting the Golden Calf: The Imaginative Potential of the Old Testament's Portrayal of Idolatry," in *Idolatry: False Worship in the Bible, Early Judaism, and Christianity*, ed. S. C. Barton (London: T&T Clark, 2007), 22-39, here 35n. 52.

Kings took place in the tenth century BCE.[4] The books of Kings present Jeroboam as a religious innovator, introducing apostate practices into Israelite religion, including the worship of golden calves. These were then revoked by King Josiah in the seventh century, who returned the religion back to its proper and original form by removing these tendencies toward idolatry and centralizing worship within the Jerusalem Temple. On the other hand, many modern scholars have asserted that it was actually Josiah who was the innovator. The reforms "introduced" by Jeroboam were once normative in ancient Israel.[5] In particular, bull imagery is frequently associated with worship of Yahweh in the Hebrew Bible[6] and in fact with Northwest Semitic deities in general (so the Canaanite deity El in the texts recovered from Ras Shamra[7]). By couching the traditional bull imagery of Yahweh in terms of the "golden calves," the Deuteronomistic Historian is attempting to hide normative Israelite practices in a polemic, utilizing a young animal in order to intend some derogatory meaning—as Jeremy Hutton has noted, the term "calf" occurs in other intentionally polemic passages associated with the Bethel and Samaria cults, too.[8]

Josiah's reforms were predicated upon his "discovery" of a Book of Law in the Jerusalem Temple. According to modern scholarship, this Book of Law is to be identified as an early core of the book of Deuteronomy.[9] As many have noted, the motif of book-finding in holy places was common in antiquity, where it served to legitimate cultic reform by couching the innovation either as a "return" to behaviors of the past or by providing a divine origin for the impulse.[10] Both are at play in the books of Kings, and so the discovered scroll serves to legitimate

---

4. See Moses Aberbach and Leivy Smolar, "Aaron, Jeroboam and the Golden Calves," *JBL* 86 (1967): 129–40.

5. See Ziony Zevit, *The Religions of Ancient Israel: A Synthesis of Parallactic Approaches* (London: Continuum, 2001), 449.

6. Gen 49:24; Num 23:22; 24:8; Deut 33:17; Isa 1:24; 49:26; 60:16; Ps 132:2, 5. On bull symbolism in Israelite and ancient Near Eastern religion, see J. Gerald Janzen, "The Character of the Calf and Its Cult in Exodus 32," *CBQ* 52 (1990): 597–607.

7. Daniel E. Fleming, "If El Is a Bull, Who Is a Calf? Reflections on Religion in Second-Millennium Syria Palestine," *EI* 26 (1999): 23–7.

8. As well as the obvious case of Exodus 32, see Deut 9:16, 21; 2 Kgs 10:29; 17:16; 2 Chr 11:15; 13:8; Neh 9:18; Ps 106:19; Hos 8:5–6; 10:5. In Hos 10:5 the feminine form of "calf" is used, which Hutton suggests is a further example of an intended insult. See Jeremy M. Hutton, "Southern, Northern and Transjordanian Perspectives," in *Religious Diversity in Ancient Israel and Judah*, ed. Francesca Stavrakopoulou and John Barton (London: T&T Clark, 2010), 149–76.

9. Affinities between Josiah's reforms and the concerns of Deuteronomy include Deut 17:3 // 2 Kgs 23:4, 5, 11; Deut 12:2–3. // 2 Kgs 23:8, 13, 14; Deut 18:8 // 2 Kgs 23:9; Deut 16:5–8. // 2 Kgs 23:22, 23. For a recent assessment, see Michael Pietsche, *Die Kultreform Josias: Studien zur Religionsgeschichte Israels in der späten Königszeit* (FAT 86; Tübingen: Mohr Siebeck, 2013).

10. See Katherine M. Stott, "Finding the Lost Book of the Law: Re-Reading the Story of 'The Book of the Law' (Deuteronomy—2 Kings) in Light of Classical Literature," *JSOT* 30 (2005): 153–69.

or undergird Josiah's cultic and religious innovations. Alongside the composition of Deuteronomy, Josiah's religious movement was further legitimated by the composition of the "Deuteronomistic History," the books of Joshua, Judges, Samuel, and Kings.[11] These texts reflect upon the kings and queens who had ruled over Israel and Judah, assessing their relative success or failure on the basis of the theological suppositions of the book of Deuteronomy, and so Josiah's reform movement of cultic centralization. Accordingly, Jeroboam and the other kings of the Northern Kingdom of Israel, with their sanctuaries (and calves) at Bethel and Dan, are condemned; Josiah, on the other hand, is held up for high praise.

In this context, the parallel between Moses' destruction of the golden calf with Josiah's destruction of the cultic objects of idol worship is significant. In 2 Kgs 23:6 we learn,

He removed the Asherah pole[12] from the Lord's temple and took it outside Jerusalem to the brook of Kidron, where he burned it. He smashed it to dust and then threw the dust in the public graveyard.

In v. 12 Josiah employs a similar method with the altars established by Manasseh:

The king tore down the altars the kings of Judah had set up on the roof of Ahaz's upper room, as well as the altars Manasseh had set up in the two courtyards of the Lord's temple. He crushed them up[13] and threw the dust in the brook of Kidron.

---

11. Martin Noth (*Überlieferungsgeschichtliche Studien 1* [Halle: Niemeyer, 1943]) originally argued that the entire Deuteronomistic History was written during the Babylonian exile. Following Frank Moore Cross (*Canaanite Myth and Hebrew Epic: Essays in the History of the Religion of Israel* [Cambridge, MA: Harvard University Press, 1973], 274–89), it is usually agreed that Joshua–2 Kings were initially compiled during the time of Josiah, and so contemporary to parts of the book of Deuteronomy, in the seventh century. Following the Babylonian exile, the Deuteronomistic History was revised again to explain these events. Moreover, the Deuteronomistic Historian continually refers to his sources (e.g., the "Scroll of the Upright One" in Josh 10:13 and 2 Sam 1:8), preserving accounts and traditions that don't always agree with each other (compare, e.g., the conquest accounts in the books of Joshua and Judges). Thus, the compositional history of this body of text is complex and likely preserves earlier traditions. For a recent overview of the theory of the Deuteronomistic History, see Thomas C. Römer, "Deuteronomistic History," *EBR* 6 (2013): 648–53.

12. In the Hebrew Bible the word אשרה is used in two related senses, sometimes as the name of the goddess Asherah and sometimes as a wooden representation of her.

13. The MT reads "he ran from there"; however, this makes little contextual sense. Mordechai Cogan and Hayim Tadmor (*II Kings: A New Translation* [AB; Garden City, NY: Doubleday, 1988], 289) therefore emend the verbal form from a qal to a hiphil with third-person plural suffix, translating "he quickly removed them." The suffix may have been lost in the MT due to haplography with the *mem* that immediately follows the verb on the form משם, "from there." However, in light of the similarities of this verse to the other descriptions

In the first account, Josiah first burns then beats the Asherah pole to dust, finally sprinkling the dust upon the graves located in the Kidron Valley. In the second, Josiah omits the burning of the altars, but crushes them to dust before scattering the dust into the brook of Kidron, the river that flowed through the Kidron Valley. Both accounts are highly similar, although not identical, to Moses' destruction of the golden calf, incorporating the tropes of burning, crushing, and scattering, although only in the second account is the ash dissolved into water. Josiah is reversing the cultic "innovations" of Jeroboam, in a literary depiction that characterizes him as a second Moses. Consequently, the story of the golden calf in the book of Exodus reached its final form in response to the reforms of Josiah,[14] creating a literary paradigm for the destruction of idolatrous cultic objects. The story of the golden calf and in particular its destruction at the hands of Moses is thus related to both the description of Jeroboam's cultic reforms in 1 Kings 12, as well as Josiah's reversal of these reforms in 2 Kings 23.

3. The Destruction of the Golden Calf as Ordeal and Annihilation

As well as the literary similarities that scholars have observed between the story of the calf and the cultic reform of Jeroboam in the books of Kings, a secondary concern has been to explicate the ritualistic nature of Moses' acts of destruction wrought upon the calf. A fairly typical explanation is that this text describes a "trial by ordeal," a process designed to determine guilt or innocence by subjecting the accused to hazardous tests thought to be under divine control. This was how the episode was understood already in antiquity. Rabbinic exegesis connected the incident of the calf to the Soṭah ritual in Numbers 5:

> The priest will then take holy water in a pottery jar and take some of the dust that is on the floor of the tabernacle and put it into the water.
>
> …
>
> Then the priest will put the woman under oath and say to her, "If no other man has had sexual relations with you, and if you have not gone astray and become defiled while under your husband's authority, may you be free from this bitter water that brings a curse. But if you have gone astray while under your husband's authority, and if you have defiled yourself and some man other than your husband has had sexual relations with you. …" Then the priest will put the woman under the oath of the curse and will say to her, "The Lord make you

---

of the destruction of religious objects both here in the books of Kings as well as in Exodus 32, it makes better sense to amend the verb from רוץ, "run," to the piel of רצץ, "to crush," again with a third plural suffix.

14. To be sure, there may be a core pre-Deuteronomistic tradition in Exodus 32; the narrative has clearly been subject to some interpolations. On the compositional history of the chapter, see Christine E. Hayes, "Golden Calf Stories: The Relationship of Exodus

an attested curse among your people, if the Lord makes your thigh fall away and your abdomen swell; and this water that causes the curse will go into your stomach, and make your abdomen swell and your thigh rot."

...

Then the priest will write these curses in a scroll and then scrape them off into the bitter water. He will make the woman drink the bitter water that brings a curse, and the water that brings a curse will enter into her to produce bitterness. (vv. 17–24)

Here the drinking of the "bitter water" produces an efficacious effect.[15] According to the traditional rabbinic view, the effect of the potion upon an adulterous woman—the rupture of her thighs—caused the woman's death.[16] However, many modern scholars have interpreted "thigh" here as a euphemism for the reproductive organs,[17] and the ritual applied to a woman who has become pregnant by her alleged lover. If so, the result of the ritual is a miscarriage of the fetus, with the woman herself surviving.[18] But in either case, the ritual functions to produce a visible

---

32 and Deuteronomy 9-10," in *The Idea of Biblical Interpretation: Essays in Honor of James L. Kugel*, ed. Hindy Najman and Judith H. Newman (Leiden: Brill, 2003), 45–93.

15. The usual interpretation of this ritual relates the potency of the drink to the magical qualities of the dust from the temple floor used in its preparation. See, e.g, Daniel Miller, "Another Look at the Magical Ritual for a Suspected Adulteress in Numbers 5:11-31," *Magic, Ritual, and Witchcraft* 5 (2010): 1–16; and Francesca Stavrakopoulou, "Materialist Reading: Materialism, Materiality, and Biblical Cults of Writing," in *Biblical Interpretation and Method: Essays in Honour of John Barton*, ed. Katharine J. Dell and Paul M. Joyce (Oxford: Oxford University Press, 2013), 223–42, here 231. Alternatively, the "holy water" is considered to activate the curse (although the Septuagint merely specifies "running water," LXX Exod 5:17). See, e.g., Tikva Frymer-Kensky, "The Strange Case of the Suspected Sotah (Numbers V 11-31)," *VT* 34 (1984): 11–26; and Ann Jeffers, *Magic and Divination in Ancient Palestine and Syria* (HCANE 8; Leiden: Brill, 1996), 163-4. However, these interpretations overlook the focus of the ritual upon the *writing* of the curses, and the subsequent dissolution of the written text into water. On the importance of the written word in the context of the Soṭah ritual, see Alice Mandell, '"I Bless You to YHWH and His Asherah"—Writing and Performativity at Kuntillet ʿAjrud," *Maarav* 19 (2012): 131–62, here 151-2. As such, holy water, temple dust, and written curse work together to bring about the efficacious ordeal.

16. m. Soṭah 3.16–17.

17. For ירך, "thigh," with the implication of "genitalia," see, e.g., Gen 46:26; Judg 8:30; Song 7:2. See also the contribution of Ekaterina E. Kozlova in this volume, who provides a number of examples where ירך must refer euphemistically to the genitals.

18. See already Charles J. Brim, *Medicine in the Bible: The Pentateuch* (New York: Forben Press, 1936), 373; followed by G. R. Driver, "Two Problems in the Old Testament Examined in the Light of Assyriology," *Syria* 33 (1956): 70-8; William McKane, "Poison, Trial by Ordeal and the Cup of Wrath," *VT* 30 (1980): 474–92; Richard S. Briggs, "Reading the Sotah Text (Numbers 5:11-31): Holiness and a Hermeneutic Fit for Suspicion," *BibInt* 17 (2009): 288–319; and Nissim Amzallag and Shamir Yona, "The Kenite Origin of the Sotah Prescription," *JSOT* 41 (2017): 383–412.

outworking of the woman's guilt: it is a trial by ordeal.[19] By comparing the golden calf episode to the Soṭah ritual, early exegesis upon this text thus understood the drinking of the calf to have a similar function, identifying those who had sinned by worshipping the calf.[20] More recently, a number of modern scholars have renewed this interpretation.[21] Yet while Moses' actions are certainly ritualistic, there is no connection between the drinking of the calf with the identification of guilty parties—the Israelites have already been caught red-handed. Instead the chapter as a whole is concerned with the *eradication* of guilt, rather than its ascertainment.[22] The golden calf episode cannot be understood as a trial by ordeal.

A second explanation for these destructive acts utilizes comparative evidence to demonstrate that the text of Exodus 32 is invoking a literary trope. This was first suggested by Samuel Loewenstamm,[23] who compared the description to the destruction of Mot by Anat in Ugaritic literature:

tiḥd/bn.ilm.mt.	She seizes Divine Mot,
bḥrb/tbqʿnn./	With a sword she splits him,
bḫṭr.tdry/nn	With a sieve she winnows him.
bišt.tšrpnn/	With a fire she burns him,
brḥm.tṭḥnn	With millstones she grinds him,
bšd/tdrʿ.nn	In a field she sows him.
širh.ltikl/ʿṣrm[.]	The birds eat his flesh,
mnth.ltkly/npr[m.]	Fowl devour his parts,
šir.lšir.yṣḥ	Flesh to flesh cries out.[24]

19. On the Soṭah ritual as a trial by ordeal, see already G. C. Gray, *A Critical and Exegetical Commentary on Numbers* (ICC; New York: Charles Scribner's Sons, 1903), 43-9; W. Robertson Smith, *Lectures on the Religion of the Semites*, vol. 1: *The Fundamental Institutions* (London: A&C Black, 1894), 177-81; and Richard Press, "Das Ordal im alten Israel. I," *ZAW* 51 (1933): 122-5, here 125.

20. See b. Zar. 44a and Numbers Rabbah 9.48; *LAB* 12.7 also interprets the episode as an ordeal, causing the tongues of the guilty to fall out.

21. See David Frankel, "The Destruction of the Golden Calf: A New Solution," *VT* 44 (1994): 330-7; and Philippe Guillaume, "Drinking Golden Bull: The Erased Ordeal in Exodus 32," in *Studies on Magic and Divination in the Biblical World*, ed. Helen R. Jacobus et al. (Piscataway: Gorgias Press, 2013), 135-47.

22. Jože Krašovec, *Reward, Punishment, and Forgiveness: The Thinking and Beliefs of Ancient Israel in the Light of Greek and Modern Views* (VTSup 78; Leiden: Brill, 1999), 91 n. 16.

23. Samuel E. Loewenstamm, "The Ugaritic Fertility Myth—the Result of a Mistranslation," *IEJ* 12 (1962): 87-8; Samuel E. Loewenstamm, "The Making and Destruction of the Golden Calf," *Bib* 48 (1967): 481-90; and Samuel E. Loewenstamm, "The Making and Destroying of the Golden Calf—A Rejoinder," *Bib* 56 (1975): 330-48.

24. KTU³ 1.6 II 30-37. For the text and translation, see Mark S. Smith, "The Baal Cycle," in *Ugaritic Narrative Poetry*, ed. Simon B. Parker (Atlanta, GA: SBL Press, 1997), 81-180, here 156.

Here Anat burns Mot in fire, grinds him down, and scatters his body in a field, where birds then eat the remains. Following the death of her brother Baal at Mot's hands, Anat's treatment of Mot's corpse is an act of vengeance aiming at destroying her enemy utterly and completely.[25] Subsequently, Christopher Begg gathered a number of other examples from ancient Near Eastern literature in which total destruction is portrayed by acts of burning, grinding, and scattering the remains on water or feeding them to birds or other animals.[26] With this trope, ancient authors therefore invoke a literary stereotype to depict total annihilation.

I find this interpretation of Moses' destruction of the calf to be largely convincing. The ancient Near Eastern literary parallels demonstrate that by burning the object and grinding it down, the authors of this text are invoking a literary trope to demonstrate that Moses destroys the golden calf utterly and completely. The same can also be said for Josiah's destruction of the Asherah pole and the altars of Manasseh. At the same time, Moses engages in a further action not found in the ancient Near Eastern texts or in Josiah's acts in 2 Kings 23: Moses forces the *Israelites* to drink the remains of the calf. This is quite different from feeding the remains of the destroyed object to birds, which invokes their ability to fly away as an additional cause of annihilation. The same can be said for biblical and ancient Near Eastern rituals which utilize birds in the removal of sin or pollution. These birds carry the pollution away from the camp.[27] Indeed, biblical texts frequently utilize bird imagery as a metaphor to describe dispersal and so military conquest and exile.[28] The consumption of the calf by the Israelites would surely have the opposite effect: not dispersal but (re)incorporation. At the same time, as we have seen, the interpretation of the drink as a trial by ordeal does not make good sense either. Instead, by focusing on the effects of consumption in biblical literature, other implications to the golden calf episode can be brought to the fore.

25. Paul L. Watson, "The Death of 'Death' in the Ugaritic Texts," *JAOS* 92 (1972): 60–4.
26. Christopher T. Begg, "The Destruction of the Calf (Exod. 32,20/Deut. 9,21)," in *Das Deuteronomium: Entstehung, Gestalt und Botschaft*, ed. Norbert Lohfink (BETL 68; Leuven: Leuven University Press, 1985), 208–51; Christopher T. Begg, "The Destruction of the Golden Calf Revisited," in *Deuteronomy and Deuteronomic Literature: Festschrift C.H.W. Brekelmans*, ed. Marc Vervenne and Johan Lust (BETL 133; Leuven: Peeters, 1997), 469–79.
27. Lev 14:4–7, 49–53; cf., 16:21–22. On the use of birds in elimination rituals in biblical and ancient Near Eastern religion, see David P. Wright, *The Disposal of Impurity: Elimination Rites in the Bible and in Hittite and Mesopotamian Literature* (SBLDS 101; Atlanta, GA: Scholars Press, 1987), 75–86.
28. See Cat Quine, "The Bird and the Mountains: A Note on Psalm 11," *VT* 67 (2017): 470–9.

4. Consumption and Transformation in the Hebrew Bible

The Hebrew Bible contains a number of restrictions concerning food: humankind is initially vegetarian until meat consumption is added in Gen 9:3–4. However, various restrictions provide limitations to the eating of animals (Leviticus 11; Deuteronomy 14). At the same time, pilgrimage feasts dictate certain times at which food should be consumed (Exod 23:14, 17; 34:23; Deut 16:16). It is with these food and festival laws that much of the scholarship on eating in biblical literature has been concerned.[29] More recently, a number of scholars have begun to consider food as a key component of ritual and religious life, utilizing anthropological and literary readings to consider the role of consumption within wider social and narrative contexts—albeit none of these studies have considered the consumption of the golden calf.[30] In particular, Meredith Warren has considered acts of transformative eating in Mediterranean literature, a category she terms *hierophagy*. By consuming an otherworldly item, characters cross boundaries from one realm to another: "the character ingests something from that realm, and the act of eating precipitates a change in the character such that the character is more closely related to the other realm."[31] Warren explores this literary trope in a variety of ancient Mediterranean texts, including traditions about Persephone, *4 Ezra*, the book of Revelation, *Joseph and Aseneth*, Apuleius' *Metamorphoses*, and *The Passion of Perpetua and Felicitas*. As such, she demonstrates that this trope was common across religious and geographical boundaries in the eastern Mediterranean world. From the Hebrew Bible, we might consider Ezekiel's consumption of an otherworldly scroll, through which he gains the ability to provide otherworldly knowledge in the form of prophecy, as an act of hierophagy.[32] Warren's arguments cohere well

---

29. On the biblical food laws, see Mary Douglas, *Purity and Danger: An Analysis of the Concepts of Pollution and Taboo* (London: Routledge, 1966), 51–71; and Seth Kunin, *We Think What We Eat: Neo-Structuralist Analysis of Israelite Food Rules and Other Cultural and Textual Practices* (JSOTS 412; Edinburgh: T&T Clark, 2004). On food festivals, see Jonathan Brumberg-Kraus, "'Not By Bread Slone …': The Ritualization of Food and Table Talk in the Passover Seder and in the Last Supper," *Semeia* 86 (1999): 165–91; and Peter Altmann, *Festive Meals in Ancient Israel: Deuteronomy's Identity Politics in the Ancient Near Eastern Context* (BZAW 424; Berlin: de Gruyter, 2011).

30. Nathan MacDonald, *What Did the Ancient Israelites Eat? Diet in Biblical Times* (Grand Rapids, MI: Eerdmans, 2008); Nathan MacDonald, *Not Bread Alone: The Uses of Food in the Old Testament* (Oxford: Oxford University Press, 2009); Cynthia Shafer-Elliot, *Food in Ancient Israel: Domestic Cooking in the Time of the Hebrew Bible* (London: Routledge, 2012); Meredith J. C. Warren, *Food and Transformation in Ancient Mediterranean Literature* (Writings from the Greco-Roman World Supplements 14; Atlanta, GA: SBL Press, 2019); Rebekah Welton, *He Is a Glutton and a Drunkard: Deviant Consumption in the Hebrew Bible* (BINS 183; Leiden: Brill, 2020).

31. Warren, *Food and Transformation*, 3.

32. On Ezek 2:8–3:4 as hierophagy, see Warren, *Food and Transformation*, 69.

with recent research on taste metaphors in biblical literature, where the gustatory sense is used to conceptualize direct and personal experience: since the sense object is internalized by the eater, taste becomes a source of knowledge.[33] Foods therefore have direct ontological repercussions upon the consumer, affecting a transformation.

Warren has aptly demonstrated that food is a social agent: something that affects a change upon the consumer, and hence when the food is otherworldly, it affects an otherworldly change. Yet as Rebekah Welton reminds us, this actually goes both ways: food is both agent but also patient, itself transformed through acts of preparation.[34] In fact, food is transformed not only through preparation but through consumption itself: the process of eating materially transforms the ontological status of the food item. Scholars of the golden calf have typically focused upon the effect of consuming the object upon the Israelites, hence the common interpretation of the episode as a trial by ordeal: this reading assumes that the consumption of the destroyed calf would affect some sort of visible outworking of the Israelite's guilt. Yet this neglects the effect of the consumption upon the calf. On the other hand, by looking at the consumption of the calf purely as a means to destroy the object in light of ancient Near Eastern literature, scholars have neglected the transformative effect of eating. Unlike the ancient Near Eastern material, where the objects are consumed by birds or animals who can then carry them far away, affecting their dispersal and so annihilation, in Exodus 32 the Israelites themselves consume the calf. Rather than dispersed and destroyed, the object is transformed through this act of consumption, incorporated into the bodies of the Israelites. This suggests that we reconsider acts of consumption and their function at the literary level of the golden calf story.

5. *Drinking the Golden Calf in Exodus 32:20*

In fact, Exodus 32 contains two acts of consumption. Following the construction of the calf, Aaron makes a proclamation: "Tomorrow will be a feast to the Lord" (v. 5). The next day the Israelites rise early in order to offer burnt offerings and peace offerings, to eat and drink, and to play (v. 6). The form לצחק, a piel infinitive construct, has been connected by a number of scholars to some sort of Canaanite orgiastic ritual, thus according to Walter Kaiser the word describes "drunken immoral orgies and sexual play."[35] However, elsewhere the word is used to describe

---

33. See Pierre Van Hecke, "Tasting Metaphor in Ancient Israel," in *Sounding Sensory Profiles in Antiquity: On the Role of Senses in Ancient Israel, Mesopotamia, and Egypt*, ed. Annette Schellenberg and Thomas Krüger (ANEM 25; Atlanta, GA: SBL Press, 2019), 99–118.

34. Rebekah Welton, "Ritual and the Agency of Food in Ancient Israel and Judah: Food Futures in Biblical Studies," *BibInt* 25 (2017): 609–24.

35. Walter C. Kaiser Jr., *Exodus* (EBC; Grand Rapids, MI: Zovervan, 1990), 478.

situations of play and mocking, without any sexual implications (Gen 21:6; 39:14, 17; Ezek 23:32). It is unlikely therefore to refer to "an orgy of drinking and sex."[36] In fact, Aaron seems instead to be attempting to mimic normative worship practices, thus he fashions the calf, somewhat surprisingly, with a חרט, a stylus or writing tool, suggesting an equivalence to the tablets of Moses. The festival he ordains is a חג, the same term used to describe the pilgrimage festivals earlier proclaimed by Moses (Exod 10:9; 12:14; 13:6; 23:15, 16). The burnt and peace offerings clearly recall the ritual prescriptions that had been outlined by Yahweh himself in Exod 20:24. With Nathan MacDonald, we must conclude that rather than any sort of Canaanite ritual, Exodus 32 describes "a parody of the cult of YHWH."[37] And this includes the consumption of food and drink. Elsewhere in biblical literature, ritual consumption is connected to a variety of worship contexts, both legitimate in the case of the pilgrimage festivals (Exod 23:14, 17; 34:23; Deut 16:16), as well as illegitimate practices, in the context of mortuary rituals (Isa 65:2–5; cf., Jer 16:5–8), or the consumption of food that has been sacrificed to other deities (Exod 34:13–16).[38] The Israelites are treating the golden calf under the aegis of proper ritual and cult, and in so doing they recognize that the golden calf is a sacred object.

Through this act of recognition, these cultic acts of eating, drinking, play, and sacrifice therefore imbue the object with power as a plausible alternative to the cult of Yahweh. We might then interpret their second act of ingestion as a *ritual inversion* of this initial feast, reversing the meal described in vv. 5–6. The longest and most important Mesopotamian anti-witchcraft ritual is known as the *Maqlû*.[39] The texts describe various rituals performed in order to remove maledictions from a person. In these rituals, a "mirror-image" performance is often used in order to rid the sufferer of his complaint. This is a type of "sympathetic magic," magic based on imitation or correspondence.[40] By inverting the original pronouncement or ritual performance, the malediction can be inverted and so removed.[41] Saul Olyan has shown that this ritual strategy is also operative in biblical rites, exploring ritual

---

36. Contra the TEV translation.
37. MacDonald, "Recasting the Golden Calf," 35.
38. For a discussion of these and other acts of "deviant consumption," see Welton, *He Is a Glutton and a Drunkard*, 224–82.
39. For the text and translation, see Tzvi Abusch, *The Magical Ceremony Maqlû: A Critical Edition* (Leiden: Brill, 2016); and Daniel Schwemer, *The Anti-Witchcraft Ritual Maqlû: The Cuneiform Sources of a Magic Ceremony from Ancient Mesopotamia* (Wiesbaden: Harrassowitz, 2017).
40. On sympathetic magic, see already James G. Frazer, *The Golden Bough: A Study in Magic and Religion*, vol. 1, *Abridged Edition* (New York: Macmillan, 1922), 12–15, 43.
41. Daniel Schwemer, "The Ancient Near East," in *The Cambridge History of Magic and Witchcraft in the West: From Antiquity to the Present*, ed. David J. Collins (Cambridge: Cambridge University Press, 2015), 17–51, here 33.

inversion in the context of rituals employed for punitive purposes.[42] The second act of consumption in Exodus 32 thus mirrors the first—only this time as an inversion it functions to take away the power of the calf that had been activated through the original ritual behaviors.[43] The act of consumption is thus transformative not for the Israelites but for the calf.

This is even more the case since in its consumption, the calf is returned back to the bodies from which it was originally derived: the calf had been produced from jewelry taken directly from the bodies of the Israelite women, sons, and daughters.[44] In the Hebrew Bible and the ancient eastern Mediterranean, items of adornment worn directly on the body were substantivized as a constituent part of the body from which they came. As such, items of clothing or jewelry transferred

---

42. Saul M. Olyan, "Ritual Inversion in Biblical Representations of Punitive Rites," in *Worship, Women and War: Essays in Honor of Susan Niditch*, ed. John J. Collins et al. (Brown Judaic Studies; Atlanta, GA: SBL Press, 2015), 135–44. On ritual inversion as a strategy for avoiding curses in the Hebrew Bible, see Laura Quick, "Averting Curses in the Law of War (Deuteronomy 20)," *ZAW* 132 (2020): 209–23.

43. The comparison between the ritual actions employed in Exodus 32 with the *Maqlû* anti-witchcraft series is all the more apposite since these tablets also describe comparable ritual strategies including burning, sprinkling, and ritual consumption. The burning of various figurines is employed in multiple rites, and in fact *Maqlû* means "burning." For "sprinkling" (Akk. *salāʔu*), including the sprinkling of river water, sea water, and various aromatics, see *Maqlû* I 28′-29′; V 94′-109-110′; VIII 177′-179′. Bread is placed inside figurines representing a witch and warlock, probably a ritual strategy of forced eating upon a party not present for the ritual (VII 171′-172′). I owe this helpful observation to Melissa Ramos (personal communication). Given that the consumption of "bewitched" food and water (*kaššāpūti ušākilūʔinni mê kaššāpūti*; I 103-104) is given as a cause of the original malediction, these ritual actions involving water and (forced) consumption could be understood as examples of ritual inversion, employed in order to rid the sufferer of his complaint, which was itself brought about through an initial act of consumption.

44. Judges 8:27 also depicts an object to be used in idol worship that is composed from jewelry. This item is described as an *ʔēpōd*, the term elsewhere used to describe an item of dress worn by the High Priest (Exodus 28). Some scholars therefore interpret the item fashioned by Gideon in Judg 8:27 as a type of garment. For discussion see Roland de Vaux, *Ancient Israel: Its Life and Institutions*, trans. John McHugh (Winona Lake, IN: Eerdmans, 1997), 349–52. However, it is noteworthy that the *ʔēpōd* in Judg 8:27 is made from golden jewelry including earrings (v. 26), recalling the golden earrings used to fashion the calf in Exod 32:2. While Gideon also uses "purple clothing worn by Midianite kings" to fashion this *ʔēpōd*, in light of the connections in the text to the story of the golden calf it is likely that rather than any sort of garment this *ʔēpōd* in fact describes the cult image of a god, made from the melted down earrings and then clothed in purple garments. A number of biblical texts attest to the "dressing" of cult statues, see 2 Kgs 23:7; Jer 10:9; Ezek 16:18. In Jer 10:9, cult statues are dressed in purple garments, as is the case of Gideon's *ʔēpōd*. Jewelry taken from the body is thus particularly appropriate for the fashioning of cultic objects.

between individuals could also transfer their ethnicity or royal status. Royalty can therefore be conferred between one individual to another through the transfer of items of royal dress: by gifting his signet ring or other items of clothing, the king could confer prestige and even royal status onto an individual.[45] Thus the gifting of Pharaoh's signet ring to Joseph, along with fine linen garments and a gold chain, symbolizes Joseph's royal power and authority, as second only to Pharaoh (Gen 41:42).[46] The calf started as a mundane item of the body. Through Aaron's fashioning and the cultic activities of sacrifice, meal, and play, it was transformed into a sacred object. In so doing, Aaron was claiming that something human was actually divine. But the act of consumption is a further act of transformation, incorporating the calf back into the bodies of the Israelites, to become once again a mundane object of the body. The human is not divine after all. Like the transformational acts of eating outlined by Meredith Warren, this is another transformative act: but rather than aiding the eater to cross boundaries from the mundane to the otherworldly, this act transforms the object that is eaten back to the mundane realm. The calf is no longer a danger to the Yahweh cult—through its consumption, its divinity is denied. Consumption functions in this narrative as part of a ritual act of desacralization.

6. Revising a Ritual Act in Deuteronomy 9

Thus far I have argued that the consumption of the golden calf should be understood as an act of transformation in which the calf is converted from a sacred to a mundane object. It thus constitutes an important but underacknowledged aspect of ancient Israelite ritual practice incorporating ritual inversion as well as transformative consumption. Yet despite the importance of this particular aspect of the story of the golden calf, in retellings of the story elsewhere in the Hebrew Bible it is conspicuously absent. The earliest reception of Exodus 32 is found in Deuteronomy 9:

> As for your sinful thing that you had made, the calf, I took it, burnt it with fire, ground it up until it was as fine as dust, and tossed the dust into the stream that flows down the mountain. (v. 21)[47]

---

45. For further implications to signet seals in the ancient Levant, see also the contribution of Alice Mandell in this volume.

46. For more instances in which clothing and jewelry transfers ethnicity or royal status between individuals, see Laura Quick, "Clothed in Curses: Ritual, Curse and Story in the Deir ʕAlla Plaster Inscription," in *To Gaul, to Greece and into Noah's Ark: Essays in Honour of Kevin J. Cathcart on the Occasion of His Eightieth Birthday*, ed. Laura Quick, Ekaterina E. Kozlova, Sonja Noll, and Phillip Y. Yoo (JSSS 44; Oxford: Oxford University Press, 2019), 95–109.

47. While all scholars recognize the literary dependence of these two units, there is some diversity in opinions concerning the directionality of the influence. I follow Christine

The order of the process of destruction is an exact match in each account, the only difference being that in Deuteronomy 9 it is Moses who describes the scene as first-person narrator, and hence utilizes first-person verbal forms: in both, Moses first takes (לקח) the calf and burns (שׂרף) it in fire (אשׁ). The further decomposition of the calf differs in each telling: in Exodus 32, Moses grinds the calf, using the verb טחן, "to grind." This word elsewhere describes the actions of millstones in the production of flour (Num 11:8; Isa 47:2): the result is that the calf becomes a powder (דק). In Deuteronomy 9, Moses beats or crushes the calf, utilizing the verb כתת, which has more violent, martial implications.[48] Indeed, in Isa 30:14 it describes an act that shatters a piece of pottery such that it can never be salvaged. The result of this action is that the calf becomes "fine grindings," בטיה טחון, utilizing the qal infinitive absolute of טחן. The dispersal of these grindings is again more violent in Deuteronomy: Moses throws (שׁלך) the dust into the water, rather than the scattering or sprinkling (זרה) described in Exodus.

Thus while the accounts are nearly exact, there is an intensification in Moses' actions in Deuteronomy 9. In this context, the omission of Moses causing the Israelites to drink the mixture in the Deuteronomy account is surprising: elsewhere the calf had been subject to more violent treatment in the Deuteronomic retelling. Why then omit to mention the consumption of the calf, the final step in its obliteration? Arguably, the absence of this episode from Deuteronomy 9 is consistent with a larger Deuteronomic polemic against magic and divination (see, e.g., Deuteronomy 13). This is similarly the case with other biblical retellings of the golden calf story, in Neh 9:16–18 and Ps 106:19–23. As demonstrated in the accounts of hierophagy uncovered by Meredith Warren, the ritual potential of acts of transformative eating go both ways—to consume an object imbued with otherworldly power is a potentially dangerous ritual strategy. Consequently, the later biblical accounts revise this ritual of inversion and transformation from their accounts of the golden calf episode. The calf is destroyed—but no longer consumed.

7. Conclusion

In this chapter, I have considered the ritualistic destruction of the golden calf by Moses in Exodus 32. Accepting the links posited between this episode with the sins of Jeroboam and his golden calves described in 1 Kings 12, I have extended this argument to connect the episode with Josiah's destruction of illegitimate cultic

---

Hayes in interpreting Exodus 32 as the prior text. Hayes has convincingly demonstrated that Deuteronomy 9–10 makes modifications to the story of Exodus 32 in line with the exegetical stance of the Deuteronomist, and accordingly is the secondary retelling. See "Golden Calf Stories," 45–93.

48. See Num 14:45; Deut 1:44; 2 Kgs 18:4; Isa 2:4; 24:2; Jer 46:5; Joel 3:10; Mic 1:7; 4:3; Zech 11:6; Ps 89:23; Job 4:20; 2 Chr 15:6; 34:7.

items in 2 Kings 23. Like Exodus 32, in 2 Kings 23 Josiah embarks on a process of destruction incorporating acts of burning, grinding, and sprinkling into water. This is in common with ancient Near Eastern literature, where these actions are invoked as a literary stereotype in order to depict the total annihilation of the destroyed object. Yet Moses embarks on a further destructive act that is not paralleled in the ancient Near Eastern material or in the books of Kings: he forces the Israelites to consume the water. In contrast to commentators both ancient and modern who assert that this action constitutes a trial by ordeal, I have argued that Exodus 32 is not concerned with identifying the guilty parties but rather with the eradication of guilt. Accordingly, by burning, grinding, and sprinkling the golden calf into water, Moses invokes a literary trope of utter destruction. And by forcing the Israelites to drink the remainder, he further limits the power of the calf. In light of recent research into transformative acts of eating in biblical and eastern Mediterranean literature, I have argued that the consumption of the calf be understood as a ritual of inversion aimed not at transforming the *Israelites* but the *calf*. The danger of the calf is mitigated as its divinity is denied and the calf incorporated back into the human bodies from which it came. At the same time, the dangerous potential of this transformative ritual act saw the account become controversial in the hands of the Deuteronomic retelling, and consequently it was revised from the account of the golden calf story in Deuteronomy 9. Interpreting the golden calf episode in light of rituals of inversion and transformative eating therefore unpacks an important but little understood aspect of ancient Israelite religious practice, as well as the reception of this story in Deuteronomy and beyond.

Part II

MAGIC AND RITUAL

Chapter 5

SATAN AND THE HIGH PRIEST: ZECHARIAH 3 AS EXORCISM

Isabel Cranz

1. Introduction

Zechariah 3 describes a vision in which Joshua stands accused in a divine courtroom but is acquitted by Yahweh. He then undergoes a change of clothing and is confirmed as priest.[1] This chapter explores the parallels between Neo-Assyrian Namburbi rituals and the vision in Zechariah 3. It highlights how the vision in Zechariah 3 employs and modifies ritual imagery and language to communicate God's intent to restore the priesthood and install Joshua as high priest in Jerusalem. Reading Zechariah 3 against the backdrop of a ritual brings fresh insight to the imagery used in communicating Zechariah's message of restoration and renewal.

---

1. Many scholars believe that Zechariah 3 was integrated at a later stage in the composition of Zechariah's vision cycle. Zechariah 3 is set apart from the remainder of Zechariah's visions by the fact that the meaning of this vision is not secondarily revealed. In addition, the angel is referred to as "angel of Yahweh" (מלאך יהוה) rather than "the angel who spoke to me" (המלאך הדובר בי). For the notion that this vision was added secondarily, see, e.g., Klaus Seybold, *Bilder zum Tempelbau: Die Visionen des Propheten Sacharja* (SBS 70; Stuttgart: KBW Verlag, 1974), 16–17; Christian Jeremias, *Die Nachtgesichte des Sacharja: Untersuchungen zu ihrer Stellung im Zusammenhang der Visionsberichte im Alten Testament und zu ihrem Bildmaterial* (Göttingen: Vandenhoeck & Ruprecht, 1977), 201–3; Holger Delkurt, *Sacharjas Nachtgesichte: Zur Aufnahme und Abwandlung prophetischer Tradition* (Berlin: de Gruyter, 2000), 146–7; Thomas Pola, *Das Priestertum bei Sacharja* (FAT 35; Tübingen: Mohr Siebeck, 2003), 35, 221–3, 261–2; Antti Laato, "Temple Building and the Book of Zechariah," in *From the Foundations to the Crenellations: Essays on Temple Building in the Ancient Near East and the Hebrew Bible*, ed. Richard S. Ellis (AOAT 366; Münster, 2010), 381–2; and Martin Hallaschka, *Haggai und Sacharja 1–8: Eine redaktionsgeschichtliche Untersuchung* (BZAW 411; Berlin: de Gruyter, 2011), 139–41, 193–4, 306–7.

Modern commentators have sought parallels between Zechariah 3 and other Hebrew traditions such as the divine council in the book of Job or Isaiah's vision of Yahweh's court in Isaiah 6.[2] Mark Boda summarizes these views by stating that Zechariah 3 "represents an amalgamation of several socio-ritual types evident elsewhere in Hebrew literature plucked from royal, priestly, and prophetic worlds."[3] Others have reached beyond the corpus of Hebrew traditions by arguing that the vision combines aspects of ancient Near Eastern law with customs of the Achaemenid administration. Thus, Jason Silverman suggests that the vision "uses ANE law and structures as they were adapted by the Achaemenids to ensure loyalty throughout their large realm."[4] By comparing Zechariah 3 to Neo-Assyrian Namburbi rituals, this essay will combine the two approaches by placing the spotlight both on the ritual aspects of the vision and its ties to the ancient Near East. Although I postulate a conceptual link between the vision and the Neo-Assyrian ritual, it is important to note that I do not assume a direct dependence between the two traditions. Instead, I will use the Namburbi to point to the fact that Zechariah's vision draws from shared ancient Near Eastern conceptions of evil, guilt, expiation, and forgiveness. For this purpose, I will first discuss three Namburbi that require a change of clothing before analyzing the prophetic vision.[5]

In this essay, I will show that the prophetic vision and the Namburbi ritual share common terminology and imagery. Both Zechariah 3 and the Namburbi contain an interplay between sign- and speech-acts, which can be understood as an attempt at communication between the divine and human worlds.[6] Yet, despite

2. The association between Zechariah 3 and the divine council in the book of Job has been observed, for instance, by N. L. A. Tidwell, "'Waʾomar' (Zech 3:5) and the Genre of Zechariah's Fourth Vision," *JBL* 94 (1975): 343–55, here 343; Peggy L. Day, *An Adversary in Heaven: Satan in the Hebrew Bible* (HSM 43; Atlanta, GA: Scholars Press, 1988), 33. See further David L. Petersen, who detects a parallel between Isaiah 6 and 1 Kings 22. See *Haggai and Zechariah 1–8: A Commentary* (Philadelphia, PA: Westminster Press, 1984), 190; cf. Jeremias, *Die Nachtgesichte des Sacharja*, 203–4.

3. See Mark J. Boda, *Exploring Zechariah*, vol. 2: *The Development and Role of Biblical Traditions in Zechariah* (SBLANEM 17; Atlanta, GA: SBL Press, 2017), 63. For other scholars who detect a ritual background in Zechariah's vision cycle, see Baruch Halpern, "The Ritual Background of Zechariah's Temple Song," *CBQ* 40 (1978): 167–90; Isabel Cranz, "The Ritual Elements in Zechariah 5:5-11," *Biblica* 96 (2015): 586–98; Isabel Cranz, "Magic and Maledictions: Zechariah 5:1-4 in Its Ancient Near Eastern Context," *ZAW* 128 (2016): 404–18.

4. See Jason M. Silverman, "Vetting the Priest in Zechariah 3: The Satan between Divine and Achaemenid Administration," *JHS* 14 (2014): 1–27, here 8–9.

5. Special focus will be placed on vv. 1–2, 3–5, and 8–10 respectively. For different views regarding the internal division of Zechariah 3, see Rüdiger Lux, *Sacharja 1–8: Übersetzt und ausgelegt* (HTKzAT; Freiburg: Herder, 2019), 249–54.

6. For the conception of ritual as an interplay of verbal and nonverbal forms of communication, see Eftychia Stavrianopoulou, "Introduction," in *Ritual and*

this conceptual similarity, one major difference exists. While the Namburbi provide ritual instructions on attaining divine forgiveness, the vision uses ritual terminology to signal that divine forgiveness has been granted. Consequently, the vision account confirms what the ritual is requesting.

2. Comparative Material

We begin with a brief overview of the Neo-Assyrian Namburbi rituals. The notion of a divine council deciding the fate of humans is well known in ancient Near Eastern ritual texts and glyptic art. Numerous depictions of so-called introduction scenes are preserved on cylinder seals, showing the supplicant's personal deity introducing him to a higher ranking god.[7] Similarly, the incantation series against curses, *Šurpu*, and the ritual against witchcraft, *Maqlû*, seem to be aware of a divine council, as different deities are addressed and asked to help the supplicants resolve their dire situation.[8] The notion of a divine council is also a central component in the non-canonical Namburbi rituals. These rituals are aimed at reversing impending doom that was announced through an unfavorable omen.[9] Namburbi typically require that the supplicant and the incantation priest prepare a ritual arrangement before Šamaš, the god of justice. Since the evil omen is the result of divine disfavor, which is itself caused by sinful behavior, the affected individual is placed on trial by the evil omen itself. With support of the incantation priest (*āšipu*), the supplicant appeals to the gods.[10] The incantation priests represent the supplicant before the gods and mediate between the human and divine world by reciting incantations

---

Communication in the Graeco-Roman World, ed. Eftychia Stavrianopoulou (Centre International d'Étude de la Religion Grecque Antique Liège, 2006), 7–22, here 8. For scholars who hold the view that ritual has a distinct communicative function, see Edmund R. Leach, "Ritual," in *The International Encyclopedia of the Social Sciences*, ed. William A. Darity Jr. (New York: Macmillan, 2008), 13:523. Roy Rappaport, *Ritual and Religion in the Making of Humanity* (Cambridge: Cambridge University Press, 1999), 50–2; Eric W. Rothenbuhler, *Ritual Communication: From Everyday Conversation to Mediated Ceremony* (Thousand Oaks: Sage, 1998), 53–4.

7. Cylinder seals carrying this motif are particularly prevalent from the Old Akkadian to the Kassite Period. See Thomas Staubli, "Images of Justification," in *Image, Text, Exegesis: Iconographic Interpretation and the Hebrew Bible*, ed. I. J. De Hulster and J. M. Lemon (London: T&T Clark, 2014), 164–5.

8. For the divine council in *Maqlû* specifically, see Tzvi Abusch, "Divine Judges on Earth and in Heaven," in *Divine Courtroom in Comparative Perspective*, ed. A. Mermelstein and S.E. Holtz (BINS 132; Leiden: Brill, 2015), 6–24.

9. For Namburbi rituals in general, see Stefan M. Maul, *Zukunftsbewältigung: Eine Untersuchung altorientalischen Denkens anhand der babylonisch-assyrischen Löserituale (Namburbi)* (BaF 18; Mainz am Rhein: Verlag Philipp von Zabern, 1994).

10. Maul, *Zukunftsbewältigung*, 60–71.

and by carrying out purificatory rites to prepare the client for his trial in the divine court.[11] During the unfolding trial, the affected individuals present themselves before Šamaš, who is implored to judge in favor of the supplicants standing accused by the evil omen. Often the gods Ea and Asalluhi are addressed as part of the ritual procedure.[12] The trial is typically accompanied by ritual acts meant to anticipate divine forgiveness and the dissolution of guilt. These acts can include the peeling of an onion, bathing or sprinkling with specially prepared water, or other rites of disposal.[13] What is particularly interesting for our purposes is that some Namburbi require the supplicant to change his clothing, with a striking parallel to Joshua's attire change in Zechariah 3. Additional features the Namburbi share in common with Zechariah 3 include an appeal to let the evil pass, the embodiment of evil through feces, as well as the presentation and application of apotropaic stones.

The first example appears in a Namburbi against an evil that is announced by the howling of a wild cat (LKA N.111).[14] The Namburbi begin with instruction, unfortunately quite fragmentary, for preparing the ritual. Following the instructions, the ritual lists an incantation addressing Šamaš, who is described as "the one who lets (the evil of) the Namburbi-(cases) pass, of the forces and omens, as many as come into being" (mu-še-tiq NAM.BÚR.BI.MEŠ Á.MEŠ GISKIM.MEŠ/ma-la it-ta-nab-šá-a ...).[15] After the incantation is repeated three times, the supplicant has to undergo the following procedure: "He takes off his garment and bathes in holy water. He dresses in a bright white garment. You pass the incense container and torch over him" (TÚG-su i-šá-aḫ-ḫáṭ A.GÚB.BA TU$_5$/TÚG DADDAG MU$_4$MU$_4$-aš NÍG.NA GI.IZI.LÁ tuš-ba-a?-šu). The incantation priest performs several rites of purification before the supplicant enters the brewery. As a final rite, the supplicant's house is purified with various substances, including a goat, copper, the hide of a bull, seeds, and incense.

The second Namburbi to be discussed is meant to ward off evil that was announced by the appearance of intertwined snakes in a house (AO 8871).[16] First

---

11. See ibid. For the different obligations and incantations associated with the profession of the incantation priest, see Cynthia Jean, *La Magie Néo-Assyrienne en Contexte: Recherches sur le Métier d'Exorciste et le Concept d'Āšipūtu* (SAAS 17; Helsinki: Neo-Assyrian Text Corpus Project, 2006), 83–110. For the different terms used for the incantation priest, see Markham J. Geller, *Ancient Babylonian Medicine: Theory and Practice* (Chichester: Wiley & Blackwell, 2010), 43–50.

12. Maul, *Zukunftsbewältigung*, 60.

13. A possible interpretation of these activities based on Hittite and biblical rituals is offered by David P. Wright, "Analogy in Biblical and Hittite Ritual," in *Religionsgeschichtliche Beziehungen zwischen Kleinasien, Nordsyrien und dem Alten Testament*, ed. Bernd Janowski, Klaus Koch and Gernot Wilhelm (OBO 129; Göttingen: Vandenhoeck & Ruprecht, 1993), 473–506.

14. For a translation and transliteration of this text, see Maul, *Zukunftsbewältigung*, 330–2.

15. For this transliteration, see ibid., 330.

16. For a translation and transliteration of this text, see ibid., 270–5.

the incantation priest prepares the ritual arrangement and fashions figurines of snakes. Then Šamaš is conjured to forgive the supplicant's guilt and to keep the evil away. An additional incantation is recited before the god Ea, who is asked to ward off the evil. The ritual arrangement is removed and the river is asked to receive the evil. The supplicant asks for the evil to pass him. The incantation priest and supplicant then have to carry out the following ritual:

[xxx] MUŠ.MEŠ *šú-nu-ti ina muḫ-ḫi pu-ut-ri* GAR-*an-ma*
[*mê ta*]-[*ḫa*₁-*bu* (!) *u ka*[*m**] 3-*šú* DUG₄.GA *na-as-ḫa-tu-nu*
[*tardātu-n*]*u uk-ku-šá-tu-nu ina* SU.MU LÚ BI TÚG-*su*¹ *i-šá-ḫaṭ-ma*
[A].[GÚB₁.BA¹? (?)] TU₅-*šú* Ì.DÙG.GA ŠÉŠ-*su* TÚG¹DADDAG
[MU₄.MU₄-*aš* N]ÍG.NA GI.IZI.LÁ ᵈᵘᵍA.GÚB.BA *túl-lal-ma*

You place the snakes onto the dung.

Then [you draw? water] and he says three times: "you are uprooted,

You are driven out, you are cut off from my body." The affected person takes off his garment.

And you bathe him in ho[ly water?]. With "good oil" you anoint him. He [puts on] a bright white garment. You purify him [with censer], torch and *aggubû* vessel.

The final Namburbi are performed against evil announced by birds entering a house (K 2999+Sm 810 (bab.)).[17] The supplicant is required to purify himself and wear a white garment over his usual clothing. At dawn the incantation priest sets up a ritual arrangement on top of the house and an incantation is recited. The supplicant confesses his guilt and circles the arrangement several times before it is removed.[18] The supplicant then undergoes the following procedure:

NÍG.NA GI.IZI.LÁ *uš-ba-a?-šú* KI?³¹ GUB.BA TÚG-*su ú-nak-kar*
TÚG *ša-nam-ma* MU₄ MU₄-*aš* Ú.MEŠ ᵍⁱˢKIRI₆ *šú-nu-tú ana* EDIN *ú-še-e*[*ṣ-ṣ*]*i*
KAŠ.SAG NAG KÙ.BABBAR KÙ.SI₂₂ AN.BAR AN.ZAḪ ⁿᵃ⁴GUG ⁿᵃ⁴ZA.[GÌN]
[ⁿᵃ⁴]NÍR ⁿᵃ⁴MUŠ.GÍR ⁿᵃ⁴BABBAR.DILI *ina* GU GADA È-*ma* UD.[7.KAM*]
[*ina* GÚ]-[*šú*]₁... GAR-*an*

Then he (the incantation priest) passes the censer and the torch over him. Where (?) he (the supplicant) stands, he changes his garment.

And he puts on a different garment. These garden herbs he brings out to the steppe.

---

17. For a translation and transliteration of this text, see ibid., 235–48.

18. The process of walking around the ritual arrangement several times is referred to as *merditu redû*. See ibid., 56–7.

He drinks beer. Silver, gold, iron, glass, carnelian, lapis lazuli, agate (ḫulālu), muššaru-stone (and) pappardilû-stone you thread onto a linen string and you place it for seven days on [his neck.]

This ritual is followed by an incantation that appeals to Ea and Asalluḫi, asking them to judge the case with the hopes that the evil will be banished.

As we will see, the three Namburbi share many features with Zechariah 3. The prophetic vision and the ritual texts overlap to the extent that guilt and expiation are envisioned in similar terms and using comparable imagery. Yet we encounter a fundamental difference when it comes to depiction and function of evil in the respective traditions. In the Namburbi, evil is a threat that needs to be averted. Consequently, the Namburbi instruct the incantation priest in rites, procedures, and incantations that persuade the gods to forgive the supplicant's guilt, which has been signaled by an evil omen. In the prophetic vision, by contrast, the evil has become wholly powerless. The figure of the Satan is necessitated only to emphasize Yahweh's all-encompassing support for rebuilding the temple and reestablishing the sacrificial service under the auspices of Joshua. As such, the prophetic vision employs ritual imagery and terminology to signal that Yahweh has forgiven his people and is ready to return to his sanctuary. In the following, the deliberations of the divine council, the process of forgiveness, and the aftermath of forgiveness will be of particular interest.

3. The Configuration of the Divine Courtroom and Satan's Charge in Zechariah 3:1–2

We first turn to the members of the divine courtroom as they are presented in Zechariah 3. The notion that Yahweh presides over a divine council is not unique to Zechariah. We encounter this council, for instance, in 1 Kings 22 or Isaiah 6. Likewise, Job 1–2 reflects the notion that the divine council assembles regularly to discuss human affairs. It is in the latter context that we hear about a character referred to as "the satan." This character incites Yahweh to challenge the piety of his servant Job. The same character appears in Zechariah 3, only in this context he is successfully opposed by the messenger of Yahweh, who seems to have merged with Yahweh himself.[19] This merging warrants attention because it reflects the status of the incantation priest in the Namburbi. The messenger of Yahweh defends Joshua against the satan, but at the same time the messenger resembles Yahweh. Similar to the incantation priest in the Namburbi, the messenger is here used purposefully as mediator because Joshua in his state of impurity cannot stand before Yahweh

---

19. See Henrike Frey-Anthes, *Unheilswesen und Schutzgenien, Antiwesen und Grenzgänger: Vorstellungen von «Dämonen» im alten Israel* (OBO 227; Göttingen: Vandenhoeck & Ruprecht, 2007), 254.

directly.[20] Like the incantation priest in the Namburbi, the messenger mediates between humans and their deities. Yet, the direction of the mediation is reversed. Rather than speaking before Yahweh in the name of the supplicant, the interpreting angel speaks before the supplicant in the name of Yahweh.

Likewise of interest is the character of "satan" or "the satan," which is a superhuman entity that appears multiple times in the Hebrew Bible.[21] As already mentioned, the satan plays a central role in the prologue to the book of Job. The satan appears also in Num 22:22, 32 in the form of Yahweh's messenger, who blocks the way of Balaam's she-ass. Satan is further responsible for inciting David to carry out a census in 1 Chronicles 21. With the exception of 1 Chronicles 21, the designation "satan" carries a definite article.[22] This suggests that "satan" is probably not a proper name but rather designates an independent divine entity that can be seen to fulfill a certain role—namely the role of accusing, inciting, and confronting.[23]

20. See Miloš Bič, *Das Buch Sacharja* (Berlin: Evangelische Verlagsanstalt, 1962), 44; Jeremias, *Die Nachtgesichte des Sacharja*, 208. Because Yahweh in v. 2 seems to be speaking about himself in the third person, the *Peshitta* emends מלאך יהוה to ויאמר יהוה. However, this amendment is not necessary. See Albert M. Wolters, *Zechariah* (Historical Commentary on the Old Testament; Leuven: Peeters, 2014).

21. Humans can also be referred to as "satan" when they function as adversaries. See 1 Sam 29:4; 2 Sam 19:23; 1 Kgs 5:18; 11:14, 23, 25; Ps 109:6. For this observation, see Rüdiger Lux, "Hat auch der Satan seine Zeit? Zur Niederlage des Widersachers JHWHs in Sacharja 3 und Hiob 1-2," in *Nichts Neues unter der Sonne: Zeitvorstellungen im Alten Testament: Festschrift für Ernst Joachim Waschke*, ed. Jen Kotjatko-Reed (BZAW 450; Berlin: de Gruyter, 2014), 293-316, here 294 n. 6. Scholars disagree about the root of the term. Heinz-Josef Fabry, for instance, suggested that "satan" either has the root שוט or שטה. See "'Satan'—Begriff und Wirklichkeit Untersuchungen zur Dämonologie der alttestamentlichen Weisheitsliteratur," in *Die Dämonen: Die Dämonologie der israelitischen-jüdischen und frühchristlichen Literatur*, ed. Armin Lange, Hermann Lichtenberger and Diethard Römheld (Tübingen: Mohr Siebeck, 2003), 277. Yet, it is possible that the term "satan" derives from the root שטן or שטם. See Cilliers Breytenbach and Peggy L. Day, "Satan שטן Σατάν, Σατανᾶς," *DDD* (1999): 726.

22. Because the term "satan" in 1 Chronicles 21 does not carry a definite article, many scholars assume that this is evidence for a gradual development of "satan" as an independent divine entity to a proper name for Yahweh's counterpart who represents pure evil. See Frey-Anthes, *Unheilswesen*, 270 n. 1535. However, this need not be the case. The reference to "satan" in 1 Chronicles 21 is roughly contemporary to the appearance of "satan" in Zechariah 3. Satan as Yahweh's evil counterpart is first referenced in *As. Mos.* 10:1 and *Jub.* 23:29. See Breytenbach and Day, "Satan," 730.

23. See Breytenbach and Day, "Satan," 727. As of late, Ryan Stokes has argued that "satan" should in fact be understood as divine executioner or attacker. See "Satan, Yhwh's Executioner," *JBL* 133 (2014): 251-70; and Ryan Stokes, "Airing the High Priests Dirty Laundry," in *Sibyls, Scriptures and Scrolls: John Collins at Seventy*, ed. Joel Baden, Hindy Najman and Eibert Tigchelaar (Leiden: Brill, 2016), 1247-64. While this alternative translation of the term "satan" is an intriguing possibility, it will not be further pursued

In the specific case of Zechariah 3, Satan stands to the right of Joshua and accuses him. This configuration is not unique to Zechariah 3. We encounter it in Psalm 109, where this setup is used when the Psalmist envisions the downfall of his opponent.²⁴ Ps 109:6 states, "Appoint a wicked man against him, may an accuser (lit. satan) stand to his right" (הפקיד עליו רשע ושטן יעוד על־ימינו).²⁵ The reverse setup appears in the Namburbi, where the figurine presenting the evil omen functions as accuser and is placed to the left of the supplicant.²⁶ In either case, Zechariah 3 does not inform us directly about the nature of the charges that are being leveled against the high priest. It is likely that the satan cannot articulate the charges because he is silenced by the messenger of Yahweh.²⁷ Before the satan can raise his voice, the messenger states in v. 2, "May Yahweh rebuke you satan, satan may Yahweh, who has chosen Jerusalem, rebuke you! Is he not like a brand plucked from the fire?!"²⁸ Although the satan is not given the opportunity to elaborate on his charges, the messenger's statement contains some clues concerning the satan's accusation. Of particular interest is the statement that Yahweh has chosen Jerusalem, which reinforces the view that Yahweh is resolved to return to his city.²⁹ Furthermore, the statement that Joshua is "a brand plucked from the fire" calls to mind Amos 4:11,

---

here, since it has no implications concerning Zechariah 3 within its ancient Near Eastern contexts.

24. See Delkurt, *Sacharjas Nachtgesichte*, 148.

25. For this observation, see Petersen, *Haggai and Zechariah 1-8*, 189. Scholars disagree whether Ps 109:6 describes a heavenly council or whether the trial is set in the world of the humans. For scholars who assume that the Psalm describes a mundane precursor to the heavenly council in Zechariah 3, see Robert Hanhart, *Sacharja* (BKAT 14.7; Neukirchen-Vluyn: Neukirchener Verlag, 1990–8); and Lux, "Satan," 294. For a scholar who stresses that both Zechariah 3 and Psalm 109 presuppose a heavenly setting for their respective trials, see Hallaschka, *Haggai und Sacharja*, 199.

26. For the setup of the divine trial during a Namburbi, see Maul, *Zukunftsbewältigung*, 70.

27. See Hinckley G. T. Mitchell, Julius A. Bewer and J. M. Powis Smith, *Haggai, Zechariah, Malachi and Jonah* (ICC; New York: Scribner, 1912), 151. Contra Petersen, who argues that Satan does articulate an official charge that is not spelled out. See *Haggai and Zechariah 1-8*, 191.

28. My translation reflects the jussive, which is in alignment with the Septuagint and the Vulgate. See Robert Hanhart, *Sacharja* (BKAT XIV; Neukirchen-Vluyn: Neukirchner Verlag, 1990–1), 168' and Wolters, *Zechariah*, 92–3. However, some modern commentators suggest translating the verse as imperfect. See André Caquot, "גער-$gā'ar$," *TDOT* (1978): 52 and Ina Willi-Plein, *Haggai, Sacharja, Maleachi* (Zürcher Bibelkommentare; Zürich: TVZ, 2007), 85.

29. Additional references to the notion that Yahweh has chosen (בחר) Jerusalem appear in Zech 1:17 and 2:12. According to Lena-Sofia Tiemeyer, the statement of Yahweh having chosen Jerusalem further underscores his mercy toward Joshua. See "The Guilty Priesthood (Zech 3)," in *The Book of Zechariah and Her Influence*, ed. Christopher M. Tuckett (Aldershot: Ashgate, 2003), 1–19, here 5–6. Martin Hallaschka argues Yahweh's choice of Jerusalem has been added by a later hand. Yahweh's choice becomes manifest in Joshua the

in which Yahweh places Israel on the same level as Sodom and Gomorrah and states that although the few survivors of Israel are like a brand snatched from the fire (אוד מצל משרפה), they do not return to God. In the statement of the messenger in Zechariah 3:2, the allusion to Amos 4:11 implies that Joshua has escaped a dangerous situation. The rescue of Joshua, then, functions as an expression of Yahweh's all-encompassing mercy and confirms the notion that the office of the high priest will be restored and the service at the temple will resume.[30] Thus, it seems that the satan was intent on raising objections against Yahweh's return to Jerusalem. The satan's accusations would most likely have been justified, but still, according to the messenger, God has dropped all charges, a fact forcefully underscored by the usage of the verb גער.

This verb is typically employed in situations that require God to overpower forces of chaos (Ps 106:7, 9; Isa 50:2; Nah 1:4) or foreign nations (Ps 9:6; MT Isa 17:3).[31] The usage of the verb here signifies that the satan resembles a negative force that stands in opposition to the high priest and hence threatens the restoration of the temple. Yet, at the same time, the presence of the satan allows the messenger to declare Yahweh's unreserved commitment to Joshua and to Jerusalem. Interestingly, the verb גער is used in apotropaic contexts like the Ketef Hinnom amulets and the verse itself is frequently quoted in incantation bowls.[32] A possible association with exorcisms is, therefore, already implied within the vision proper.[33]

---

high priest, which is why the particle עוד is missing. See *Haggai und Sacharja*, 204. A few translations and commentators assume that the subject of בחר is "the satan," although this understanding requires the verb to take on a different meaning. See Wolters, *Zechariah*, 92.

30. Nevertheless, Joshua is not innocent; rather, Yahweh's grace has saved him and his people from disaster. See Carol L. Meyers and Eric M. Meyers, *Haggai, Zechariah 1-8*, 186–7; Tiemeyer, "The Guilty Priesthood," 7; Michael R. Stead, *The Intertextuality of Zechariah 1-8* (LHBOTS; New York: T&T Clark, 2009), 158–9; Tiemeyer, *Zechariah and His Visions*, 125–6.

31. See Petersen, *Haggai and Zechariah 1-8*, 191; Meyers and Meyers, *Haggai, Zechariah 1-8*, 186–7; Frey-Anthes, *Unheilswesen*, 255; Lux, "Satan," 297–8. In some situations, however, גער can have humans as their subject. See Frey-Anthes, *Unheilswesen*, 255 n. 1424.

32. The phrase reappears in Jude 1:9, b. Ber. 51a, and at Qumran. See Caquot, "גער-gāʿar," 52. For the occurrence of גער in the Ketef Hinnom inscriptions and its significance in the classification of these amulets as apotropaic, see Theodore J. Lewis, "Job 19 in the Light of the Ketef Hinnom Inscriptions and Amulets," in *Puzzling Out the Past: Studies in Northwest Semitic Languages and Literatures in Honor of Bruce Zuckerman*, ed. Steve Fine (Leiden: Brill, 2012), 99–113, here 107–8.

33. The association between the vision and exorcisms is indicated by the fact that the phrase יגער בך השטן appears retrospectively in Jude 10, b. Ber. 51a, and Incantation Bowls. Nevertheless, it is not clear whether the phrase was integrated into Zechariah 3 from a previously existing exorcistic formula or whether Zechariah 3 functions as a starting point for later exorcistic texts. See Caquot, "גער-gāʿar," 52 and Wolters, *Zechariah 1-8*, 92.

In sum, the setup of the divine council as it is presented in Zechariah 3 contains many parallels to the Namburbi. Like in the Namburbi, Zechariah 3 is set in a divine council. Like the Namburbi, Zechariah 3 features an individual standing accused by one divinely sent entity. Both in the Namburbi and in Zechariah 3, we encounter an individual who is tasked with mediating between the accused individual and the deity. Despite these parallels, we encounter some differences, such as the observation that the accuser in Zechariah 3 is silenced and the accused individual is acquitted on ground of Yahweh's infinite mercy. Likewise, the mediator in the vision represents God before the individual, while the incantation priest represents the supplicant before the gods. These differences suggest that although the vision account uses ritual imagery and language, it still operates on a different level, since the evil is completely neutralized and Yahweh's support is guaranteed from the beginning.

4. Joshua's Acquittal (vv. 3–5): Change of Clothing and Forgiveness

The acquittal of Joshua, which was already announced in vv. 1–2, is continued in more concrete terms in the next three verses. In v. 4, we are informed that Joshua is dressed in filthy clothing, but "(Yahweh's messenger) spoke to the attendants: 'Take the filthy clothing from him.' And to him he said, 'See I have removed your guilt from you, and I will dress you in clean garments'" (ויען ויאמר אל־העמדים לפניו לאמר הסירו הבגדים הצאים מעליו ויאמר אליו ראה העברתי מעליך עונך" "והלבש אתך מחלצות). At this point the prophet himself gets involved by stating, "Place a pure turban on his head, and clothe him in robes" (וישימו צניף טהור על ראשו וילבשהו בגדים).[34] Three points are of interest here: the nature of the dirt on his clothing; the significance of the fact that he changes his clothing; and the statement that Joshua's guilt is forgiven.

Joshua's filthy clothing is referred to as בגדים צאים. The usage of the adjective צאים is significant insofar as that the term is one employed in contexts of extreme filthiness. Nouns with the root צוא appear, for example, in Deut 23:14; Ezek 4:12; 2 Kgs 18:27 // Isa 36:12; Isa 4:4; 28:8; and Prov 30:12, where they come to be applied to feces and vomit.[35] In this context, then, the prophetic vision account can be shown to visualize guilt in terms of excrement. We encounter the same tendency

---

34. The involvement of Zechariah is apparent through the first person of the verb ואמר that precedes v. 5. Some scholars follow the Vulgate and suggest amending the first person to the third person. As such, the statement is assigned to the interpreting angel rather than Zechariah. See, for instance, Petersen, *Haggai and Zechariah 1-8*, 197; and Hanhart, *Sacharja*, 170–1. Yet the involvement of prophetic characters is a typical feature in visions of a divine council. See Tidwell, "'Wa'omar' (Zech 3:5)," 354. See further, Wolters, *Zechariah*, 94–5.

35. See Petersen, *Haggai and Zechariah 1-8*, 193–4; Tiemeyer, "The Guilty Priesthood," 7; Rudman, "Zechariah," 193–4. In Isa 4:4 and Prov 30:12 the noun צואה applies to ritual

in the Namburbi against snakes, in which the evil omen is placed on a dung heap to underscore the baselessness of its accusation.³⁶ Nevertheless, in the eyes of Zechariah even this extreme level of filthiness does not prevent Yahweh from forgiving the high priest and ordering a change of clothing. The term used for the fresh clothing in Zechariah 3 is מחלצות, from the root חלץ that appears in Akkadian and Arabic with the meaning "to purify" or "to be pure."³⁷ Again, a parallel to the Namburbi can be detected. In the three Namburbi, the supplicants are required to change their clothing as part of the expiatory process. Contrary to the vision, however, the new change of clothing is referred to as "bright white" (DADDAG), not as pure. Although neither the Namburbi nor the prophetic vision account explain why the change of clothing is required, three interrelated possibilities exist. For one, donning clean (or in the case of the Namburbi, bright white) garments can signalize the completion of one ritual stage and the beginning of a new phase of ritual. The interpretation as transitional rite is applicable to both the vision and the Namburbi. It can also be observed for the Day of Atonement ritual in Leviticus 16 and the priestly inauguration in Exodus 29 and Leviticus 8.³⁸ Secondly, it is possible that the change of clothing is meant to signalize purification and atonement. This is most clearly expressed in the Namburbi in which the change of clothing is typically followed by purification with holy water and plant materials. Purification and atonement also play a role in the vision account, where the change of clothing is followed by the statement that Joshua's guilt is pardoned. This

impurity while the other occurrences of this noun relate to feces. Nevertheless, although Zechariah's vision report does address impurity in relation to the priesthood, we do not encounter terms that are commonly employed in Priestly contexts of ritual impurity such as טמא. See Tiemeyer, *Zechariah and His Visions*, 127. Possibly, the choice of words reflects the wish to employ a more broadly applicable term for defilement and guilt. See Delkurt, *Sacharjas Nachtgesichte*, 160-2; Hanhart, *Sacharja*, 188.

36. Most scholars assume some link between the filthiness of Joshua's clothing and his guilt referenced in the second half of the verse. See Tiemeyer, *Zechariah and His Visions*, 127; Hanhart, *Sacharja*, 185; Delkurt, *Die Nachtgesichte des Sacharjas*, 160-2; Meyers and Meyers, *Haggai, Zechariah 1-8*, 187. Ina Willi Plein formulates a more differentiated view regarding the filthy clothing by stating that they reflect Joshua's imprisonment in Babylon and his low social standing. See *Haggai, Sacharja, Maleachi*, 86. An additional angle of interpretation is presented by Miloš Bič, for whom the filthiness displays the high priest's status as an act of penance and his inability to function as high priest. See *Das Buch Sacharja*, 46.

37. Dale Winton Thomas, "A Note on *mḥlṣwt* in Zech 3:4," *JTS* 33 (1931-2): 279-80. Cf. Tiemeyer, "The Guilty Priesthood," 8; James C. Vanderkam, "Joshua the High Priest and the Interpretation of Zechariah 3," *CBQ* 53 (1991): 553-70, here 556; Meyers and Meyers, *Haggai, Zechariah 1-8*, 190.

38. For the link between Exodus 29, Leviticus 8, 16, and Zechariah 3, see Tiemeyer, *Zechariah and His Visions*, 209; and Jeremias, *Die Nachtgesichte des Sacharja*, 209. For the nature of Joshua's change of clothing as a rite of transition, see Lux, "Satan," 299.

observation leads us to the next point, namely, that both the Namburbi and the prophetic vision contain a declaration of forgiveness.

As already mentioned, for all three Namburbi, incantations are recited that refer to Šamaš as "the one who lets (the evil of) the Namburbi-(cases) pass, of the forces and omens, as many as come into being" (*mu-še-tiq* NAM.BÚR.BI.MEŠ Á. MEŠ GISKIM.MEŠ/*ma-la it-ta-nab-šá-a* ...).[39] Furthermore, we find requests like "Let me pass the evil of the snakes, may their evil not approach me and not come close. (May it) not come near and not catch up with me. Its evil from my body may it be released" (ḪUL MUŠ.MEŠ *šú-n[u-ti] šu-ti-qa-in-ni-ma* ḪUL-*šú-nu a-a* TE-*a a-a* KU.N[U] [*a*]-*a* DIM₄.MÀ *a-a* KUR-*an-ni* ḪUL-*šú-nu ina* SU.M[U] [*lip*]-[*pa₁-ṭir*]).[40] A similar tendency of associating expiation with the power of a deity can be observed for the prophetic vision, in which the change of Joshua's garments is followed by the statement, "See, I have caused your iniquity to pass from you" (ראה העברתי מעליך עונך). It is noteworthy that the hiphil verb with the root עבר is comparable to the Š-stem of the Akkadian *etēqu*. The usage of the hiphil and Š-stem respectively gives expression to the causative action of divine forgiveness.[41] Finally, the statement that Yahweh has let Joshua's guilt pass can be understood as a "performative utterance."[42] Similar to the Namburbi, in which acts of purification are accompanied by incantations, this utterance is accompanied by the description of a sign act when Joshua undergoes his change of clothing.[43]

In the vision, Yahweh grants forgiveness regardless of whether Joshua is deserving of this forgiveness or not. To a certain degree, this is comparable to the Namburbi against the wild cat that ends with the declaration that "this is its

---

39. This statement is repeated in several Namburbi that call for a change of garment. See Maul, *Zukunftsbewältigung*, 450, 331, 275.

40. Maul, *Zukunftsbewältigung*, 275.

41. It is further noteworthy that the usage of the hiphil of עבר stands in contrast to the verb כפר, which is typically used for priestly contexts of forgiveness. Although Zecheriah's vision appears to presuppose a priestly setting, the usage of העביר is emblematic for prophetic descriptions of atonement as they appear in historiographic texts and wisdom literature (2 Sam 12:13; 24:10; 1 Chr 21:8). The qal with the root עבר appears in Amos 7:8; 8:2; and Micah 7:18, suggesting that the usage of עבר in the context of forgiveness is a marker of the prophetic take on atonement. See Delkurt, *Die Nachtgesichte des Sacharjas*, 167–8.

42. For the notion that the statement is a performative declaration, see Al Wolters, *Zechariah*, 93. Wolters bases himself on Dilbert Hillers's classification of performative utterances that he describes as "verbs usually in the first person singular perfect" that do not describe a past act but "an action in the present that is accomplished ... by the speaker's pronouncement of the utterance under appropriate circumstances." See "Some Performative Utterances in the Bible," in *Pomegranates and Golden Bells*, ed. David P. Wright et al. (Winona Lake, IN: Eisenbrauns, 1995), 757–66, here 760, 762.

43. See Mark J. Boda, *Haggai, Zechariah* (The NIV Application Commentary; Grand Rapids, MI: Zondervan, 2004), 256. For the observation that the utterance is not "just a pure word-event," see Petersen, *Haggai and Zechariah 1-8*, 194.

release"; yet for the most part, the incantations in the Namburbi are phrased as petitions rather than statements that the gods have forgiven the supplicant's guilt. Consequently, although the prophetic vision can be shown to use ritual imagery and terminology, the vision still differs from the Namburbi because it is phrased as divine response granting forgiveness rather than a human request for forgiveness.

5. Joshua's Commissioning as High Priest and Yahweh's Promise (vv. 8–10)

After the change of clothing and Yahweh's declaration of forgiveness, Joshua is sworn in and confirmed as high priest. Verses 8–10 contain a plethora of fascinating and in many parts baffling imagery and statements. For the purpose of this chapter, I want to draw specific attention to v. 9, which contains the image of a stone placed before Joshua with seven eyes engraved on it and Yahweh's declaration that "I will forgive the iniquity of the land in one day."

The meaning of the stone with the seven eyes has been subject to considerable discussion. Some scholars have speculated that the stone is instrumental in the rebuilding of the temple, which anticipates the fourth vision account in Zech 4:6ab–10a where Zerubbabel is presented with the top stone for the temple.[44] Nevertheless, for the most part, scholars prefer reading the vision in the context of atonement. This interpretation is supported by the fact that it reflects the direct setting of the vision that dealt with the attire of the high priest and Yahweh's ability of granting forgiveness. In this case, then, the stone that will be engraved can be likened to the breastplate of the high priest, which, according to Exod 28:9, 21, is adorned with fourteen engraved stones representing the Israelite tribes. In Exod 28:36 we learn that the breastplate is paired with a plate the high priest carries on his forehead, which carries the inscription "Holy for Yahweh" (קדש ליהוה). In the continuation of this passage, this plate is meant to avert the guilt of the Israelites as is explained in Exod 28:38 where it is stated, "that Aaron may bear the guilt from all the holy things that the Israelites consecrates, from all their holy donations" (נשא אהרן את עון הקדשים אשר יקדישו בני ישראל לכל מתנות קדשיהם).[45]

---

44. See, for instance, Halpern, "The Ritual Background," 169–70; and Hallaschka, *Haggai und Sacharja*, 206, 220. The visions presented by Zechariah are purposefully ambivalent such that a definite interpretation is probably out of reach. See Meyers and Meyers, *Haggai, Zechariah 1-8*, 222–5. Still, the notion that the stone in Zech 3:9 is the top stone of the temple has some serious drawbacks. Thus, the immediate context of Zechariah 3 does not deal with the building of the temple. Likewise, elsewhere in the vision cycle, it is Zerubbabel who is associated with the rebuilding of the temple. See Mitchell et al., *Haggai, Zechariah, Malachi and Jonah*, 157. See further, Tiemeyer, *Zechariah and His Visions*, 144–5.

45. Mitchell et al., *Haggai, Zechariah, Malachi and Jonah*, 157–8; Petersen, *Haggai and Zechariah 1-8*, 211; Hanhart, *Sacharja*, 199; Delkurt, *Die Nachtgesichte des Sacharjas*, 193–4; Stead, *The Intertextuality of Zechariah 1-8*, 169–70; Tiemeyer, *Zechariah and his Visions*, 144–5.

Understanding the stone in Zech 3:9 as part of the priestly vestments would explain the nature of the "eyes" as "facets."[46] Since the eyes are dual, they equal the facets of the fourteen inscribed stones of the high priestly attire.[47] The unusual choice of the term עינים to describe the facets may be an attempt to link the process of atonement to Yahweh's power, which is expressed through seven eyes in the next chapter.[48] Therefore, the stone with which the high priest is presented at the end of the vision has an apotropaic function. It is this stone that will allow Yahweh to remove the guilt of the land in one day.

A similar conclusion to the divine trial and ritual purification is presented in the Namburbi against evil announced by birds. Here we learn how the supplicant is presented with several precious and semiprecious stones that he has to wear around his neck to prevent the evil from approaching him. Nevertheless, we encounter a major difference, namely, that the forgiveness is not extended to the whole land but rather limited to one person. As such, the vision can be shown to instrumentalize ritual imagery and language and yet reaches beyond the ritual by extending forgiveness to the whole land and facilitating the inauguration of a ritual apparatus in the form of a temple that will allow for the future expiation of the people's guilt.

6. Conclusion

This essay has shown how the prophetic vision account in Zechariah 3 uses ritual imagery and language to convey the notion that Yahweh has forgiven his people and is ready to return to his land, his city, and his sanctuary. The vision account shares several similarities with the three Namburbi. These similarities include the process of a divine trial, the presence of a mediator, the change of clothing, and the combination of sign- and speech-acts. Likewise, we find sporadic parallels like the usage of feces to signify guilt and the presentation of apotropaic stones at the conclusion of the ritual. Despite the similarities, it could be shown how ritual and vision operate on different levels. While the ritual employs sign- and speech-acts to request forgiveness, the vision employs the same imagery and language to signify that forgiveness has already been granted. The difference in setting also affects the presentation of evil. The evil portrayed by the omen is virulent and dangerous, and even when it is contained, it can reappear at any time. The evil portrayed by the satan and the guilt of priest and people has lost its potency as Yahweh has raised his voice, silenced the satan, and has forgiven the guilt, signaling that the time of punishment is over and the age of restoration has begun.

---

46. Tiemeyer, *Zechariah and His Visions*, 141; Vanderkam, "Joshua the High Priest," 568.
47. See Vanderkam, "Joshua the High Priest," 568.
48. See Hanhart, *Sacharja*, 226–7. For the links of Zech 3:9 and the remainder of the prophetic cycle, see Delkurt, *Die Nachtgesichte des Sacharjas*, 192–4.

Chapter 6

CONTESTED DIVINATION: BIBLICAL NECROMANCY AND COMPETITION AMONG RITUAL SPECIALISTS IN ANCIENT ISRAEL

Kerry M. Sonia

1. Introduction

The elements of the narrative in 1 Samuel 28 are well-known. King Saul is desperate. The armies of the Philistines and Israelites are poised for battle. As any prudent king would, Saul seeks guidance from Yahweh concerning the imminent conflict. But Yahweh refuses to answer him through dreams, priestly divination of the Urim, or prophecy. Ultimately, Saul must find a necromancer at Endor, who is able to summon the ghost of Samuel, the great Yahwistic prophet whose prophecies concerning Saul had proven accurate in the past. Indeed, Samuel had accurately prophesied to Saul the whereabouts of his father's missing asses (1 Sam 9:20) and Saul's rise to the kingship of Israel (1 Sam 10:1, 24). It is fitting, then, that Samuel would pronounce the demise of Saul's kingship, effectively bookending his reign with prophetic oracles. Samuel explains to Saul why Yahweh has turned against him and predicts both Saul's imminent defeat in battle and David's rise to the throne.

The ensuing narrative confirms Samuel's predictions, which suggests that the necromancer at Endor successfully facilitates the delivery of the Yahwistic oracle from the dead prophet to Saul. It is difficult to interpret this encounter as anything but successful. Even though the information Saul receives is not the outcome he desires, the necromancer and her method of divination prove effective. We can evaluate Samuel's oracle in 1 Samuel 28 through the lens of "true prophecy" described in Deut 18:22 or Jer 28:9. According to the Deuteronomy passage, "If a prophet speaks in the name of Yahweh but the thing does not take place or prove true, it is a word that Yahweh has not spoken." The Jeremiah passage similarly states, "As for the prophet who prophesies peace, when the word of that prophet comes true, then it will be known that Yahweh has truly sent the prophet." By the standards of these texts, the necromantic encounter in 1 Samuel 28 is an instance of true Yahwistic divination. It is successful, notably, despite the fact that Yahweh has repeatedly refused to answer Saul just prior to this encounter. It is almost as if both Samuel and Yahweh have been compelled to communicate with Saul against their will, which speaks perhaps to the perceived power and efficacy of necromancy in this text.

However, as Karen Smelik notes in her study of 1 Samuel 28's long history of interpretation, both ancient and modern treatments of the text have struggled with this aspect of the story—the apparent success of the necromantic encounter—and how it could possibly be consistent with so-called "biblical monotheism."[1] More recently, Esther Hamori has argued against the assumption that the necromancer at Endor is foreign or practicing a foreign form of cult: "It is not generally imagined that she could simply be an Israelite woman practicing Israelite religion."[2] Hamori claims that the message delivered by the necromancer is "overtly Yahwistic."[3] There is no indication in this text, she points out, that the necromancer is engaged in any non-Yahwistic activity. Further, Hamori troubles the sharp distinction often made in biblical scholarship between prophecy and other forms of divination, including necromancy. She notes that this scholarly distinction stems in part from taking biblical polemic at face value and in part from outdated theories of religion, pitting foreign, illicit "magic" against sanctioned "religion."[4]

What 1 Samuel 28 highlights and other biblical texts tend to obscure is the overlap between the work of necromancers and other ritual specialists, particularly prophets. This essay examines the dynamic between necromancers and prophets in the Hebrew Bible and offers some correctives for the discourse surrounding "biblical necromancy." Firstly, biblical texts depicting necromancy are not univocal in their evaluation of the practice. More specifically, 1 Samuel 28 challenges the notion that necromancy is universally viewed by biblical writers as ineffective or antithetical to Yahwistic religion. Secondly, the polemic of foreignness and illegitimacy, so often found in biblical texts depicting necromancy, tends to obscure the competition between necromancers and other ritual specialists. While many studies of necromancy analyze biblical rhetoric against necromancy on theological grounds—as the result of an incompatibility with normative Yahwism—this essay shifts the focus to dynamics between necromancers and prophets in the biblical text, how different writers draw distinctions between them, and what might be at stake in articulating these boundaries.

I begin by addressing the category "necromancy" and previous attempts to identify a coherent theological rationale for its negative portrayal in the Hebrew Bible. Then I turn to the depiction of necromancy in 1 Samuel 28 and other texts (e.g., Isa 8:19; 1 Chr 10:13–14) and consider what these passages suggest about the

---

1. Karen Smelik, "The Witch of Endor: I Samuel 28 in Rabbinic and Christian Exegesis Till 800 A.D," *Vigiliae Christianae* 33 (1979): 160–79.
2. Esther J. Hamori, *Women's Divination in Biblical Literature: Prophecy, Necromancy, and Other Arts of Knowledge* (New Haven, CT: Yale University Press, 2015), 111.
3. Ibid., 112.
4. Esther J. Hamori, "The Prophet and the Necromancer: Women's Divination for Kings," *JBL* 132 (2013): 827–43.

relationship between necromancers and prophets. Ultimately, I suggest we reframe the discourse about necromancy in biblical scholarship to adequately consider the overlap and, thus, competition among ritual specialists in ancient Israel and how this dynamic shapes biblical rhetoric about necromancy.

2. Definitions and Previous Reconstructions

There is some debate among scholars about how to define the category "necromancy" in the broader study of religion. While some regard necromancy as the attempt to procure privileged information from the dead,[5] others have broadened this definition to include the invocation of the dead in general.[6] I opt for the former; in my view, the dead may be invoked for different reasons and by different means. Conflating these different modes of invocation obscures how they function in their particular contexts. Necromancy constitutes one mode of such invocation and focuses particularly on the acquisition of privileged information— information that is otherwise difficult to obtain or inaccessible to living human beings, such as knowledge of the future. In this regard, necromancy is quite similar to other modes of divination, such as prophecy, but differs in the means by which it attains this knowledge.

Though there are relatively few references to necromancy in the Hebrew Bible, it looms large as a category in the study of Israelite religion and ancient religion more generally. This emphasis is no doubt due in part to the predominantly negative portrayal of necromancy in the Hebrew Bible and its association with so-called "foreign" cult or what nineteenth-century scholars called "magic" or "primitive religion." There is a tendency among biblical scholars to separate necromancy from other forms of divination, especially prophecy, based partly on biblical rhetoric and partly on this outdated paradigm—necromancy often assigned to the sphere of "magic" or "primitive religion" and prophecy to the

---

5. "Necromancy, the art or practice of conjuring up the souls of the dead, is primarily a form of divination. The principle purpose of seeking such communication with the dead is to obtain information from them, generally regarding the revelation of unknown causes or the future course of events." See Erika Bourguignon, "Necromancy," in *The Encyclopedia of Religion*, vol. 10, ed. M. Eliade (New York: Macmillan, 1987), 345–7. See, similarly, Ann Jeffers, *Magic and Divination in Ancient Palestine and Syria* (Leiden: Brill, 1996), 167; Brian Schmidt, *Israel's Beneficent Dead: Ancestor Cult and Necromancy in Ancient Israelite Religion and Tradition* (Winona Lake, IN: Eisenbrauns, 1994), 11; Christophe Nihan, "1 Samuel 28 and the Condemnation of Necromancy in Persian Yehud," in *Magic in the Biblical World: From the Rod of Aaron to the Ring of Solomon*, ed. Todd E. Klutz (London: T&T Clark, 2003), 24; and Christopher B. Hays, *Death in the Iron Age II and in First Isaiah* (Tübingen: Mohr Siebeck, 2011), 47.

6. Josef Tropper, *Nekromantie: Totenbefragung im Alten Orient und im Alten Testament* (Neukirchen-Vluyn: Neukirchener, 1989), 14–15.

sphere of supposedly more evolved or legitimate religion. However, recent studies have emphasized that both prophecy and necromancy belong to the broader ritual category of divination, which Hamori defines as "any type of action culturally understood to allow acquisition of knowledge otherwise restricted to the divine realm."[7] This reframing of necromancy and prophecy as part of the same ritual genus, divination, casts a different light on biblical texts that depict them together.

Biblical depictions of necromancy often characterize it as illicit and non-Yahwistic. Leviticus 19:31 construes necromancy as defiling, while Lev 20:6 depicts it as a form of cultic disloyalty. Deuteronomy 18:20–12 refers to necromancy as an abomination to Yahweh, and both 2 Kgs 21:6 and 2 Chr 33:6 consider it evil in the eyes of Yahweh. Finally, 1 Chr 10:13–14 construes necromancy as sacrilege. Furthermore, necromancy is often associated in these texts with other cult practices considered illicit by the biblical writers, especially child sacrifice (e.g., Deut 18:10–11; Lev 20:2–6; 2 Kgs 21:6; 2 Chr 33:6). Such biblical depictions make it easy for scholars to fall into a similar pattern of privileging the prophets and the ritual work they do. This scholarly bias toward the prophets likely stems from a long history of biblical interpretation in which scholars unconsciously align themselves with the polemic of the prophets and against their ritual rivals.[8] Thus, previous studies have often rationalized biblical polemic against necromancy by resorting to theological arguments about the nature of Yahwistic religion and its inherent incompatibility with necromancy. This is often couched in binary terms: necromancy is associated with death and, thus, corpse and grave pollution, while

---

7. Hamori, *Women's Divination*, 4.

8. In an essay on the supposed antagonism between priests and prophets in the Hebrew Bible, Ziony Zevit argues that biblical interpreters from various historical periods often side with the prophets, a bias that may stem from the New Testament rivalry between Jesus and temple personnel—most notably, the high priest Caiaphas ("The Prophet Versus the Priest Antagonism Hypothesis," in *The Priests in the Prophets: The Portrayal of Priests, Prophets and Other Religious Specialists in the Latter Prophets*, ed. Lester L. Grabbe and Alice Ogden Bellis [New York: T&T Clark International, 2004], 210–13). Zevit argues that the antagonism between priests and prophets has been overstated in scholarly reconstructions, due in part to backreading the tension between temple personnel (such as Caiaphas in Matt 26:57–68; Mark 14:53–65; Luke 22:64) and Jesus in the New Testament into the dynamic between figures in the Hebrew Bible. This motif of temple elites versus charismatic reformers continues to appeal to later generations of interpreters, especially those who align themselves with the Protestant Reformation. The prophets, then, become analogous to the charismatic religious authorities in direct communication with God charged with condemning the corrupt religious activity of cultic elites. Though we are not concerned at present with the dynamic between priests and prophets in the Hebrew Bible, Zevit's argument identifies ways in which modern scholarly bias may unconsciously influence reconstructions of "legitimate" and "illegitimate" ritual and ritual specialists in Israelite religion.

Yahweh is the god of life and requires purity.⁹ Other studies suggest that necromancy and its reliance upon the, perhaps divine, dead (as use of the term אלהים in 1 Sam 28:13 and Isa 8:19 suggests) for information violates the primacy of Yahweh and what some have called "monotheism" in Israelite religion.

The general lack of evidence detailing necromantic ritual in the Hebrew Bible contributes to an overreliance upon this anti-necromancy rhetoric. To be sure, what we do not know about biblical necromancy outweighs what we do. For example, we do not know the incantations or ritual acts by which necromancers summon the dead. Similarly, we do not know who among the dead are typically summoned—a famous prophet like Samuel or less prominent laypersons.¹⁰ We do not know who is able to summon the dead—only ritual specialists or laypersons as well. We also do not know where these rituals typically take place. 1 Samuel 28 is the only detailed account of necromancy in the Hebrew Bible, and it lacks many of these features. It does, however, caution against some common misconceptions of necromancy. For instance, previous treatments of necromancy often assume that people summon their own ancestors during necromancy; however, the fact that Saul summons Samuel (with whom he has no kinship bond) in 1 Samuel 28 challenges such a generalization.¹¹

Although the necromancer invokes the dead Samuel at Endor, the text never refers to the presence of Samuel's corpse in the ritual. In fact, the notice in 1 Sam 28:3 about the prophet's burial in Ramah argues against the notion that the summoning of Samuel *at Endor* requires his corpse. This observation challenges the argument that necromancy poses a threat to Yahwism as expressed in the Deuteronomistic ideology because it troubles the binaries of life/purity and death/impurity. Therefore, the argument that polemic against necromancy assumes an anxiety about pollution through corpse or grave contact is unsupported by this

---

9. See, e.g., Rainer Albertz and Rüdiger Schmitt, *Household and Family Religion in Ancient Israel and the Levant* (Winona Lake, IN: Eisenbrauns, 2012), 470; Stephen L. Cook, "Death, Kinship, and Community: Afterlife and the חסד Ideal in Israel," in *The Family in Life and in Death: The Family in Ancient Israel—Sociological and Archaeological Perspectives*, ed. Patricia Dutcher-Walls (New York: T&T Clark, 2009), 119.

10. It is possible that exceptional figures like Samuel are capable of exhibiting similar powers in death as they did in life. We find an analogous example in the power of the dead prophet Elisha's bones to revivify a man who touches them in 2 Kgs 13:21. While living, Elisha is credited with the resurrection of a dead child in 2 Kgs 4:32–35. Would this way of understanding the powers of the dead help elucidate 1 Samuel 28? Perhaps only a prophet like Samuel, a mouthpiece of the divine, is able to effectively communicate divine knowledge in death. However, we can hardly reconstruct such a principle on the basis of one text, leaving us to speculate on what it may or may not indicate with regard to broader conceptions of the practice.

11. For further discussion of the distinction between necromancy and the cult of dead kin in Israelite religion, see Kerry M. Sonia, *Caring for the Dead in Ancient Israel* (Archaeology and Biblical Studies 27; Atlanta, GA: SBL Press, 2020), 65–128.

text, which is by far our most descriptive evidence for necromantic ritual in the Hebrew Bible.

The argument that inquiring of the dead in necromancy violates the primacy of Yahweh also ignores the fact that 1 Samuel 28 seems to depict successful Yahwistic divination: a necromancer summons a dead prophet of Yahweh who delivers what turns out to be an accurate oracle. The success of this necromantic encounter suggests that not all biblical writers believe necromancy to be incompatible with Yahwistic religion. At the same time, it is notable that while this text depicts Yahwistic divination through necromancy, it is not concerned with promoting a supposed "monotheistic" agenda. After all, the dead Samuel is referred to as an אלהים in 1 Sam 28:13, which suggests that this text is not interested in portraying Yahweh as the sole divine being capable of interceding in the world of the living.[12]

In short, scholars have struggled to identify a consistent theological rationale for the biblical polemic against necromancy. What I propose instead is that we examine this polemic through the lens of competition among ritual specialists in ancient Israel and ask what this rhetoric against necromancy might seek to accomplish. While biblical writers often positively construe the activity of priests and prophets and their access to Yahweh, most of these writers push necromancers to the margins of Israelite society, depicting them as aberrant, foreign, and antithetical to Yahwistic religion. That biblical writers should use the rhetoric of foreignness to condemn necromantic ritual is hardly surprising—in fact, several biblical texts use this polemic against rituals they seek to marginalize.[13] This association between "foreignness" and "illicit" ritual activity is a recurring trope

---

12. Brian Schmidt argues that אלהים in 28:13 refers not to the ghost of Samuel but to the "gods known to be summoned" in other ancient Near Eastern necromantic texts ("The 'Witch' of En-Dor, 1 Samuel 28, and Ancient Near Eastern Necromancy," in *Ancient Magic and Ritual Power*, ed. Marvin Meyer and Paul Mirecki [New York: Brill, 1995], 120–6). This interpretation, he argues, helps account for the fact that the אלהים in v. 13 takes a plural participle (אלהים ראיתי עלים מן־הארץ) but the אלהים in v. 15 takes a singular verb (ואלהים סר מעלי). Schmidt argues that the first אלהים in v. 13 refers to multiple netherworld divinities that accompany the dead person invoked in the ritual, while the second refers to Yahweh. Ultimately, this argument is unconvincing. When Saul asks what "his/its form" looks like in v. 14, it seems clear based on the flow of the narrative that Saul is referring to the appearance of the אלהים in the previous verse and, thus, a singular entity. Furthermore, 1 Sam 28:13 is not the only place where אלהים, construed as a singular, takes a plural form. In Josh 24:19, e.g., אלהים (referring to Yahweh) takes both a singular verb (יֻשִּׁ֖יא) and a plural adjective (קדשׁים). Furthermore, Waltke and O'Connor (7.4.3d) note that the "honorific plural" is often used for participles referring to Yahweh (Job 35:10; Ps 118:7). Thus, the plurality of the participle in this verse need not lead to speculative interpretations of אלהים as referring to any divine being other than the dead Samuel invoked during the necromantic ritual depicted in this text.

13. Some texts, for instance, associate foreigners with various kinds of negatively construed cultic practices. See Christopher T. Begg, "Foreigner," *ABD* 2 (1992): 829–30,

throughout much of the Hebrew Bible. Instead of recognizing this polemic as a reflection of competition among ritual specialists, many treatments of biblical necromancy have taken these negative characterizations at face value—that the practice originates outside of Israel and is prohibited on theological grounds. In doing so, they replicate the rhetoric of ancient writers, obscuring the nuances in biblical depictions of divination and its practitioners.

Finally, a brief word is necessary to clarify what I mean by "competition" among "ritual specialists" in the Hebrew Bible. Certain individuals (and sometimes groups of individuals) are recognized as proficient performers of ritual in the biblical text. Sometimes they explicitly compete against each other, as in the case of Qoraḥ rebellion (Num 16:1–35) and Elijah's showdown against the prophets of Baal (1 Kgs 18:19–40). In these cases, successful performance of ritual entails specialized knowledge and skill as well as access to the divine. The stakes of this competition may include religious authority, social privilege, and material wealth. Individual ritual specialists are sometimes hired and paid for their services, both in and outside of the royal court. Although the biblical text does not depict the payment of a necromancer, there are several references to the payment of prophets and priests. In 1 Sam 9:6–9, a young Saul and his servant discuss what they might pay the prophet Samuel (food or silver) for his assistance in locating the missing asses of Kish. In Judg 17:10, Micah similarly offers food and silver to the Levite from Bethlehem in exchange for his work as a priest in Micah's sanctuary.

Other texts evaluate the payment of ritual specialists more negatively. Micah 3:11 alleges that judges, prophets, and priests accept payment for favorable legal judgments and ritual outcomes regardless of divine will. The text vehemently condemns this practice, blaming it for the destruction of Jerusalem. Lester Grabbe similarly interprets Amos 7:12–15 as an allegation by a rival prophet that Amos is merely a prophet for hire.[14] While priests are often associated with fixed

---

for a brief survey of the terminology and depiction of foreigners in the Hebrew Bible. For a discussion of the "Canaanite" origins of practices such as child sacrifice, Asherah worship, and necromancy, see Schmidt, *Israel's Beneficent Dead*, 138–9, in which he argues that this association is a deliberate distortion by the biblical writers that serves their polemic against such practices. See, similarly, the discussion of "willful confusion" regarding cultic practices in Deuteronomistic polemics in Saul M. Olyan, *Asherah and the Cult of Yahweh in Israel* (Atlanta, GA: Scholars Press, 1988), 11–13. For a broader discussion of the stigmatizing rhetoric against foreigners and foreignness in different biblical texts, see Saul M. Olyan, "Stigmatizing Associations: The Alien, Things Alien, and Practices Associated with Aliens in Biblical Classification Schemas," in *The Foreigner and the Law: Perspectives from the Hebrew Bible and the Ancient Near East*, ed. Reinhard Achenbach, Rainer Albertz and Jakob Wöhrle (Wiesbaden: Harrassowitz Verlag, 2011), 17–28.

14. Lester L. Grabbe, "A Priest Is without Honor in His Own Prophet," in *The Priests in the Prophets: The Portrayal of Priests, Prophets and Other Religious Specialists in the Latter Prophets*, ed. Lester L. Grabbe and Alice Ogden Bellis (JSOTS 408; London: T&T Clark, 2004), 81.

ritual spaces, other kinds of ritual specialists are depicted as relatively itinerant and, perhaps, more dependent on freelance work. While previous studies have examined the tension among rival priests and prophets and the representation of this conflict in the Hebrew Bible, they have overlooked the role of necromancers in this competitive ritual landscape.

3. Necromancers and Prophets

The Endor encounter raises questions regarding the relationship between necromancy and other forms of divination, including prophecy. The narrative of 1 Samuel 28 seems to consider the similarity between necromancer and prophet relatively unproblematic: the necromancer at Endor successfully summons a dead Yahwistic prophet in order to deliver a Yahwistic oracle. At no point does 1 Samuel 28 condemn the activity of the necromancer. This depiction of Yahwistic divination through necromancy may explain the context in which the writer of 1 Chr 10:13–14 must clearly state that Saul's necromantic encounter in 1 Samuel 28 does not involve Yahweh:

> Saul died on account of his transgression, which he committed against Yahweh, because he did not keep the word of Yahweh. He also inquired through a ghost (אוב) for divination and did not divine through Yahweh. Therefore, he (Yahweh) killed him and turned the kingdom over to David, the son of Jesse.

This text could not be more explicit: the necromantic encounter at Endor is *not* Yahwistic. Moreover, resorting to a ghost rather than Yahweh for divination results in Saul's death and the fall of his dynasty. This unequivocal statement in 1 Chronicles 10 may be an attempt to refute the idea that 1 Samuel 28 depicts a Yahwistic oracle via necromancy, an indication that this interpretation persists into the Persian period and must be adamantly refuted.[15]

Indeed, unlike 1 Samuel 28, texts such as Isa 8:19 and Deut 18:9–11 are very concerned with drawing sharp distinctions between the work of necromancers and prophets. For instance, Isa 8:18–20 sets up a contrast between the prophet and his children, who will act as signs and portents for Yahweh, and those who practice necromancy:

---

15. Details both within Chronicles and its use by later sources suggest that it was composed during the Persian period (539–332 BCE). For a discussion of the issues related to the dating of Chronicles, see Gary N. Knoppers, *1 Chronicles 1–9: A New Translation with Introduction and Commentary* (AB; Garden City, NY: Doubleday, 2004), 101–17. The clear allusion to the Endor narrative in 1 Chr 10:13–14 suggests it was relatively well-known by the Persian period and necessitated further commentary by the writer(s) of Chronicles.

I[16] and the children that Yahweh has given me will become signs and wonders in Israel from Yahweh of hosts who dwells on Mount Zion. Surely, they will say to you, "Consult ghosts and spirits (האבות והידענים)[17] that chirp[18] and mutter, for shouldn't a people consult their אלהים,[19] the dead for instruction and a message on

16. Presumably, the prophet himself. For a discussion of the difficulties in distinguishing the quoted speech, speaker, and audience of this passage, see Robert P. Carroll, "Translation and Attribution in Isaiah 8:19f," *Bible Translator* 31 (1980): 126–34. The division of the passage in this way seems more logical than understanding the phrase, "shouldn't a people consult their god(s)," as a negative retort to the people's request for necromantic oracles. Interpreting the phrase as a negative retort would render the passage as follows: "Surely, they will say to you, 'Consult האבות והידענים that chirp and mutter.' Shouldn't a people (instead) consult their God (אלהים) [rather than] the dead for instruction and a message on behalf of the living? Surely, they will say such a futile thing."

Yet, in this division of the passage, it is unclear how the phrase "the dead ... on behalf of the living" fits with the material surrounding it. Interpreting the אלהים as Yahweh does not account for the apparent parallelism between אלהים and "the dead." It would not make sense for the biblical writer to refer to Yahweh as dead, a characterization reserved for allegedly "foreign," ineffective divine beings. Instead, the reference to "the dead" seems to refer back to the האבות והידענים earlier in the verse, a reference to the dead invoked in necromantic ritual. Therefore, the apparent parallelism of these two phrases suggests that they belong to the same quotation in which the people request necromantic oracles. Additional support for interpreting the material from "Consult האבות והידענים" to "the dead ... on behalf of the living" as a single quotation comes from the fact that the notice "Surely, they will say such a thing" seems to mark the end of that quotation. For a similar division of this passage, see Joseph Blenkinsopp, *Isaiah 1-39: A New Translation with Introduction and Commentary* (Garden City, NY: Doubleday, 2000), 242; Schmidt, *Israel's Beneficent Dead*, 148; and Karel van der Toorn, *Family Religion in Babylonia, Ugarit, and Israel: Continuity and Changes in the Forms of Religious Life* (Leiden: Brill, 1996), 222n. 70.

17. In different biblical texts, this phrase refers either to ghosts and spirits summoned during necromancy or the necromancers themselves. The first sense of the phrase seems to make better sense in this particular text. For a discussion of the components of this phrase and their history of interpretation, see Tropper, *Nekromantie*, 189–201. More recently, Christopher Hays has proposed a new etymology of the Hebrew אוב as deriving from the Egyptian term for an ancestor statue (*Death in the Iron Age II*, 170–4). See also Christopher B. Hays and Joel M. LeMon, "The Dead and Their Images: An Egyptian Etymology for Hebrew אוב," *Journal of Ancient Egyptian Interconnections* 1 (2009): 1–4.

18. This form is a pilpel participle of צפף, "to cheep, whisper" (HALOT 2: 1050). In addition to the necromantic context of Isa 8:19 and 29:4, this form of the verb also appears in Isa 10:14 and 38:14, where it refers to the sound of birds.

19. Contra Schmidt, *Israel's Beneficent Dead*, 150, who interprets the אלהים in this passage, as in 1 Sam 28:13, as netherworld deities summoned during necromancy, not the dead. As I note above, the term seems to function here as a reference to the dead invoked in necromantic ritual.

behalf of the living?" Surely, they will say such a futile[20] thing. The hard-pressed and hungry will pass by. When they are hungry and angry, they will curse their king and אלהים. Whether they look above or to the netherworld (ארץ),[21] they will look and find distress and darkness, the gloom of anguish and thick darkness.

It is clear that this passage wants to distinguish prophet from necromancer. It emphasizes the inefficacy of summoning the dead, depicting the speech of the dead as mere "chirps" and "mutters." Yet, the people's request that the prophet perform divination through the dead implies that some Israelites may have assumed that prophets perform such a ritual. Perhaps necromancy was merely one method in the prophet's divinatory repertoire, according to this view. In fact, the rhetorical question, "Shouldn't a people consult their אלהים?," suggests the extent to which the people take for granted (1) the importance of consulting the dead; and (2) the prophet as an appropriate intermediary. Yet, the text goes on to undermine the efficacy of necromancy in the verses that follow. Thus, it is possible that Isa 8:18–20 reflects the notion that people may ask prophets to perform necromancy on their behalf, and the passage is formulated in such a way as to mock such a request.

This is a recurring theme elsewhere in the book of Isaiah, especially in passages depicting acute crisis. These passages depict those who seek necromantic divination as no better than the dead they invoke, condemned to a world of darkness and distress typified by ancient West Asian depictions of the netherworld. Like Isa 8:19, they often undermine necromancy by emphasizing the unintelligibility and inefficacy of necromantic speech. For instance, Isa 29:4 refers to the lowliness of Jerusalem by comparing it with a ghost "chirping" from the earth:

You will be brought low and will speak from the netherworld (ארץ);[22] your speech will be uttered from the dust. Your voice will be like a ghost (אוב) from the netherworld (ארץ); your voice will chirp (תצפצף) from the dust (עפר).

20. The phrase אשר אין־לו שחר is difficult. The contrast between שחר, "dawn," and the darkness imagery in v. 22 seems to underscore the ineffectiveness of necromancy in the passage. Other interpretations have amended the MT using the LXX, which has δῶρον, apparently reading שׂחד, "bribe," instead of שחר. Others translate שחר according to Arabic *saḥara*, "put to forced labor," which would then render the phrase, "which has no force." For these and other interpretations of the phrase, see Theodore J. Lewis, *Cults of the Dead in Ancient Israel and Ugarit* (Atlanta, GA: Scholars Press, 1989), 132n. 13. While the meaning of שחר is unclear, its context indicates that the phrase is meant to emphasize the fact that necromancy is ultimately futile and will not improve the situation of those who seek its aid, which is how I have rendered it above.

21. The use of the term ארץ here may be a reference to the netherworld, since the passage is concerned with various modes by which the distressed seek divine assistance, including consultation of the dead.

22. Concerning the pair ארץ//עפר, see my note above regarding possible references to the netherworld in Isa 8:19.

6. Contested Divination

Although Isa 29:4 is not explicitly an attack on necromancy, its negative depiction of ghosts and their ability to speak from the netherworld suggest a similar bias against the powers of the dead and their ability to communicate effectively with the living.

Some scholars argue that Isa 28:7-22 contains a similar bias against necromancy that emphasizes the unintelligible speech of the dead:[23]

> Whom shall he[24] teach knowledge? To whom shall he explain the message? Those who are weaned from milk and taken from the breasts? For—צו לצו צו לצו קו לקו קו לקו, a little here, a little there—with stammering speech and strange language it is spoken to this people ... To them the word of Yahweh is צו לצו צו לצו קו לקו קו לקו, a little here, a little there, so that they go, stumble backward, are broken, ensnared, and taken. Therefore, hear the word of the Yahweh, you scoffers who rule this people in Jerusalem. Because you have said, "We have made a covenant with death, and with Sheol we have an agreement."

The meaning of the lexical string (צו לצו צו לצו קו לקו קו לקו) is unclear, and different scholars have offered several interpretations.[25] The most convincing interpretation, in my view, is that this alliterative string is intended to mimic unintelligible speech—perhaps a foreign language, the babble of children, or the supposedly garbled speech of the dead. The repetitive sounds in the phrase may imitate the babbling of recently weaned infants, referenced in Isa 28:9. If the lexical string in Isaiah 28 is meant to evoke the "chirps" and "muttering" of the dead, then its association with the babbling of infants further emphasizes the inefficacy of the dead and their ability to communicate true knowledge of Yahweh. In short, these Isaiah texts depict necromancy as ineffective in large part because of the unintelligibility and powerlessness of the dead.

The reference to necromancy in Deut 18:11 is similar in some ways to the treatment of necromancy in the book of Isaiah. Deuteronomy 18:11 refers to the

---

23. Karel van der Toorn, "Echoes of Judean Necromancy in Isaiah 28,7-22," *ZAW* 100 (1988): 199–217. Though van der Toorn has become one of its more recent proponents, this interpretation is not new. Previous scholars who have advocated for this reading of Isa 28:7–22 include G. W. Wade, *The Book of the Prophet Isaiah* (London: Methuen, 1911), 180; Samuel Daiches, *Isaiah and Spiritualism: A New Explanation of Isaiah XXVIII, 5-22* (London: Jewish Chronicle Supplement, 1926): 6; E. König, *Das Buch Jesaja* (Gütersloh: Bertelsmann, 1926), 254; and Baruch Halpern, "'The Excremental Vision': The Doomed Priests of Doom in Isaiah 28," *HAR* 10 (1986): 109–21.

24. Presumably, Yahweh, whose word is unintelligible to inhabitants of Jerusalem later in this passage.

25. For a summary of these interpretations, see HALOT, 1009. Interpretations cited in this entry include: (1) צו and קו are names for letters, being taught to a child; (2) these terms are translated "precept" and "(measuring) line," respectively; (3) the phrase comes from Akkadian *ṣi lūṣi qî luqqi*, "Go out, let him go out; wait, let him wait."

practice of necromancy, the consultation of the אוב וידעני (cf. Lev 20:27), and those who seek the dead (דרש המתים). This condemnation of necromancy appears before the Israelites' entrance into the land of Canaan, and the text bases its condemnation of necromancy on the notion that the Israelites must avoid the supposed rituals of the Canaanites, necromancy being chief among them. Verse 11 belongs to a larger passage in 18:10–12 that lists necromancy alongside child sacrifice (cf. Lev 20:6) and refers to the activity of different ritual specialists as abominations (תועבת) committed by the Canaanites before Israel's entry into the land:

> When you enter the land that Yahweh your god is giving to you, you shall not learn to act in accordance with the abominations of those nations. There shall not be found among you one who makes his son or daughter pass through the fire, a קסם קסמים מעונן ומנחש ומכשף חבר חבר,[26] one who inquires of אוב וידעני, and one who seeks the dead, because anyone who does these things is an abomination to Yahweh. Because of these abominations, Yahweh your god is dispossessing them before you. (Deut 18:9–12)

It is important to note that this passage referring to the necromancer is bookended in the chapter by, first, an explanation of what is owed to the Levites for their temple service in vv. 1–8 and, last, by the promise that Yahweh will raise up a prophet from the midst of the people in vv. 15–16, 18–22. The juxtaposition of these ritual specialists in the chapter—the Levites, the necromancer (and other practitioners of supposedly Canaanite ritual), and the prophet—emphasizes the endorsement or condemnation of different ritual specialists by this text.

The placement of the polemic against necromancy in this narrative moment, just before the Israelites enter the land of Canaan, is an example of biblical mythmaking[27] at its most effective. Projected back to this moment in Israelite history, the pronouncement of Deut 18:11 against necromancy, among other rituals, creates an unassailable argument against this kind of ritual specialist.

---

26. I have left these specialized terms untranslated, primarily because it is difficult to reconstruct their individual practices or to distinguish them from each other with any certainty. Clearly, they are ritual practices negatively construed by the text. The appearance of קסם and necromancy in this passage suggests that most of them are methods of divination, while כשף (and its Akkadian cognate *kašāpu*) suggests an association with rituals meant to manipulate divine forces for benevolent or malevolent purposes, CAD K 284. For an examination of נחש in biblical contexts and its possible Aramean origin, see Gary A. Rendsburg, *Israelian Hebrew in the Book of Kings* (Bethesda: CDL Press, 2002), 66–7.

27. I use the term "mythmaking" here in reference to the work of Russell T. McCutcheon, who defines "mythmaking" as: "a species of ideology production, of ideal-making, where 'ideal' is conceived not as an abstract, absolute value but as a contingent, localized construct that comes to represent and simultaneously reproduce certain specific social values *as if* they were inevitable and universal" ("Myth," in *Guide to the Study of Religion*, ed. Willi Braun and Russell McCutcheon [New York: Cassell, 2000], 204).

Necromancy is not merely ineffective, as the Isaiah passages assert; it endangers the very foundations of Israel itself. Thus, the reference to necromancy in Deuteronomy 18 is part of a larger polemic in the chapter that distinguishes supposedly illegitimate ritual specialists, including necromancers, from others in Israel, including the priests and prophets.

4. Reframing Discussions of Necromancy

So, what might these different passages suggest about biblical necromancy as a ritual category? The nature of biblical polemic against necromancy becomes more apparent when 1 Samuel 28 is taken into consideration. In this text, the activity of the necromancer seems compatible with Yahwism, an interpretation of the text that appears to persist in the Persian period as indicated by its refutation in 1 Chr 10:13-14. The contrast between the ritual work of the prophet and the necromancer in both Isa 8:19-20 and Deut 18:10-11 suggests a tension between these ritual specialists that must be addressed by the biblical writers. The prophetic polemic against necromancy in the book of Isaiah focuses on the unintelligibility and inefficacy of the speech of the dead. Such rhetoric against necromancy makes particular sense in a prophetic book, as it seeks to undermine not only the practices of rival ritual specialists but also the power of the dead themselves. They may chirp and mutter, but they cannot communicate with the living. The Deut 18:10-11 passage uses alienating rhetoric to marginalize necromancy and set it in opposition to the work of Yahwistic priests and prophets. Yet, the biblical texts are not univocal in this depiction of necromancy, as 1 Samuel 28 demonstrates. The narrative about the necromancer at Endor is striking because it depicts necromantic ritual so differently than these other biblical texts. The speech of the dead prophet Samuel, summoned through necromancy, is not only articulate but also accurate, conveying what other biblical texts would characterize as a "true" Yahwistic oracle.

In light of these observations, I propose that we give due consideration to the dynamic between these religious specialists and how it influences evaluations of necromancy in the biblical text as non-normative Yahwism.[28] Necromancy provides an alternate means of petitioning divine beings for privileged information, and this

---

28. Indeed, both Elizabeth Bloch-Smith and Mark Smith argue that polemics against consulting the dead through intermediaries date to the Hezekiah and Josiah reforms of the eighth century BCE and are later incorporated into Deuteronomic legal material, the Holiness Code, and the writings of Isaiah. See Elizabeth Bloch-Smith, *Judahite Burial Practices and Beliefs about the Dead* (JSOTS 123; Sheffield: Sheffield Academic Press, 1992), 146-7; Mark S. Smith and Elizabeth Bloch-Smith, "Death and Afterlife in Ugarit and Israel: Review of Beatific Afterlife in Ancient Israel and in the Ancient Near East," *JAOS* 108 (1988): 277-84. Bloch-Smith attributes these changes to the influx of refugee cultic personnel from the north and the threat they posed to Judahite cultic and political figures.

service may threaten prophets in their roles as intermediaries between the Israelites and the divine. Biblical polemic against necromancy makes sense in this context, as it seeks to undermine not only the practices of these ritual specialists but also the efficacy of the dead themselves. Yet, the persistence of the people and kings in seeking necromantic oracles suggests that they continue to view necromancy as an effective means of divination, and both they and the specialists who invoke the dead likely view necromancy as legitimate within Yahwistic religion.

Chapter 7

BINDING ASMODEUS: A LEXICAL ANALYSIS OF THE RITUAL AND MEDICAL USE OF FISH IN TOBIT

Lindsey A. Askin

1. Introduction

In the book of Tobit, a fumigation ritual involving fish heart, liver, and burning incense exorcises a demon, and fish gall heals an eye disease that had been causing deteriorating vision. A few studies on the medical use of fish in Tobit explore equivalents in Babylonian medicine,[1] while others appeal to Tobit as evidence of shifting Hellenistic Jewish attitudes to medicine.[2] While establishing a contemporary context for the medical use of fish may be straightforward, arguing for a broad cultural shift in Hellenistic Judaism is less justifiable. Detecting continuity and discontinuity in attitudes to medicine can be more effective when using a variety of analytical methods.

---

1. Annie Attia, "Disease and Healing in the Book of Tobit and in Mesopotamian Medicine," in *Mesopotamian Medicine and Magic: Studies in Honor of Markham J. Geller*, ed. Strahil V. Panayotov and Luděk Vacín (Ancient Magic and Divination 14; Leiden: Brill, 2018), 36–68; Hans J. Lundager Jensen, "Family, Fertility and Foul Smell: Tobit and Judith," in *Studies in the Book of Tobit: A Multidisciplinary Approach*, ed. Mark Bredin (Library of Second Temple Studies 55; London: T&T Clark, 2006), 129–39; Bernd Kollmann, "Göttliche Offenbarung magisch-pharmakologischer Heilkunst im Buch Tobit," *ZAW* 106 (1994): 289–99; Wolfram von Soden, "Fischgalle als Heilmittel für Augen," in *Bibel und alter orient: altorientalische Beiträge zum Alten Testament*, ed. Hans-Peter Müller (BZAW 162; Berlin: de Gruyter, 1985), 76–7; I. Papayannopoulos, J. Laskaratos, and S. Marketos, "Remarks on Tobit's Blindness," *Korot* 9 (1985): 181–7.

2. Pieter W. van der Horst, "Early Jewish Knowledge of Greek Medicine," in *Strength to Strength: Essays in Honor of Shaye J.D. Cohen* (BJS 363; Providence: Brown University Press, 2018), 103–13; Maria Chrysovergi, "Contrasting Views on Physicians in Tobit and Sirach," *JSP* 21 (2011): 37–54; Maria Chrysovergi, "Attitudes towards the Use of Medicine in Jewish Literature from the Third and Second Centuries BCE" (PhD Thesis, Durham University, 2011); Larry P. Hogan, *Healing in the Second Temple Period* (NTOA 21; Göttingen: Vandenhoeck & Ruprecht, 1992).

An exploration of Tobit's vocabulary for describing medicine and exorcistic ritual would bring new data to this area of research. It is illuminating to look at Greek Tobit lexicographically, not just in light of LXX Greek but also Greek literature, epigraphy, and papyri.[3] Medical texts and magical formulaic writing sometimes draw upon specialist technical terms. The degree to which the textual witnesses of Tobit use or eschew such technical vocabulary from wider contexts can thus shed light on Tobit's attitudes to medicine and exorcism as a whole.

As a story set in Babylonia and Media, this study argues that Tobit may be understood better in light of Babylonian medicine as well as Greek traditions. The aim of this chapter is to investigate Tobit's ritualistic use of incense and potent ingredients in exorcism and medicine through lexical analysis, or the exploration of vocabulary. If Tobit does reflect one or more traditions of medicine and of exorcistic ritual—Jewish, Near Eastern, and Hellenistic Mediterranean—such contexts should shine through in Tobit's choice of words. Detecting the presence of specialist or technical terms would be particularly revealing of Tobit's historical contexts, audience, attitudes to medicine or to exorcistic ritual, and textual history.

Tobit has a complex textual history that has made speculation about some of the oddities of this text all the more attractive, such as the mysterious dog. Tobiah's dog appears at varying points in the Greek and Latin versions, with internal disagreements, and in all cases the dog is rather disconnected from the plot. This study will focus on each version's differences at the lexical level: choices of vocabulary and technical terms. In this way, this study aims to offer fresh lexical and text-critical insights into Tobit's attitudes to medicine and exorcistic ritual. While far from exhaustive, four key passages will be considered: Tob 6:4–9 (getting the fish); 6:17 (Azariah's instructions); 8:1–9 (the ritual of exorcism); and 11:4, 7–15 (the dog, the healing of the eyes).

2. Textual History

The textual history of Tobit is crucial to understand before beginning an exploration of vocabulary terms. Most researchers favor an Aramaic original,[4] while a Hebrew original is proposed by Esther Eshel.[5] There are three Aramaic manuscripts (4Q196–199) and one Hebrew (4Q200).[6] Greek Tobit has at

---

3. John A. L. Lee, *A Lexical Study of the Septuagint Version of the Pentateuch* (SCS 14; Chico: Scholars Press, 1983); James K. Aitken, *No Stone Unturned: Greek Inscriptions and Septuagint Vocabulary* (CSHB 5; Winona Lake, IN: Eisenbrauns, 2014).

4. Andrew B. Perrin, "An Almanac of Tobit Studies: 2000-2014," CBR 13 (2014): 111–13.

5. Esther Eshel, "Biblical Apocrypha and Pseudepigrapha in the Light of the Qumran Scrolls," in *The Qumran Scrolls and Their World*, ed. Menahem Kister (Ancient Literature of Eretz Israel and Its World: Between Bible and Mishnah; Jerusalem: Yad Ben-Zvi, 2009), 590–1.

6. A claimed new Aramaic fragment (Tob 14.3-4) in the Schøyen collection may be a forgery. Kipp Davis, Ira Rabin, Ines Feldman and Myriam Krutzsch, "Nine Dubious 'Dead

7. Binding Asmodeus 119

least three known text-types: the Long Recension G^{II}; Short Recension G^{I}; and Intermediary G^{III}.[7] Egypt is a possible location for Greek translation, but variants make a diachronic study of the Greek impossible.[8] The VL has both short and long recensions. The Vulgate is probably based on G^{I}, VL, and a Hebrew version specially translated orally for Jerome from Aramaic. While the Syriac Peshitta is now lost, several Syriac textual witnesses show at least two text-types. One text-type is in the seventh-/eighth-century Syro-Hexaplaric MS 8fl (Tob 1:1–14:15), a copy of Paul of Tella's 616 CE Syro-Hexapla, which is based on the intermediary G^{III}. Another Syriac text-type (Tob 7:11b–14:15, excluding 13:9–18) is found in the same manuscript and a few others.[9] Ethiopic and Coptic versions are dependent on G^{I}.[10] Several medieval Hebrew and Aramaic manuscripts exist, all of which seem to be translations from a Greek *Vorlage*,[11] including a rediscovered medieval Hebrew manuscript in the Taylor-Schechter Cairo Genizah collection.[12] Simply put, the complex transmission of Tobit should alert the reader to the fact that not every version is in agreement, and that some differences in translation may result in interesting implications for research of Tobit's vocabulary.

Text-critical studies have aided our understanding of the versions and their relationships to one another.[13] For example, while G^{II} has priority over

Sea Scrolls' Fragments from the Twenty-First Century," *DSD* 24 (2017): 220–1; Michaela Hallermayer and Torleif Elgvin, "Schøyen Ms. 5234: ein neues 'Tobit'-Fragment vom toten Meer," *RevQ* 22 (2006): 451–61.

7. G^{II} is mainly represented by Sinaiticus, P.Oxy 1076 [MS 910] (sixth century CE; Tob 2:2–5, 8), and MS 319 (eleventh century CE minuscule, Tob 3:6–6:16). G^{I} is mainly: Vaticanus, Alexandrinus, Venetus, and P.Oxy 1594 [MS 990] (third century CE, Tob 12:14–19). G^{III} is: Codex Cittaviensis (MS 44) and Codex Ferrariensis (MS 106), and Codex Ferrariensis c.1337 CE (MS 107). For a clear introduction to Greek Tobit, see Loren T. Stuckenbruck and Stuart Weeks, "Tobit," in *T&T Clark Companion to the Septuagint*, ed. James K. Aitken (London: T&T Clark, 2015), 237–60.

8. Stuckenbruck and Weeks, "Tobit," 239–42.

9. J. C. H. Lebram, "Die Peschitta zu Tobit 7,11-14,15," *ZAW* 69 (1957): 185–211.

10. Joseph A. Fitzmyer, *Tobit* (Commentaries on Early Jewish Literature; Berlin: de Gruyter, 2002), 3–15.

11. Ibid., 12–14.

12. Siam Bhayro, "A Leaf from a Medieval Hebrew Book of Tobit: Jacques Mosseri Genizah Collection at Cambridge University Library, Mosseri I.38 (with a Note on the Dating of T-S A45.25)," in *With Wisdom as a Robe: Qumran and Other Jewish Studies in Honour of Ida Frölich*, ed. K. D. Dobos and M. Köszeghy (Sheffield: Sheffield Phoenix, 2009), 163–73.

13. See Stuart Weeks, "Restoring the Greek Tobit," *JSJ* 44 (2013): 1–15; Géza G. Xeravits and József Zsengellér, eds., *The Book of Tobit: Text, Tradition, Theology: Papers of the First International Conference on the Deuterocanonical Books, Pápa, Hungary, 20-21 May, 2004* (JSJSup 98; Leiden: Brill, 2005); Vincent T. M. Skemp, *The Vulgate of Tobit Compared with Other Ancient Witnesses* (SBLDS 180; Atlanta, GA: SBL Press, 2000); Edward M. Cook, "Our Translated Tobit," in *Targumic and Cognate Studies: Essays in Honour of Martin McNamara*,

G^I,[14] the search for a Greek *Urtext* is still far from clear. Correspondences between G^I and the intermediary G^{III} suggest that G^I still has value.[15] Loren Stuckenbruck and Stuart Weeks note that G^{II} witnesses do not have "a monopoly on early readings" and, considering occasional Qumran agreements with G^I and G^{III}, in some cases G^{II} may preserve later readings.[16] Therefore, in this study G^{II} and G^I will be analyzed as evenly as possible. The differences between G^I and G^{II} vocabulary could offer clues about register, provenance, or setting.

Recent critical editions aid researchers in navigating the complex textual history of Tobit. Editions of the Qumran fragments are a considerable gift to Tobit studies,[17] as are polyglots.[18] That being said, studies and commentaries on Tobit

ed. Kevin J. Cathcart and Michael Maher (JSOTS 230; Sheffield: Sheffield Academic, 1996), 153–62; Merten Rabenau, *Studien zum Buch Tobit* (BZAW 220; Berlin: de Gruyter, 1994); Paul Deselaers, *Das Buch Tobit: Studien zu seiner Enstehung, Komposition und Theologie* (OBO 43; Freiburg: Vandenhoeck & Ruprecht, 1982).

14. The Short Recension (G^I) is a redacted abbreviation of the Long Recension (G^{II}), stylistically adding more coherence and eliminating Semitisms. See Fitzmyer, *Tobit*, 5.

15. Stuart Weeks, "Some Neglected Texts of Tobit: The Third Greek Version," in *Studies in the Book of Tobit: A Multidisciplinary Approach*, ed. Mark Bredin (LSTS 55; London: T&T Clark, 2006), 12–42. Compare Fitzmyer, *Tobit*, 5, who argues G^{III} is a compromise but closer to G^{II}.

16. Stuckenbruck and Weeks, "Tobit," 238, 244.

17. Aramaic and Hebrew fragments from Qumran: Joseph A. Fitzmyer in Magen Broshi, Joseph A. Fitzmyer and Esther Eshel, *Qumran Cave 4. XIV: Parabiblical Texts, Part 2* (DJD 19; Oxford: Clarendon Press, 1995), 1–76 + plates i–x; Joseph A. Fitzmyer, "The Aramaic and Hebrew Fragments of Tobit from Qumran Cave 4," *CBQ* 57 (1995): 655–75; Klaus Beyer, *Die aramäischen Texte vom Toten Meer samt den Inschriften aus Palästina, dem Testament Levis aus der Kairoer Genisa, der Fastenrolle und den alten talmudischen Zitaten. Band 1* (Göttingen: Vandenhoeck & Ruprecht, 1984), 298–300; Klaus Beyer, *Die aramäischen Texte vom Toten Meer samt den Inschriften aus Palästina, dem Testament Levis aus der Kairoer Genisa, der Fastenrolle und den alten talmudischen Zitaten: Ergänzungsband* (Göttingen: Vandenhoeck & Ruprecht, 1994), 134–47; Klaus Beyer, *Die aramäischen Texte vom Toten Meer samt den Inschriften aus Palästina, dem Testament Levis aus der Kairoer Genisa, der Fastenrolle und den alten talmudischen Zitaten. Band 2*. (Göttingen: Vandenhoeck & Ruprecht, 2004), 172–86; Michaela Hallermayer, *Text und Überlieferung des Buches Tobit* (DCLS 3; Berlin: de Gruyter, 2008).

18. Stuart Weeks, Simon J. Gathercole and Loren T. Stuckenbruck, eds., *The Book of Tobit: Texts from the Principal Ancient and Medieval Traditions: With Synopsis, Concordances, and Annotated Texts in Aramaic, Hebrew, Greek, Latin, and Syriac* (FSBP 3; Berlin: de Gruyter, 2004); Christian J. Wagner, *Polyglotte Tobit-Synopse: Griechisch, Lateinisch, Syrisch, Hebräisch, Aramäisch; mit einem Index zu den Tobit-Fragmenten vom Toten Meer* (Abhandlungen der Akademie der Wissenschaften zu Göttingen, Philologisch-Historische Klasse 3 258; Göttingen: Vandenhoeck & Ruprecht, 2003). Greek editions: Alfred Rahlfs and Robert Hanhart, eds., *Septuaginta* (Stuttgart: Deutsche Bibelgesellschaft, 2006); Robert Hanhart, *Tobit* (Septuaginta. Vetus Testamentum Graecum 8/5; Göttingen: Vandenhoeck &

7. *Binding Asmodeus* 121

tend to focus on single versions, literary landscape, and narrative.[19] By comparison, early twentieth-century scholarship on Tobit's demonology and angelology remains underdeveloped. Some promising research on the angel Raphael has come out in recent years,[20] while far fewer studies are dedicated to Ašmodai.[21]

As mentioned, some studies appeal to Tobit as an example of developing Jewish views of medicine directly due to Hellenism,[22] while others recognize the Babylonian use of fish gall in eye medicine.[23] There may be an incongruity in pointing to Tobit as evidence of Hellenized Jewish attitudes to medicine when Babylonian medicine provides a precedent for medical practices witnessed by the Hebrew Bible, particularly for a story set in Babylonia and Media.[24]

3. *Textual and Lexical Analysis*

A fresh focus on vocabulary, particularly as terms cross with medical and magical terminology, will be useful to ritual studies and Tobit research in general for historical and textual reasons, as stated above. Each vocabulary term is analyzed in turn here, subdivided into sections of the text, before overall patterns are examined for significance.

Ruprecht, 1983); H. B. Swete, *The Old Testament in Greek According to the Septuagint*, 3 vols. (Cambridge: Cambridge University Press, 1894), 2: 815-48. The NETS translation of Tobit contains parallel G^I/G^{II} columns.

19. See Perrin's update of new and forthcoming critical editions and commentaries: Perrin, "Almanac of Tobit."

20. Géza G. Xeravits, "The Angel's Self-Revelation in Tobit 12," in *Sibyls, Scriptures, and Scrolls: John Collins at Seventy*, ed. Joel S. Baden, Hindy Najman, and Eibert J. C. Tigchelaar, 2 vols. (JSJSup 175; Leiden: Brill, 2017), 1399-417; Phillip Muñoa, "Raphael the Savior: Tobit's Adaptation of the Angel of the Lord Tradition," *JSP* 25 (2016): 228-43; Margaret Barker, "Archangel Raphael in the Book of Tobit," in *Studies in the Book of Tobit: A Multidisciplinary Approach*, ed. Mark Bredin (LSTS 55; London: T&T Clark, 2006), 118-28.

21. Beate Ego, "Textual Variants as a Result of Enculturation: The Banishment of the Demon in Tobit," in *Septuagint Research: Issues and Challenges in the Study of the Greek Jewish Scriptures*, ed. Wolfgang Kraus and R. Glenn Wooden (SBLSCS 53; Atlanta, GA: SBL Press, 2006), 371-8; Louis H. Gray, "The Meaning of the Name Asmodaeus," *JRAS* 4 (1934): 790-2.

22. van der Horst, "Early Jewish Knowledge"; Chrysovergi, "Attitudes"; Chrysovergi, "Contrasting"; Hogan, *Healing*.

23. Attia, "Disease"; Jensen, "Family"; Kollmann, "Göttliche Offenbarung"; von Soden, "Fischgalle."

24. By comparison, for example, Jensen rightly recognizes biblical mentions of ointments (1 Kgs 20:7; Luke 10:34) having Near Eastern and Greek equivalents. See Jensen, "Family," 168n. 15.

3.1. Tob 6:4–9

3.1.1: *Tob 6:4–6* נון *(4Q197 4.i.7–10)* Naturally נון (נונא, fish) is used throughout the extant Aramaic witnesses,[25] while Hebrew Tobit (4Q200) uses דג.[26] Greek Tobit uses ἰχθύς, but the rarity of fish in extant Aramaic scriptural texts means that Tobit is our only example of the Greek rendering of נון.[27] It is not clear that נון meaning fish is adopted into Late Biblical Hebrew despite the shared verbal root in Hebrew נין or נון (to increase, have descendants), semantically similar to דגה (to increase, multiply).[28] Given the importance of the fish in Tobit, the assonance between נונא and נינוה is striking. Potentially, if assonance were intentional, it would be an argument in favor of an Aramaic original. However, such an argument is unprovable given the lack of synonyms for fish in Aramaic.[29]

3.1.2: *Tob 6:5* ἀνάτεμε *(G^I)* and ἀνάσχισον *(G^{II})* Azariah's instructions to Tobiah include how to prepare the fish. Azariah says to "dissect" the fish, using ἀνάτεμε (ἀνατέμνω) in G^I and ἀνάσχισον (ἀνασχίζω) in G^{II}. Both words are rare.[30] The word ἀνατέμνω in other uses refers to dissection of bodies by embalmers (Herodotus 2.87) and butchering an eagle (Lucian, *Prometheus* 21), but its only LXX occurrence is in Tobit. The more common τέμνω shares a similar semantic range and occurs more frequently in the LXX.[31] In light of Lucian and Herodotus, ἀνατέμνω is appropriate for Tobit since the context is dissecting an animal or dead thing. Likewise ἀνασχίζω (G^{II}) has similar usages to ἀνατέμνω.[32] In both cases, G^I and G^{II} opted for verbs with slightly more explicit contexts (or more sophisticated tone?) than τέμνω.

---

25. HALOT 2:682. Jastrow 888. Compare also the Akkadian cognate *nūnu* (and fish deity *Nūnu*) and Syriac ܢܘܢܐ. See Payne-Smith 333; and Jeremy A. Black, Andrew George, and Nicholas Postgate, eds., *A Concise Dictionary of Akkadian*, 2nd ed. (SANTAG 5; Wiesbaden: Harrassowitz, 2012), 258.

26. Also across the medieval Hebrew witnesses (Tob 6:3–7, 17; 8:2; 11:4, 7, 11; 12:3) Weeks, Gathercole, and Stuckenbruck, *The Book of Tobit*.

27. Rahlfs and Hanhart, *Septuaginta*; T. Muraoka, *A Greek-Hebrew/Aramaic Two-Way Index to the Septuagint* (Louvain: Peeters, 2010), 274. The Greek translation of Hebrew דג is ἰχθύς in most cases, with three exceptions: Jonah 2:1, 11 (κῆτος) and Num 11:22 (τὸ ὄψος τῆς θαλάσσης).

28. Compare BDB 630 (נון, נין).

29. Although the biblicizing דג is found in the Babylonian Talmud, it is less common than נון. Jastrow 279.

30. LSJ. LEH 42, 44. One inscriptional use refers to cutting a projecting rafter (IG II² 462, Attica 307/6 BCE).

31. The verb τέμνω is common and versatile, e.g., in medical contexts (Hippocrates, *Aphorisms* 7.44) and hunting and cutting up a small bird (Aristotle, *On Breath* 484b).

32. E.g., Herodotus 1.123 (cutting up a hare), 3.35 (dissecting a boy's dead body); Aristotle, *Nich.* 1148b.20 (describing legendary feminine creatures that rip open pregnant women's bodies to eat their fetuses).

3.1.3. *Tob 6:8: ὀχληθῇ (G¹)* G¹ concludes that once the demon or evil spirit is driven away, they will no longer "disturb/annoy/distress" (ὀχλέω) the patient: οὐ μηκέτι ὀχληθῇ, echoing earlier in the line ὀχλῇ δαιμόνιον. G¹¹ reads instead μὴ μείνωσιν μετ' αὐτοῦ εἰς τὸν αἰῶνα. Forms of ὀχλεω occur in some medical contexts[33] as well as general senses of "disturb."

3.1.4. *Tob 6:9: ἐγχρῖσαι (G¹, G¹¹)* Less common in LXX vocabulary, ἐγχρίω (to anoint/smear) appears only in Tob 6:9 (G¹, G¹¹), 11:8 (G¹, but G¹¹ ἔνπλασον) and Jer 4:30, where it also refers to the eyes:[34]

καὶ ἐὰν ἐγχρίσῃ στίβι τοὺς ὀφθαλμούς σου

and that you anoint your eyes with paint

Another related context regarding anointing eyes is Rev 3:18:

καὶ κολλούριον ἔγχρισον τοὺς ὀφθαλμούς σου, ἵνα βλέπῃς

and *collyrium* to anoint your eyes so that you may see

In each example, the verb refers to anointing eyes in both medical and beautification contexts. While medical terminology adopts rather generic words sometimes, these examples show a flexible though still quite specific semantic range for ἐγχρίω. There are various Greek words for "anoint," but χρίω is more common across LXX and classical sources, including medical texts.[35] The word ἐγχρίω appears infrequently in Greek sources and can mean anoint or sting.[36] An associative sense of stinging may suggest ἐγχρίω either is or becomes particularly appropriate for *eyes*, as seen in Tobit, Jeremiah, and Revelation.

3.2. *Tob 6:17*

3.2.1. *Differences in the Greek versions* In this verse, incense forms a base for the fish liver and heart to fumigate the room.[37] Azariah's instructions in G¹¹ are to put the liver and heart on embers of incense (not aforementioned), from which an aroma is given off, which the demon smells and flees from. G¹ instructs to take

---

33. Hippocrates, *Epidemics* 1.19, 2.1.3; *Prorrh*. 1.147; Vettius Valens, *Anthol*. 167.20; Cornutus, *De natura deorum* 33. LSJ.

34. LEH 171. Here I follow Hanhart and Rahlfs-Hanhart: ἐνγχρῖσαι. Swete reads ἐνχρῖσαι for both G¹, G¹¹, but notes ἐγχρῖσαι is possible.

35. E.g., in anointing eyes: Hippocrates, *De morbis Mul*. 1.105.1–2. LSJ.

36. Sting: Plato, *Phaedrus* 251d. Poison injected by stinging: Claudius Aelianus, *De natura animal*. 1.54.4. LSJ.

37. G¹ mentions smoke rising, but not a "stench." Compare Moore's translation at 6.17: "When the stench rises" for "so to make the smoke rise." Carey A. Moore, *Tobit: A New Translation with Introduction and Commentary* (AB 40A; Garden City, NY: Doubleday, 1996), 206.

incense embers first, put the heart and liver on them, and make it smoke, which the demon smells and flees. 4Q196 is too fragmentary to know the order.³⁸ The VL seems to follow the structure of G^II more closely in this passage.³⁹ The Vulgate is different here, focusing on prayer first, and does not mention the fish organs specifically. The original order is unknowable, but the variation may suggest that the Aramaic may not have made sense to translators, and that G^I in condensing G^II felt the need to reorder the instructions for sense:

(G^I) καὶ ἐὰν εἰσέλθῃς εἰς τὸν νυμφῶνα, λήμψῃ τέφραν θυμιαμάτων καὶ ἐπιθήσεις ἀπὸ τῆς καρδίας καὶ τοῦ ἥπατος τοῦ ἰχθύος καὶ καπνίσεις, καὶ ὀσφρανθήσεται τὸ δαιμόνιον καὶ φεύξεται καὶ οὐκ ἐπανελεύσεται τὸν αἰῶνα τοῦ αἰῶνος. ὅταν δὲ προσπορεύῃ αὐτῇ.

(G^II) καὶ ὅταν εἰσέλθῃς εἰς τὸν νυμφῶνα, λαβὲ ἐκ τοῦ ἥπατος τοῦ ἰχθύος καὶ τὴν καρδίαν καὶ ἐπίθες ἐπὶ τὴν τέφραν τῶν θυμιαμάτων καὶ ἡ ὀσμὴ πορεύσεται, καὶ ὀσφρανθήσεται τὸ δαιμόνιον καὶ φεύξεται καὶ οὐκέτι μὴ φανῇ περὶ αὐτὴν τὸν πάντα αἰῶνα καὶ ὅταν μέλλῃς γίνεσθαι μετ᾽ αὐτῆς.

(VL) *et cum intraueris in cubiculum, tolle iecor et cor piscis illius, et pone super carbones, et odor manabit, et odorabitur illud daemonium, et fugiet, et non apparebit circa illam omnino in perpetuum.*

(Vg [**Amiatinus**]) *tu autem cum acceperis eam ingressus cubiculum tuum per tres dies contine te ab ea et nihil aliud nisi orationi uacabis cum ea. ipsa autem nocte incenso iecore piscis fugabitur daemonium*

4Q196 14.i.11-13 [... ב]ס ... נונא] [ערק]וֹ שדא ה[ויר]י ...] [עמה מהוה]ל [תצבי וכדי
[...] לבב מן

3.2.2. καπνίσεις *(G^I) and ἡ ὀσμὴ πορεύσεται (G^II)* In both cases, the verb is not θυμιάω, a choice that is not too problematic given the ranges of καπνίζω and ὀσμή. With καπνίζω (G^I), the usual verb for "to smoke,"⁴⁰ Paul of Aegina (seventh century CE) uses καπνίζω in his medical treatise in reference to fumigation for a continuous cough.⁴¹ Three cognate verbs with prefixes exist for καπνίζω, all of which

---

38. *DJD* 19, 20, Plate III. A large amount of space ... is estimated for column width, as only the right edges have been preserved.

39. VL does not always follow G^II. Weeks proposes a G^III *Vorlage* for VL. Weeks notices, e.g., that both G^III and VL make noticeable reordering and stylistic changes to improve the text, or possibly to popularize G^II without abbreviating it, and some minor changes such as rendering "demon" as "unclean spirit" (Weeks, "Some Neglected," 20).

40. For other LXX uses: Gen 15:17; Exod 19:18; 20:18; Isa 7:4; 42:3. LEH 305.

41. Paul of Aegina 3.28:

A trochisk is to be inhaled for a continued cough. Of storax, of pepper, of mastich, of Macedonian parsley, of each oz. i; of sandarach, scr. vi; two bay-berries; mix with honey; and fumigate (κάπνιζε) by throwing them upon coals, so that the person

relate to fumigation: ἀποκαπνίζω (*PGM* 2.23), περικαπνίζω (P.Mag.Leid.W1.33), and ὑποκαπνίζω (Hipp. *De morbis Mul.* 2.117).⁴² The first and second uses are in magical incantations, and the third is in a Hippocratic remedy for white flux for women.⁴³ The word ὀσμή (G^II) can refer to good or foul smells, as with the verb ὄζω, but often appears with a modifier if the type of smell is important.⁴⁴ The text and vocabulary here do not give enough information to presume the fish fumigation smell was bad (note the neutrality of G^II: ἡ ὀσμὴ πορεύσεται, and see below §3). Ritually and contextually, the type of smell is less significant for the practitioner than the meaning of the ingredients being smoked.

3.2.3. *Aramaic Tob 6:17:* שׁד (*4 Q196 14.i.12*) The lexeme שׁד (Aramaic שׁידא) is an Akkadian loanword (*šēdu*); the plural is more common in Biblical Hebrew while the singular rises in prominence in Qumranic Hebrew,⁴⁵ Mishnaic Hebrew, Aramaic, and Syriac.⁴⁶ Here and elsewhere שׁד is rendered by δαιμόνιον (Deut 32:17 and Ps 106:37) although δαιμόνιον is used to translate various words.⁴⁷ The netherworld in Mesopotamian traditions is located geographically far to the west,⁴⁸ from which

affected with the cough may inhale the vapour through a funnel. It answers also with those affected by cold in anywise.
Francis Adams, *The Seven Books of Paulus Ægineta*, 3 vols. (London: Syndeham Society, 1844), 473.

42. LSJ. Forms of θυμιάω and καπνίζω appear with similar frequency in inscriptions (https://epigraphy.packhum.org/).

43. "Fumigate (ὑποκάπνιζε) below with rice-wheat, winter wild figs, leaves and scab of the olive, and a third portion of skin peeled from a bottle gourd—the rest in an equal amount." The first part of the flux remedy is an astringent wine-based drug concoction. LCL 538:282–3.

44. It is unclear what other Greek word could have been used, and the absence of a modifier for ὀσμή is worth noting. For pleasant odors, a rare poetic compound word εὐοσμία exists, but the more common thing is to add a modifier to describe the smell, e.g., κακὴ ὀσμή (Sophocles, *Philoctetes* 890–1), καλὴν ὀσμὴν (Euripedes, *Cyclops* 153), or διὰ δὲ τῶν ῥινῶν ὀσμαῖς (Xenophon, *Hier.* 1.4). LSJ. LEH 448.

45. DCH 8:266.

46. HALOT 4:1417–18. BDB 993. Jastrow 1523–4.

47. Muraoka, *Greek-Hebrew/Aramaic*, 26, 360. Isa 13:21 with שׂעירים, Isa 34:14 with ציים, and interestingly Ps 95:5 with אלילים.

48. Piotr Michalowski, "Masters of the Four Corners of the Heavens: Views of the Universe in Early Mesopotamian Writing," in *Geography and Ethnography*, ed. Kurt A. Raaflaub and Richard J. A. Talbert (The Ancient World: Comparative Histories; London: Wiley-Blackwell, 2010), 147–68; Nikita Artemov, "The Elusive Beyond: Some Notes on the Netherworld Geography in Sumerian Tradition," in *Altorientalische Studien zu Ehren von Pascal Attinger: mu-ni u4 ul-li2-a-ašĝa2-ĝa2-de3*, ed. Catherine Mittermayer and Sabine Ecklin (OBO 256; Göttingen: Vandenhoeck & Ruprecht, 2012), 1–30.

roving ghosts can escape,⁴⁹ and where netherworld deities and demons originate, an interesting consideration for Tobit since Ašmodai flees far in a westward direction (Egypt being west of Ecbatana). Regarding words that relate to the demon's appearance and departure, G^II uses φανῇ (φαίνω, to appear): μὴ φανῇ περὶ αὐτήν. This construction may give a sense that the demon appeared around Sarah or showed itself around her.⁵⁰ Again, G^I is different: οὐκ ἐπανελεύσεται (it will not recur/return).

3.3. *Tob 8:1–9*

3.3.1. *Tob 8:3:* τὰ ἀνώτατα Αἰγύπτου *(G^I) and* τὰ μέρη Αἰγύπτου *(G^II)* In G^I Ašmodai flees to Upper Egypt, though in G^II reads τὰ μέρη Αἰγύπτου (region/district of Egypt).⁵¹ One occurrence of μέρος in papyri has the meaning of local district (P.Oxy 2113.25), which matches the sense of μέρος as "district" in NT texts with specific locales.⁵² References to demon-like entities in Hebrew texts place them in barren wildernesses.⁵³ Magic incantations bowls are not normally specific about where the demon is to go once divorced or driven away from the client, though cardinal directions often feature in incantations.⁵⁴

3.3.2. *Tob 8:3* ἔδησεν *(G^I) and* ἐπέδησεν *(G^II)* The compound verb ἐπιδέω occurs mostly in medical contexts for bandaging or binding a wound.⁵⁵ In this case, G^II (ἐπιδέω) is slightly medical in context while G^I (δέω) is slightly magical.⁵⁶ It is worth investigating the full textual evidence for the verb "to bind" (δέω) in magical and exorcistic senses. In Greek magical papyri, binding is frequent in magical charms and spells.⁵⁷ An epigram of Lucillius (first century CE) includes a use of δέω in a context of a bound (or charmed) tongue: Ἂν τοῦ γραμματικοῦ μνησθῶ

---

49. JoAnn Scurlock, "Ghosts in the Ancient Near East: Weak or Powerful?" *HUCA* 68 (1997): 77–96.

50. Compare occurrences of lexeme φανῇ in Rom 7:13 and Rev 18:23 (μὴ φανῇ).

51. G^II strangely has prepositions ἄνω εἰς, possibly a scribal corruption (Fitzmyer, *Tobit*, 242).

52. Matt 2:22; 15:21; 16:13; Mark 8:10; John 19:23; 21:6; Acts 2:10. Nonspecific "region": Acts 19:1, 20:2; Eph 4:9; Rev 16:19. Louw 122. LSJ. The word μέρος is extremely common in inscriptions.

53. Henrike Frey-Anthes, "Concepts of 'Demons' in Ancient Israel," *WO* 38 (2008): 38–52. Fitzmyer mentions 1 En. 10:4, Matt 12:42, Luke 11:24, Rev 18:2, and the wilderness in Lev 16:10. Fitzmyer, *Tobit*, 243.

54. I am grateful to Matt Bartlett and Siam Bhayro for their advice here.

55. Hippocrates, *De capitis vulner.* 13, *De fracturis* 21, *De articulis* 14; Xenophon, *Cyr.* 5.2.43. Only two other cases exist, both fastening the crest on a horse (Herodotus 1.171; Aristophanes, *Ranae* 1038).

56. LSJ.

57. Binding mentioned in spells, often using δέω: *PGM* IV.83, 350, 395, 590, 1246, 2247, 2326, 2904–5, 3094, 3100; VII.455, 985; XV.1, 20; XII.63; XXVIIIa.4; XXVIIIc.5;

μόνον Ἡλιοδώρου, εὐθὺ σολοικίζον τὸ στόμα μου δέδεται, "If I only think of the grammarian Heliodorus, my tongue at once commits solecisms and I suffer from impediment of speech."[58]

In Ezek 37:17, binding is found in a metaphorical sense:[59]

καὶ συνάψεις αὐτὰς πρὸς ἀλλήλας σαυτῷ εἰς ῥάβδον μίαν τοῦ **δῆσαι** αὐτάς, καὶ ἔσονται ἐν τῇ χειρί σου

and join them together into one stick, so that they may become as one in your hand.[60]

In Tob 3:17, a literal use of binding is found, worth comparing with 8:3:

καὶ **δῆσαι** Ασμοδαυν τὸ πονηρὸν δαιμόνιον

and to bind Asmodeus the wicked demon.

Given the versatile adoption of δέω in magical contexts, it is not that Tobit adopts a technical term from magic so much as that δέω is a common term. Magical spells and amulets bind deities, demons, and the objects of spells, such as a desired lover in a binding love spell. The frequency of binding in incantations and creating magical objects indicates that such a context would not be lost in articulating cosmologically how Raphael binds Ašmodai.

3.3.3. *Tob 8:4 συνεκλείσθησαν (G¹)* The phrase ὡς δὲ συνεκλείσθησαν ἀμφότεροι could refer not to Tobiah and Sarah (NETS) but to Raphael and Ašmodai, especially given the conjunction ὡς, "while."[61] G^II by contrast reads καὶ ἐξῆλθον. The verb συγκλείω (to shut/enclose) has a sense of "confined together" and can even mean "locked together" in combat.[62] The urgency of Tobiah and Sarah's prayer for

XXXII.1, 15; XXXVI.157; LVII.5; CI. 17, 36; CII.44. Binding spells in instructions or titles: *PGM* III.163, 277; IV.296, 335, 1875; VII.297, 877, 913; VIII.1; XII.163. Binding objects in instructions: *PGM* II.71-2; IV.1381, 3196; V.389; VII.453; XII.464; XXXVI.330; *PDM* XIV.637. Hans Dieter Betz, ed., *The Greek Magical Papyri in Translation: Including the Demotic Spells* (Chicago: University of Chicago Press, 1986); Karl Preisendanz, *Papyri Graecae Magicae*, ed. Albert Henrichs, 2 vols. (Stuttgart: Teubner, 1973).

58. LCL 85:138–9.

59. Other LXX uses: Gen 38:28; 42:24; Judg 15:10, 12.

60. Translations of the LXX are based on the New English Translation of the Septuagint (NETS).

61. The Vulgate lacks an equivalent phrase, beginning both 8:3, 4 with *tunc*. Compare VL: *et exierunt, et clauserunt ostium cubiculi*, which could again refer to Raphael and Ašmodai.

62. Euripedes, *Andromacha* 122. LSJ. In epigraphy, two occurrences: one for shutting a door (IG I³ 52, Attica 434/3 BCE) and fastened threads (IosPE I² 352, Chersonesos c. 107 BCE) (https://epigraphy.packhum.org/).

mercy makes sense if they are praying just at the moment "while" Raphael and Ašmodai are in Egypt, simultaneous action being a feature of Tobit (3:7, 17).

3.3.4. *Tob 8:6 (G^I, G^{II})* The prayer of Tobit contains a quotation from LXX Gen 2:18, which contains a similar phrase from Gen 2:20:

Tob 8:6b:

(G^I) σὺ εἶπας Οὐ καλὸν εἶναι τὸν ἄνθρωπον μόνον, ποιήσωμεν αὐτῷ **βοηθὸν ὅμοιον αὐτῷ**.

(G^{II}) σὺ εἶπας ὅτι Οὐ καλὸν εἶναι τὸν ἄνθρωπον μόνον, ποιήσωμεν αὐτῷ **βοηθὸν ὅμοιον αὐτῷ**.

LXX Gen 2:18: καὶ εἶπεν κύριος ὁ θεός Οὐ καλὸν εἶναι τὸν ἄνθρωπον μόνον· ποιήσωμεν αὐτῷ **βοηθὸν κατ' αὐτόν**.

LXX Gen 2:20b: τῷ δὲ Αδαμ οὐχ εὑρέθη **βοηθὸς ὅμοιος αὐτῷ**.

G^I and G^{II} both replace κατ' αὐτόν (Gen 2:18) with ὅμοιον αὐτῷ (Gen 2:20). The rest of the quotation from Gen 2:18 is unchanged. Rather than posit a *Vorlage* of LXX Gen 2:18 identical to Tob 8:6, or suggest that Tobit is being creative here, the quotation more plausibly conflates the final three words of Gen 2:18 and 2:20.

3.4. *Tob 11:4, 7–15*

3.4.1. *Tob 11:4: The Dog (or Heart)* Though it is tempting to see a Greek translator's mistake of הלב for כלב as argued by Israel Abrahams,[63] problems arise in consideration. While Abrahams posited a Hebrew or Aramaic original for Tobit and noted the dog's absence from the Vulgate at 11:4, he erroneously stated that the Greek witnesses had the dog and that no Semitic witnesses included it. Only G^I has the dog at both 5:17 and 11:4. The reverse is true for Tob 6:2, where the dog appears in G^{II} but not G^I. At least two Syriac manuscript witnesses include the dog at 11:4 (Syro-Hexapla and Buchanan Bible), but not at 6:2. Most of the medieval Hebrew and Aramaic manuscripts do lack the dog at 11:4 and 6:2, but one witness (MS Constantinople 1519) includes it at 11:4. Furthermore, the Vulgate lacks the dog at 11:4 but includes it at 11:9 and 6:2. The reconstructions of Fitzmyer, Milik, and Beyer are admirable, but the line is fragmentary.[64]

The answer may lie in the Greek. At 11:4, G^{II} has ὁ κ(υριο)ς, where G^I reads ὁ κύων. Another manuscript, Ferrara 187 I, representing G^{III},[65] has a large ⌒ or ~ above κυ indicating (ων) in Greek miniscule.[66] Since κ(υριο)ς is abbreviated with

---

63. Israel Abrahams, "Tobit's Dog," *JQR* 1 (1888): 288.
64. Fitzmyer, *Tobit*, 204.
65. Stuckenbruck and Weeks, "Tobit," 14.
66. Viktor Emil Gardthausen, *Griechische palaeographie: die Schrift, Unterschriften und Chronologie im alterum und im byzantinschen Mittelalter*, 2 vols. (Leipzig: Verlag von Veit & Comp., 1911), 2:341.

a straight line above it as a *nomina sacra*, the textual error is more likely to have arisen in Greek, from G¹'s misreading of G^II κ(υριο)ς with a straight line, as κυ with a curvy line for κύ(ων).⁶⁷ Tob 5:17, which includes the dog only in G¹, is Tobit's expressed wish for God to accompany Tobiah on his journey. If this suggestion is correct, then the dog began life in Tobit as a result of error in Greek-to-Greek transmission, not Aramaic/Hebrew-to-Greek, about God accompanying Tobiah's righteous quest. A full survey of all extant Greek manuscript witnesses would be necessary but is beyond the scope of this study.

3.4.2. *Tob 11:8: ἔγχρισον (G¹) and ἔνπλασον (G^II)* See above for ἔγχρισον (G¹). The verb ἔνπλασον (G^II) is difficult to interpret. If correctly transcribed,⁶⁸ ἔνπλασον (G^II) might be a scribal error of ἔμπλασον (ἔμπλασσω, to mold/plaster). The verbs ἔμπλασσω and related ἐκπλάσσω both mean "to plaster." Forms of ἔνπλασσω also occur in two papyri; in another case nominal forms of both ἔμπλασσω and ἔνπλασσω occur in the same text.⁶⁹ The word ἔμπλαστρον "plaster" is common in Hippocratic and other medical texts.

3.4.3. *Tob 11:8, 12: λευκώματα (G¹, G^II)* Here a technical term is used (white spots in the cornea, today called leukoma), found throughout Tobit (2:10; 3:17; 6:9; 11:8, 12) but not elsewhere in LXX or NT sources. The word λεύκωμα has two distinct meanings: one is a tablet covered with gypsum for displaying notices (from which we get the word *album*) and the other is leukoma. The latter is found in medical contexts as well as papyri.⁷⁰ At Tob 6:8 the Qumran Aramaic preserves "scales" חרריא (Q197 4.i.15)⁷¹ translated at 6:8 by λευκώματα.

3.4.4. *Tob 11:11: נפוץ (4 Q200 5.2)* Tobiah spreads the ointment in his father's eyes. The line reads [ומר]ורת הדג בידו ונפוץ [בעיניו --]. Here the choice of פוץ (niphal) was difficult for the Greek translators.⁷² A reconstruction could be "was spread [in his eyes]" or "it (the scales) was scattered [from his eyes]." Another word that

---

67. Whether G^III misread G^II or copied G¹ is unknown, but the latter seems more likely.
68. Hanhart reads ἔμπλασον. Rahlfs and Hanhart, *Septuaginta*.
69. Both ἔμπλασσω (5×) and ἔνπλασσω (2×): P.Mich.17.758 (collection of medical prescriptions, fourth century CE). ἐνπλαστρος (fol.F r. 10), ἐνπλάστρι[ον] (fol.L r. 6). Papyri with ἔνπλασσω: SB.28.17139 (medical receipt, fifth century CE) and SB.16.12694 (letter, 200–400 CE).
70. Aristotle, *Physiognomonica* 8813a.28, Dioscorides, *MM* 3.84, Galen, *De simplicium med* 14.775, Aëtius, *Iatric.* 7.39. In papyri: P.Grenf.1.33 (second century BCE), SB.20.14471 and SB.20.14481 (160 BCE), BGU.3.834 (125 CE), SB.1.4414 (143 CE), P.Grenf.2.51 (143 CE), SB.V.7515 (155 CE).
71. From חרר (to burn). HALOT 1:357. DCH 3:322. Another medical word from חרר is חַרְחֻר (Deut 28:22), burning fever.
72. *Qal*: I) scatter (people), II) overflow. DCH 6:667–8. HALOT 3:918–9. BDB 807. Jastrow 1145.

might have been chosen is מרח as in Isa 38:21 (applying an ointment made from a cake of figs), but it was not. Since different vocabulary is used at 11:8 for "spread" (G¹ ἔγχρισον; G^II ἔνπλασον), the Hebrew and Aramaic at 11:8 likewise may have been different from נפוץ at 11:11. Since 11:8 does not survive in the Qumran fragments, we cannot know.

3.4.5. *Tob 11:11 ἐνεφύσησεν (G^II)* While NETS and Moore translate "blew on his eyes,"[73] identifying with ἐμφυσάω (cf. LXX 3 Kgdms 17:21). The phrase is not matched by the Latin, Syriac, G¹, or even G^III (ἐκάμμυσε). Yet another possible translation might be "it was cloudy in his eyes," conjecturing the existence of a verbal neologism cognate to νεφόομαι and νεφελίζω. Given the morphological variety of νεφ-, another verb akin to "cloudy" would not be out of place in Koine. Related lexemes νεφέλιον and νεφελώδης (cloudiness) appear in medical texts related to eyes.[74] The similarity between eye and cloud in Hebrew and Aramaic might also explain a Greek translator's confusion if the text was damaged.

3.4.6. *Tob 11:11: προσέπασεν (G¹)* Where G^II has ἐνεφύσησεν, G¹ reads προσέπασεν. Contrary to LEH, προσπάσσω (sprinkle upon) does not seem to be a neologism.[75] There are three extant examples of προσπάσσω besides Tobit, all of which are medical: Dioscorides (*MM* 1.52), Orobasius (*Collectiones medicae* 7.21.6), and Nicander (*Alexipharmaka* 563).[76] Since Nicander lived in the second century BCE in Colophon, it is more likely that the word already existed in Koine.

3.4.7. *Tob 11:12: חרוק (4 Q200 5.2)* Because the Hebrew text does not survive, theoretically it is possible that here Tobit gnashes his teeth (חרק + acc.) in pain rather than scraping/incising the scales, but this is not held out by the other versions.[77] Furthermore, a Late Biblical Hebrew use in a documentary text (חרקק "Scar" or

---

73. Moore confidently calls it a "important procedural step," Moore, *Tobit*, 263.

74. Cloudiness of eyes: νεφέλιον (Dioscorides, *MM* 2.151); νεφελώδης (Galen, *De methodo medendi* 14.10.1019). Cloudiness in urine: νεφέλιον (Hippocrates *Coa praesagia* 571); νεφέλη (Hippocrates, *Prorrh.* 2.20, *Prog.* 12; Galen, *De sanitate tuenda* 6.252).

75. LEH 528. LSJ. Katrin Hauspie, "Further Literary Observations in Both Tobit Versions," in *Die Septuaginta—Entstehung, Sprache, Geschichte: 3. Internationale Fachtagung Veranstaltet von Septuaginta Deutsch (LXX.D), Wuppertal 22.-25. Juli 2010*, ed. Siegfried Kreuzer, Martin Meiser, and Marcus Sigismund (WUNT 286; Tübingen: Mohr Siebeck, 2012), 238–48.

76. Nicander of Colophon flourished *c.* 130 BCE. Nicander reads: ὅ ἐστιν εἶδος βοτάνης, προσπάσσων ἀμμωνιακὸν καὶ χορτάσας, ὑγιάσεις τὸν κάμνοντα. See Alain Touwaide, Christian Förstel, and Grégoire Aslanoff, *Theriaka y Alexipharmaka di Nicandro* (Barcelona: M. Moleiro, 1997).

77. HALOT 1:356-7. Jastrow 506. DCH 3:322. Lam 2:16; Pss 35:16; 37:12; 112:10; Job 16:9; 1QH^a 9:41, 10:13; 4Q171 f1-2.ii.12.

"Scarface") indicates that the latter, "incising/scraping out" the scales, may be more precise.[78]

4. Fish Heart and Liver Fumigation in Exorcism

Exorcism is categorized as a magical practice, and the best attested form of Jewish magic, with evidence such as bowls and manuscripts, including from Qumran (4Q560).[79] Jewish exorcistic techniques rely on "the innate natural powers of various substances" and the powers of the exorcist, and often include incantations.[80] Josephus writes of a plant with exorcistic powers called *baʿaras* root (Josephus, *War* 7.180–185).[81] A rabbinic method of exorcism involves bringing roots, fumigating them under the afflicted person, and pouring water over the demon.[82] The apotropaic use of fish organs in Egypt and Mesopotamia is noted by Bernd Kollmann,[83] but Tobit is our only extant example of fish in a Jewish exorcistic ritual.

The use of smoke or incense (Tob 8:2) and its smell requires some further attention: ת[אתנה] (4Q197 4.i.12), τέφραν τῶν θυμιαμάτων and ἐκάπνισεν (G¹), τέφραν τοῦ θυμιάματος (G¹¹), *carbones vivos* (VL, Vg). Here the Syriac witnesses have ashes of incense ܕܒܣܡܐ ܩܛܡܐ which smoke (ܘܐܬܢܢ) (Syro-Hexapla, agreeing with G¹ ἐκάπνισεν), or incense ܒܣܡܐ (Buchanan Bible), on which the heart and liver are placed.[84] Smoke, often made with incense, is used to invoke or adjure divine assistance in cultic and magical contexts.[85] Smoke is also employed for increased efficacy, for example, in a charm for bloody flux (*PGM* XXIIa.7) and a tablet charm to subject others (*PGM* VII.929). A common and versatile Egyptian purification rite was fumigation by incense (*sn-nṯr*).[86] Egyptian herbalists also fumigated herbs while praying to make them more potent before harvesting (*PGM*

---

78. *DJD* 2 8.4 in a name: ישוע בר חרקק. Milik translates "inciser" or "Balafré" (Scar). Pierre Benoît and Roland de Vaux, *Les Grottes de Murabbaʿât* (DJD 2; Oxford: Clarendon Press, 1961), 87–9.

79. Gideon Bohak, *Ancient Jewish Magic: A History* (Cambridge: Cambridge University Press, 2008), 88–114.

80. Ibid., 94.

81. Ibid., 90–1.

82. *Pirke de-Rab Kahana* 4.7. See Bohak, *Ancient Jewish Magic*, 90.

83. Kollmann, "Göttliche Offenbarung," 292.

84. ܒܣܡܐ is related to Hebrew בֶּשֶׂם or בֹּשֶׂם and Aramaic בוסמא, meaning balsam, perfume, spice, or fragrance.

85. Some examples of magical contexts: *PGM* VII.639 (invoking Asklepios), XII.216 (gods of the heavens), etc.

86. J. F. Bourghouts, "Witchcraft, Magic, and Divination in Ancient Egypt," in *Civilizations of the Ancient Near East*, ed. Jack M. Sasson, 4 vols. (New York: Scribner, 1995), 3:1779.

IV.2970). Incense use in Israelite cultic contexts is well known (e.g., Num 16:7, Exod 30:7–8, Lev 2:1, Jer 6:20, et al.).[87]

Aramaic incantation bowls invoke God and angels to drive away forces that affect clients, as do most magical and prayer formulae.[88] In Tobit, God is thanked in prayer (Tob 8:5–8) immediately after Ašmodai is exorcised. Though the ritual is carried out by human hands and according to angelic instruction, the power to drive away demons only works with God's authority.

In rituals seeking to dispel negative forces, a common refrain in Babylonian anti-witchcraft spells is that the witch will go up in smoke (e.g., *Maqlû* III 74–75), while another spell invokes the smoke of Girra to cover the witch's face and scatter the witch (*Maqlû* III 166–169). In general, the Babylonian physician *asû*, exorcist-priest *āšipu*, and *mašmaššu* frequently employed fumigation to administer drugs and drive away gods, demons, and ghosts causing disease.[89]

It is slightly beyond the text to state that the fish smoke's "vile" smell was what drove away Ašmodai, when linguistically and contextually the power is attributed to fumigation, an odor (textually neutral),[90] and the symbolic efficacy of fish heart and liver with added incense. The potency and symbolism of the ingredients that invoke a higher power and correct ritual performance are what drives away a demon. The focus on smell among commentators is reminiscent of the misconception, also fish-related, that Roman *garum* stank. In truth, making *garum* from fermented mackerel intestines and blood was smelly, but the final product itself was odorless and *umami*. Furthermore, the Qumran witnesses most likely mentioned salting the fish (6:6), agreeing with the Syriac and VL.[91] Therefore

---

87. Kjeld Nielsen, *Incense in Ancient Israel* (VTSup 38; Leiden: Brill, 1986).

88. Shaul Shaked, James Nathan Ford, and Siam Bhayro, *Aramaic Bowl Spells: Jewish Babylonian Aramaic Bowls, Volume 1* (MRLA 1; Manuscripts in the Schøyen Collection 20; Leiden: Brill, 2013); Dan Levine, *A Corpus of Magic Bowls* (New York: Columbia University Press, 2003); Joseph Naveh and Shaul Shaked, *Amulets and Magic Bowls: Aramaic Incantations of Late Antiquity*, 2 vols. (Jerusalem: Magnes, 1985).

89. Markham J. Geller, *Ancient Babylonian Medicine* (London: Blackwell, 2010), 20, 127; JoAnn Scurlock, *Sourcebook for Ancient Mesopotamian Medicine* (SBLWAW 36; Atlanta, GA: SBL Press, 2014); JoAnn Scurlock and Burton R. Andersen, *Diagnoses in Assyrian and Babylonian Medicine: Ancient Sources, Translations, and Modern Medical Analyses* (Urbana: University of Illinois Press, 2005).

90. G[I]: ὠσφράνθη (he smelled, ὄζω), ὀσμῆς (fragrance or odor); G[II] ὀσμή; G[III]: no equivalent; VL: *odor*; Vg: no equivalent; Syr: ܐܪܝܚ (and he smelled it).

91. Naomi S. S. Jacobs, *Delicious Prose: Reading the Tale of Tobit with Food and Drink: A Commentary* (JSJSup 188; Leiden: Brill, 2019), 111; Fitzmyer, *Tobit*, 207. Jacobs at one point calls the smoke "malodorous," but argues Tobiah could easily preserve fish organs with butter or salt: Jacobs, *Delicious Prose*, 126, 129. Moore writes of 8:2: "The burning organs, many days ripe, would have produced a wretched odor," although he acknowledges that the Aramaic may have included salting the fish at 6:6. See Moore, *Tobit*, 200–1, 236. Somewhat less clearly, Moore comments elsewhere (Tob 6:8) that "the use of vile-smelling smoke to

the fish organs might have been preserved for the journey, due to increased fish consumption in the Hellenistic Mediterranean world, including salted fish.[92] The rabbis agreed that salted fish tasted better than unsalted.[93]

The textual witnesses offer neutral language regarding the type of smell. On the one hand, what is pleasant to humans and gods may be disagreeable to demons and ghosts. On the other hand, ingredients in magical and medical contexts were not always nice. Medicine sometimes contained emetics and some toxic substances in small doses. Thus the universal complaint of patients refusing life-saving medicine on the basis of taste is noted in Hippocratic tradition: Keep a watch also on the faults of the patients, which often make them lie about the taking of things prescribed. For through not taking disagreeable drinks, purgative or other, they sometimes die. What they have done never results in a confession, but the blame is thrown upon the physician (*Decorum* 14).[94] This section has explored a sample of the exorcistic and medical roles of fish and fumigation, showing clear and foundational historical contexts for the status of fish use in Tobit's exorcistic ritual of fumigation. Fish is used not only in a ritual of exorcism but also in a medical treatment for the eye—another practice that is better understood with historical context.

5. Fish Gall in Eye Medicine

The use of fish gall in eye medicine in Mesopotamian and Greek medicine has been surveyed elsewhere. Several studies have explored Babylonian medicine in comparison with Tobit, with an extensive survey by Annie Attia.[95] Naomi Jacobs provides an overview of Babylonian, Greek, and Egyptian fish remedies and consumption.[96] There is a considerable amount of cultural overlap in ingredients for eye ointments. Most rabbinic *collyria* references mention the liquid serving as the ointment base but not other ingredients,[97] though one mentions bitter substances (Chul 111b). Fish is a medicine for the eyes according to Rabbi Shmuel.[98]

---

exorcise an evil spirit was a widespread technique throughout the ancient world" (201), though no citation is given.

92. Jacobs, *Delicious Prose*, 113.

93. BB 74b.

94. LCL 148:296–7.

95. Attia, "Disease"; Kollmann, "Göttliche Offenbarung"; von Soden, "Fischgalle"; Papayannopoulos, Laskaratos, and Marketos, "Remarks on Tobit's Blindness."

96. Jacobs, *Delicious Prose*, 108–35.

97. Liquids used as bases: water (Shab 8:1, 77b), wine (Nid 19b, Shab 109b), spittle (BB 126b, Shab 108b), breastmilk (tos Shab 8:8), dew (y Shab 8:11), or egg white (Shab 77b). Some include flour (tos Pesach 2:3). Mar Samuel made a *collyrium* for Judah ha-Nasi (Shab 108b). Some poisoned *collyria* (Nid 55b). Fred Rosner, *Encyclopedia of Medicine in the Bible and Talmud* (Jerusalem: Jason Aronson, 2000), 83.

98. Nedar 54b: דהא אמר שמואל נון סמך עין נונא סמא לעינים.

Babylonian remedies for eye ailments included *kuppû* fish gall.[99] *CAD* suggests the unidentified *kuppû* fish is perhaps an "eel-like fish," its ideogram being shared with a snake.[100] In Hittite culture, where fish consumption was lower, fish play an infrequent role in sacrifice[101] and are absent from blood rituals.[102] Rabbinic texts record that fish are impervious to the evil eye.[103] The Egyptian medical text P.Ebers has a variety of eye treatments. Tortoise gall with honey is a cure for leukoma (Ebers §LVII) and a cure for trachoma when mixed with labdanum (§LVII). A remedy for an eye "in which all evil things has arisen" includes human gall (§LXI). To "improve the sight," one remedy is *abdju*—fish gall and stibium ground fine and put into the eyes (§LXII).[104]

Greek and Roman traditions preserve various medical uses for marine life. Cuttlefish relieve hemorrhoids (Hippocrates, *Haem.* 8), oysters settle the stomach and restore appetite (Pliny, *NH* 32.21), shells restore hair loss (*NH* 32.23), and jellyfish cure chilblains and gout (Dioscorides, *MM* 2.39). Among Roman *collyrium* stamps, used by military physicians to label eye ointments on the frontier, two stamps list ox gall as an ingredient.[105]

The most detailed information on fish in eye medicine comes from Pliny, Hippocrates, and Dioscorides. Pliny writes that fish fat, sun-dried and mixed with honey, improves clearness of vision, and that stargazer (Uranoscopidae) gall heals vision, cataracts, scars, and "superfluous flesh" around the eyes, due to its "abundance of gall":

> Of all fish, river or sea, the fats, melted in the sun and mixed with honey, are very good for clearness of vision, and so is beaver oil and honey. The gall of the star-gazer heals scars and removes superfluous flesh about the eyes. No other fish has a greater abundance of gall; this opinion, Menander too expresses in his comedies. This fish is also called uranoscopos, from the eye which it has in its head. The gall of the coracinus too improves vision, and that of the red

---

99. *CAD* 8:551–2. *CAD* lists medical uses of *kuppû* fish: AMT 66, 7:14; BAM 12:13; 14:2; 18:14; 22:20; 23:9. Kollmann, "Göttliche Offenbarung"; von Soden, "Fischgalle."

100. *CAD* 8:551–2.

101. Alice Mouton, "Animal Sacrifice in Hittite Anatolia," in *Animal Sacrifice in the Ancient Greek World*, ed. Sarah Hitch and Ian Rutherford (Cambridge: Cambridge University Press, 2017), 239–52.

102. Gary Beckman, "Blood in Hittite Ritual," *JCS* 63 (2011): 95–102, here 98n. 28.

103. BM 84a; Ber. 55b; cf. Rashi on Gen 48:16.

104. Cyril P. Bryan, trans., *The Papyrus Ebers* (London: Geoffrey Bles, 1930), 98; B. Ebbell, trans., *The Papyrus Ebers: The Greatest Egyptian Medical Document* (Copenhagen: Levin & Munksgaard, 1937), 69, 74.

105. Most of the military *collyrium* recipes have plant and mineral ingredients. See Harald Nielsen, *Ancient Ophthalmological Agents: A Pharmaco-Historical Study of the Collyria and Seals for Collyria Used during Roman Antiquity, as Well as of the Most Frequent Components of the Collyria* (AHSNM 31; Odense: Odense University Press, 1974).

sea-scorpion with old oil and Attic honey disperses incipient cataract; it should be applied as ointment three times, once every other day. The same treatment removes albugo from the eyes. (*NH* 32.24)[106]

Hippocrates describes several ointments for the eyes: honey and sweet wine, or black poplar tree resin and breastmilk, pomegranate juice, or white grape juice (*de morbis Mul.* 1.105). In another case, he recommends agents for the eyes: dissolve burned copper, verdigris, and myrrh in goat's gall, grind them all together fine, and dissolve this in white wine; then place this in a copper vessel and expose it to the sun, and after that put it into a reed and employ it dry (Hipp. *De morbis mul.* 1.102).[107]

Dioscorides expounds upon the medical efficacy of gall, noting that ox gall is better than that of other land animals (2.96), although for vision improvement, the most effective kinds are galls from sea scorpions, the fish called callionymus (uranoscopus [stargazers]), sea turtles, and hyenas seem to be more effective; as well as that of partridge, eagle, white hens, and wild she-goats (*MM* 2.96).[108]

Dioscorides confirms elsewhere sea scorpion gall for bathing eyes, leukoma, and excessive moisture in the eyes (*MM* 2.14) and that cuttlefish cure pterygium and white spots on the cornea (*MM* 2.23). Elsewhere Pliny writes extensively of ox gall and tortoise gall for all kinds of eye ailments including cataracts (*NH* 28.47, 32.14). Thus on most points Dioscorides and Pliny agree on the efficacy of stargazer, sea scorpion, tortoise, and ox gall for eyes. Pliny seems unaware of the medical uses of cuttlefish. Given Hippocrates' recommendation (goat gall), it might be suggested that fish gall was not used in Greek and Roman eye medicine until the Hellenistic period, despite long-standing use in Egypt and Babylon.

Stargazers (Uranoscopidae) have venomous spines, eyes on top of their heads, and rows of exposed teeth. They are found worldwide, measure up to 24 inches, and some species give electric shocks. If one were to speculate a big, scary-looking fish which would (1) attack Tobiah's submerged foot; (2) possess scales and fins; and (3) whose gall was a renowned cure in ancient eye medicine, one might be tempted to choose the stargazer.[109] Alas, the stargazer is a saltwater fish, so it would not be found in the Tigris. One could, however, propose that a stargazer-like fish, one that is a danger to humans but celebrated in eye medicine, might have been imagined for the consistently unidentified Tobit fish. Given the evolution and

---

106. LCL 418:506–7.

107. LCL 538:242–243.

108. Dioscorides Pedanius, *Dioscorides de Materia Medica: Being an Herbal with Many Other Medicinal Materials*, trans. T. A. Osbaldeston and R. P. A. Wood (Johannesburg: IBIDIS, 2000).

109. Moore gives an overview of other commentators' speculations on the fish species, all of whom focus on size: crocodile, hippopotamus, pike, shad, or the enormous Nile perch. Moore, *Tobit*, 199.

variety of local preferences discussed above, Tobit's fish is ultimately unknown but likely had a realistic (not fantastical) target based on local medical preferences and availability.

6. Conclusions

Given the difficulty of the text's vocabulary and versions, lexicography is an illuminating approach to Tobit. In Aramaic the use of נונא/נינוה (fish/Nineveh) could plausibly reflect intentional assonance, but the lack of other Aramaic fish terms makes this unprovable. It has been proposed that the mysterious dog began life as a scribal error in Greek-to-Greek transmission, not Aramaic-to-Greek. The conflation of Gen 2:18 with 2:20 within Tobiah's prayer (Tob 8:6) is relevant for scribal composition and citations. The use of ἐγχρίω (G^I, G^I) in medicine as well as Jer 4:30 and Rev 3:18 is pertinent for the study of early Jewish and Christian medicine. More research could be done on Jewish and Christian contexts of familiarity with ophthalmology and eye ointments (*collyria*).

Out of twelve Greek vocabulary examples examined in general, there were three cases where G^I uses a medical term (ὀχλέω, καπνιζω, προσέπασσω) when G^{II} did not, one case where it is G^{II} but not G^I (ἐπιδέω), and four cases where both text-types use medical terms (ἀνατέμνω/ἀνάσχιζω, ἐγχρίω, λευκώματα, ἐγχρίω/ [ἔν/ἔμ]πλασσω). Interestingly, in the one case where G^{II} uses medical terminology ἐπιδέω when G^I does not (δέω), it was shown that δέω, while having a general sense, is frequent in magic papyri. In this small sample of relevant passages, this study shows that G^I appears to opt for more medical, and in one case magical, terminology.

Building upon Stuckenbruck's proposal that G^I may have toned down magical connotations of exorcism,[110] this study shows that G^I seems to positively medicalize neutral terms in G^{II}. It is not possible to prove that this is due to redaction, since G^{II} may not always preserve the earlier reading.[111] A more thorough survey of both texts would be necessary to build upon this proposal that G^I is more medical.

The Greco-Roman use of fish gall in eye medicine appears to be a Hellenistic innovation, while being long-standing in Babylonian and Egyptian ophthalmology. This finding aligns with evidence of increased fish consumption in the Hellenistic Mediterranean. Nevertheless, Hellenistic and Roman eye medicine continued using animal gall and mineral ingredients alongside fish gall. The most effective fish in eye medicine, the stargazer, is large and dangerous to humans. Although the stargazer could not be found in a river as a saltwater fish, it is proposed that a local stargazer-like fish might have been imagined for Aramaic/Hebrew Tobit. Indeed,

---

110. Loren T. Stuckenbruck, "The Book of Tobit and the Problem of 'Magic'," in *Jüdische Schriften in ihrem antik-jüdischen und urchristlichen Kontext*, ed. Hermann Lichtenberger and Gerbern S. Oegema (SJSHRZ 1; Gütersloh: Gütersloher, 2002), 258–69.

111. Stuckenbruck and Weeks, "Tobit," 238, 244.

ancient readers of Greek and Latin Tobit nevertheless might have imagined the stargazer as Tobiah's fish regardless of fresh/saltwater origin, since stargazer gall was so legendary in eye medicine. This proposal remains one of many unprovable theories about the fish species, but the stargazer theory is at least coherent with Hellenistic-Roman-era medicine.

Nevertheless, it is unwise to conjecture Tobit as evidence of "Hellenized" Jewish medicine since fish gall use has such long-term continuity in Babylonian and Egyptian medicine. Regardless of Hellenistic innovations, the Tobit fish owes more to the *kuppû*-fish or *abdju*-fish than Greco-Roman fish gall use. In Greek and Latin versions, though, it is plain that Tobit's fish use would be more realistic and popular to a Hellenistic and Roman audience than a pre-Hellenistic one. It has been shown that ancients used smoke to increase the efficacy of magic. Furthermore, a "vile stench" does not seem to accord with ancient Jewish magic, since exorcistic rituals derived their potency from ingredient symbolism and the authority of the practitioner. It is also more likely that Tobiah salted the fish so that it would not be rotten.[112] Finally, the vocabulary of the fumigation ritual gives neutral language regarding its smell. The language of "binding" throughout is notable in light of magic papyri and incantations driving away demons.

In sum, this lexical analysis has shown that Tobit's ritualistic use of incense and potent ingredients in exorcism reflects known Jewish magical tradition, while the medical use of fish suggests knowledge of long-standing Near Eastern and Hellenistic Mediterranean ophthalmological treatments. Altogether, with word choices varying between the neutral and technical, Tobit's vocabularies of magic and medicine indicate a setting in which such knowledge is acceptable and common, and that lexicological research should be of considerable priority in future studies of Tobit and ritual.

112. Jacobs, *Delicious Prose*, 111; Fitzmyer, *Tobit*, 207.

Chapter 8

ENCHANT THE SABBATH DAY TO MAKE IT HOLY: CONJURATION AND PERFORMATIVITY IN EXODUS 20:8-11

Timothy Hogue

1. Introduction

What does it mean to זכור את־יום השבת לקדשו? If this is really a command to "remember the Sabbath Day" as it is typically translated, how can remembering a day "make it holy"? Many commentaries are quick to point out that this commandment entails something more than a passive cognitive activity but rather some ritual action intimately connected to the observance of the Sabbath.[1] Nevertheless, the translation of זכור as "remember" persists. If this translation must constantly be explained away, it is time for a new one. Clearly, the Decalogue's Sabbath commandment prescribes some form of ritual engagement, but as this is the only place in the Hebrew Bible where the enjoinder is to זכור the Sabbath, that ritual engagement is challenging to envision.

Translating terms in ritual contexts must always be done with some measure of caution. As Catherine Bell argues, "the most symbolic action, even the basic symbols of a community's ritual life, can be very unclear to participants or interpreted by them in very dissimilar ways."[2] Nevertheless, surely something more specific can be said about the command to זכור את־יום השבת. Hermann

---

1. Cf. Brevard S. Childs, *Memory and Tradition in Israel* (London: SCM Press, 1962), 50-5; Brevard S. Childs, *The Book of Exodus* (Philadelphia, PA: Westminster Press, 1974), 412-17; Frank-Lothar Hossfeld, *Der Dekalog: Seine Späten Fassungen, Die Originale Komposition Und Seine Vorstuten* (OBO 45; Fribourg: Universitätsverlag, 1982), 40-2; John I. Durham, *Exodus* (WBC 3; Grand Rapids, MI: Zondervan, 1987), 276; William Johnstone, *Exodus* (Sheffield: JSOT Press, 1990), 91; Nahum M. Sarna, *Exodus Commentary* (The JPS Torah Commentary; Philadelphia, PA: Jewish Publication Society, 1991), 13, 111-12; William H. C. Propp, *Exodus 1-18: A New Translation with Introduction and Commentary* (AB; Garden City, NY: Doubleday, 1998), 421.

2. Catherine Bell, *Ritual Theory, Ritual Practice* (New York: Oxford University Press, 1992), 183.

Eising argues that "remember" here "can hardly represent its [zkr's] basic meaning" and that the verb זכר instead entails "active cognitive occupation" to which often "an act of concrete performance is added."[3] Similarly, the noun אזכרה "memorial/invocation offering" is so designated because it is an offering paired with an invocation of Yahweh's name (cf. Lev 24:7).[4] Though unusual, the most telling use of the root may be the causative form in Amos 6:10. In this passage, an illegitimate funerary ritual is described, in which one practitioner warns another that, יהוה משב להזכיר לא יכ"one must not invoke the name of Yahweh." Hans Wolff is undoubtedly correct to conclude that "undertones of magic accompany this expression, the notion being that to name Yahweh's name is necessarily to invoke the presence of Yahweh himself."[5] This raises the possibility of a magical nuance to the occurrence in Exodus 20 as well. This study will argue that the commandment in Exod 20:8 is not simply to remember the Sabbath. Rather, the Sabbath is made holy through enchantment—that is, interactive fascination that culminates in embodied action.

2. The Core of the Sabbath Commandment in Exodus 20

The Sabbath commandment is admittedly the most reworked portion of the Decalogue, showing evidence of transformation extending perhaps throughout the exilic and post-exilic periods.[6] Nevertheless, various lines of evidence leave room for an ancient core of the Sabbath commandment from the pre-exilic period that grew out of Levantine ritual traditions. While many scholars deny the possibility of a pre-exilic Sabbath—at least as a weekly observance[7]—and thus exclude it from the Decalogue, there are good reasons to accept some form of early Sabbath practice. I will connect this early practice to the Decalogue more specifically below.[8] But before commencing the comparative study, it is worth

---

3. Hermann Eising, "Zkr," in *Theological Dictionary of the Old Testament*, ed. G. Johannes Botterweck and Helmer Ringgren, trans. David E. Green, vol. IV (Grand Rapids, MI: Eerdmans, 1980), 66.

4. Ibid., 80–1.

5. Hans Walter Wolff, *Joel and Amos* (Hermeneia; Philadelphia, PA: Fortress Press, 1977), 283 n. 31.

6. Cf., Childs, *The Book of Exodus*, 415; Hossfeld, *Der Dekalog*, 40–2; Jean-Louis Ska, *Introduction to Reading the Pentateuch* (Winona Lake, IN: Eisenbrauns, 2006), 49–50.

7. Though it is disputed, the appearance of the time designation *šbt* in the seventh-century Metsed Hashavyahu inscription at least suggests a pre-exilic Sabbath if not its precise nature. Oded Tammuz argues convincingly that a pre-Persian weekly Sabbath may even have been practiced. See Oded Tammuz, "The Sabbath as the Seventh Day of the Week and a Day of Rest: Since When?," *ZAW* 131 (2019): 287–94.

8. Johannes Meinhold was the first to argue for a Persian period origin for the Sabbath, which has become a common position. Even while allowing for a nonweekly Sabbath

beginning with a brief literary critical study to better reconstruct the content of the original commandment. It is worth establishing the antiquity of the command to זכר the Sabbath because this will place it in the same sociohistorical context as the Levantine rituals I use in my comparison.

2.1 Uncovering the Core of the Sabbath Commandment

The Sabbath is only the object of the verb זכר in one instance in the Hebrew Bible— Exod 20:8. By contrast, the Sabbath is the object of the verb שמר "keep" some ten times, including the Sabbath Commandment in the repetition of the Decalogue in Deut 5:12.[9] On the basis of *lectio difficilior*, we can propose that this less attested reading reflects a remarkably different tradition and may even be earlier than the version in Deuteronomy. Lauren Monroe argues that

> more difficult (i.e., less well attested) terminology is more likely to be original than added, as an addition usually serves the purpose of bringing a text into alignment with larger theological, ideological, historiographic, or narrative interests that are part and parcel of later editorial processes. Unique features may be witness to literary creativity that is not motivated by integration into an extended collection or ideological program but rather served the author's more limited narrative goals.[10]

It is easy to see how the use of שמור in Deut 5:12 brought that version of the Sabbath commandment into conversation with other legal corpora in the Pentateuch, such as the Holiness Code and the larger context of Deuteronomy 5–11.[11] The tradition preserving זכור, however, accomplishes no such thing. While the Sabbath does become an אות, "sign," and a ברית, "covenant," in P and H—objects that might be

---

during the monarchic period, Erhard Blum excludes the Sabbath commandment from his reconstruction of the pre-exilic Decalogue on this basis. Compare D. Johannes Meinhold, "Zur Sabbatfrage," *ZAW* 48 (1930): 121–38; with Erhard Blum, "The Decalogue and the Composition History of the Pentateuch," in *The Pentateuch: International Perspectives on Current Research*, ed. Thomas B. Dozeman, Konrad Schmid, and Baruch J. Schwartz (Tübingen: Mohr Siebeck, 2011), 289–302, here 298.

9. The additional occurrences are in Exod 31:13, 14, 16; Lev 19:3, 30; 26:2; and Isa 56:2, 4, 6. Thus, outside of Deuteronomy, the Sabbath is only "kept" in Holiness or Holiness-influenced contexts. Benjamin D. Sommer, *A Prophet Reads Scripture: Allusion in Isaiah 40–66* (Stanford, CA: Stanford University Press, 1998), 169; Saul M. Olyan, "Exodus 31:12-17: The Sabbath According to H, or the Sabbath According to P and H?," *JBL* 124 (2005): 201–9.

10. Lauren A. S. Monroe, *Josiah's Reform and the Dynamics of Defilement: Israelite Rites of Violence and the Making of a Biblical Text* (Oxford: Oxford University Press, 2011), 84.

11. Jack R. Lundbom, "The Inclusio and Other Framing Devices in Deuteronomy I–XXVIII," *VT* 46 (1996): 296–315, here 304–6.

remembered—these texts never connect the Sabbath to the verb זכר.¹² This is especially remarkable given that ברית is the object of זכר thirteen times in the Hebrew Bible, including multiple occurrences in P and H.¹³ Even if the tradition in Exod 20:8 is not precisely earlier, it fails to connect the Sabbath commandment to other traditions in the way that Deut 5:12 does. The cluster of terms in the Sabbath commandment in the Exodus Decalogue is unique, and it cannot be compared to other legal corpora to provide either a relative date or an intertextual explanation.

Not only is the root of the verb in Exod 20:8 unique in its connection to the Sabbath, its form is also unusual. There are only three other cases of a command to זכר a specific day, but only one is in the infinitive absolute.¹⁴ Esther 9:28 is a prescription for the festival of Purim using a niphal plural participle. Deuteronomy 16:3 uses a qal singular imperfect, and this command concerns the festival of Unleavened Bread rather than the Sabbath.¹⁵ Only in Exod 13:3 is there a command to remember a day—again the festival of Unleavened Bread—that uses the infinitive absolute as in Exodus 20.¹⁶ This last passage is typically considered either Deuteronomic or post-Deuteronomic,¹⁷ and it actually has more in common with the Deuteronomic Decalogue—which requires observing the Sabbath and remembering the Exodus event—than it does with the Decalogue in Exodus. In fact, Exod 13:3 may be drawing upon the same Deuteronomic tradition expressed

---

12. Jeffrey Stackert, "How the Priestly Sabbaths Work: Innovation in Pentateuchal Priestly Ritual," in *Ritual Innovation in the Hebrew Bible and Ancient Judaism*, ed. Nathan MacDonald (BZAW 468; Berlin: de Gruyter, 2016), 85–98.

13. Gen 9:15, 16; Exod 2:24; 6:5; Lev 26:42, 45; Ezek 16:60; Amos 1:9; Pss 105:8; 106:45; 111:5; 1 Chr 16:15.

14. Hossfeld, *Der Dekalog*, 40–2.

15. On the date of the Deuteronomic Code (Deuteronomy 12–26) see Eckart Otto, "The History of the Legal-Religious Hermeneutics of the Book of Deuteronomy from the Assyrian to the Hellenistic Period," in *From Antiquity to Early Islam* (Oxford: Oxford University Press, 2013), 228–33. On the relative dating of the various prescriptions of the Festival of Unleavened Bread, see Rainer Albertz, *Exodus, Band I: Ex 1-18* (Zürich: Theologischer Verlag Zürich, 2012), 211–12.

16. The use of the infinitive absolute in Exodus 20 serves to demarcate the boundaries between rhetorical units. Only the positive commands in the Decalogue are phrased as infinitives. The Sabbath commandment closes a divinely focused unit while the command concerning parents opens a collection of commands regarding action toward other people. This rhetorical strategy is also attested in Northwest Semitic inscriptions—such as the Kulamuwa inscription—and it may be another indication of the antiquity of Exod 20:8. The same rhetorical purpose does not appear to have informed the use of the infinitive in Exod 13:3, however. See Timothy Hogue, "The Monumentality of the Sinaitic Decalogue: Reading Exodus 20 in Light of Northwest Semitic Monument-Making Practices," *JBL* 138 (2019): 79–99, here 93.

17. Molly M. Zahn, "Reexamining Empirical Models: The Case of Exodus 13," in *Das Deuteronomium Zwischen Pentateuch Und Deuteronomistischem Geschictswerk*, ed. Eckart

in Deut 16:3 as well as in Deut 5:15; 7:18; 9:7; 15:15; 16:12; 24:9, 18, 22; and 25:17.[18] Alternatively, William Propp proposes that Exod 13:3 may be the "D-like" or Elohistic source material for the Deuteronomic expressions.[19] Regardless, a connection to the feast of Unleavened Bread or the commemoration of the Exodus event is unlikely to explain the pairing of זכר and the Sabbath in Exod 20:8. Absent any other references to these traditions, it is a tall order to propose that the writer of Exod 20:8 intended to integrate the Sabbath with these other festivals using the verb זכר alone.

What these other instances of זכר do suggest is that Exod 20:8 is using the root with a ritual nuance. Of the 221 uses of זכר in the Hebrew Bible, roughly 65 percent occur in cultic contexts such as these prescriptions concerning festival days and the connections to covenant discussed above. In addition, זכר regularly takes as its object God,[20] the name of God or other deities,[21] the law of God,[22] and ritual paraphernalia.[23] In at least one instance (Isa 66:3), the Hiphil מזכיר cannot be understood except as some form of ritual manipulation of blood. While none of these instances can suggest a direct relationship between the Sabbath and specific traditions recorded in the Hebrew Bible, they do demonstrate a broader ritual usage of the root זכר that should inform our interpretation of Exod 20:8.

Apart from the initial verb, the connection of the Sabbath to a seventh day of rest is sometimes used as evidence for the lateness of the commandment as a whole. However, the specific prescriptions concerning the seventh day—or at least most of them—were likely later additions to an earlier core. Erhard Blum argues that the material in Exod 20:9–10 was initially added in Deut 5:13–14 and later transposed to Exodus 20 to better align it with the text in Deuteronomy.[24] Supporting this assertion is Bernhard Lang's argument that the phrase כאשר צוך יהוה, "thus Yahweh commanded you," in Deut 5:12 is an introductory formula for a command derived from Judahite royal administration. It implies that the material to follow constitutes the content of the command, suggesting that this phrase appears in Deuteronomy to introduce additional verses meant to explain how the

Otto and Reinhard Achenbach (Göttingen: Vandenhoeck & Ruprecht, 2004), 36–55; David Carr, *The Formation of the Hebrew Bible: A New Reconstruction* (Oxford: Oxford University Press, 2011), 267.

18. Hendrik Bosman, "From 'Sign/אות' to 'Memorial/זכרון' in Exodus 13:1-16," *Scriptura* 112 (2013): 52–62, here 55.

19. Propp, *Exodus 1-18*, 377–9.

20. Cf., Deut 8:18; Judg 8:34; 2 Sam 14:11; Isa 17:10; 48:1; 57:11; 62:6; 64:4; Jer 20:9; 51:50; Ezek 6:9; Jon 2:8; Zech 10:9; Pss 22:28; 42:8; 63:7; 77:4; Eccl 12:1; Neh 4:8; 1 Chr 16:4.

21. Cf., Exod 20:23; 23:13; Josh 23:7; 2 Sam 18:18; Isa 26:13; 49:1; Jer 11:19; Hos 2:19; Amos 6:10; Zech 13:2; Pss 20:8; 45:18; 83:5; 119:55.

22. Cf., Num 15:39, 40; Josh 1:13; Mal 4:4; Pss 103:18; 105:53; 119:49, 52; Neh 1:8.

23. Cf., 1 Sam 4:18; Jer 3:16; 17:2; 44:21; Ps 20:4.

24. Blum, "The Decalogue and the Composition History of the Pentateuch," 293–4.

Sabbath is to be kept.²⁵ These additional verses are consistent with—perhaps even quotations of—Sabbath commandments from priestly/Holiness texts (Exod 31:12–17),²⁶ the Covenant Code (Exod 23:12), and the Holiness Code (Lev 23:3), suggesting that they were added to bring the Decalogue's Sabbath commandment into conversation with these corpora. Exod 20:9–10 is thus likely additional and editorial, but the Sabbath commandment in Exod 20:8 is original.²⁷ A connection between the seventh day and the Sabbath cannot be used to securely date the core of the Sabbath commandment, nor can it disambiguate our primary object of inquiry: the use of the verb זכר in this context. While the verses concerning the seventh day do suggest connections to other legal corpora, they do not suggest that the core of the commandment was composed with similar motivations.

An approach to Exod 20:8–11 based on inner biblical exegesis leads to the same conclusions by different means. In Deut 5:12, the phrase כאשר צוך יהוה, "thus Yahweh commanded you," does not merely introduce the material to follow. It also opens a resumptive repetition that closes in Deut 5:15 with the phrase על־כן צוך יהוה, "therefore Yahweh commanded you." The resumptive repetition is a typical exegetical marker that indicates all the material contained within the resumption is additional and editorial.²⁸ While the specifically Deuteronomic language of צוך יהוה has been removed from the Exodus Decalogue,²⁹ the additional verses are still framed by the words ששת ימים תעבד, "six days you shall work," in Exod 20:9; and כי ששת ימים עשה יהוה, "for in six days Yahweh made," in 20:11. This is another resumptive repetition marking inserted material—namely, the commands concerning the seventh day of rest.³⁰ These editorial markers suggest that the

---

25. Lang's argument is based on the similar use of such introductory phrases in Hebrew inscriptions. See Bernhard Lang, "The Decalogue in the Light of a Newly Published Palaeo-Hebrew Inscription (Hebrew Ostracon Moussaieff No. 1)," *JSOT* 77 (1998): 21–5.

26. There is some debate over how much of the material in Exodus 31 should be assigned to P as opposed to H. Compare Olyan, "Exodus 31:12-17"; with Jeffrey Stackert, "The Holiness Legislation and Its Pentateuchal Sources: Revision, Supplementation, and Replacement," in *The Strata of the Priestly Writings: Contemporary Debate and Future Directions*, ed. Sarah Shectman and Joel Baden (Zurich: Theologischer Verlag Zürich, 2009), 173–90.

27. Childs, *The Book of Exodus*, 415; Jeffrey Stackert, "The Sabbath of the Land in the Holiness Legislation: Combining Priestly and Non-Priestly Perspectives," *CBQ* 73 (2011): 239–50, here 241 n. 4; Ottilia Lukács, "The Inner-Biblical Interpretation of the Sabbath Commandment," in *Hiszek, Hogy Megértsem!: Konferenciakötet–Doktoranduszok Országos Szövetsége Hittudományi Osztály Fiatal Kutatók És Doktoranduszok IV. Nemzetközi Teológuskonferenciája, Budapest, 2013. November 30* (Budapest: Károli Gáspár Református Egyetem, 2015), 37–45, here 43.

28. Bernard M. Levinson, *Deuteronomy and the Hermeneutics of Legal Innovation* (New York: Oxford University Press, 1997), 18–20; Ska, *Introduction to Reading the Pentateuch*, 77–8.

29. Blum, "The Decalogue and the Composition History of the Pentateuch," 294n. 16.

30. Lukács, "The Inner-Biblical Interpretation of the Sabbath Commandment," 44–5.

commands concerning the seventh day were added by later editor, so however one dates these verses they do not reflect directly on the antiquity of v. 8.

The relationship of Exod 20:11 to 20:8 and whether it was part of an earlier edition of the commandment is more difficult to determine. This verse is a motivation clause introduced by the particle כי. It is debated whether or not these clauses are original or editorial.[31] These motivation clauses also appear in the image commandment (Exod 20:5) and name commandment (Exod 20:7), so they may be motivated by the immediate context of the Decalogue rather than an attempt to integrate the commandments into a broader collection. The motivation clause marked by כי also contains a resumptive repetition from the motivation clause of the image commandment. The image commandment opens in Exod 20:4 by forbidding כל־תמונה אשר בשמים ממעל ואשר בארץ מתחת ואשר במים מתחת לארץ, "any likeness that is in heaven above or that is on the earth below or that is in the waters beneath the earth." The Sabbath commandment closes in Exod 20:11 by noting that Yahweh created את־השמים ואת־הארץ את־הים ואת־כל אשר בם, "the heavens and the earth and the sea and all that is in them." This repetition brackets the divine-focused unit of the Decalogue, ties the motivation clauses of the image commandment and Sabbath commandment together, and strongly suggests that these were composed by the same individual and may even be original to the Decalogue.[32]

Based on the other motivation clauses in the Decalogue, we might reasonably expect the entire divine-focused unit to end with the Sabbath's כי-clause. This is not the case. Instead, it is followed by the phrase וינח ביום השבעי, "and he rested on the seventh day," in Exod 20:11, which echoes the appearance of the seventh day in v. 10 and perhaps marks an additional insertion. This is then followed by a second motivation clause marked with על־כן, "therefore." This is unlike any of the other motivation clauses in the Exodus Decalogue, but it does resemble the motivation inserted into the Sabbath commandment in Deut 5:15. This is probably an additional insertion, but it is tied to the rest of the commandment by its resumptive repetition of the root *qdš*, "to consecrate," which now forms a bracket around the preserved version of the Sabbath Commandment in Exodus 20.

In summary, v. 8 is likely the core of the earliest form of the Decalogue's Sabbath commandment. The material in v. 11 has clearly been modified, but some of it may be original as well. The original commandment was an enjoinder to זכר the Sabbath, perhaps with some motivation based on relevant action by Yahweh. The material concerning the seventh day of rest was likely added in an attempt to merge that tradition with the Decalogue's Sabbath and to connect it with other legal corpora. That is not to say that this additional material could not also have been relatively early, but it is less obviously connected to Levantine conjuration rituals. Actions and objects denoted by the root *zkr*, however, are central to such rituals.

---

31. Cf., Christoph Levin, "Der Dekalog Am Sinai," *VT* 35 (1985): 165–91, here 170; Blum, "The Decalogue and the Composition History of the Pentateuch," 299.

32. Hogue, "The Monumentality of the Sinaitic Decalogue," 94–5.

3. Conjuration in the Ancient Near East

Before turning to other uses of the root *zkr*, it is important to take note of the ancient ontological conceptions that informed its use. Eve Sweetser argues that ritual "both acknowledges (or affirms) a particular ontology as prevailing, and is also intended to assist in maintaining it, or keeping it in being."[33] In general, the cultures of the ancient Near East embraced nondualist ontologies. Perhaps the best example of this understanding is the Mesopotamian concept of the *ṣalmu*. Typically translated "image," *ṣalmu* was actually a distinct ontological category that is not coextensive with modern notions of representation. The word certainly could refer to objects like statues and stelae, but these objects were not symbols of a person present elsewhere; rather, objects designated as *ṣalmu* became extensions of that individual and could therefore substitute that individual in ritual contexts. In the words of Zainab Bahrani, "instead of being a means of signifying an original real, it was seen as ontologically equivalent to it, existing in the same register of reality."[34] The category of *ṣalmu* even included human actors in ritual performances. The human substitute in rituals was not merely a representation but "a living human image" and "a material replacement" ontologically equivalent to the person or god thus replaced.[35] Ritual actions and objects thus had the effect of "conjuring rather than reconstructing the real."[36] This understanding can shed significant light on the various uses of the root *zkr*.

3.1. The Root zkr and Levantine Conjuration

The most basic meaning of the root *zkr* is "to name" or "to mention." On this basis, it is easily extended "to invoke." While this definition can account for many of the uses of the verb and its derivations, some remain difficult to explain.[37] I propose that this is because the sense of this verb is often understood representationally. In ritual contexts, the term is understood as describing the cause—that is, the action—of the ritual rather than its effect or outcome. These distinctions are not necessary to maintain in light of the nondualist ontology of the ancient Near East. Ritual actions blended cause and effect and the identities of ritual agent and patient. The performance of ritual did not result in an immaterial effect elsewhere; rather, some rituals were understood to include their own results. For example, in the Mesopotamian sacred marriage ceremony—sometimes a component of new

---

33. Eve Sweetser, "Blended Spaces and Performativity," *Cognitive Linguistics* 11 (2000): 305–33, here 314.
34. Zainab Bahrani, *The Infinite Image: Art, Time and the Aesthetic Dimension in Antiquity* (London: Reaktion Books, 2014), 73.
35. Bahrani, *The Infinite Image*, 68–9.
36. Ibid., 24.
37. Daniel E. Fleming, *Time at Emar: The Cultic Calendar and the Rituals from the Diviner's Archive* (Winona Lake, IN: Eisenbrauns, 2000), 122–4.

year's celebrations—the king was wedded to the goddess Inana/Ishtar through a ritual he performed with a priestess. In this ritual, the priestess was not understood as simply symbolizing or representing the goddess. Rather, the priestess actually brought forth and embodied the goddess in the context of the ritual performance. According to Bahrani, "without this uncertainty of identities, the ritual would be useless."[38] To *zkr* an entity need not mean simply naming it. To *zkr* an entity actually brings it forth or conjures it. This understanding can also explain the relationship between actions and artifacts designated by the root *zkr*.

Akkadian instances of the root *zkr* can have verbal, material/iconographic, or even cognitive referents, but these various semantic ranges can be combined if we approach them in light of conjuration. For example, the *CAD* defines the term *zikru* as "discourse, utterance, pronouncement, words" as well as "name," but it also records a secondary meaning of "image, counterpart, replica" or "idea, concept."[39] Some examples will demonstrate that these two meanings are more connected than they at first appear. Gilgamesh I ii 31 recounts that the goddess Aruru was commanded to create Gilgamesh's counterpart (*zikiršu*). Line 33 follows with the explanation that "she created a replica of Anu in her heart and created Enkidu" (*zik-ru ša ᵈA-nin ibtani ina libbiša ... Enkidu ibtani*). Similarly, the Descent of Ištar (KAR 1 r. 5) recounts that "Ea created an idea and then created Aṣūšu-namir" (*Ea ... ibtani zikru ibnīma Aṣūšu-namir*).[40] In both cases, the actor produces a cognitive model and then brings it forth as a material reality. The word *zikru* encapsulates both the cognitive form it sometimes indicates and the newly wrought physical presence. *Zikru* describes something that simultaneously conjures and contains the result of that conjuration. This recalls Bahrani's observation that in Mesopotamia "the act of naming ... is a performative one; it is even alchemical in its force"[41] and transforms the named entity into a "facet of being or emanation."[42] The extension from a performative act (as in naming) to a cultic artifact (as an image) is unproblematic within the ancient nondualist ontology; the same semantic range is expressed in *ṣalmu*. A similar range of meanings can be observed in ritual uses of *zkr* in the Levant.

Perhaps the most elaborate of the known Levantine conjuration rituals was the Zukru Festival of Emar as recorded on tablets dating to the thirteenth century BCE. This multiday festival culminated in a public invocation of the city's chief deity Dagan accompanied by offerings.[43] In ritual contexts, there is no distinction between naming or invoking a thing and bringing about its presence. Daniel Fleming argues, for instance, that "when worshippers name a god ... they invite the god's presence."[44] In fact, the relationship may be even more direct. When

---

38. Bahrani, *The Infinite Image*, 201.
39. Fleming, *Time at Emar*, 123–4n. 326.
40. CAD_z, 116.
41. Bahrani, *The Infinite Image*, 191.
42. Ibid., 43.
43. Fleming, *Time at Emar*, 120–6.
44. Ibid., 124.

ritual actors name or invoke a god—or otherwise act on the deity's behalf—they actually bring about the god's presence. Dagan was thus conjured or summoned through the Zukru Festival. This function can be further substantiated in light of the festival's central event.

On the first and last day of the Zukru as well as on "the consecration day" (*ūmu qaddusi*), the ritual practitioners repeated a special manipulation of the cult statue of Dagan. After feasting within the city on these days, they would transport the statue outside where it was driven between two or more aniconic stelae. These stelae were anointed with oil and blood beforehand, thus receiving offerings apart from the statue. Based on parallels to other ritual uses of stelae at Emar and in the Hittite world, Fleming argues that these stelae were likely alternative embodiments of Dagan himself. That is, both the statue and the stelae conjured Dagan, but in different contexts—urban and non-urban space. In the Zukru Festival, these two conjurations of Dagan were brought together. After this procession out of the city and through the stelae, the statue of Dagan was returned to Emar.[45] The ritual feast, invocation, transport of the statue, and anointing of the stones all contributed to the enchanted atmosphere of the Zukru, allowing these mundane elements to blend with numinous ones. As a result, these material and performative aspects of the ritual contributed together to the conjuration of Dagan before the Emarites. While the title of "Zukru" may have originally intended the invocation in particular, naming the festival in this way suggests that the term had already gained a much broader meaning, referring to the complex set of practices and artifacts that facilitated Dagan's conjuration.[46] The Zukru Festival was a time of conjuring, an enchanted time, so it was named accordingly. The Zukru Festival was also not unique; similar ritual practices are attested during the Iron Age.

At Iron Age Samʔal (Zincirli Höyük), the root *zkr* appears in contexts strongly suggestive of conjuration rituals. The best example to demonstrate this comes from the Hadad Inscription (*KAI* 214)—a royal monumental inscription dating to the eighth century BCE. Lines 17–18a of that inscription relate an invocation or incantation to be spoken before the monument. These lines read as follows:

יאמר [תא]כל נבש פנמו עמך ותש[תי נ]בש פנמו עמך עד יזכר נבש פנמו עם [ה]דד

Let him say: "May the personhood of Panamuwa eat with you, and may the personhood of Panamuwa drink with you." Henceforth, may he conjure the personhood of Panamuwa with Hadad.

Leaving aside the tendentious term *nbš*, these lines are significant for what they imply about the meaning of the verb *zkr*. The entire ritual action is summarized by this verb. To *zkr* thus includes the incantation, the offerings it mentions, and perhaps even the speaker's subsequent acts of eating and drinking. More importantly, though, when we view this incantation in light of a nondualist

---

45. Ibid., 82–7.
46. Ibid., 138–40.

ontology, we must recall that the very act of performing it brought about its numinous effect. In other words, *zkr* also includes Panamuwa's manifestation and his ritual participation. To זכר נבש פנמו involved a blending of the actions of the ritual agent (speaking, offering, eating, and drinking) with the imagined participation of the ritual subject (Panamuwa's—and by extension Hadad's— speaking, eating, and drinking).[47] The presence and ritual agency of Panamuwa and Hadad are conjured by the ritual actions of the practitioner.

Clearly, the verb *zkr* refers to the conjuring of Panamuwa's presence through the proper activation of the monument. Based on its usage in the Hadad Inscription, we may propose that the range of meanings of the verb *zkr* in ritual contexts should also include "to incant," "to enchant," and "to conjure." Panamuwa is not simply invoked or remembered in this prescription. He is conjured in the minds of the monument's users as they activate his monument. A noun זכר is also attested in Sam'alian as a description of a stele, probably on the basis that stelae were a material means of conjuration.[48] In light of the verbal use of the term, the noun זכר was probably not a "memorial" in the sense of a symbolic object pointing to a past entity. It is an enchanted object that facilitates that entity's conjuration. It is thus better translated as "fetish," following Lambros Malafouris and Roy Ellen's understanding of fetishes as animate artifacts that conflate signifier and signified.[49] Underlying both of these meanings is a process of enchantment and conjuration that can be further fleshed out by recent theoretical work on ritual.

4. Technologies of Enchantment

The root *zkr* is used to denote various actions and objects that conflate ritual cause and effect and signifier and signified. All of these material practices can be analyzed in terms of enchantment. Jane Bennett describes enchantment as "a state of interactive fascination" accompanied by an "odd combination of somatic effects."[50] Ritual performances and artifacts are a means of bringing about this

---

47. Seth Sanders, "The Appetites of the Dead: West Semitic Linguistic and Ritual Aspects of the Katumuwa Stele," *BASOR* 369 (2013): 35–55, here 48–9; Timothy Hogue, "I Am: The Function, History, and Diffusion of the Fronted First-Person Pronoun in Syro-Anatolian Monumental Discourse," *JNES* 78 (2019): 323–39, here 336.

48. Timothy Hogue, "Abracadabra or I Create as I Speak: A Reanalysis of the First Verb in the Katumuwa Inscription in Light of Northwest Semitic and Hieroglyphic Luwian Parallels," *BASOR* 381 (2019): 193–202, here 194; Hogue, "I Am," 325–6.

49. Roy Ellen, "Fetishism," *Man* 23 (1988): 219–29; Lambros Malafouris, *How Things Shape the Mind: A Theory of Material Engagement* (Cambridge, MA: MIT Press, 2013), 133–4.

50. Jane Bennett, *The Enchantment of Modern Life: Attachments, Crossings, and Ethics* (Princeton, NJ: Princeton University Press, 2001), 5.

interactive fascination. Alfred Gell argues that ritual is a means of "casting a spell over us so that we see the world in an enchanted form."[51] Gell accordingly labels ritual practices and artifacts as *"technologies of enchantment."* That is, ritual is material engagement that draws attention to itself through its blurring of identities and ontological boundaries. Ancient Near Eastern conjuration practices performatively called people and deities into being in specific locales. This comports well with Gell's explanation of technologies of enchantment; he argued that as a result of such practices and artifacts "we are fascinated because we are essentially at a loss to explain how such an object comes to exist in the world."[52] Enchantment is a useful concept to explore in relation to the Sabbath commandment because it encapsulates well Nahum Sarna's understanding of זכר as involving a "sharp focusing of attention" that "eventuates in action."[53] In other words, to זכר entails interactive fascination. More than this, the ritual actions involved in this interaction bring forth new realities. In short, to זכר is to engage in enchantment—to enchant and be enchanted. Enchantment also permits us to move from memory to a more active cognitive process that underlies ritual more broadly: conceptual blending.[54]

Conceptual blending is a cognitive process in which two or more mental spaces are selectively projected onto a combined space. Mental spaces are defined as "small conceptual packets constructed as we think and talk, for purposes of local understanding and action."[55] These conceptual packets are coactivated in the mind and blended to produce a new integrated mental space. This blended space contains some of the same concepts as the input spaces but in new relationships to each other. Conceptual blending can be used to explain more well-known operations like metaphors, in which we make sense of one concept in terms of another. For example, in the well-known biblical metaphor "God is king," some aspects of God are described and understood in terms of features usually linked to human kings.[56] The metaphor results from the projection of a source mental space (human king) onto a target space (God), resulting in a blend (divine king). Conceptual blending is broader than metaphor, however, in that the blended mental spaces may relate

---

51. Alfred Gell, "The Technology of Enchantment and the Enchantment of Technology," in *Anthropology, Art and Aesthetics*, ed. Jeremy Coote and Anthony Shelton (Oxford: Clarendon Press, 1992), 44.
52. Gell, "The Technology of Enchantment and the Enchantment of Technology," 62.
53. Sarna, *Exodus*, 13.
54. Jill Stevenson, "Embodied Enchantments: Cognitive Theory and the York Mystery Plays," in *The York Mystery Plays: Performance in the City*, ed. Margaret Rogerson (Woodbridge: York Medieval Press, 2011), 91–112, here 111.
55. Gilles Fauconnier and Mark Turner, *The Way We Think: Conceptual Blending and the Mind's Hidden Complexities* (New York: Basic Books, 2002), 102.
56. Marc Zvi Brettler, *God Is King: Understanding an Israelite Metaphor* (Journal for the Study of the Old Testament Supplement Series 76; Sheffield: JSOT Press, 1989).

to each other in more varied ways than the source-target relationship that defines metaphors specifically.[57]

The explanatory power of conceptual blending—especially for ritual—lies in its proposition that new structures emerge in the blended space as a result of the new and unique relationships formed between the concepts from the input mental spaces.[58] For example, the divine king blend discussed above includes new concepts—such as an eternal reign—that did not exist in either of the inputs. This concept only emerges in the blend. The process of emergence explains how a mundane action or object can have profound magical and social effects. The relevance of this theory of emergence to ritual can be more easily demonstrated by means of an example—the ritual of the Baby's Ascent.

The Baby's Ascent was a ritual performed in some Italian villages in which a newborn baby was carried up a flight of stairs in order to ensure the child's future prosperity. In Sweetser's analysis of the ritual, a mental space of climbing stairs is blended with one of social ascendancy. The parent reaching the top of the stairs with the baby represents the desired effect of the ritual: the child's later success in life. But reaching the top of the stairs is also the cause of the child's success.[59] The parent's actions are blended with those of the child as are the causal relationships between them. Jill Stevenson argues that this sort of blending of cause and effect in the ritual's emergent structure is precisely what enchants its audience and participants. When our attention is drawn to blends by means of ritual performances, the emergent structure becomes fascinating because it appears by means of combining relatively mundane activities with profound concepts to create a new relationship between them that is more than their sum and basic interrelation.[60] This fascination with conceptual blends in rituals—that is, their power to enchant—is part of what is entailed by the root *zkr* in ritual contexts.[61]

Blending and enchantment point to another significant aspect of rituals: their performativity. Performativity refers to an action's ability to actually bring about something rather than simply depict something.[62] Sweetser explains this using the Christian practice of Communion as an example. In Communion, the bread and the wine may be seen as only representing the body and blood of Christ, and similarly their consumption may be seen to represent union between the participants and Christ. Such is certainly the case in some Protestant traditions. But Communion can also be understood "as intending to bring about this spiritual

---

57. Rafael E. Núñez, "Enacting Infinity: Bringing Transfinite Cardinals into Being," in *Enaction: Toward a New Paradigm for Cognitive Science*, ed. John Stewart, Olivier Gapenne, and Ezequiel A. Di Paolo (Cambridge, MA: MIT Press, 2010), 320.

58. Fauconnier and Turner, *The Way We Think*, 40–4.

59. Sweetser, "Blended Spaces and Performativity," 312; Fauconnier and Turner, *The Way We Think*, 81.

60. Stevenson, "Embodied Enchantments," 110–12.

61. Sarna, *Exodus*, 13.

62. John Searle, "How Performatives Work," *Linguistics and Philosophy* 12 (1989): 535–58.

union via the consumption of the bread and wine."[63] For example, in Roman Catholic or Lutheran contexts the ritual does not merely symbolize or represent the union of believer and deity; it also causes it. The bread and the wine bring about the body and blood of Christ rather than simply representing them. Blending makes this performativity possible. Due to the coactivation of mundane and profound conceptual spaces, walking up stairs can change a child's life, and eating a piece of bread dipped in wine can unite one with a powerful deity. Emergence and enchantment provide an etic framework for engaging the mysteries of rituals on their own terms. This framework is particularly helpful for gaining new insights into the command: זכור את-יום השבת.

5. Enchantment and the Sabbath Commandment

What is most clear about the Sabbath commandment is that it was a time of ritual engagement. Other scholars have suggested that the pre-exilic Sabbath was a rite celebrated on the day of the new moon or full moon, both of which could be enchanted in Levantine ritual systems. The suggestion of the full moon is most associated with Johannes Meinhold, who argued that שבת was actually loaned into Hebrew based on the Akkadian *šapattu*, a technical designation for the fifteenth day of the month.[64] Though lasting multiple days, the Zukru festival was also initiated on the fifteenth day of the first month of Emar's year, which is specified as the day of the full moon.[65] The possibility of *šbt* originally designating the full moon is particularly striking given its close association with the new moon.

A number of texts mention the new moon and the Sabbath in the same breath and even appear to equate the two (2 Kgs 4:23; Isa 1:13; Hos 2:13; Amos 8:5). Daniel Fleming proposes that the terms חדש and שבת referred to special celebrations in the midst of major festivals during the pre-exilic period; they may not have been synonymous but may well have been components of the same festivals.[66] If this is so, the mention of the new moon (חדש) and Sabbath (שבת) alongside each other may have served as a hendiadys for the most important days in particular festivals, the new moon and perhaps the full moon. Hosea 2:13 may thus be using חדשה ושבתה, "her new moon and her Sabbath," as a hendiadys in apposition to חגה, "her festival." This would parallel the usage in Ps 81:4, in which חדש and כסה, "full moon," are used in apposition to יום חגנו, "our festival day."[67] Alternatively, חדש and

---

63. Sweetser, "Blended Spaces and Performativity," 314.

64. Johannes Meinhold, *Sabbat und Woche im Alten Testament: eine Untersuchung* (Göttingen: Vandenhoeck und Ruprecht, 1905); Johannes Meinhold, "Die Entstehung des Sabbats," *ZAW* 29 (1909): 81–112.

65. Fleming, *Time at Emar*, 97.

66. Daniel E. Fleming, "The Day of Yahweh in the Book of Amos: A Rhetorical Response to Ritual Expectation," *RevBib* 117 (2010): 20–38, here 37.

67. It is somewhat problematic that another term—*ksh*—already existed for the day of the full moon. The contention that *šbt* originally meant "full moon" is also problematic

שבת may be synonymous, as they appear to be in Amos 8:5. Regardless, there is a clear relationship between the three designations, and perhaps there was some fluidity in regard to which part of the festival שבת referred.

At the very least, the term שבת referred to a particularly enchanted time within a festival. For example, the new moon was initially the most significant time during ancient Israel's autumnal New Year festival.[68] Emar's Zukru festival likewise functioned as an autumnal New Year festival, while other significant festivals were aligned with various new moons.[69] The eventual combination of Israel's New Year festival with Sukkot meant that the festivities could last at least until the full moon.[70] We might reasonably expect that one or both of these days was a time of conjuration and perhaps designated a שבת. This connection also lends itself to a comparison to Jeroboam's inauguration of the northern kingdom and its major cult sites in 1 Kgs 12:28–33. This ritual event occurred on the fifteenth day of the eighth month, potentially an autumn שבת. Among other things, Jeroboam installed a cult statue of Yahweh and even alluded to the opening line of the Decalogue while ritually inaugurating it.[71] This ritual inauguration was thus primarily intended to conjure the presence of Yahweh in particular sites in the northern kingdom and may reflect a שבת occurring during the Israelite autumnal New Year.

because there is no evidence that the term *šapattu* was used outside of southern Mesopotamia. Daniel E. Fleming, "A Break in the Line: Reconsidering the Bible's Diverse Festival Calendars," *RevBib* 106 (1999): 161–74, here 173–4.

68. Karel Van Der Toorn, "Celebrating the New Year with the Israelites: Three Extrabiblical Psalms from Papyrus Amherst 63," *JBL* 136 (2017): 633–49, here 640–1.

69. Technically, the Zukru Festival was one of two major events in the Emarite year—the other being in the spring. I thus refer to the Zukru as an autumnal New Year, while recognizing that a vernal festival existed as well. Fleming, *Time at Emar*, 127–33.

70. George W. Macrae, "The Meaning and Evolution of the Feast of Tabernacles," *CBQ* 22 (1960): 251–76, here 257; Johannes C. de Moor, *New Year with Canaanites and Israelites* (Kamper Cahiers 21–2; Kampen: J.H. Kok, 1972); William W. Hallo, "New Moons and Sabbaths: A Case-Study in the Contrastive Approach," *HUCA* 48 (1977): 1–18, here 9–10; Tryggve N. D. Mettinger, *The Dethronement of Sabbath: Studies in the Shem and Kabod Theologies* (Lund: Gleerup, 1982), 67; Sigmund Mowinckel, *The Psalms in Israel's Worship*, trans. D.R. Ap-Thomas (Grand Rapids, MI: Eerdmans, 2004), 116–23; Alexander Rofé, *Introduction to the Literature of the Hebrew Bible* (Jerusalem: Simor, 2009), 473–4; Noga Ayali-Darshan, "The Seventy Bulls Sacrificed at Sukkot (Num 29:12-34) in Light of a Ritual Text from Emar (Emar 6, 373)," *VT* 65 (2015): 9–19, here 3; Van Der Toorn, "Celebrating the New Year with the Israelites," 639.

71. Jonathan S. Greer, *Dinner at Dan: Biblical and Archaeological Evidence for Sacred Feasts at Iron Age II Tel Dan and Their Significance* (CHANE 66; Leiden: Brill, 2013), 40. If Meinhold's thesis is correct, Jeroboam inaugurated his kingdom on *šbt*—the fifteenth day of the month or the day of the full moon (Akkadian *šapattu*). Even if his thesis is not maintained, however, there is clearly an implicit connection between the two. Meinhold, *Sabbat und Woche im Alten Testament*; Meinhold, "Die Entstehung des Sabbats."

As an alternative to the above, Erhard Blum suggests that the term *šapattu* was loaned into Hebrew during the pre-exilic period to describe the seventh day of rest, which had previously had no special designation in Hebrew. This loan was based on phonological correspondence with the Hebrew verb שבת and inherited none of its meaning from the Akkadian term.[72] Fleming suggests that the seventh day derived its significance from seven-day festivals, which would have included the Sabbath in a more restricted sense.[73] Oded Tammuz's data concerning the observation of a seventh day of rest in pre-Persian Judean communities points to an earlier origin for that practice,[74] so its combination with the Sabbath may have similarly been early and based on its connection to seven-day festivals associated with major invocations of Yahweh. Thus, even if *šbt* originated as a term for the seventh day of rest, it still designated a practice intended to mark a time as enchanted.

5.1. *The Sabbath and the Decalogue*

Whether the Sabbath is understood as a full moon rite, a new moon rite, or even the seventh day of rest, a relationship to times of conjuration is probable. One final connection can make it certain. An important piece of evidence has been missing from previous discussions of the Sabbath in relation to pre-exilic ritual practice. As suggested by the principle of *lectio difficilior*, the command זכור את-יום השבת was not part of an editorial attempt to align this practice with a broader context. Rather, this ancient core of the Sabbath commandment is a "witness to literary creativity that is not motivated by integration … but rather served the author's more limited narrative goals."[75] That is, the phrasing of this commandment indicates no attempt to allude to or accommodate other legal corpora; rather, it suggests a creative Sabbath prescription that is uniquely motivated by this specific composition. In other words, the most important context for determining the meaning of the Sabbath Commandment is the Decalogue.

I have recently demonstrated that the Decalogue was composed in imitation of Levantine "I am" inscriptions—a special class of monumental inscriptions employed primarily in the Levant during the Iron Age.[76] The entire purpose of these inscriptions was to conjure the individual identified in the opening "I am …" statement, and this was sometimes buttressed with prescribed conjuration rituals as in the case of the Hadad Inscription discussed above. The "I" of these inscriptions was blended with the individual understood as speaking through

---

72. Blum, "The Decalogue and the Composition History of the Pentateuch," 293n. 15.
73. Fleming, "A Break in the Line," 173–5; Fleming, "The Day of Yahweh in the Book of Amos," 37.
74. Tammuz, "The Sabbath as the Seventh Day of the Week and a Day of Rest."
75. Monroe, *Josiah's Reform and the Dynamics of Defilement*, 84.
76. Hogue, "The Monumentality of the Sinaitic Decalogue."

it, who was also blended with the epigraphic support. That individual's presence emerged in the blend and was thus conjured before the audience.[77] In other words, "I am" inscriptions were fundamentally a technology of enchantment.

The Decalogue was modeled on artifacts intended to conjure the individuals identified in the "I am" statement opening them. As a depicted material conjuration of Yahweh, the physical text of the Decalogue—however it is imagined in the narrative world of Exodus—is a natural location for an associated conjuration ritual. This is why the original commandment was to זכור the Sabbath. The Sabbath was to be made into an enchanted time in which Yahweh's presence could be invoked by performance and extended to material implements such as the text of the Decalogue. During this time of interactive fascination, the Decalogue could fully function as a material conjuration of Yahweh and the ritual practitioner's performative acts could blend with the imagined participation of Yahweh. If the text of the Decalogue was thus an enchanted object, the Sabbath was included as a practice of enchantment to activate it.

Viewed from this perspective and in light of a broader consideration of ancient Near Eastern ritual, even the material added to the Sabbath commandment suggests a performative ritual. The ritual actors are fundamentally enjoined to imitate Yahweh by resting on the seventh day as he rested after the sixth day of creation.[78] This ritual action is similar to that of the aforementioned *ṣalmu*. By imitating Yahweh's actions, the ritual participants do not merely symbolize or indicate him. Their actions blend with his so that they become ontologically indistinct from him. His presence and activity emerge from that of the ritual participants. They *zkr* Yahweh through the Sabbath, not by remembering his act of rest but by recreating it among themselves. To rest on the Sabbath is to participate in the being of Yahweh.

6. Conclusion: Enchanting the Sabbath

To זכור את-יום השבת cannot only mean to remember the Sabbath. Ritual in the ancient Near East never entailed such passive cognitive acts, but rather actually brought things into existence and created vague boundaries between cause and effect and the identities of the ritual participants, targets, and implements. For the ancients, ritual was participation in other forms of being. To זכור the Sabbath is to recognize it as and indeed make it into a time of enchantment—a time for conjuring and participating in the presence of Yahweh, a time when ritual

---

77. Hogue, "I Am," 336.

78. Jon Levenson argues that the account of creation is a reflection of seven-day festivals such as those discussed above. The seven days of creation thus reflect these festivals as times of conjuring. Jon D. Levenson, *Creation and the Persistence of Evil: The Jewish Drama of Divine Omnipotence* (Princeton, NJ: Princeton University Press, 1988), 76–7.

performers can exist in the same register of reality as the divine. The Sabbath becomes holy because, by enchanting it, the Sabbath keeper conjures God and participates in his being. Rather than translate זכר as "remember" with a set of caveats about the ritual acts and interactive fascination it entailed, I instead translate Exod 20:8 as "Enchant the day of the Sabbath to make it holy."

Part III

TEXTUALIZATION AND RITUAL

Chapter 9

AARON'S BODY AS A RITUAL VESSEL IN THE EXODUS TABERNACLE BUILDING NARRATIVE

Alice Mandell

1. Introduction: Aaron's Inscribed Uniform: What Are These Inscriptions and What Do They Do in This Narrative?

The Tabernacle building story describes the uniform of Israel's high priest in intricate detail. Aaron's clothing sets him apart from other priests: it is distinguished by valuable materials, which mirror the colors, metals, and fabrics in the holiest areas of the Tabernacle and by precious stones that are unique in the Tabernacle.[1] His clothing is also distinguished by three sets of inscriptions, which are set into the shoulder and chest pieces on his uniform and into his headdress (Exodus 28 and 39).[2] The present study offers an analysis of these three sets of inscriptions in a way that is sensitive to how their words and design inform their ritual logic. While southern Levantine inscriptional practices might suggest that YHWH's many worshipers should be represented in the Tabernacle by inscriptions inscribed into the very structure of the Tabernacle, or onto objects set into YHWH's cultic precinct, in this narrative, only Aaron's inscribed uniform can represent Israel's body politic in the Tabernacle. And, rather than inscribed "holy" vessels, Aaron is marked as a "dedicated" thing by an inscription on his headpiece. This raises questions regarding the ritual function of the inscriptions in Aaron's uniform and what his body contributes to their ritual meaning.

In this story there is a striking contrast between ritual things that are made for YHWH's cult but are anepigraphic and Aaron's bedazzled, inscribed clothing.[3] Exodus 28:9–38 describes three sets of inscriptions: a shoulder-piece containing

---

1. See Menahem Haran, *Temples and Temple-Service in Ancient Israel* (Oxford: Clarendon Press, 1978), 149–204; esp. 158–65, 212.
2. See Wolfgang Zwickel, "Die Bedeutung des hohenpriesterlichen Brustschildes," in *Edelsteine in der Bibel*, ed. Wolfgang Zwickel (Mainz am Rhein: Verlag Philipp von Zabern, 2002), 50–70; also Cornelis Houtman, *Exodus* (Kampen: Kok, 1993), 499–502.
3. This story does not mention Aaron's inscribed staff (Num 17:17–25); in this account, the stone tablets are hidden in the ark (Exod 25:16, 21; 40:20–21). These two inscriptions are not on display in the main area of the Tabernacle but are placed into the restricted access

two engraved stones, each with six of Israel's tribal names; a breastplate holding twelve different precious stones, each engraved with a different tribal name; and a golden flower attached to Aaron's headdress, which is inscribed with the words קדש ליהוה, "dedicated to YHWH." YHWH further specifies these inscriptions are all to be inscribed in the manner of a seal inscription, as פתוחי חתם "the engravings of a seal"; this detail is repeated in YHWH's instructions in Exod 28:11, 21, 36 and in the narrative about their craft production in Exod 39:6, 14, and 30 (six times in all).

> Inscription Set 1: Exod 28:9-12; Exod 39:6-7
> Design: 2 precious stones of the same type engraved with 6 names of the 12 sons of Israel (one stone per shoulder).[4]
> Meaning: remembrance
>
> Inscription Set 2: Exod 28: 17-21, 29; 39:10-14
> Design: 12 different precious stones are arranged 4x3 on a golden breastplate; each stone is engraved with the name of a different tribe.
> Meaning: continual remembrance
>
> Inscription Set 3: Exod 28:36-38; 39:30-31
> Design: A golden flower (ציץ), a stylized rosette, is inscribed with the words קדש ליהוה, "dedicated to YHWH."[5] This inscription is attached to the high priest's headdress by a blue-purple thread.[6]
> Meaning: he takes on Israel's guilt and this headdress will enable the tribes to find favor in YHWH's presence.

These inscriptions are not mere "accessories" or signifiers of Aaron's status but are essential to the ritual power of his uniform.[7] Their importance is underscored

---

area of the tent shrine. In Exodus 28 and 39, it is suggested that Aaron's inscribed uniform is made to move about with him inside of the Tabernacle as he performs his cultic duties.

4. The LXX describes it as σμάραγδος, a green-colored stone; however, Akkadian comparative material suggests it is a reddish color in the Hebrew textual tradition (*sāmtu* AHw S 1019); see Zwickel, "Die Bedeutung des hohenpriesterlichen Brustschildes," 53.

5. The description of Aaron's staff in Num 17:23, which is also described as flowering using the word ציץ, refers specifically to the blossom of an almond tree. In Exodus 28 and 39, the term ציץ refers to a stylized flower that is inscribed in a seal script. The design of this ornament is meant to evoke the rosette used in royal clothing in the broader ancient Near East; this symbol was also incorporated into the design of administrative seals that were used in and around Jerusalem in the later monarchy of Judah (more on this below).

6. In the LXX, this ornament is described as a golden plaque (πέταλον) incised with the words Αγίασμα κυριου "Holiness of the Lord."

7. Here I draw from Alfred Gell's writings on object agency, specifically, his description of the "technology of enchantment." Things produced with skill, such as the inscriptions on the high priest's dress, can captivate audiences and demand an encounter between object and viewer. See Alfred Gell, "The Technology of Enchantment and the Enchantment of Technology," in *The Art of Anthropology: Essays and Diagrams* (Oxford: Berg, 2006), 159–86,

by the fact that this narrative consecrates much textual space to the descriptions of Aaron's dress, with a clear emphasis on the crafting and meaning of these inscriptions. This narrative also communicates their importance in overt ways: (1) YHWH, their divine designer, provides detailed instructions to Moses about their craft production and their ritual significance; and (2) their design as inscribed, precious things is unique in the Tabernacle. To this we can add that their script and layout onto Aaron's uniform also impart meaning about their ritual power and serve to infuse Aaron's uniform with the representational power connected to inscriptions from the southern Levant and broader Near East.

Scholarship that reads texts "as images" also highlights an important distinction between these inscriptions and the other ritual things crafted for the Tabernacle. Unlike other media (e.g., the other pieces of Aaron's uniform) texts are material *and* linguistic things that communicate through their design, context, and their words.[8] The inscriptions on Aaron's uniform therefore demand an approach that considers the multimodality of these inscriptions.[9] In this narrative, the design and layout of the inscriptions on Aaron's uniformed body encode a visual and spatial commentary about their ritual power that complements the message articulated by their words.[10]

To address this facet of these inscriptions, I focus upon two specific aspects of their design: their script, in the style of "seal engravings"; and their layout on Aaron's uniformed body upon the areas of his head, shoulders, and chest. I propose that the shared seal script visually unifies these three sets of inscriptions into a cohesive visual display and connects Aaron's uniform (and office) to the representational authority of seals and sealing practices in the Southern Levant. I also argue that the layout of the inscriptions on Aaron's uniform forges a spatial relationship between Aaron's body and the bodies of inscribed vessels in the southern Levant, which were used in cultic spaces. Together, these design elements communicate the idea of Aaron as an authorized ritual vessel in YHWH's Tabernacle. Instead

---

quote on 144; see also Alfred Gell, "The Critique of the Index," in *Art and Agency: An Anthropological Theory* (Oxford: Oxford University, 2013 [originally 1998]), 74–5.

8. See the approach in Gunther Kress and Theo van Leeuwen, *Reading Images: The Grammar of Visual Design* (2nd ed.; London: Routledge, [1996] 2006); and Carey Jewitt, ed., *The Routledge Handbook of Multimodal Analysis* (2nd ed.; London: Routledge, 2017).

9. For example of the association that can arise between a particular word, script, color, and medium, we might think of the iconic design of the "GOODYEAR" logo, which for many evokes the image of a blimp in the sky. This logo has become enmeshed with a specific form of advertising that is now iconic of this brand of rubber and tires.

10. For such an approach to the visual and material communicative meaning of the inscriptions in Aaron's uniform, see Christian Frevel, "On Instant Scripture and Proximal Texts: Some Insights into the Sensual Materiality of Texts and Their Ritual Roles in the Hebrew Bible and Beyond," *Postscripts* 8 (2012): 68–72; for an application of this approach to the study of Hebrew ritual texts, see James W. Watts, "The Three Dimensions of Scripture," in *Iconic Books and Texts*, ed. James W. Watts (London: Equinox, 2013), 9–32.

of a collection of dusty, inscribed pots left in the Tabernacle, Exodus 28 and 39 remake the high priest's body into a ritual vessel that plays a dual function, as both Israel's dedication and as a "holy" vessel dedicated to YHWH's cult. And, seeing that Aaron's body is the only inscribed display in the Tabernacle that serves a representational function, we might further extrapolate that in this narrative, Israel's high priest takes over the role of these ritual objects in YHWH's shrine.

2. The Meaning of the Inscriptions on the High Priest's Uniform in Exodus 28 and 39

Much of scholarship has focused upon how the design of this inscribed uniform ascribes Aaron ritual and royal power.[11] First let us consider the tribal stones set into Aaron's uniform: YHWH instructs Moses they will enable the twelve collective tribal bodies to be represented in his shrine. This suggests that the stone inscriptions do the work of inscribed dedications that represent worshipers in temples before the gods.[12] As Frevel writes, "By adding the dedicatory or votive inscription, Aaron in a way becomes himself a votive or representative gift given by the Israelite tribes."[13] The diverse and costly materials used to make these inscriptions also communicate the priesthood's economic resources to procure rare materials through long-distance trade.[14]

11. Frevel, "On Instant Scripture," 68–72; Christophe Nihan and Julia Rhyder, "Aaron's Vestments in Exodus 28 and Priestly Leadership," in *Debating Authority: Concepts of Leadership in the Pentateuch and the Former Prophets*, ed. Katharina Pyschny and Sarah Schulz (Berlin: de Gruyter, 2018), 52–7, 59–61; Christophe Nihan, "Le pectoral d'Aaron et la figure du grand prêtre dans les traditions sacerdotales du Pentateuque," in *Congress Volume Stellenbosch 2016*, ed. Louis C. Jonker, Gideon R. Kotzé, and Christl M. Maier (VTSup 177; Leiden: Brill, 2017), 38–40; and for a comparative approach to this clothing as ancient Near Eastern dress, see Carmen Joy Imes, "Between Two Worlds: The Functional and Symbolic Significance of the High Priestly Regalia," in *Dress and Clothing in the Hebrew Bible: "For All Her Household are Clothed in Crimson"*, ed. Antonios Finitsis (New York: T&T Clark, 2019), 29–62.

12. See Jeffrey Tigay, "The Priestly Reminder Stones and Ancient Near Eastern Votive Practices," in *Shai le-Sara Japhet: Studies in the Bible, Its Exegesis and Language Presented to Sara Japhet*, ed. Mosheh Bar Asher, Dalit Rom-Shiloni, Emanuel Tov and Nili Wazana (Jerusalem: Bialik, 2007), 342, 350–5; William H. Propp, *Exodus 19–40: A New Translation with Introduction and Commentary* (Garden City NY: Doubleday, 2006), 438, 523–5; and Christian Frevel, "Gifts to the Gods? Votives as Communication Markers in Sanctuaries and other Places in the Bronze and Iron Ages in Palestine/Israel," in *"From Ebla to Stellenbosch" Syro-Palestinian Religions and the Hebrew Bible*, ed. Cornelius Izak and Louis Jonker (Wiesbaden: Harrassowitz Verlag, 2008), 31–2; see also Frevel, "On Instant Scripture," 57, 68–72; and Nihan and Rhyder, "Aaron's Vestments," 559–61.

13. Frevel, "On Instant Scripture," 70.

14. Nihan and Rhyder, "Aaron's Vestments," 54–5; see too Zwickel, "Die Bedeutung des hohenpriesterlichen Brustschildes," 63–5.

9. Aaron's Body as Ritual Vessel   163

Another view is that these texts operate in the same way as inscribed foundation deposits: rather than a royal patron, however, the tribal stones commemorate how Israel's twelve tribes financed the building of the Tabernacle (Exod 25:1-7).[15] Their connection to the Ephod and the Urim and Thummim has been understood as critical evidence that these stones were seen to have divinatory power (at the very least by later Jewish audiences of this story).[16] And, as will be argued here, their design and execution as precious stones inscribed in a seal script suggest that like stone seals, the tribal inscriptions have both representative and amuletic power.[17]

The design of the inscribed golden rosette set into Aaron's headdress also conflates several forms of inscriptional and ritual power. However, this inscription differs in form and in content from the tribal stone inscriptions. Israel's dedications are incised into precious stones, a durable medium expected of seals, whereas the inscription attached to Aaron's headdress is inscribed onto pure gold, a highly malleable metal. According to YHWH, the headdress appeases YHWH when Aaron enters into his presence with Israel's gifts (Exod 28:38).[18] The design of this text as a golden ornament that is worn on the body and is marked with the deity's name evokes the image of an inscribed, golden amulet.[19]

There is another important difference. Like the tribal stones, the headdress inscription also incised in the manner of a seal. However, the formula, קדש ליהוה "dedicated to YHWH," is not the formula that we would expect for a seal but is that

---

15. See Othmar Keel, "Die Brusttasche des Hohenpriesters als Element priesterschriftlicher Theologie," in *Das Manna fällt auch heute noch. Beiträge zur Geschichte und Theologie des Alten, Ersten Testaments*, ed. Frank-Lothar Hossfeld and Ludger Schwienhorst-Schönberger (HBS 44; Freiburg: Herder, 2004), 285-6.

16. For an overview of scholarship, see Phillipe Guillaume, "Aaron and the Amazing Mantic Coat," in *Studies on Magic and Divination in the Biblical World*, ed. Helen R. Jacobus, Anne K. de Hemmer Gudme, and Phillipe Guillaume (Piscataway, NJ: Gorgias, 2013), 101-17, esp. 103-6.

17. See Judith Wegner, "The Evolution of Ancient Egyptian Seals and Sealing Systems," in *Seals and Sealing in the Ancient World: Case Studies from the Near East, Egypt, the Aegean, and South Asia*, ed. Marta Ameri, Sarah Kielt Costello, Gregg Jamison and Sarah Jarmer Scott (Cambridge: Cambridge University, 2018), 229-57; see also D. Ben-Tor, "The Administrative Use of Scarabs during the Middle Kingdom," in *Seals and Sealing in the Ancient World: Case Studies from the Near East, Egypt, the Aegean, and South Asia*, ed. Marta Ameri, Sarah Kielt Costello, Gregg Jamison and Sarah Jarmer Scott (Cambridge: Cambridge University, 2018), 289-301.

18. "It shall be on Aaron's forehead, and Aaron shall take on himself any guilt incurred in the holy offering that the Israelites consecrate as their sacred donations; it shall always be on his forehead, in order that they may find favor before the LORD" (NRSV).

19. Two silver miniature scrolls discovered in an elite burial complex in Jerusalem (late seventh-sixth centuries BCE) offer an exemplar of the use of metal to craft protective amulets. See Jeremy D. Smoak, *The Priestly Blessing in Inscription & Scripture: The Early History of Numbers 6:24-26* (Oxford: Oxford University Press, 2015).

used to mark a dedicated object. For example, the term קדש "dedicated" is attested on inscribed vessels in the southern Levant, which were dedicated to the service of a god.[20]

The golden blossom described as the site of this inscription is most likely a stylized rosette. The rosette was a well-known emblem that was used in the design of the clothing of royal and divine figures in the ancient Near East.[21] In late monarchal Judah the rosette was also used in royal sealing practices in and around Jerusalem.[22] It therefore seems significant that this icon of royal power, which was also used in Judean royal seals, is inscribed with an inscription that is inscribed using a seal script. This suggests that the seal-script and rosette design of this inscription work together as a visual means of connecting Aaron to royal administrative power. And, as a communicative complex, the seal script, dedication formula, and layout of this inscription authorize Aaron to do the work of a ritual vessel in YHWH's shrine.

3. *Aaron's Inscribed Clothing and Seals, Sealed Things, and Sealing Practices*

We might complement the above analysis of the design of these inscriptions with a more narrowed focus on the repeated detail that they are all to be incised in the manner of seals. The description of the seal script used in these inscriptions (פתוחי חתם "seal engravings" in Exod 28:11, 21, 36; 39:6, 14, 30) stands out because it is repeated so often in this passage but is otherwise unattested in the Hebrew Bible.[23]

---

20. Jeremy D. Smoak, "Holy Bowls: Inscribing Holiness in Ancient Israel and Judah," *MAARAV* 23 (2019): 69–92.

21. See A. Leo. Oppenheim, "Golden Garments of the Gods," *JNES* 8 (1949): 172–93; Jane M. Cahill, "Royal Rosettes Fit for a King," *BAR* 23 (1997): 48–57, 68–9; and Salvatore Gaspa, "Golden Decorations in Assyrian Textiles: An Interdisciplinary Approach," in *Prehistoric, Ancient Near Eastern and Aegean Textiles and Dress*, ed. Mary Harlow, Cécile Michel, and Marie-Louise Nosch (Oxford: Oxbow Books, 2015), 227–44.

22. Jane M. Cahill, "Rosette Stamp Seal Impressions from Ancient Judah," *IEJ* 45 (1995): 230–52; and Ido Koch and Oded Lipschits, "The Rosette Stamped Jar Handle System and the Kingdom of Judah at the End of the First Temple Period," *ZDPV* 129 (2013): 55–78.

23. Indeed, we might ask why it is that the narrative repeats this detail six times but is silent about the arrangement of the tribal stones. YHWH specifies that they are to be arranged according to the tribal ancestors' birth orders (perhaps that in Gen 35:22–26). However, he does not list the names of the tribes, or clarify which set of six tribal names is assigned to which shoulder piece, or what the different stones and their colors signify or their connection to specific tribes; we also do not know why the headpiece text is inscribed in gold rather than a precious stone. For a summary of later traditions about the meaning and placement of the stones, see Houtman, *Exodus*, 487, 497–8, 502–3.

Scholars overwhelmingly understand this detail as a reflection of the technical expertise needed to create these inscriptions. Accordingly, the phrase פתוחי חתם is most commonly understood to be a reference to "mirror writing" (the inscription of these words *intaglio*), which is assumed by many scholars to be the technique used to incise these texts into the tribal stones and into the golden ornament.[24] This engraving technique was used to ensure a text's correct orientation when a seal was impressed onto a surface.[25]

While it is true that seals created as legal/economic authorizing text-objects, made to be impressed into a text, were inscribed in "mirror" or "reverse" writing (*intaglio*), the explanation that this expression is a reference to "mirror writing" does not account for the fact that the inscriptions in Exodus 28 and 39 are not actually seals, made for impression, but are created to be displayed, ritual objects. Seals that were made to be used as votives or dedications were not inscribed in "mirror" writing but were inscribed in the positive. In such cases, there was no need to inscribe the seal *intaglio*, because it was not made to be impressed into another medium but was in and of itself accessed as a text.[26] All of this suggests that in the literary imagination of this story, where P is crafting an image of the high priest's clothing, this detail does not signify that the inscriptions are incised in reverse writing (YHWH is not reading these words backward).[27] Limiting this expression to a technical term related to their crafting overlooks how this script operates in this story as a critical part of the visual design of Aaron's uniform. Rather, this detail visually interconnects the three sets of inscriptions and associates them with the authority of seals and sealing practices.

If we are to take a visual design approach to these inscriptions, we must also look to the broader design of personal seals and to the script used in seal inscriptions. A more fruitful comparison is to consider how this script connects the inscribed priestly stones to the representational power of seals in economic and legal contexts, as well as to the use of precious stone seals as personalized objects that represented worshipers before the gods.[28] Moreover, scholarship that approaches writing as a facet of visual culture increasingly highlights how the

---

24. E.g., Houtman translates this phrase as follows: "Through application of the seal engraving technique" (*Exodus*, 476, 490, 512); see also Nihan, "Le Pectoral," 37; Frevel, "On Instant Scripture," 71; contra Tigay, "Priestly Reminder Stones," 353.

25. See Holly Pittman, "Seals and Sealings in the Sumerian World," in *The Sumerian World*, ed. Harriet Crawford (New York: Routledge, 2013), 321; Ruth Hestrin and Michal Dayagi-Mendels, *Inscribed Seals: First Temple Period Hebrew, Ammonite, Moabite, Phoenician and Aramaic from the Collections of the Israel Museum and the Israel Department of Antiquities and Museums* (Jerusalem: Israel Museum, 1979), 8–10.

26. Pittman, "Seals and Sealings," 321.

27. Tigay also doubts that these inscriptions are incised in "mirror" writing in this story ("Priestly Reminder Stones," 353).

28. See Nihan and Rhyder, "Aaron's Vestments," 54; also William W. Hallo, "'As the Seal Upon Thy Heart': Glyptic Roles in the Biblical World," *BR* 1 (1985): 20–7.

choices made in the display of texts—including their layout and script (or font)—and the broader spatial and social contexts in which they are used—contribute to their iconic load.[29]

As an example of how this principle operates in the analysis of a text created in a literary space, we might look to the slogan inscribed into the façade of the headquarters of the Ministry of Truth in George Orwell's novel *1984*. The ekphrastic description of this writing and its setting (the headquarters of The Ministry of Truth) highlights how this slogan mirrors both the language ideologies and oppressive policies of the Party in this story:

> The Ministry of Truth—Minitrue, in Newspeak—was startlingly different from any other object in sight. It was an enormous pyramidal structure of glittering white concrete, soaring up, terrace after terrace, three hundred meters into the air. From where Winston stood it was just possible to read, picked out on its white face in elegant lettering, the three slogans of the Party:
>
> WAR IS PEACE
> FREEDOM IS SLAVERY
> IGNORANCE IS STRENGTH.[30]

These words, when disassociated from the towering façade of this building and their terrifying effect, take on a different meaning (e.g., scrawled onto a bathroom wall, or set onto a bumper sticker, or printed onto a coffee mug). This example reminds us that when we analyze texts, context is everything—and that a text's context can extend beyond its material form to include the broader social spaces in which it is viewed, used, or discussed.

With this understanding in mind, the seal-style script in Exodus 28 and 39 creates an image of these inscriptions in the mind of the audiences of this story in a way that connects these inscriptions, and Aaron's uniform, to the crafting, use, and power of seals in diverse contexts. In the ancient Near East, seals were not merely a measure of the person or emblematic of economic authority, but they conferred status in their own right as coveted things and icons of social status, representative power, and economic authority.[31] This is in part because seals in the ancient Near East were a written representational medium perhaps more deeply connected to

---

29. See Peter Unseth, "Sociolinguistic Parallels between Choosing Scripts and Languages," *Written Language and Literacy* 8 (2005): 19–42; Jürgen Spitzmüller, "Floating Ideologies: Metamorphoses of Graphic 'Germanness,'" in *Orthography as Social Action: Scripts, Spelling, Identity and Power*, ed. Alexandra Jaffe, Jannis Androutsopoulos, Mark Sebba and Sally Johnson (Berlin: de Gruyter, 2009), 255–88; Alice Mandell, "Reading and Writing Remembrance in Canaan: Early Alphabetic Inscriptions as Multimodal Objects," *HeBAI* 2 (2018): 253–84.

30. George Orwell, *1984* (Boston: Houghton Mifflin Harcourt, [1949] 2020), 5.

31. Leonard Gorelick and A. John Gwinnett, "The Ancient Near Eastern Cylinder Seal as Social Emblem and Status Symbol," *JNES* 49 (1990): 45–56, here 45, 47.

the body than any other type of text—seals were designed to be used by and worn on the body—and to signify individual and institutional bodies.[32]

The connection between seals and the human body is an important one and perhaps explains, in part, why it was important for the ritual logic of these inscriptions that they be worn on Aaron's body through the medium of his clothing, as opposed to being incised on objects and placed in the Tabernacle or carved into the structure of this tent. Seals were made according to the scale of the human body, as they were typically crafted to be held, manipulated, and impressed by the human hand.[33] For example, cylinder seals were designed to be rolled, whereas stamp seals were scaled to be impressed by the hand.[34] Seals were also made to be worn on the bodies of their owners as jewelry, as bracelets or necklaces, or attached to their clothing with a seal-pin; signet seals were also worn as rings or on necklaces.[35] As precious and portable things worn on the body, seals also functioned as amulets that conferred protection on their wearers.[36] In burial practices, those seals placed "by the shoulders, hands, and waist" suggests a similar placement during the life of the interred, either on clothing or as jewelry

---

32. See Dominique Collon, "How Seals Were Worn and Carried: The Archaeological and Iconographic Evidence," in *Proceedings of the XLVe Rencontre Assyriologique Internationale Part II: Yale University: Seals and Seal Impressions*, ed. William W. Hallo and Irene J. Winter (Bethesda, MD: CDL, 2001), 15–30; see also Joanna S. Smith, "Authenticity, Seal Recarving, and Authority in the Ancient Near East and Eastern Mediterranean," in *Seals and Sealing in the Ancient World: Case Studies from the Near East, Egypt, the Aegean, and South Asia*, ed. Marta Ameri, Sarah Kielt Costello, Gregg Jamison and Sarah Jarmer Scott (Cambridge: Cambridge University Press, 2018), 100–1.

33. The terminology of seals in the ancient Near East also reflects this inherent connection between seals and the body: e.g., the Sumerian ⁿᵃ⁴*kišib* (i.e., stone object *kišib*) has the meaning "seal" but also the meaning of "hand" (*kišib* without the determinative); this is loaned into Akkadian as a noun *kišibbu* "seal," though the logogram KIŠIB represents the word *kunukku* "seal" in Akkadian. The Egyptian term *djebat*, which refers to a New Kingdom Period signet seal, derives from the word "finger." For a discussion, see Smith, "Authenticity, Seal Recarving, and Authority," 101; Wegner, "The Evolution of Ancient Egyptian Seals and Sealing Systems," 231; see also Karen Radner, "Siegelpraxis (Sealing Practice): A. Philologisch," *Reallexikon der Assyriologie und Vorderasiatischen Archäologie* 12 (2010): 466–9.

34. Edith Porada, "Why Cylinder Seals? Engraved Cylindrical Seal Stones of the Ancient Near East, Fourth to First Millennium B.C.," *Art Bulletin* 75 (1993): 563–82; Pittman, "Seals and Sealings," 324–9.

35. Beatrice Teissier, *Ancient Near Eastern Cylinder Seals from the Marcopolic Collection* (Berkeley: University of California Press, 1984), xiii–xiv.

36. Collon, "How Seals Were Worn," 21; see also the amuletic and administrative use of scarab seals in Egypt and the Levant in the first and second millennium BCE in Wegner, "The Evolution of Ancient Egyptian Seals," 229–57; see also Ben-Tor, "The Administrative Use of Scarabs," 289–301.

directly worn on the body.[37] In Exodus 28 and 39, this relationship between the body and seals is reflected in the placement of these inscribed stone inscriptions, which are attached to Aaron's body through the medium of his uniform.[38] This is also expressed in their representational function, to signify the bodies of the tribes in YHWH's presence.

While seals were used to represent people in economic and legal interactions, their representative power could extend to ritual spaces.[39] Seals created specifically for a ritual purpose or as prestige display objects, to be deposited in a shrine or temple, were crafted to be more visually appealing and tended to be made of finer materials than seals used only for transactions. Those seals, like Israel's inscribed stones, that served a dedicatory or votive function, operated differently than those used with a signature function; such objects invested their representative power in representing people before deities.[40] When left near a cult statue or worn on a deity's body, they functioned as reminders of a worshiper's presence and their gift.[41]

In addition, the high degree of skill needed to produce seals is referenced through the elite status and cross-specialization of Bezalel and Oholiab, the craft specialists who make these seal-script inscriptions (see Exod 38:22–23; 39:6, 14, 30).[42] The materials used to make these seal-script inscriptions—precious stones and gold—rather than stone, bone, clay, or a less costly medium—distinguish these inscriptions as seals made for a special use. Israel's stones stand out in the Tabernacle space as costly and exotic materials that required access to long distance trade. It is also implied in this narrative, in the crafting of the tribal names into a hard medium, that these objects are meant to be permanent representatives of the tribes. Their use in the Tabernacle, a restricted-access space that is under YHWH's watchful gaze, also communicates that these seals are forever protected from recarving.[43] In this story, the tribal stones are eternal ambassadors for Israel in YHWH's presence; their design as a permanent part of Aaron's uniform speaks

---

37. Collon cites burials in the Royal Cemetery at Ur as well as exemplars from the Levant that date to the second and first millennia BCE ("How Seals Were Worn," 19–21). See also Gorelick and Gwinnett, "The Ancient Near Eastern Cylinder Seal," 45, 47.

38. See also Jer 22:24 and Hag 2:23 for the intimate connection between seals and the bodies they represent.

39. Hallo, "As a Seal Upon Thy Heart," 24–6. See, too, the use of seals in the *maqlû* series to seal the lips of figurines who represent an enemy (Teissier, *Ancient Near Eastern Cylinder Seals*, xxvii).

40. Pittman, "Seals and Sealings," 321.

41. Hallo, "As a Seal Upon Thy Heart," 25.

42. For this reminder of the diverse skill sets needed by seal makers, I am indebted to Nadia Ben-Marzouk.

43. The act of recarving a seal not only enacted a change in its representational authority but also was a statement about both the former owner and the person whom it represented moving forward. See Smith, "Authenticity, Seal Recarving, and Authority," 120–1.

to his role as the conduit for this interaction. All of this suggests that the references to "seal engravings" in this story therefore are not merely a comment about the craft production but connect these inscriptions (and Aaron's uniform) to the power of seals to represent human bodies and institutions in these diverse settings.

To better understand what the specific reference to the design of all of the tribal stones in a "seal script" might mean to an audience of this story, either in late monarchic Judah or in the Yehud, we must also consider the broader design and iconicity of seals in the southern Levant.[44] As discussed, a visual design perspective suggests that all three texts are to be written in the style of "seal engravings" (פתוחי חתם), in part, to visually connect them as a cohesive textual unit on the high priest's uniform, in spite of the differences in their words, medium (diverse precious stones and a golden ornament), color (the tribal stones are made of different stone types), or location on Aaron's uniform. We can now step outside of the immediate narrative to consider the iconic load of these inscriptions, set into a first millennium BCE context. Thinking about the script as an integral aspect of the visual design of these inscriptions raises the question of how we might use this detail to anchor the description of these inscriptions into a particular period in Israel's history. This raises the question of what these inscriptions "looked" like to the writers and ancient audiences of this narrative. If we posit that Exodus 28 and 39 were composed sometime during the later phase of the Judean monarchy shortly after the destruction of the temple (the Iron IIIC Neo-Babylonian Period), we might consider the script described in this narrative to be a reference to the script style associated with Hebrew seals in the first millennium BCE. The letter forms in Old Hebrew seals tend to be less cursive than when the Hebrew Script was used in other inscriptional types, for example, in those texts executed in ink on pottery sherds. For this reason, the script used in seals is described as "formal," "lapidary," and most recently as "a formal cursive script."[45] Over time, this script

---

44. See the exemplars in Nahman Avigad, *Hebrew Bullae from the Time of Jeremiah: Remnants of a Burnt Archive* (Jerusalem: Israel Exploration Society, 1986); Nahman Avigad and Benjamin Sass, *Corpus of West Semitic Stamp Seals* (Jerusalem: Israel Academy of Sciences and Humanities, 1997); Nahman Avigad, "Bullae and Seals from a Post-Exilic Judean Archive/בולות וחותמות מתוך ארכיון ממלכתי מימי שיבת ציון." *Qedem* 4 (1976): 1–36; Benjamin Sass, "The Pre-Exilic Hebrew Seals: Iconism vs. Aniconism," in *Studies in the Iconography of Northwest Semitic Inscribed Seals: Proceedings of a Symposium Held in Fribourg on April 17–20, 1991*, ed. Benjamin Sass and Christoph Uehlinger (OBO 125; Fribourg: University Press, 1993), 194–256.

45. To be clear, not all seals were written in a less cursive or earlier script style; however, because seals were written in a hard, durable medium, they tended to be written in a less fluid script than texts created out of other media. See Avigad, *Hebrew Bullae*, 113; see Larry G. Herr, *The Scripts of Ancient Northwest Semitic Seals* (Missoula, MT: Scholars Press for the Harvard Semitic Museum, 1978), 79–80; Christopher A. Rollston, *Writing and Literacy In the World of Ancient Israel: Epigraphic Evidence From the Iron Age* (Atlanta, GA: SBL

style, which was more conservative, became iconic both of seals and of their authority.⁴⁶

If we view the design of the stones to reflect actual sealing practices in the southern Levant, particularly those in and around Jerusalem, their design points to sealing practices after the ninth century BCE. Only after the ninth century is there evidence for the use of writing on seals.⁴⁷ The aniconism of the stone seals in this narrative further places their design no earlier than the late seventh–early sixth centuries BCE, a period corresponding to the end of the Judean monarchy and the Neo-Babylonian period.⁴⁸ It is debated whether or not the trend in aniconic seals in Judah was religiously motivated, as it is also attested in Trans-Jordanian seals from the late seventh–sixth centuries BCE.⁴⁹ Anchoring this story in a later monarchal context raises the question of what non-linguistic marks might have been associated with the design of these aniconic stone seals. And while this narrative does not mention borders and registers, such markings provided internal organization to inscribed seals, which were aniconic during the late

Press, 2010), 96–7; also Andrew G. Vaughn, "Paleographic Dating of Judean Seals and Its Significance for Biblical Research," *BASOR* 313 (1999): 58–9; see also Phillip Zhakevich, "The Tools of an Israelite Scribe: A Semantic Study of the Terms Signifying the Tools and Materials of Writing in Biblical Hebrew" (PhD diss., University of Texas Austin, 2015), 55–7; 147–9; see also the section on glyptics in Philip Zhakevich, *Scribal Tools in Ancient Israel: A Study of Biblical Hebrew Terms for Writing Materials and Implements*, History, Archaeology, and Culture of the Levant 9 (University Park, Pennsylvania: Eisenbrauns/The Pennsylvania State University Press, 2020).

46. E.g., Times New Roman font is a H(igh)-register font used for writings considered to be authoritative (hopefully, like this essay); Comic Sans, however, is viewed as a L(ow)-register font and is considered to be more appropriate for less formal writings.

47. See Oded Lipschits and David S. Vanderhooft, "Yehud Stamp Impressions in the Fourth Century B.C.E., A Time of Administrative Consolidation?" in *Judah and the Judeans in the 4th Century BCE*, ed. Oded Lipschits, Gary N. Knoppers, and Rainer Albertz (Winona Lake, IN: Eisenbrauns, 2007), 75–94; and Lipschits and Vanderhooft, *The Yehud Stamp Impressions*.

48. The ninth-century bullae found in the City of David are anepigraphic, whereas there is an increase in inscribed seals in the later eighth century BCE. See Ronny Reich, Eli Shukron, and Omri Lernau, "Recent Discoveries in the City of David, Jerusalem," *IEJ* 57 (2007): 156, 162; and William M. Schniedewind, *A Social History of Hebrew* (New Haven, CT: Yale University Press, 2013), 103–4.

49. See Mitka R. Golub, "Aniconism and Personal Names on Iron Age II Inscribed Stamp Seals from Judah, Israel and Neighbouring Kingdoms," *TA* 45 (2018): 164; Christoph Uehlinger, "Northwest Semitic Inscribed Seals, Iconography and Syro-Palestinian Religions of Iron Age II: Some Afterthoughts and Conclusions," in *Studies in the Iconography of Northwest Semitic Inscribed Seals: Proceedings of a Symposium Held in Fribourg on April 17–20, 1991*, ed. Benjamin Sass and Christoph Uehlinger (OBO 125; Fribourg: University Press, 1993), 283–4; and Ariel Winderbaum, "The Iconic Seals and Bullae of the Iron Age," in *The Summit of the City of David Excavations 2005–2008 Final Reports Vol. 1*, ed. Eliat Mazar (Jerusalem: Shoham, 2015), 363–420.

monarchic period.[50] Perhaps such design elements were also a part of the image that this description of the stone seals conjured in the minds of the audiences of this narrative.[51]

Before we conclusively date this description of the tribal stones to the late seventh–early sixth centuries BCE based on this criteria, it is important to remember that: (1) these inscriptions are in an imaginative narrative, which conflates aspects of diverse text types; and (2) that seals are typically more conservative text types than more ephemeral writings.[52] This means that the design of the tribal stones in this story might also reflect inscriptional traditions from a slightly earlier period than the composition of this story. For example, early Yehud stamp seals reflect an Aramaic scribal tradition, and yet seals produced in and around Jerusalem retained the earlier layout used by the Judean chancellery.[53] The descriptions of these inscriptions therefore do not conclusively pinpoint a date for the composition of this story but rather suggest that the inscriptions are modeled after inscriptions that spanned the seventh—fifth centuries BCE (at the very least, after the eighth century BCE).

As discussed, scripts can become highly iconic and derive importance as visual indexes of linguistic communities that use writing, as well as of communities that share a geopolitical or religious identity.[54] While the Old Hebrew script is associated with the Iron Age, audiences engaging with this narrative in the periods following

---

50. See Sass, "The Pre-Exilic Hebrew Seals," 204–6.

51. The issue of the aniconic design of the tribal stones also raises the question of whether or not YHWH's decision that the tribes are to be represented by aniconic stones in this narrative takes an ideological stance regarding the design of personal seals more broadly. Are Israel's seals, which are inscribed but otherwise unadorned in this narrative, meant to set a precedent/model for aniconic seals? That is, do the tribal stones serve as ideal proto-seals in a similar way that the Tabernacle operates as a proto-temple (to establish that this was the proper way to design a seal and that this practice was mandated by YHWH in Israel's formative years)?

52. E.g., Type 1 (eighteen according to Oded Lipschits and David S. Vanderhooft's classificatory scheme) uses the formula *l*+PN; a doubled line-register intersects the seal's inscription. See Oded Lipschits and David S. Vanderhooft, *The Yehud Stamp Impressions: A Corpus of Inscribed Impressions from the Persian and Hellenistic Periods in Judah* (Winona Lake, IN: Eisenbrauns, 2011), 84–8. A further complication is that a seal script can represent the cultural identity of the craftspeople making a text, rather than the person who commissioned the seal. See André Lemaire, "Les critères non-iconographiques de la classification des sceaux nord-ouest sémitiques inscrits," in *Studies in the Iconography of Northwest Semitic Inscribed Seals: Proceedings of a Symposium Held in Fribourg on April 17–20, 1991*, ed. Benjamin Sass and Christoph Uehlinger (OBO 125; Fribourg: Vandenheoch & Ruprecht, 1993), 5–7, 21.

53. Several scholars date this story to the fifth–fourth centuries BCE and connect these inscriptions (or their literary forms) to the Yehud seals. See Nihan, "Le Pectoral," 37; Zwickel, *Edelsteine*, 45–9; and Keel, "Die Brusttasche des Hohenpriesters," 384–6.

54. See, e.g., Amir Sharifi, "Orthography and Calligraphic Ideology in an Iranian-American Heritage School," in *Orthography as Social Action: Scripts, Spelling, Identity*

the fall of Judah most likely associated the description of a seal-style (i.e., more conservative) script in this story with the Paleo- or Neo-Hebrew script, which continued to be used in limited contexts in the southern Levant.[55] Specifically, later Jewish descriptions of the high priest's garments speak to a widespread tradition that the Paleo- or Neo-Hebrew script was used to write the headdress inscription.[56] This interest in the inscription is in part due to its content, which references the name YHWH in this story. In the second half of the first millennium BCE, the use of this script to write Hebrew, rather than the Aramaic-derived Hebrew script, was highly ideological. The more archaic Hebrew script was used in this period for a more limited range of writings and was iconic of Judah's former political and religious institutions.[57] This custom suggests that this older script phase evolved into a high register script.

Turning to the headdress inscription, it is an inscribed ornament that is shaped like a rosette. As discussed, this symbol was used in royal costumes in the broader ancient Near East, but also in Judean stamp seals from the later seventh century BCE (see Figure 1).[58] This suggests that this inscription conjured both the royal power of foreign kings and local administrative practices in and around Jerusalem.[59] The metal medium into which this text is inscribed may have also evoked metal signets, or perhaps coinage—both of which transposed the authority of sealing practices and their script style into the medium of precious metals.[60] The rosette

and Power, ed. Alexandra Jaffe, Jannis Androutsopoulos, Mark Sebba and Sally Johnson (Berlin: de Gruyter, 2009), 225-54.

55. This is also the understanding in Zwickel, "Die Bedeutung des hohenpriesterlichen Brustschildes," 46.

56. E.g., Josephus views the divine name to be written in "sacred letters with the name of God," which seems to refer to the Paleo-Hebrew script (Josephus *Ant.* 3.176).

57. The iconic load of the Old Hebrew script is perhaps clearest in the practice of writers to shift to the Paleo-Hebrew script when writing out the divine name. See R. S. Hanson, "Paleo-Hebrew Scripts of the Hasmonaean Age," *BASOR* 175 (1964): 26-42; Joseph Naveh, *Early History of the Alphabet. An Introduction to West Semitic Epigraphy and Paleography* (Jerusalem: Magnes Press, 1997), 112-24; J. Naveh, "Scripts and Inscriptions in Ancient Samaria," *IEJ* 48.1/2 (1998): 91-100; Schniedewind, *A Social History of Hebrew*, 171-2.

58. See Oppenheim, "Golden Garments," 172-93; Gaspa, "Golden Decorations," 227-44; Koch and Lipschits, "The Rosette Stamped Jar Handle System," 68-9; and Cahill, "Rosette Stamp Seal Impressions," 230-52.

59. Ido Koch further argues that the usurpation of such Neo-Assyrian imperial emblems speak to King Josiah's political ambitions ("Pictorial Novelties in Context: Assyrian Iconography in Judah," in *The Last Century in the History of Judah: The Seventh Century BCE in Archaeological, Historical, and Biblical Perspectives*, ed. Filip Čapek and Oded Lipschits [Atlanta, GA: SBL Press, 2019], 154-9).

60. See Ephraim Stern, "Notes on the Development of Stamp-glyptic Art in Palestine during the Assyrian and Persian Periods," in *Uncovering Ancient Stones: Essays in Memory*

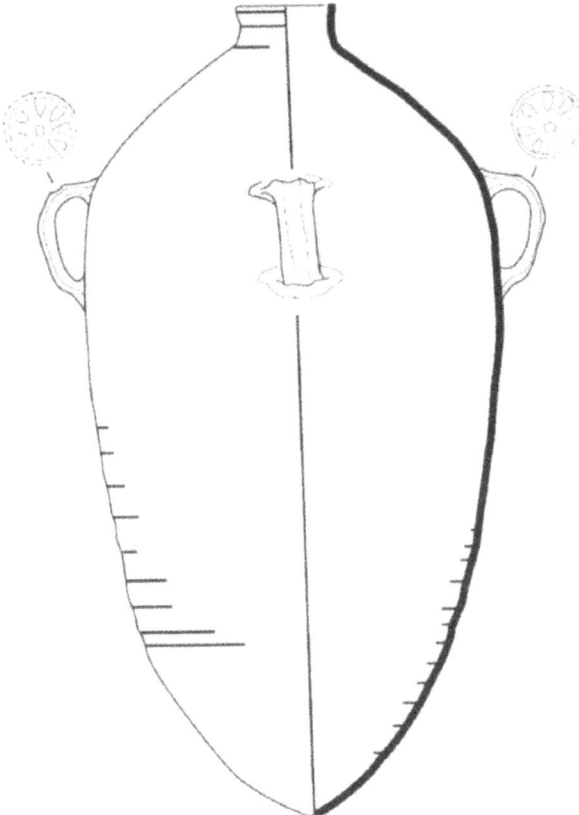

Figure 1 Rosette Stamp Seal Impressions on a Storage Jar (Site of Khirbet el-Garra). From Ido Koch and Oded Lipschits, "The Rosette Stamped Jar Handle System and the Kingdom of Judah at the End of the First Temple Period," *Zeitschrift des Deutschen Palästina-Vereins*, 59/1 (2013): 56, fig. 1. Used with permission. Image by I. Beit Arieh.

inscription is therefore doubly marked as a seal—it is a text that is written in a way that connects it to seals—and it is incised into an ornament that was shaped like a rosette, a form used in seals in the later Judean monarchy.

In summary, the repeated reference that these three sets of inscriptions are incised using a "seal" script is not merely a description of the technique used to incise words on a stone or metal medium. And this is not a reference to "reverse" writing. This detail is used here to add texture to their design and to their meaning. This shared script style is a powerful communicative mode, which visually connects these inscriptions into a cohesive display and ascribes them the authority of seals written in a high-register script. Seen in a Second Temple Period context, the seal script used to craft these three inscriptions marks them as important, authoritative, and highlights that these texts, which include the divine name, are written in a Hebrew, rather than an Aramaic script. In this way, the design of these inscriptions in the manner of seal inscriptions confers legal and royal authority and evokes the mystique of antiquity to both Aaron's uniform and his office.

4. Beyond the Words of the Text: Aaron's Body as an Inscribed Ritual Vessel

Now that we have addressed the materiality and design of these inscriptions, it is worth reconsidering their spatial layout on Aaron's uniform using the framework of multimodality. If we understand Aaron's uniformed body to operate as ritual vessel in the Tabernacle, it makes sense that the tribal names and words קדש ליהוה (holy to YHWH) should conform to the placement of similar words found on vessels used in temple, shrine, and domestic cultic contexts.[61] Studies of this narrative have argued that the layout of these inscriptions onto Aaron's uniform is meant to engage their readership. For example, the shoulder texts are seen to communicate vertically to a heavenly audience whereas the chest texts communicate horizontally to an earthy audience.[62] Another proposal about their placement relates more specifically to the position of the tribal stone inscriptions next to the Ephod and the Urim and Thummim. The placement of the stones is seen to relate to their function in priestly ritual and divination.[63] The placement of these inscriptions is also connected to the symbolic meanings associated with specific parts of Aaron's body. Aaron's head and chest are also those areas of the human body that are connected in the Hebrew Bible to complex emotions, cognitive abilities, and psychological states (e.g., the heart as the seat of understanding).[64] While these explanations rightfully take into consideration the display aspect of these three sets of inscriptions, it is important to keep in mind

---

of H. Neil Richardson, ed. L. M. Hopfe (Winona Lake, IN: Eisenbrauns, 1994), 245–55, here 246.

61. As a convenient reference, see the placement of the inscriptions on the corpus of inscribed dedicatory vessels and קדש bowls in Shmuel Ahituv, *Echoes from the Past: Hebrew and Cognate Inscriptions from the Biblical Period* (Jerusalem: Carta, 2008), 342–5.

62. See Propp, *Exodus*, 524; Tigay, "Priestly Reminder Stones," 342; Umberto Cassuto, *A Commentary on the Book of Exodus* (Jerusalem: Magnes Press, 1967), 376–7. Houtman views the shiny metal and placement of the inscription on Aaron's headdress to be a means of attracting YHWH's attention (*Exodus*, 516–17).

63. E.g., Guillaume argues that the tribal stones are dice. The design of the shoulder-piece masked certain tribal names; the chest piece stones are arranged in a way to ensure that all tribal names are always visible on Aaron's uniform. See Guillaume, "Aaron and the Amazing Mantic Coat," 110–11.

64. Propp connects these three parts of the high priest's body to "perception, thought, and agency" (*Exodus*, 524); in Frevel's study, their placement over Aaron's heart connects the inscribed gems to "the volitional, cognitive, and emotional center of a person" ("On Instant Scripture," 70). Houtman writes, "the high priest 'body and *soul*' must be Israel's representative" (*Exodus*, 497).

that they are not designed merely as texts made for reading or for viewing but to act as representational things in the Tabernacle. Any meaning that they have is entangled with the high priest's body and his movement in this ritual space.[65]

4.1 Inscription as a Visual and Material Act on Iron Age Dedicatory Vessels

To the arguments above about the ways in which the design of the inscriptions on Aaron's uniform was central to their ritual logic, we can add that the location of these inscriptions on Aaron's uniformed body mirrors the placement of similar formulae on the bodies of inscribed vessels filling a cultic function. This creates a spatial connection between Aaron's body and his cultic work and the design and function of inscribed ritual vessels in the Southern Levant. Such personalized dedications and "holy bowls" were typically inscribed on their rims, shoulders, and upper bodies—the areas corresponding to the head, shoulders, and chest of the human body.[66] First, I will examine the Iron Age Hebrew dedicatory formulae and its layout on vessels; then I will analyze the layout of the $qdš$ formula on vessels dedicated to the service of a god. At the end of this analysis, I will offer some suggestions as to why it is that P replaces the dedications and other types of inscribed cultic vessels that we might expect in a temple or shrine with an inscribed uniform, which is only worn by Israel's high priest (Figure 2).

According to YHWH, the tribal stones are inscribed dedications that ensure that Israel is represented in his presence. The power of such inscribed objects was activated or (perhaps better) enhanced by their degree of proximity to the deity's presence.[67] This explains why this narrative takes an interest in assuring that Israel's inscriptional representation remains inside of the Tabernacle.[68] Dedications in the southern Levant typically offer little more than the formula l-PN ("for PN"), and sometimes the name of a deity or a reference to the object itself (e.g., cup) being

---

65. Here I borrow from I. Hodder's writings regarding the "dialectic of dependence and dependency between humans and things" (*Studies in Human-Thing Entanglement* [2016], 14).

66. There is also an analogous spatial relationship between the placement of the words of the Shema in Deut 6:8 on the hand and forehead of the human body, and their inscription on the doorposts and entryways of homes and cities (6:9). The placement of the tefillin also transposes such practice onto the human body. See also Frevel, "On Instant Scripture," 62–8.

67. As Gudme writes, the "physical nearness" to the god's presence was the key to unlocking the power of such objects "as both a representation of the worshiper and a memento of the worshiper's gift" (Anne K. de Hemmer Gudme, *Before the God in This Place for Good Remembrance: A Comparative Analysis of the Aramaic Votive Inscriptions from Mount Gerizim*, [Berlin: de Gruyter, 2013], 89; see also 147). See the analysis of the dedicatory inscriptions from Gerizim, which span the fifth–second centuries BCE in Gudme, *Before the God in This Place for Good Remembrance*.

68. See Frevel, "On Instant Scripture," 70–1.

Figure 2 Inscribed Rim of a Stone Bowl, šmʿyw son of ʿzr (ninth–eighth century BCE). Shmuel Aḥituv, Esther Eshel, and Zeʾev Meshel, "The Inscriptions." Pages 75–6 in *Kuntillet ʿAjrud (Ḥorvat Teman): An Iron Age II Religious Site on the Judah-Sinai Border* (ed. Zeʾev Meshel; Jerusalem: Israel Exploration Society, 2012), Fig. 5.2, Inscription 1.1. Used with permission.

presented to the deity.[69] And yet, these inscriptions (and the very act of inscribing) transformed their medium (e.g., a seal or stone or ceramic vessel) into ritual agents that petitioned the gods for worshipers.[70]

By way of example, a 200 kg stone basin at the site of Kuntillet ʿAjrud contains a longer dedicatory formula than that of the tribal stones and includes a verb of blessing and a reference to the deity conferring the blessing (Figure 3).[71]

לעבדיו בן עדנה ברכ הא ליהו

(Stone Bowl) Belonging to Ōbadyāw, son of ʿAdnā. May he be blessed by YHW.

This inscription is located on the rim of the vessel, marking it as having a dedicatory function. While the bowl itself is not referred to directly in the inscription, it is

---

69. In such dedications the preposition *lamed* (here the *lamed* of ownership or *lamed auctoris*) connected people to ritual vessels and the presence of the gods. For a discussion of the genitive function of *lamed* (and parallels using the *lamed auctoris*), see GKC §29a-c; Joüon §130b. See also Yigael Yadin, "Recipients or Owners: A Note on the Samaria Ostraca," *IEJ* 9 (1959): 184–7; Yigael Yadin, "A Further Note on the Samaria Ostraca," *IEJ* 12 (1962): 64–6; contra Anson F. Rainey, "Private Seal-Impressions: A Note on Semantics," *IEJ* 16 (1966): 187–90; and Anson F. Rainey, "The Sitz im Leben of the Samaria Ostraca," *TA* 6 (1979): 91–4.

70. To be clear, I view the act of writing this formulary on a vessel to be a performative act in and of itself. See Mandell, "'I Bless You to YHWH," 150–3.

71. See Aḥituv, Eshel and Meshel, "The Inscriptions," 75–7.

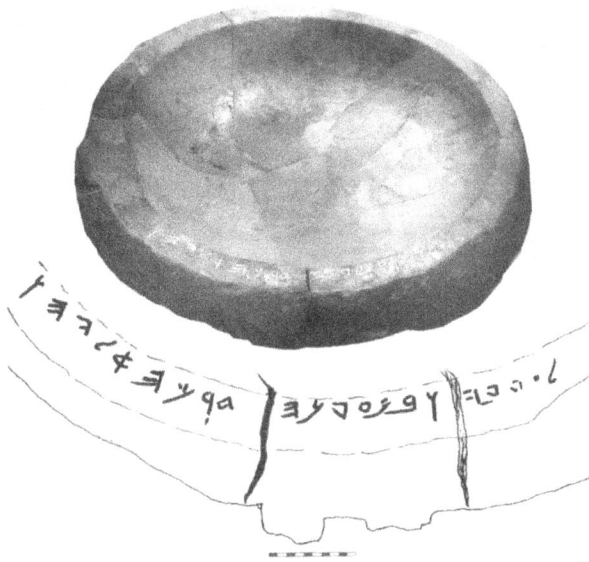

Figure 3 Kuntillet 'Ajrud Inscribed Stone Bowl (ninth–eighth century BCE). Aḥituv, Eshel and Meshel, "The Inscriptions," Fig. 5.3, Inscription 1.2. Used with permission.

implied that the inscribed object itself, a stone basin, is among the things dedicated to the deity by Ōbadyāw.

4.2 Inscription as a Visual and Material Act on Iron Age Holy Bowls

While the tribal stones do the work of dedications, the headdress inscription marks Aaron as a ritual vessel dedicated to YHWH's service (Figure 4). It comprises three parts: קדש "dedicated, holy," followed by the preposition ל, which functions as a possessive, and the name of the deity being venerated, YHWH: "dedicated to YHWH."

The use of the word *qdš* as a means of marking Aaron as an ritual actor in YHWH's Tabernacle is perhaps best paralleled in the growing corpus of southern Levantine "holy bowls," which were marked with this same terminology. While most of these vessels date to the eighth–seventh centuries BCE, two vessels date to the Second Temple Period, speaking to the continuity of this practice beyond the destruction of earlier Iron Age cultic structures in Judah and Philistia and their cultic implements.[72] As seen from J. Smoak's survey, *qdš* was inscribed on a range of vessel types post-firing, which suggests

---

72. For a bibliography and images, see Ahituv, *Echoes from the Past*, 342–5; and Smoak, "Holy Bowls," 70–1.

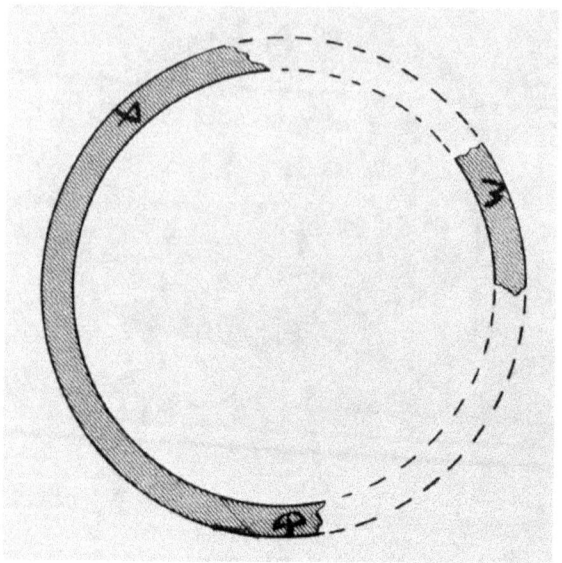

Figure 4 Rim Inscription.
Y. Yadin, A. Ben-Tor, and Sh. Geva, *Hazor, III–IV. An Account of the Third and Fourth Seasons of Excavation, 1957–1958* (Jerusalem: Israel Exploration Society, 1989), Plate 182. Used with permission.

a process by which a standard vessel was transformed into a ritual vessel by the addition of *q-d-š* (Figure 5).[73]

Inscribing this terminology was not merely a way to distinguish or classify ritual vessels, but was "a material, visual, and embodied act."[74] As J. D. Smoak writes,

> "Holy" not only indexed hand and eyes in relation to the object, but also the ritual movements of the object as it passed between bodies and spaces. That is, the inscription created the idea that the vessel was a holy object that was employed in holy action by holy bodies.[75]

The words of these inscriptions were more than mere labels signaling that these objects belonged to the service of a god. These inscriptions and the forms of these

---

73. A shorted variant attested in two bowls, which were found at Arad near to an altar (Locus 394; Stratum X), comprises just the two graphemes קש. Cross identifies the use of such an abbreviation and the form of these two inscriptions as evidence that these vessels derive from "a Phoenician center." See Frank Moore Cross, "Two Offering Dishes with Phoenician Inscriptions from the Sanctuary of Arad," *BASOR* 235 (1979): 75–8, here 78.

74. Smoak, "Holy Bowls," 71.

75. Ibid., 84.

VESSELS INSCRIBED WITH Q-D-Š

LOCATION	VESSEL TYPE	TEXT	RELATIVE DATE
Hazor	Deep Bowl	Rim: *q-d-š* Side: *q-d-š*	eighth century BCE
Arad	Shallow Bowl	Bowl 1: *q-š* Bowl 2: *q-š*	eighth–seventh centuries BCE
Arad	Potsherd	*q-d-š*	Unknown
Beersheba	Krater	*q-d-š*	eighth century BCE
Tel Miqne-Ekron	Four Potsherds	*q-d-š*	eighth century BCE
Unprovenanced	Bowl	*q-d-š*	eighth century BCE (?)

Figure 5 Chart of Vessels Inscribed with QDŠ.
Jeremy D. Smoak, "Holy Bowls: Inscribing Holiness in Ancient Israel and Judah," *Maarav* 23 (2019): 69–92, here 72. Used with permission.

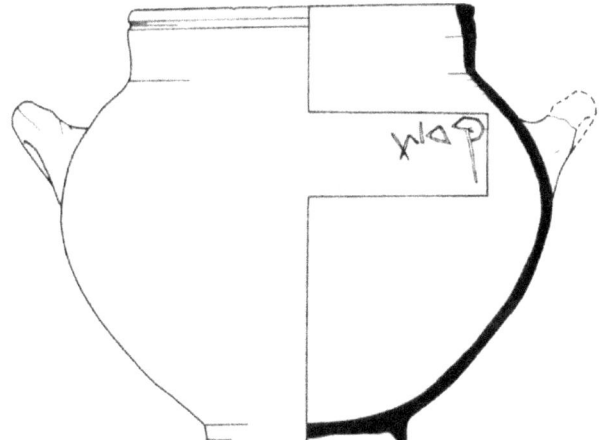

Figure 6 Shoulder Inscription on a Krater, Beersheba.
G. Bachi, "Several Kraters from Stratum II," in *Beersheba I* (ed. Yohanan Aharoni; Tel Aviv: Tel Aviv University, 1973), 38–42; plate 69.2. Used with permission.

vessels guided worshipers about how their human bodies were to interact with the bodies of these "holy bowls" (Figure 6).[76]

When we turn to the function of the *qdš* formula on Aaron's headdress, this formula of dedication functions elliptically to include the inscribed object as the "thing" being dedicated to the service of a deity. With this in mind, we might read the headdress formula קדש ליהוה in the following way: קדש ליהוה (אַהֲרֹן) (Aaron): dedicated to YHWH.[77]

5. When Pots Are People and High Priests Are Pots: The Relationship between Ritual Bodies in Exodus 28 and 39

In the previous section, I argued that the design of Aaron's uniform creates a connection between diverse ritual bodies: Aaron's uniformed body, Israel's tribes (human bodies), and ritual vessels (crafted, cultic bodies). The description of the inscriptions on Aaron's uniform and their function in Exodus 28 and 39 taps into the conceptual metaphor THE BODY IS A VESSEL, through the spatial connection made between Aaron's uniformed body and the bodies of ritual vessels.[78] Thinking about these inscriptions from the perspective of visual design highlights the importance of their layout as critical to the ritual logic of these inscriptions. As Karen Polinger reminds us there is also an inherent spatial relationship between human bodies and those vessels that are designed to be used by human bodies.[79] Polinger writes, "As vessels may have not only lips, but mouths, necks, shoulders, bodies and feet, so may human beings be seen as vessels."[80]

The comparison between the bodies of humans and vessels is reflected in scholarly treatments of vessels in the way that we describe pots as having body parts (e.g., the lip, mouth, neck, shoulder, body, or foot of a vessel).[81] This metaphor

---

76. Ibid., 81.

77. See also the discussion of the function of this inscription in Houtman, *Exodus*, 516-17.

78. I propose this to be a variant of the well-established conceptual metaphor, THE BODY IS A CONTAINER, which highlights the spatial relationship between the human body and containers. See George Lakoff and Mark Johnson, *Metaphors We Live By* (Chicago: University of Chicago Press, 2003 [originally published 1980]); and Mark Johnson, *The Body in the Mind: The Bodily Basis. Meaning, Imagination, and Reason* (Chicago: University of Chicago Press, 1987).

79. See Karen Polinger, "Ceramic Imagery in Ancient Near Eastern Literature," *MRS Proceedings* 185 (1990): 391.

80. Ibid., 411.

81. See also the metaphoric relationship between pots and bodies in Joanna Brück, "Body Metaphors and Technologies of Transformation in the English Middle and Late Bronze Age," in *Bronze Age Landscapes: Tradition and Transformation*, ed. Joanna Brück (Oxford: Oxbow Books, 2001), 152-3; and M. A. Torres de Souza and Camilla Agostini,

also pervades ancient Israelite literature, where human bodies are often described and conceptualized as vessels.[82] The most well-known connection between a body and a vessel in the Hebrew Bible is, perhaps, the image of a human form crafted by YHWH, the divine potter in Gen 2:7. Conversely the destruction of the human body is compared in the biblical text to the smashing of a vessel (Pss 2:9; 31:13 [Heb.]; Jer 19:11; 22:28; 48:38; 51:34), whereas the description of coarse vessels masked with glaze serves as a metaphor for human deception (Prov 26:23). This understanding reinforces the deeper play upon the body–vessel relationship in the placement of the inscriptions onto Aaron's uniform. With this understanding in mind, it seems significant that the three inscriptions described in Exodus 28 and 39 mark Aaron's priestly body in a similar way to inscribed vessels set into cultic spaces:

Aaron: Head-Shoulders-Chest
Ritual Vessel: Rim-Shoulder-Body.

This suggests that the spatial properties of these texts is also a mode that communicates that Aaron's priestly body is taking on the work of the ritual bodies of ceramic, stone, and metal that we would expect in the temple of a god.

6. Conclusion

In this essay, I have joined those scholars who argue that the Tabernacle building narrative in Exodus creates three sets of inscriptions that communicate Aaron's royal, economic, and ritual power. However, I have taken a different methodological approach and have considered their multimodality, focusing on how not only their words but also their script and layout on Aaron's uniform communicate that Aaron's uniformed body operates as a ritual vessel in the Tabernacle. Through the story of the crafting of these inscriptions, this narrative inscribes Levantine dedicatory practices and their power into the very fabric of the high priest's uniform and office—transforming him into the supreme ritual vessel. This narrative thereby replaces the individual dedications and inscribed vessels expected in cultic places with an idealized ritual vessel: the priestly body.

"Body Marks, Pots, and Pipes: Some Correlations between African Scarifications and Pottery Decoration in Eighteenth- and Nineteenth-Century Brazil," *Historical Archaeology* 46 (2012): 102–23.

82. For an overview, see Polinger, "Ceramic Imagery: 409–13.

Chapter 10

THE LITERARY REPRESENTATION OF SACRIFICE IN BIBLICAL NARRATIVE

Liane M. Feldman

1. Introduction

To a modern reader, sacrifice is one of the more foreign concepts found in the Hebrew Bible, and yet it is pervasive throughout biblical thought. Nearly half of the Pentateuch is concerned with the details of sacrificial offerings and a sacrificial cult. One of the preoccupations of the stories of the early monarchy in the books of Samuel and Kings is cultic—from the exploits of Yahweh's ark in 1 Samuel 4–6 to the building of Yahweh's temple and its sacrifice-filled inauguration in 1 Kings 5–8. Prophets such as Isaiah, Jeremiah, Amos, and Micah devote some of their energies to critiques of the sacrificial cult, whereas prophets such as Ezekiel, Haggai, and Malachi devote a significant portion of their energy to reimagining a second iteration of Yahweh's temple and sacrificial cult in Jerusalem. Even some of the psalms are steeped in ideas, themes, and technical language from the cultic sphere. Sacrifice is far from a marginal element of the Hebrew Bible, and yet it has often been marginalized by those interested in studying the Bible as literature.

When considering aspects of literary artistry such as characterization, narrative development, poetic structures, complex imagery, and wordplay, texts that describe the slaughter, butchering, and burning of animals are understandably not the first to come to mind. The banality and, to put it plainly, the ickiness factor of such graphic and detailed descriptions has mainly provoked two types of responses among scholars: to ignore these texts entirely or to treat them as representative of a version of actual historical practice. In both cases, this removes texts about sacrifice from the realm of literary analysis. Unlike many sacrificial texts found elsewhere in the ancient world, sacrificial texts in the Hebrew Bible are nearly always embedded in larger literary compositions.[1] The question asked of these

---

1. Sacrificial texts from Ugarit or Carthage, for example, are typically descriptions or instructions for a particular ritual written on a single tablet. In the Hebrew Bible, sacrificial texts are almost always framed as the direct speech of a character within a narrative story or prophetic vision. For the Ugaritic material, see Dennis Pardee, *Ritual and Cult at Ugarit*

texts should not be "are they literature?" but rather "how do they work within the literary composition?"

In recent years, there have been a number of studies of the sacrificial materials in Leviticus from a more-or-less literary perspective. James Watts, for example, has pushed for scholars to make the important distinction between rituals and texts about rituals, arguing that Leviticus is first and foremost a text and needs to be interpreted as such. Watts then focuses his analysis on the rhetorical function of texts that describe ritual, ultimately arguing that they serve a persuasive, didactic purpose for both ancient Israelite priests and laypeople.[2] This type of approach walks the line between literary criticism and historical criticism, between acknowledging the textualized nature of the biblical ritual materials and attempting to posit their historical functions and audiences. In his book, Bryan Bibb goes further than Watts and argues that questions about compositional history and historical practice should be set aside.[3] Bibb's work takes seriously the textualized nature of the ritual writings in Leviticus but disappointingly continues to use literary readings to make historical arguments about aspects of the Israelite cult.[4] Even when scholars have fought the impulse to historicize sacrificial texts, they have often slipped back into such arguments. The lure of reconstructing ancient Israelite religious practice is a strong one, and given the paucity of non-biblical, nontextual evidence for sacrificial practices, it is no surprise that the detailed descriptions we have in places like Leviticus and Ezekiel become fodder for such enterprises.

The question at the heart of this chapter is a simple one: what happens if we take seriously the literary nature of the biblical sacrificial materials? What if we set aside questions related to recovering historical practice and instead read texts like Leviticus like we read Job—as a complex piece of literature with multiple modes of discourse, a dynamic story world, and complex characters. In this chapter, I will discuss two examples of sacrificial texts in the biblical narrative and analyze each from a decidedly literary perspective. I will turn first to the story of Elijah and the prophets of Baʿal in 1 Kings 18 to explore how detailed descriptions of sacrifice are used to create a satirical episode in the larger Elijah cycle. Then I will take up the most well-known sacrificial text in the Hebrew Bible, Leviticus, in order to discuss the use of textualized sacrificial instructions in the construction and subversion of boundaries. In both examples, the primary question will be the same: how should

---

(Atlanta, GA: SBL Press, 2002). For examples of sacrificial texts framed as narrative speech, see Exodus 29, Leviticus 1–7, 11–17; Numbers 5–6, 8, 19.

2. James W. Watts, *Ritual and Rhetoric in Leviticus: From Sacrifice to Scripture* (Cambridge: Cambridge University Press, 2007), esp. 27–36.

3. Bryan D. Bibb, *Ritual Words and Narrative Worlds in the Book of Leviticus* (Bloomsbury: T&T Clark, 2009), 1–2.

4. For example, he makes the claim that women have complete access to the "sacrificial cult," which seems to push beyond the world of the story (his "narrative world") and into the historical world of ancient Israel. See Bibb, *Ritual Words and Narrative Worlds*, 89.

we read literary representations of sacrifice in narrative texts? I will suggest that texts about sacrifice in the Hebrew Bible cannot and should not be divorced from their narrative contexts. In order to understand anything about sacrifice, I will argue that one must understand both its presence within biblical literature and the interpretive possibilities raised by the fact of its textualization.

2. Sacrifice and Humor in the Prophets of Baʿal

In sacrifice, as in comedy, timing is everything. In comedy it is often all about the comedian's pacing in their telling of a joke. This much is also true in the case of a narrator's telling of a story—narrators can choose to speed up or slow down the progression of events in the world of the story for dramatic effect. In some cases, however, it is the characters within the story who take advantage of timing for dramatic effect, as in the case of the story of Elijah and the prophets of Baʿal on Mount Carmel in 1 Kings 18. This story falls in the middle of a three-part episode about the exploits of the prophet Elijah (1 Kings 17–19). In this episode, Elijah commands Ahab to gather 450 Baʿal prophets and all of the Israelites at Mount Carmel where he intends to stage a battle of the gods: two altars will be prepared— one for Baʿal and one for Yahweh—and whichever prophets are able to compel their god to light their offering on fire will prevail.

The fact that this battle of the gods takes the form of competing sacrificial offerings is one that has long been taken as a given by scholars or simply glossed over.[5] The point of the story, of course, is that Yahweh is the Israelites' god, not Baʿal, and however Elijah chooses to prove that is fine. Yet the use of sacrifice in this story is not accidental, coincidental, or simply theatrical. As several scholars have noted, the use of sacrifice is evocative of the covenants made between Yahweh and Israel on Mount Sinai, and this medium for proving Yahweh's superiority is a rebuke to the Israelites and a reminder of their failure to uphold that covenant.[6] While this is undoubtedly one of the layers of meaning in the use of sacrifice in this story, it is not the only one. Careful attention to the norms of sacrificial

---

5. See, e.g., Arthur E. Zannoni, "Elijah: The Contest on Mount Carmel and Naboth's Vineyard," *Saint Luke's Journal of Theology* 27 (1984): 265–77; Charles E. Baukal, Jr., "Pyrotechnics on Mount Carmel," *Bibliotheca Sacra* 171 (2014): 289–306; and John A. Beck, "Geography as Irony the Narrative-Geographical Shaping of Elijah's Duel with the Prophets of Baal (1 Kings 18)," *SJOT* 17 (2003): 291–302. For her part, while she devotes an entire section of her article to "the sacrifice," Else Holt argues that it is not the slaughter of the bulls and their burning that constitutes the true sacrifice in this story, but rather it is the slaughter of the prophets of Baʿal. See Else K. Holt, "'… Urged on by his wife Jezebel.'—A literary reading of 1 Kgs 18 in context," *SJOT* 9 (1995): 83–96, here 86–9.

6. See Mordechai Cogan, *I Kings* (AB; New Haven, CT: Yale University Press, 1974), 443; Holt, "'… Urged on by His Wife Jezebel,'" 85.

offerings and the use of chronology in the story world pave the way for another interpretation of this story.

It is often an uncritical reflex of readers to see the presence of sacrifice in a story and presume a level of solemnity and seriousness, and in some cases even historical reality. Numerous interpretations of the story of Elijah and the prophets of Baʿal have seen its sacrificial elements as a window into historical religious practice, with some even going so far as to suggest that the descriptions of sacrificial procedures in this passage accurately reflect practices of the ninth-century northern cult. But must sacrifice always be seen as an opportunity for historical reconstruction? Were ancient authors limited to including sacrificial scenes only in order to increase the veracity of the tale? Or might sacrifice appear in stories for other reasons as well? As he sets up his battle of the gods, Elijah ostensibly gives every advantage to the prophets of Baʿal—they outnumber him 450 to one, they are given first pick of the two bulls, and they are given the first opportunity and most of the day to summon their god. In short, the narrator makes it appear as though this is another David versus Goliath moment, which serves to cast Elijah's eventual victory in even more of a miraculous light. Yet the norms of sacrifice and the mechanics of summoning one's god tip the scales in Elijah's favor here. While Elijah explicitly mocks the prophets of Baʿal, he implicitly mocks the Israelites as well by taking advantage of their lack of knowledge of these norms. There are two main ways in which Elijah manipulates sacrifice to his dramatic advantage in this scene: (1) his insistence on the absence of fire; and (2) his control of the timing of the attempted offerings. In this section I will look at each of these in turn and argue not only that they contribute to the broader theme of Elijah's condemnation of the Israelites for their lack of loyalty to Yahweh but also that for those who do understand sacrificial norms, these elements introduce a touch of humor into the scene.

According to Elijah's instructions, when the prophets of Baʿal prepare their offering, they must refrain from one step: lighting the offering on fire (18:23). This is presented as the resolution of the battle: the god who sends forth fire to burn their offering is the more powerful god. The idea that gods consume offerings via fire is one that is found throughout the Hebrew Bible.[7] The details of Elijah's instructions matter here, however. In his description of the offering procedure, he

---

7. See, e.g., Lev 9:24; 10:2; Deut 4:24; Judg 6:21; 2 Sam 22:9; 2 Kgs 1:10; Isa 30:27; Ezek 42:13. For discussions of gods consuming food or other offerings via fire, see William H. C. Propp, *Exodus 1-18: A New Translation with Introduction and Commentary* (Garden City, NY: Doubleday, 1999), 409; William H. C. Propp, *Exodus 19-40: A New Translation with Introduction and Commentary* (Garden City, NY: Doubleday, 2006), 460; Jacob Milgrom, *Leviticus 1-16: A New Translation with Introduction and Commentary* (AB; New Haven, CT: Yale University Press, 1991), 389; W. G. Lambert, "Donations of Food and Drink to the Gods in Ancient Mesopotamia," in *Ritual and Sacrifice in the Ancient Near East*, ed. Jan Quaegebeur (Leuven: Uitgeverij Peeters, 1993); and Mark E. Smith, "Like Deities, Like Temples (Like People)," in *Temple and Worship in Biblical Israel*, ed. John Day (London: T&T Clark, 2004), 3–27.

specifies that the animal should be burned in its entirety by the fire, suggesting that this type of offering is a whole burnt offering or an עלה. Indeed, when the offering finally succeeds at the end of the story, it is described as a whole burnt offering (18:38). As Baruch Levine established nearly half a century ago, one of the primary functions of the whole burnt offering in the Hebrew Bible is as a means to attract the attention of a god and to summon that god to come to the place of the offering.[8]

The presence of a cut-up animal on an altar is not enough to summon a god, though. It is the smoke from a burning offering that wafts heavenward that captures a deity's attention and brings him to the altar to consume that offering. The very name of the offering itself implies a type of ascent (עלה) in the procedure. In a somewhat anomalous moment in the Priestly Narrative in Exodus 40, Moses is said to "send up a whole burnt offering" (ויעל עליו את העלה).[9] This is the first offering ever offered on that particular altar, and it is the only time in the Priestly Narrative that the verb describing the sacrifice of a whole burnt offering is על״ה. From that point onward in that story, Yahweh is present in the tabernacle and no longer needs to be summoned from the heavens. In the story of Elijah and the prophets of Baʿal, like many of the biblical stories of sacrifice outside of the Priestly Narrative, there is no tabernacle and no established altar. Yahweh or Baʿal must be summoned to the site of the offering. Elijah suggests that this summoning occur auditorily— the prophets will simply ask their god to come down. Yet there is little evidence that a simple petition on its own is enough to move a deity from heaven to earth unless it is the deity's own idea.[10] Such a movement usually requires some kind of enticement, typically in the form of a sacrifice for the god to consume. Because Elijah specifically stipulates that the offerings may not be burned, he immediately removes one of the primary means of attracting a deity's attention and eliciting a response. Butchered meat on an unkindled altar is simply not enough to capture the attention of a god residing in the heavens. Elijah sets up this battle of the gods to subvert one of the main ways in which sacrifices work—where there is no fire, there can be no enticing smoke to waft heavenward.

The prophets of Baʿal seem to be entirely aware of this fact. While they begin their quest for Baʿal's attention with simple petitions lasting from morning until midday (18:26), they eventually realize that they need to up the ante. They add

---

8. "The essential role of the ʿōlâ seems to have been that of *attraction*. The ʿōlâ was offered up with the objective of evoking an initial response from the deity prior to bringing the primary concerns of his worshippers to his attention." See Baruch A. Levine, *In the Presence of the Lord: A Study of Cult and Some Cultic Terms in Ancient Israel*, Studies in Judaism in Late Antiquity (Leiden: Brill, 1974), 22.

9. Exod 40:29.

10. When Yahweh comes to meet a human being on earth, it typically seems to be on his terms or on his timeline. For example, in Gen 18:1, Yahweh simply appears to Abraham. Similarly, in Exodus 3, the angel of Yahweh appears to Moses. Likewise, in Numbers 22, the angel of Yahweh appears to Balaam's donkey. Yahweh can be summoned via sacrifice, and this is often why the patriarchs build altars and offer sacrifices in places.

movement (dancing) to try to catch Baʿal's attention and then when that fails, prompted by the mockery of Elijah they shout even louder (18:27–28). In what seems like a last-ditch effort, they begin to cut themselves, drawing their own blood in an effort to pique Baʿal's interest.[11] While these actions—shouting, dancing and blood-drawing—seem to be unrelated, they are all choreographed to disturb a god at rest. There is good reason to think that the natural state of Yahweh (and likely any god imagined in a similar way) is at rest, benignly disengaged from his creation.[12] Movement, sound, and the odor of blood appeal to the god's senses of sight, hearing, and smell in an attempt to disturb that divine repose and provoke a response. In short, while the structuring of the storytelling in vv. 20–29 looks at first glance as though it is mocking the ineffectual and perhaps even barbaric behaviors of the prophets of Baʿal, the prophets themselves are using what tools they do have at their disposal in an attempt to rouse their god, unfortunately for them unsuccessfully. The blood-letting in particular has another function in the narrative, as it foreshadows the wholesale slaughter of these prophets by the Israelites at the end of this scene. At this point in the story the prophets are spilling their blood for Baʿal, while in a few hours the Israelites will spill that same blood for Yahweh. If the efforts of the prophets of Baʿal fail to capture their god's attention, then why is Elijah's far simpler petition successful, especially in light of the fact that he seems to make matters more difficult for himself by drenching the altar and the cut-up bull with water? Is it simply that Yahweh is more attentive, or that Elijah's voice is more worthy of being heeded, or that Baʿal just does not exist? Perhaps Elijah intends the gathered Israelites to come to these very conclusions.[13] However, these are not the only possible explanations.

Part of the answer to Elijah's success and the failure of the prophets of Baʿal is found in his control of the progression of events in the story, and thus in the timing of these offerings. As the one who set the terms of the battle, Elijah serves as a master of ceremonies for the entire day. His deference to the prophets of Baʿal at the beginning of the scene may appear to mitigate that fact and level the playing field, but in reality, it is pointedly strategic from the perspective of sacrificial norms. The proceedings begin at some point in the morning, after everyone has been assembled at the mountain and preparations have taken place. The prophets of Baʿal carry on with their unheeded summons until noontime. Rather than take

---

11. There seems to be some evidence that human blood was thought to "cry out" to a god, thus disturbing his respite (see Gen 4:10; Job 16:18). For an argument that human blood was more potent and thus more disturbing than animal blood for a god, see Simeon Chavel *Oracular Law and Priestly Historiography in the Torah* (FAT II; Tübingen: Mohr Siebeck, 2014), 74.

12. For a description of Yahweh's benign inattentiveness, see Jeffrey Stackert, "How the Priestly Sabbaths Work: Innovation in Pentateuchal Priestly Ritual," in *Ritual Innovation in the Hebrew Bible and Ancient Judaism*, ed. Nathan MacDonald (BZAW 468; Berlin: de Gruyter, 2016), 79–111, here 83.

13. See 1 Kgs 18:36–37.

his turn at this point, Elijah goads them on, mocking their god by suggesting that he is off relieving himself, sleeping or simply on a walk somewhere.[14] This threefold insult prompts the prophets of Baʿal to redouble their efforts. This both advances the timeline in the story world and sets up an even more stark contrast between the failure of the prophets of Baʿal and the success of Elijah. Elijah leaves them to shout more loudly, dance more wildly, and gash themselves with knives "until the time for the grain offering" (עד לעלות המנחה), at which point he has them cease their efforts.[15] This enigmatic phrase raises a number of questions, first and foremost, what is the time of the grain offering? And why does Elijah allow the prophets of Baʿal to persist only until this point?

While the actions of the prophets of Baʿal are, from their own perspective, designed to capture the attention of Baʿal by appealing to the senses of Baʿal available to them, they are, from the perspective of Elijah, simply a way to pass the time. The time for the grain offering almost certainly refers to the evening iteration of the twice-daily regular offering made to Yahweh. This offering happened early in the morning and in the evening.[16] The most comprehensive instructions for this offering are found in the Priestly Narrative in Exod 29:38–42, which describes the offering of a single year-old male lamb combined with a grain offering and a libation twice each day. Elsewhere in the book of Kings, the twice-daily offering is described differently, with a morning meat offering and an evening grain offering (2 Kgs 16:15). Despite the disagreements between biblical texts about the specifics of this offering, one thing remains stable: the timing. Twice a day, early in the morning and in the evening, Yahweh is conditioned to expect an offering; they are his regular meals.[17]

This battle of the gods begins in the morning, but by the time the stage is set, the time of the early morning offering has passed. By allowing the prophets of Baʿal to go first, Elijah strategically buys himself time. His mockery of their god serves to spur them on in their attempts to summon Baʿal longer. The derisive comments Elijah makes are all geared toward imagining Baʿal as an oversized human being.[18] First he suggests that Baʿal is too busy shitting and pissing to answer their pleas.[19] This is perhaps the basest of human and animal activities and the fact that Elijah raises this possibility provides shock value and adds an edge to his mockery. By then suggesting that Baʿal is traveling or sleeping, Elijah tones down his rhetoric

---

14. 1 Kgs 18:27.

15. 1 Kgs 18:29.

16. See 2 Kgs 6:20 for the morning offering and 2 Kgs 16:15 for the evening offering.

17. The importance of the time of day is also noted by Baukal, though he argues that the evening timing is simply to "intensify the impact" of the fire against a dusk sky. See "Pyrotechnics on Mount Carmel," 293.

18. Smith, "Like Deities, Like Temples," 16–20.

19. For this translation, see Gary A. Rendsburg, "The Mock of Baal in 1 Kings 18:27," *CBQ* 50 (1988): 414–17, here 416–17. A similar hendiadys is used to mock the drunkenness of the god ʾIlu in RS 24.258:21.

but keeps the same underlying supposition: Baʕal acts like a human. One might expect that Elijah is mocking the belief that a god can and does behave in the manner of human beings with these comments. But is this truly the source of Elijah's mockery? Is it that the prophets of Baʕal do not understand how their god functions?

This seems not to be the case, especially given Elijah's reliance on timing in this story. The one activity that Elijah does not mention when he mocks Baʕal's silence is that "perhaps Baʕal is not hungry!" But in truth, this might well be the case. Faced with the lack of a strong, pleasing smell to waft heavenward to capture his attention, what else could redirect a god's gaze to this prophetic battleground? Hunger. Similar to a dog who perks up and becomes attentive to their owner's every move in the minutes leading up to dinner time, it is reasonable to expect that Yahweh and Baʕal would be aware of their own mealtimes and more attentive to human beings than usual around those times. By waiting until the time for the grain offering, Elijah is stacking the deck for Yahweh to answer his summons by banking on the fact that Yahweh will be looking for his next meal.

Elijah could have called on Yahweh right there and then, but he does not do that. Instead he delays further. These delays serve two purposes: they ensure that Yahweh is awaiting his next meal and, more significantly, they remind the Israelites of their infidelity. Elijah's careful rebuilding of the destroyed altar along with his placement of twelve stones, one for each tribe of Israel, has absolutely nothing to do with capturing Yahweh's attention. Instead, such a demonstration has everything to do with reminding the Israelites of the loyalty they owe to their god. When he calls for water to be brought and poured over the altar and offering, Elijah again mocks the Israelites. In the broader context of the story, they are now three years into a drought so severe that it has caused widespread famine and death, yet the water has nothing to do with capturing Yahweh's attention.[20] Water is as precious a resource as one can come by, and Elijah is calling for buckets of it to be found, collected and dumped over this altar to Yahweh. To call for this water also calls for the Israelites themselves to sacrifice one of their most limited resources to this demonstration.

When Elijah finally gets around to calling on Yahweh after the third time water is poured over the altar, all of the Israelites and the prophets of Baʕal are paying attention. The scene before them is so patently absurd that it seems to have no chance of succeeding. If nearly a full day's worth of effort on the part of 450 prophets failed to summon Baʕal, how on earth is an altar covered in soggy bull parts going to be set aflame by Yahweh? Of course, predictably, Yahweh responds to Elijah's summons nearly right away—but not before Elijah is able to work into his plea a reminder that the point of lighting the altar on fire is so that the Israelites know that Yahweh is their god (18:37). This formulation runs parallel to the initial instructions for the regular daily offering in Exod 29:38–46, which describes the mechanics of the twice-daily offering followed by Yahweh's promise to meet the

---

20. 1 Kgs 18:1.

Israelites where it is offered (in that case at the tabernacle) so that "they shall know that I am their god who brought them out of Egypt" (Exod 29:46). Elijah's plea to Yahweh in these verses is to "answer me, O Yahweh, answer me so that these people know that you, O Yahweh, are god" (1 Kgs 18:37a). Yahweh immediately sends down fire to consume the offering (his meal), and Elijah is vindicated. The people, precisely as they do so many times elsewhere in biblical narrative when their god appears in fire, fall to their faces and praise Yahweh.[21]

Elijah and Yahweh emerge victorious in the battle of the gods due in large part to Elijah's understanding of the mechanics of sacrificial offerings and his careful attention to timing in the progression of this scene. The use of repetition, intensification, and deliberate patterning allow the sacrificial content to be read as an integral part of the development of the plot itself. It is not a given that a battle of the gods must be staged via sacrifice. The choice to use sacrifice here allows Elijah to play with time, to draw out the ways in which gods are imagined, and to mock the bodily functions of foreign gods while also conceding and taking advantage of the bodily needs of his own god. The ultimate purpose of this scene is for Elijah to win back the Israelites to the whole-hearted worship of Yahweh by showing them the impotence of Baʿal. He succeeds, in part, because the Israelites themselves do not understand enough of how sacrifice works or who their god is that they remain unaware of the trickery used by Elijah to bring about a positive result. In this case, the prophet is able to use the ignorance of the Israelites to his and Yahweh's advantage. The prophets of Baʿal for their part remain none the wiser, and the newly zealous Israelites make quick work of their slaughter before they have much of a chance to register an objection or tarnish the seemingly miraculous response of Yahweh.[22]

3. Creating and Subverting Boundaries in Leviticus

Nearly all of Leviticus is made up of a series of Yahweh's speeches that contain both instructions for performing different types of sacrifices and laws governing purity and impurity in proximity to his home, known within the story as the tent of meeting. Embedded within the seemingly endless details about slaughter, blood manipulation, and bodily impurities, Yahweh delineates spaces and creates boundaries within the tent of meeting and the Israelite encampment around it. The first set of Yahweh's instructions (Leviticus 1–7) are about the details of sacrificial procedure and are concerned primarily with the spaces inside the tent of meeting itself. The second set of instructions given by Yahweh (Leviticus 11–15) are concerned with diagnosing and treating impurity and are focused on the relationship between the Israelite encampment and the tent of meeting. In this section, I will discuss the boundary-making function of these speeches within the

---

21. Lev 9:24; Num 20:6; Judg 13:20; Ezek 3:23.
22. They go from praising with one breath to slaughtering in the next (18:39–40).

story world and the boundary-breaking function of these speeches on the level of the story's discourse.

Within the story world, Yahweh's speeches in Leviticus 1–7 implicitly draw boundaries that govern the movements and restrict the access of ordinary Israelites to large parts of the tent of meeting. In this section of his speech, Yahweh lays out basic instructions for how to offer a sacrifice and explains the differences between the different types of sacrifices. While there are five different types of sacrifices described in these chapters, there is a basic underlying pattern for all of them.[23] Taking Yahweh's first set of instructions in Lev 1:3–9 as an example, it is possible to delineate seven steps to a sacrificial offering:

1. Bringing of the animal to the tent of meeting (1:3)
2. Hand-laying to mark possession[24] (1:4)
3. Slaughter (1:5a)
4. Blood manipulation (1:5b)
5. Butchering of the animal (1:6)
6. Preparing the altar and/or butchered animal parts (1:7–9a)
7. Offering the animal on the altar (1:9b)

These seven steps can be identified across nearly all of the different types of sacrifices, with some sacrifices (such as the well-being offering or the purification offering) requiring an eighth step that divides the meat between altar, offeror, and priest.[25] In the case of every type of offering, however, the first step is for an offeror, nearly always a lay Israelite, to bring the animal or grain to the tent of meeting.[26] The second step is for the offer to lay their hand on the animal to designate ownership,[27] and the third step is for the animal to be slaughtered.[28]

---

23. The identification of this underlying pattern or structure is indebted to Naphtali Meshel's work on the grammar of priestly sacrifice. See *The "Grammar" of Sacrifice: A Generativist Study of the Israelite Sacrificial System in the Priestly Writings with The "Grammar" of *Σ* (Oxford: Oxford University Press, 2014).

24. David P. Wright, "The Gesture of Hand Placement in the Hebrew Bible and in Hittite Literature," *JAOS* 106 (1986): 433–46, here 434–9.

25. The grain offering is a special case in that a number of these steps (such as slaughter and butchering) clearly do not apply to a nonanimal sacrifice. For a further discussion of each of these steps and a more detailed explanation of how these steps manifest in forms of the sacrifice other than the whole burnt offering, see Liane M. Feldman, *The Story of Sacrifice: Ritual and Narrative in the Priestly Source* (FAT 141; Tübingen: Mohr Siebeck, 2020), 53–6.

26. See, e.g., Lev 1:10, 15; 2:2, 14; 3:1, 6, 12; 4:3, 14, 23, 28; 5:6.

27. See, e.g., Lev 1:4; 3:2, 8, 13; 4:4, 15, 24, 29, 33. For a discussion of single-hand laying as a marker of ownership, see Wright, "Hand Placement," 434–39.

28. See, e.g., Lev 1:5, 11; 3:2, 8, 13; 4:4, 15, 24, 29, 33.

What is most interesting about this third step is that there is no explicit subject for the verb: who is slaughtering the animal? In the paradigmatic case at hand, Yahweh's instructions begin in v. 3 with the general statement: "if his offering is burnt offering from the herd, he should bring it to the entrance of the tent of meeting." Who is this he? Contextually speaking, the most logical antecedent is the subject of v. 2: "a person among you who would bring an offering to Yahweh" (אדם כי יקריב מכם קרבן ליהוה). This hypothetical person remains the subject of the 3ms verbs in v. 3 (יקריבנו, יקריב) and is the implied subject of the hand-laying procedure in v. 4 (וסמך ידו). In v. 5, Yahweh describes the slaughter of the animal: ושחט את בן הבקר לפני יהוה. The verbal form in this clause, a 3ms *weqatal* form following the form in v. 4, has traditionally been translated as an impersonal verb: "the bull will be slaughtered before Yahweh."[29] More logically, however, the subject of the verb ושחט in v. 5a should be the same as the subject of the verb in v. 4—the offeror.[30] Indeed, in the very next sentence, the subject explicitly changes along with the introduction of a 3cp verbal form: "the sons of Aaron, the priests, will offer the blood" (והקריבו בני אהרן הכהנים את הדם). There is no need, other than discomfort with the idea of a lay Israelite participating in the sacrificial procedure, to think that ושחט is an impersonal verb.[31] Reading the offeror as the subject of the verb in v. 5 means that the division of sacrificial labor has to be reconsidered. In this case, the lay Israelite can and should be involved in the sacrificial procedure—up to a point. That point is as much physical as it is procedural, and the sacrificial material (the animal) changes hands when the need arises to use the altar itself. The fact that the offeror is responsible for steps 1–3 while the priests are responsible for steps 4–7 draws a boundary within the courtyard of the tent of meeting. That boundary sits at the eastern edge of the altar. An ordinary Israelite cannot pass that boundary and approach the altar. The altar and all that lies west of it becomes the purview of the priests.

In the case of the purity laws, boundaries are not drawn within the tent of meeting but at its entrance, and in some of the more severe cases, at the entrance to the Israelite camp that surrounds the tent of meeting. Impurity, unlike sin, has no stigma attached to it other than the inability to participate in or enter ritual spaces.[32] Given the wide variety of different ways that Yahweh describes Israelites

---

29. NRSV, NJPS. For this argument see also Martin Noth, *Leviticus: A Commentary* (OTL; Philadelphia, PA: Westminster Press, 1965), 22. Baruch Levine also appears to accept the NJPS translation of this verb as impersonal. See *Leviticus* (The JPS Torah Commentary; New York: Jewish Publication Society, 1989), 7.

30. Thomas Hieke has argued that the idea that an Israelite could not have performed the slaughter goes back to the LXX, which contains a third-person plural form of the verb (σφάξουσι), anticipating the introduction of the priests in the next clause. See *Levitikus 1–15* (HTKzAT; Freiburg: Herder, 2014), 150.

31. For a similar argument, see already Rashi on 1:5; Milgrom, *Leviticus 1–16*, 154; John Hartley, *Leviticus* (WBC; Nashville, TN: Thomas Nelson, 1992), 21.

32. Milgrom explicitly argues because Yahweh is himself holy, people with impurities may not enter the tabernacle complex. He makes it clear, however, that impurity presents

contracting impurity, it is safe to say that most Israelites would have been impure much of the time. Over the course of a long speech with many detailed laws about diagnosing and treating impurities, Yahweh draws several boundary lines. The first of these lines is at the entrance to the tent of meeting itself. In his instructions to a new mother, Yahweh says that she cannot touch any holy thing or enter the sanctuary until her prescribed time for purification is complete (12:4). While the specific law applies to a new mother, the general principle can be seen operating in numerous other contexts, and the idea that an impure individual cannot come into contact with sacred objects or enter sacred space becomes foundational to the working of the tent of meeting and its cult.[33] It is not enough simply to keep impure people away from the tent of meeting, however. Certain impurities are so severe that the afflicted individuals must be removed from the Israelite camp altogether, and Yahweh draws yet another boundary at the edge of the camp. The risk for contagion of severe impurity is so high that it is better to relocate the afflicted individual outside the inhabited area than risk widespread severe impurity within the Israelite camp, which would in turn risk contamination of Yahweh's home with that impurity.[34]

These three boundaries—the eastern side of the altar, the entrance to the tent of meeting, and the entrance to the camp—must be inferred from Yahweh's laws and instructions; they are not explicitly labeled or otherwise discussed in Leviticus.[35] Not all characters within the story are in an equal position to infer all of these boundaries, however. The Israelites in the story are not privy to all of Yahweh's speeches in Leviticus 1–7 and 11–16. At the beginning of many of Yahweh's speeches is a single command: "Speak to X and say to them."[36] The secondary addressee,

---

no moral or physical danger to the individual who contracts it. See *Leviticus 1-16*, 616–17. Jonathan Klawans develops the distinction between ritual and moral impurity even further and suggests explicitly that the presence of the deity is dependent on a reasonable level of purity. See *Purity, Sacrifice, and the Temple: Symbolism and Supersessionism in the Study of Ancient Judaism* (Oxford: Oxford University Press, 2009), 68–9.

33. For example, Lev 7:19–20 alluded to the prohibition on touching holy objects while impure in the case of the consumption of sanctified sacrificial portions, but it does not have a programmatic statement like Lev 12:4.

34. There is no direct evidence that the priestly author(s) implemented the quarantine due to fear of contagion of the disease. See, e.g., the discussions in Milgrom, *Leviticus 1-16*, 818; and Yitzhaq Feder, "Contagion and Cognition: Bodily Experience and the Conceptualization of Pollution (*ṭumʾah*) in the Hebrew Bible," *JNES* 72 (2013): 151–67, here 162–5.

35. It is only later in the Priestly Narrative, in Numbers 18 which is itself likely a secondary addition to the text, that these boundaries and the entities responsible for protecting them are made more explicit. See the discussion in Jacob Milgrom, *Studies in Levitical Terminology: The Encroacher and the Levite: The Term ʿaboda* (Eugene, OR: Wipf & Stock, 1970), 26.

36. See Lev 1:2; 4:2; 6:2; 11:2; 12:2; 15:2.

the "x," is not always the same. Sometimes it is the Israelites and other times it is the priests. This differentiation of secondary audiences means that the Israelites within the story never hear the instructions about procedures to be done inside the sanctuary (Leviticus 16) or about the inner workings of the cult: disposal of sacrificial remains, tending of the altar fire, distribution of sacrificial portions, and so on (Leviticus 6–7). These speeches are meant to be relayed only to Aaron and his sons. That boundary at the eastern edge of the altar governs not only their physical movements but also limits what they can witness. With very few exceptions, they can only learn about what can be seen from that line.[37] Those things that occur beyond the courtyard at the time of the offering remain beyond their knowledge. In large part, this is because they physically cannot have access to these places—only consecrated individuals (the priests) are able to enter the sanctuary or touch the altar.[38] The logic within the story seems to be that if a character cannot have access to the space, or at least the ability to witness the activity being described in that space, then they need not know about what happens.[39]

The fact remains, however, that all of these instructions are included in a larger narrative story about the history of the Israelites and their cult. This narrative, starting with the creation of the world in Genesis 1 and ending with the Israelites on the edge of the promised land in Deuteronomy 34, has its own implied

---

37. The one obvious exception is in the case of the purification offering offered on behalf of the high priest or the entire Israelite community (Lev 4:3–21). In the course of this sacrificial procedure, the priest is described as bringing the blood inside of the sanctuary; that description is part of what the Israelites are told.

38. For this argument, see Philip Peter Jenson, *Graded Holiness: A Key to the Priestly Conception of the World* (Sheffield: JSOT Press, 1992), 119–21; Liane M. Feldman, "Ritual Sequence and Narrative Constraints in Lev 9:1–10:3," *JHS* 17 (2017): 1–35, here 9–10.

39. The case of the day of atonement ritual in Leviticus 16 is particularly interesting here. The ritual described in this chapter requires that offerings be made on behalf of the people, and as such one would expect the involvement of the people in the procedure. Yet there is no indication given by Yahweh in Lev 16:1–28 that they are meant to be told about this particular ritual procedure. The active participation of the people appears only in vv. 29–34, which have typically been identified as a later addition to the chapter. See, e.g., Bruno Baentsch, *Leviticus* (Gottingen: Vandehoeck & Ruprecht, 1900), 380; Noth, *Leviticus*, 117, 126; Karl Elliger, *Leviticus* (Tübingen: Mohr, 1966), 207; Milgrom, *Leviticus 1–16*, 1061–3; Frank H. Gorman Jr., "Priestly Rituals of Founding: Time, Space, and Status," in *History and Interpretation*, ed. M. Patrick Graham, William P. Brown and Jeffrey K. Kuan (Sheffield: Sheffield University Press, 1993), 47–64; Israel Knohl, *The Sanctuary of Silence: The Priestly Torah and the Holiness School* (Winona Lake, IN: Eisenbrauns, 2007), 27–8; Christophe Nihan, *From Priestly Torah to Pentateuch: A Study in the Composition of the Book of Leviticus* (FAT; Tübingen: Mohr Siebeck, 2007), 347. As I have argued elsewhere, the only verses concerned with the people are vv. 29b–31, with the possibility that the dating formula in v. 29aβ is a later addition, harmonizing this chapter with the cultic calendar in Lev 23. See Feldman, *The Story of Sacrifice*, 166–7.

reader: a specific community of ancient Israelites.⁴⁰ If Yahweh's instructions function to create boundaries within the story world, their textualized presence in the Priestly Narrative actively subverts those boundaries. Within the world of the narrative, lay Israelites cannot enter the sanctuary, they cannot see the rituals that happen inside, they cannot witness the clean-up processes, or learn the diagnostic criteria for skin diseases that cause impurity. These things are meant only for the priests who have specially designated access. But taking a step back, from the perspective of the written narrative, ordinary Israelites suddenly have access not only to these spaces, procedures, and criteria, but they quite literally stand alongside Moses in the sanctuary as he listens to these instructions come directly from Yahweh. The narrator has chosen to tell the story in such a way that the reader stands where Moses stands and hears what Moses hears. This affords the implied reader, the ancient Israelite, a level of access to both Yahweh and his tent of meeting that goes well beyond anything given to the Israelites or even the priests within the story. The implied reader stands as Moses's equal.

An ordinary Israelite hearing Yahweh's words, seeing the innermost spaces of Yahweh's home, and learning about the procedures necessary to maintain those spaces is unthinkable within the world of this story. Recall that most Israelites were likely impure much of the time, and that impure Israelites could not even cross the threshold into the courtyard of the tent of meeting. And even if an Israelite were ritually pure, they could not go beyond the eastern edge of the altar in the courtyard, and certainly not inside the sanctuary. Such access to Yahweh and Yahweh's sancta required sanctification, something reserved only for the priests.⁴¹ Any ordinary Israelite who attempted to cross these boundaries was subject to death.⁴² Those things that prevent an ordinary Israelite from gaining access to privileged spaces within the story world—purity and sanctification—do not exist in the realm of text. One need not be pure to read a written narrative. One need not be sanctified to read about what happens inside Yahweh's inner sanctum. The boundaries so

---

40. A distinction should also be made between the actual reader and the implied reader of a text. The reader of the text is the individual who perceives the text, whereas the implied reader is a construct within the world of the text itself. "The counterpart of the implied author is the implied reader—not the flesh-and-bones you or I sitting in our living rooms reading the book, but the audience presupposed by the narrative itself" (Seymour Benjamin Chatman, *Story and Discourse: Narrative Structure in Fiction and Film* [Ithaca, NY: Cornell University Press, 1978], 149–50). In short: the reader of a text creates an image of who they think the author might be while they are reading. This is the implied author. The implied reader is then a further abstraction; it is who the reader thinks the implied author intends to have reading his or her text.

41. For a discussion of the dangerous nature of the priesthood, see Milgrom, *Leviticus 1-16*, 1035.

42. See Num 18:1–7, and for a further discussion of the issue of the encroacher, Jacob Milgrom, "Encroaching on the Sacred: Purity and Polity in Numbers 1–10," *Int* 51 (1997): 241–53, here 243–4.

carefully established for the characters within the story are subverted by the very telling of that story. It is the process of writing, the textualization of sacrifice, that in the end opens every aspect of the tent of meeting and its cult to all Israelites.

4. Conclusion

When we set aside the quest to reconstruct aspects of historical religious practice and instead consider the possibility that sacrificial materials are themselves literary and an integral part of ancient Israelite literature, new readings of these texts can emerge. This is not to say that it is unimportant to understand the details, rules, and mechanics of sacrifice presented in these texts. In the case of the prophets of Baʿal, it is only when a deeper understanding of how sacrifice works is brought to a literary reading of the story that the elements of humor and mockery of the Israelites emerge. Similarly, in the case of the Priestly Narrative in Leviticus, it is only possible to imagine the narrative subverting boundaries created within its story if one has a thorough understanding of the ways in which the author(s) of this story conceive of the role of lay Israelites and issues of purity and access to the tent of meeting complex. Sacrificial texts found in narrative contexts are not the same as all other narrative texts. On the contrary, they evoke norms that may be explicitly described elsewhere in the story or perhaps only implied at other points in the narrative. What these literary representations of sacrifice do not do, however, is demand or assume knowledge of actual historical practice in a temple or other ritual context. These narratives construct the framework needed to understand the literary functions of their sacrificial activity. Reading sacrificial texts as literature may not be intuitive to us as modern readers, but it is worth considering the ways in which these literary representations of sacrifice are integral to the construction of many biblical narratives.

Chapter 11

THE OFFERINGS OF THE TRIBAL LEADERS,
THE PURIFICATION OF THE LEVITES, AND THE
HERMENEUTICS OF RITUAL INNOVATION

Nathan MacDonald

1. *Introduction*

In Num 7:1–88 the leaders of the secular tribes on their own initiative bring identical offerings to the Tabernacle on sequential days, and in Num 8:5–22 a ritual is enjoined upon Moses and the Israelites by which the Levites might be purified and made ready for service in the sanctuary. Neither text has enjoyed the esteem of biblical scholars, and critical scholarship of the nineteenth century was particularly harsh in its judgments. Numbers 7 repeats the same detailed list of offerings twelve times with no apparent variation, which led Abraham Kuenen to complain that nowhere else was the priestly writer as "monotonous and tediously exhausting" as here.[1] Numbers 8 was rightly perceived to have a close relationship with Numbers 3, but Julius Wellhausen saw the ritualization in Numbers 8 as "frivolous" and a "mechanical historicization on the basis of legal conceptions," while Kuenen described it as a "tasteless repetition and exaggeration" of Numbers 3.[2] Such pejorative judgments are characteristic of their age and are rather more rare in contemporary scholarly discourse, but it is not clear to me that Numbers 7

---

1. "So monoton und ermüdend weitschweifig wie *N* VII ist P² übrigens nicht" (Abraham Kuenen, *Historisch-kritische Einleitung in die Bücher des alten Testaments hinsichtlich ihrer Entstehung und Sammlung* [Leipzig: Otto Schulze, 1887], 91).
2. "In einer so frivolen Weise ist die einfache Idee 3,5–13 hier auf Grund gesetzlicher Vorstellungen mechanisch vergeschichtlicht, noch einen Schritt über 3,14–51 hinaus" (Julius Wellhausen, *Die Composition des Hexateuchs und der historischen Bücher des Alten Testaments* [3rd ed.; Berlin: Georg Reimer, 1899], 178); "Dieser Abschnitt ist nämlich eine geschmacklose Wiederholung und Uebertreibung des Berichtes über die Aussonderung der Leviten zum Dienst am Heiligthum, *N* III und IV" (Kuenen, *Historisch-kritische Einleitung*, 90n. 33).

or 8 has raised significantly in scholarly assessment. They are not often traduced in the terms that were common in the nineteenth century,[3] but they are mostly ignored outside commentaries on Numbers.[4] In this chapter I argue that rather more appreciation is appropriate for the subtle intertextuality of these two rituals. By means of bricolage, the scribal author constructs two novel rituals, which provide a role for the secular tribes and the Levites in the inauguration of the Tabernacle, and interact with the existing rituals in subtle and interesting ways. Since the dependence of Numbers 7 and 8 upon texts in Exodus and Leviticus is widely recognized, it is possible to move the examination of intertextuality beyond questions of directionality to examine the complex literary moves made by the composer. To do so requires moving between historical criticism, narrative criticism, literary theory, ritual theory, and inner-biblical interpretation.

2. Chronological Deformation in Numbers 7

An important feature of the scribal method is the introduction in Num 7:1 of a significant chronological deformation. From its majestic opening lines in Genesis 1 until the death of Moses in Deuteronomy 34, the Pentateuch is a narrative that moves steadily forward through time. Retrospects may be offered by characters within the narrative, most notably by Moses in Deuteronomy, but even these occur within the narrative framework of the Pentateuch. The single exception occurs early in the book of Numbers. The census and ordering of the camp described in Numbers 1–4 continues the chronology found in Exodus and is said to occur on the first day of the second month in the second year after the departure from Egypt. With Num 7:1, however, the reader is transported back a month earlier to the first day of the first month. "On the day Moses completed setting up the Tabernacle" (ויהי ביום כלות משה להקים את המשכן). The verse clearly alludes to Exodus 40: "in the first month on the second year, on the first day of the month, the Tabernacle was set up" (ויהי בחדש הראשון בשנה השנית באחד לחדש הוקם המשכן; 40:17; cf. v. 1) and "Moses finished the work" (ויכל משה את המלאכה; v. 33), and consequently thrusts the reader back an entire biblical book. The chronological deformation is maintained in subsequent chapters. In Num 9:1–14 the instructions for the keeping of the first remembrance of the Passover on the fourteenth day of the first month are given together with the questions that arise as the result of some of the people being ritually unclean on that occasion. After the instructions for a deferred Passover, the reader's perspective is projected back for a second time to the first day of the first month—"on the day the Tabernacle was set up" (וביום הקים את המשכן; 9:15)—in order to describe the appearance of the pillar of fire and cloud. The

---

3. There are, alas, exceptions. Eryl Davies refers to the "tedious, monotonous tone" of Numbers 7 (Eryl W. Davies, *Numbers* [NCBC; London: Marshall Pickering, 1995], 70).

4. One notable exception is the thoughtful article by Jonathan Stökl on "Innovating Ordination," *HeBAI* 7 (2018): 483–99.

original chronological sequence of the book is only resumed with the departure of the Israelites from the wilderness of Sinai in Num 10:11, which is identified as the twentieth day of the second month.

Various scholarly solutions have been proposed to address the problematic chronology of these chapters. Baruch Levine reaches for a redactional solution and argues that Num 9:1 with its reference to the first month must have "appeared in the text of Numbers before the opening caption of the book was added."[5] This does not resolve the problem, it merely relocates it: why would an author or editor have mentioned the second month in Num 1:1, if there was a reference to the first month a few chapters later? Jacob Milgrom, on the other hand, suggests that we translate ביום in 7:1 with a vaguer "when."[6] This proposal was already anticipated by George Gray, who rightly observed that despite "when" being a legitimate translation of ביום the allusions to the specific occasion of Exodus 40 preclude such an indefinite rendering.[7] Eryl Davies regards it as simply evidence of an inattentive editor.[8] However, the importance of dates within the book of Numbers and the insistence with which the composer of Numbers 7–10 dates these events prior to Numbers 1–4 suggest that this is no accident.[9]

An appreciation of the scribal purposes can be best achieved by attending to the ways in which the textual material in Numbers 7–10 relates to earlier material in the Pentateuch. It does so in various ways, which we can classify into three broad categories. First, some texts repeat and revise earlier texts from Exodus and Leviticus in rather subtle ways. Secondly, some texts include novel material that has no parallel in the earlier books. Thirdly, some material sits between these two categories. Earlier textual material is reworked, but the changes are more wide-ranging and substantive.

First, some of the textual material in Numbers 7–10 repeats and revises texts from Exodus and Leviticus in subtle ways. A first example of such revision is the fragmentary Num 7:89 that presents itself as the fulfillment of Exod 25:22 by reusing the same language.[10] According to Exod 25:22 God will meet with Moses in the holy of holies and there receive the commandments. In the book of Exodus, the completion of the Tabernacle saw YHWH's glory fill the sanctuary such that Moses could not enter it (Exod 40:34–35). At no point in the subsequent narrative was it specified when or how Moses regained access to the tent of meeting. The opening of the book of Leviticus that presents God speaking to Moses "from the

---

5. Baruch A. Levine, *Numbers 1–20* (AB; Garden City, NY: Doubleday, 1993), 295.

6. Jacob Milgrom, *Numbers* במדבר (JPS Torah Commentary; Philadelphia, PA: Jewish Publication Society, 1990), 362–4.

7. George Buchanan Gray, *Numbers* (ICC; Edinburgh: T&T Clark, 1903), 75.

8. Davies, *Numbers*, 71.

9. Sturdy shows greater literary appreciation than Davies. "This is a flashback. It is not an instance of carelessness, for this earlier date comes again in 9:1 and 9:15" (John Sturdy, *Numbers* [CBC; Cambridge: Cambridge University Press, 1976], 56).

10. Gray, *Numbers*, 77.

tent of meeting" (מאהל מועד; Lev 1:1) could quite legitimately be understood to mean that Moses stood outside the tent while God spoke from its midst,[11] but in Num 1:1 God speaks to Moses a month later "in the tent of meeting" (באהל מועד). Thus, 7:89 resolves an issue created by 1:1 and suggests that after the dedication of the altar, Moses was again able to enter the Tabernacle.[12] A second example of repetition and revision is the instructions about the lampstand in 8:1–4, which repeats material found in Exodus 25, 37 and Leviticus 24. In the instructions to Moses in Exod 25:31–40, directions are given about how the light from the lampstand is to be cast: "you shall make the seven lamps, and the lamps shall be set up so as to illuminate the area in front of it" (ועשית את נרתיה שבעה והעלה את נרתיה והאיר על עבר פניה; 25:37). In the account of the lampstand's fabrication no mention is made of the orientation of the lamps, and Num 8:1–4 fills this lacuna. It also clarifies the unique expression על עבר פניה with the more familiar priestly expression אל מול פני.[13] A third example of repetition and revision is the account of the accompaniment of the cloud in Num 9:15–23, which reprises the final verses of Exodus 40. In Exodus 40 the Israelites' journeying is determined by the cloud, but a definite progress is anticipated. Whenever the cloud lifts, the Israelites set out on the next stage of their journey. The account in Num 9:15–23 is rather more convoluted and anticipates the stuttering movements in the wilderness that will characterize the Israelites' experience in the book of Numbers. Sometimes the cloud moves forward on the following day, but at other times it will rest for days, a month, or even longer (v. 22). The revision of the material from Exodus 40 also insists that the movement is always according to YHWH's mouth (על פי יהוה), a characteristic expression of the book of Numbers' framing chapters.[14]

Secondly, some of the texts in Numbers 7–10 consist of novel material that lack any parallel in Exodus and Leviticus. A first example is the lengthy list of offerings brought by the tribal leaders (Num 7:10–88) and the wagons that transported them (7:3–9), which are given to the Levitical clans of the Gershonites and the Merarites for the transportation of the Tabernacle's paraphernalia. In the initial account of the Tabernacle's first month in Exodus 25–Leviticus 8,[15] only Moses

---

11. Karl Elliger, *Leviticus* (HzAT 4; Tübingen: Mohr Siebeck), 34.

12. See also Milgrom, *Numbers*, 59, who refers to the seven-day ordination ceremony of the priests instead.

13. The expression אל עבר occurs in Exod 28:26; 39:19. Achenbach rightly describes 25:37 as an "etwas kryptischen Text" (Reinhard Achenbach, *Die Vollendung der Tora: Studien zur Redaktionsgeschichte des Numeribuches im Kontext von Hexateuch und Pentateuch* [BZABR 3; Wiesbaden: Harrassowitz Verlag, 2003], 539). Cf., Exod 26:9; 28:25, 37; 39:18; Lev 8:9. This is one reason to reject Kellermann's proposal that Exod 25:37bβ was inserted into 25:31–40 on the basis of Num 8:1–4 (Diether Kellermann, *Die Priesterschrift von Numeri 1,1 bis 10,10: literarkritisch und traditionsgeschichtlich untersucht* [BZAW 120; Berlin: de Gruyter, 1970], 111–15).

14. See Num 3:16, 39, 51; 4:37, 41, 45, 49; 9:18, 20, 23; 10:13; 13:3; 33:38; 36:5.

15. It is widely recognized that Leviticus 8–10 is not a compositional unit. Although Achenbach and Nihan view Leviticus 9 as part of the original priestly account of the

11. Tribal Leaders, Levites, and Ritual Innovation 203

together with Aaron and his sons have a significant role in the functioning of the cult. The people—treated as a unit, the sons of Israel (בני ישראל)—do no more than witness the opening ceremonies around the ordination of the priests, who are then sequestered away for seven days. As is well known, the Levites are almost entirely absent from Exodus to Leviticus, and their occasional appearance is to be attributed to later redactional hands.[16] It is only with Numbers 1–2 that the theocratic ideal of an ordered twelve-tribe camp is presented and with Numbers 3–4, the tribe of Levi. The sacrificial offerings of the tribal leaders retell the earliest days of the Tabernacle's functioning in order to provide a role for the twelve secular tribes,

---

Tabernacle and see Leviticus 10 as a later addition (Reinhard Achenbach, "Das Versagen der Aaroniden: Erwägungen zum literarhistorischen Ort von Leviticus 10," in *"Basel und Bibel": Collected Communications to the XVIIth Congress of the International Organization for the Study of the Old Testament, Basel 2001*, ed. Matthias Augustin and Hermann Michael Niemann [Frankfurt am Main: Peter Lang, 2004], 55–70; Christophe Nihan, *From Priestly Torah to Pentateuch: A Study in the Composition of the Book of Leviticus* [FAT II/25; Tübingen: Mohr Siebeck, 2007], 111–50, 576–607), the ritual of the eighth day in Leviticus 9 is entirely unanticipated. The primary reason for seeing a caesura between chs 9 and 10 is the sudden change of mood, but this is an ingredient to the narrative of Aaron's sons. The novelty of Leviticus 9 means that we would be better to see a literary-critical rupture between chs 8 and 9 (cf., Gary A. Anderson, "'Through Those Who Are Near to Me, I Will Show Myself Holy': Nadab and Abihu and Apophatic Theology," *CBQ* 77 [2015]: 1–19 [here 8 n.17]; Andreas Ruwe, "Das Reden und Verstummen Aarons vor Mose: Leviticus 9–10 im Buch Leviticus," in *Behutsames Lesen: Alttestamentliche Exegese im interdisziplinären Methodendiskurs. Christof Hardmeier zum 65. Geburtstag*, ed. Louis C. Jonker et al. [Arbeiten zur Bibel und ihrer Geschichte 28; Leipzig: Evangelische Verlagsanstalt, 2007], 169–96). The addition of Leviticus 9 itself transforms the first month of the Tabernacle's operation by having the people contribute an offering and witnessing the appearance of the divine presence.

16. The exceptions are Exod 6:25; 32:25–28; 38:21; Lev 25:32–33. Exodus 6:25 concludes the genealogy of Moses and Aaron (6:14–25), a text that has long been recognized as intrusive and has affinities with some of the latest parts of the Pentateuch including texts in Numbers (Achenbach, *Vollendung*, 110–24). Similarly, the reference to the Levites in the story of the Golden Calf (Exod 32:25–28) has also been judged an addition. Their appearance is unanticipated and the slaughter of just 3,000 when the entire people are guilty is unexplained. (For a recent examination coming to a different view, see Harald Samuel, *Von Priestern zum Patriarchen: Levi und die Leviten im Alten Testament* [BZAW 448; Berlin: de Gruyter, 2014], 270–94.) The mention of the Levites in Exod 38:21 is entirely unanticipated and seems to have in view their work of transportation. It appears rather oddly in a text that is concerned with the fabrication of the Tabernacle (S. R. Driver, *The Book of Exodus* [CBC; Cambridge: Cambridge University Press, 1911], 392; Samuel, *Von Priestern*, 294–5). The reference to the Levites in the Jubilee legislation (Lev 25:32–33) presupposes the legislation about the Levitical cities and is usually judged an interpolation (Nihan, *Priestly Torah*, 522n. 503).

their leaders, and the Levites. A second example is the instructions about the silver trumpets in Num 10:1–10. The instructions presuppose the organization of the camp described in Numbers 1–2. The sounding of a trumpet is already mentioned in relation to the holy convocation on the first day of the seventh month (Lev 23:24) and on Yom Kippur (25:9), and these could be reflected in the requirement that the trumpets be blown on festival days (Num 10:10). The use of the trumpets on other occasions sees this practice extended in various directions perhaps under the influence of other biblical texts, such as the account of the fall of Jericho (Joshua 6).[17]

Thirdly, some of the texts rework earlier texts with changes that are wide-ranging and substantive. A first example is the instructions for a deferred Passover in Num 9:1–14. The Israelites are instructed to keep the Passover at the appointed time on the fourteenth day of the first month (vv. 1–5), but some are prevented from offering the Passover because they have corpse impurity (vv. 6–8). Consequently, they find themselves in breach of Numbers 28, which requires that offerings be made at their appointed time (v. 2; cf. 9:13).[18] The issue could only have arisen with the instructions that those with corpse impurity be expelled from the camp (Num 5:1–4; 19:1–22). A deferred Passover is permitted a month later, and the language of the Passover instructions in Exodus 12 is reused to insist that the same regulations apply to the deferred Passover as the one held in the first month.[19] A second example is the ritual for the purification of the Levites in Num 8:5–22, which reworks the divine speech in Numbers 3 into a ritual. As already noted, the Levites are hardly present in Exodus and Leviticus, and it is only in the book of Numbers that they emerge with any clarity. This is most persuasively explained by recognizing the references to the Levites in Exodus and Leviticus as late redactional insertions, and the lower clergy as a distinctive contribution of the book of Numbers.[20] According to Num 3:5–13, the Levites substitute for the firstborn male Israelites and assist Aaron and his sons in the Tabernacle service. The offering of the Levites to the priesthood is realized through a ritual in which the Levites are given as a "presentation" (תנופה). This ritual reflects the manipulation undergone by the brisket of the well-being offering, which was given to the entire priesthood by the offerers. Its altered status was realized through the rite of תנופה in which the brisket was presented in the direction of the deity (Lev 7:28–36).[21]

---

17. Achenbach, *Vollendung*, 553–6.
18. Ibid., 548.
19. There are numerous textual links between Exodus 12 and Numbers 9: vv. 2, 5 (Exod 12:6), v. 11 (Exod 12:8), v. 12 (Exod 12:10, 43, 46), v. 14 (Exod 12:48–49). For a nuanced discussion, see Simeon Chavel, *Oracular Law and Priestly Historiography in the Torah* (FAT II/71; Tübingen: Mohr Siebeck, 2014), 93–164.
20. See especially Samuel, *Von Priestern*.
21. For discussion of the rite of *tenupah* see Jacob Milgrom, "*Hattĕnûpâ*," in *Studies in Cultic Theology and Terminology* (Studies in Judaism in Late Antiquity 36; Leiden: Brill, 1983), 139–58; Jacob Milgrom, "The Alleged Wave-Offering in Israel and in the Ancient

Thus, just as the brisket was given to the entire priesthood through the rite of תנופה so also the Levites are given to the entire priesthood through the rite of תנופה.

In every case that we have examined, Numbers 7–10 address perceived lacuna within existing Pentateuchal legislation, often lacuna that have emerged only as a result of shifts stemming from the introduction of novel perspectives elsewhere in the book of Numbers. The two rituals that are our especial concern—the offerings of the tribal leaders and the purification of the Levites—arise from the addition of novel material in Numbers 1–4, which describe a hierarchical and differentiated community with twelves tribes positioned around the Tabernacle and three Levitical septs tasked with particular duties for the Tabernacle and the priests. The issue that the scribal author of Numbers 7–10 addresses is how the twelve tribes and the Levites relate to the cult of Exodus and Leviticus focused entirely around the Aaronide priests. The offerings of the tribal leaders and the purification of the Levites seek to retell the first month of the second year in light of the new information contained in Numbers 1–4. By deforming the chronology and revisiting the first month of the Tabernacle's functioning the people and the Levites are given important roles in the cult's inauguration but without by any means diminishing the priesthood's supremacy.

3. *Rewritten Scripture, Intertextuality, and Ritual Innovation*

Why did the author of these new rituals choose to locate them here, rather than in their proper chronological location within the books of Exodus and Leviticus? The idea that those books of Leviticus were closed and were no longer open to editing should be excluded. As Simeon Chavel observes,

> The idea that the interpolator could not add it somewhere in Exodus or Leviticus because these scrolls were somehow closed, namely, seen to be in a kind of final form that should not be tampered with, must be discounted at the very outset as fundamentally anachronistic; the idea is totally belied by the wide range of revisionary activity attested in the scrolls found at Qumran, in which one encounters all manner of manipulation of received text, from small insertions to large-scale excerpting to comprehensive recomposition.[22]

Further, some current redactional models allow for very late reworking of the texts of Exodus and Leviticus.[23] The problem facing our author was that locating these new rituals in their chronological place in Exodus and Leviticus would also have

---

Near East," *IEJ* 22 (1972): 33–8; Nathan MacDonald, "Scribalism and Ritual Innovation," *HeBAI* 7 (2018): 415–29.

22. Chavel, *Oracular Law*, 116.

23. See, e.g., Nihan and Achenbach's arguments about the late insertion of Leviticus 10 (see n. 16 above).

required inserting all the material in Numbers 1–4 at earlier points. Narratively rewinding the clock by a month is a simpler and more elegant solution. In its own way this scribal technique provides an interesting insight into the aesthetic sensibilities of the composer of these chapters.[24]

We might describe the composition of Numbers 7–10 by appeal to the notion of rewritten Scripture. In other words, Numbers 7–10 is a *rewriting* of the first month after the Tabernacle's completion, and here I am understanding *rewriting* as an exegetical technique, rather than as a genre.[25] One of the advantages of rewriting, rather than inserting the material of Numbers 7–10 into their expected position in Exodus and Leviticus, is that it allows parallel versions of the narrative to coexist without forcing the writer to explicate their precise relationships. This is especially apparent if we try to reflect on how the offerings of the tribal leaders relate to the seven-day ordination ceremony, for attempting to enact the ceremony would have generated some significant difficulties.

The date at the beginning of Exodus 40 indicates that the completion of the Tabernacle occurred on the first day of the first month and we would naturally expect that the seven-day ordination ceremony took place on the first seven days of the first month. But if the chieftains approached Moses on the first day of the

---

24. As already appreciated by Gordon J. Wenham,

> It would no doubt have been possible to have included the material in Numbers 7–9 at appropriate points in the main narrative of Exodus 40 to Numbers 1. But the present arrangement makes for a clearer exposition of the main themes of Leviticus and at the same time permits the reader to see the full significance of the tribal gifts to the altar. Had the narrative in Leviticus been interrupted by twelve notices of tribal gifts on twelve consecutive days, it would have obscured the focus of that book on the sacrifices and the ordination of Aaron. (*Numbers* [TOTC; Leicester: Inter-Varsity Press, 1981], 92)

25. In his seminal essay on "rewritten Bible," Philip Alexander identifies a number of characteristics of rewritten Bible that would also apply to Numbers 7–10: (1) These chapters form a sequential narrative; (2) They are not intended to replace or supersede the texts they reproduce; (3) Readers are expected to call the originals to mind as they read; (4) The retelling is highly selective and includes expansions; (5) The texts produce an interpretive reading of Scripture. In some other respects, of course, these chapters do not correspond with Alexander's characterization of late Second Temple rewritten Bible. In particular, these chapters are not free-standing compositions nor do they cover a substantial portion of the Bible (Philip S. Alexander, "Retelling the Old Testament," in *It Is Written: Scripture Citing Scripture: Essays in Honour of Barnabas Lindars, SSF*, ed. Donald A. Carson and Hugh G. M. Williamson [Cambridge: Cambridge University Press, 1988], 99–121). The comparison is easier to make if we understand "rewritten scripture" as an exegetical technique, as some do, rather than as a genre, as Alexander does in this essay. It is also possible if we view "rewritten scripture" as an exegetical technique with fuzzy boundaries, which overlapped with other exegetical techniques. For discussion see Molly M. Zahn, "Genre and Rewritten Scripture: A Reassessment," *JBL* 131 (2012): 271–88.

first month with their offerings, this would see the first seven chieftains offering their gifts while the priests were sequestered in the tent of meeting during the ordination ritual. Rashi follows the rabbis in arguing that the ordination ritual took place during the final days of the twelfth month, which would allow the leaders to bring their offerings on the first twelve days of the first month. Ramban rejects this approach and argues that the seven-day ordination ritual took place at the beginning of the first month, and the offerings of the leaders took place on the eighth to the nineteenth days of the first month.[26] Yet, as Jacob Milgrom observes that would mean the offerings of the tribal leaders overlapped with the celebration of Passover.[27] All of these proposals also stumble over Num 7:10, which would identify the first day of the chieftains' offerings with the day that the altar was anointed, which was the first day of the seven-day ordination ceremony (Lev 8:10). Milgrom's own solution is "that none of these offerings were actually sacrificed on the day it was brought to the Tabernacle."[28] This seems far from satisfactory either, for in the sacrificial legislation of Leviticus the offerer plays a role in the sacrificial ritual. Were the tribal leaders meant to return to the Tabernacle a few days later to reclaim their animals and only then sacrifice them?

The relationship between the two texts can be illuminated through the image of the palimpsest that Gérard Genette used as his overarching metaphor for describing intertextuality.[29] A palimpsest is a text that is overwritten by another text such that the original text is still visible below it. The repurposing of textual

---

26. Michael Carasik, *The Commentators' Bible. The JPS Miqra'ot Gedolot. Numbers* במדבר (Philadelphia, PA: Jewish Publication Society, 2011), 44–5.
27. Milgrom, *Numbers*, 362.
28. Ibid., 363.
29. Gérard Genette, *Palimpsest: Literature in the Second Degree*, trans. Channa Newman and Claude Doubinsky (Lincoln: University of Nebraska Press, 1997). More accurately, in this volume Genette addresses what he calls "hypertextuality." The deriving of one text, the *hypertext*, from another, the *hypotext*. Although Genette explores six categories of hypertextuality in all their variety, his definition of hypertextuality is also rather restricted. "I will ... deal here with ... [cases] in which the shift from hypotext to hypertext is both massive (an entire work B deriving from an entire work A) and more or less officially stated" (Genette, *Palimpsest*, 9). Genette's concern here is to avoid diluting hypertextuality into a characteristic of all literature since no literary work avoids evoking some other literary work to some degree. Genette's concern is to analyze the ways in which texts are manipulated, rather than create a poststructuralist philosophy in the manner of Julia Kristeva. Genette classifies two types of relations that hypertexts have to their hypotexts: transformation and imitation. Hypertextuality is just one instance of what Genette calls "transtextuality," the others being paratextuality, metatextuality, architextuality and what Genette labels "intertextuality," the direction citation of one text by another. For the various ways in which the metaphor of the palimpsest has been used in thinking about literature from Thomas De Quincey to Genette, see Sarah Dillon, *The Palimpsest: Literature, Criticism and Theory* (London: Bloomsbury, 2007).

material from Exodus 25–40 means the knowledgeable reader is very well aware of one text being taken into another and the two accounts inhabiting the same space in a complicated manner. This is the kind of meaning that Genette has in mind with the application of the palimpsest as a metaphor for intertextuality. Yet, we can also pursue this metaphor of a palimpsest further, for in a palimpsest two very different texts inhabit the same space, not related texts as in theories of intertextuality. We might find, for example, an ancient treatise of Aristotle in Greek partially erased and replaced by a liturgical text in Latin. An important consequence is that it is not possible to read both texts simultaneously. To read one, we must consciously suppress the other text in our mind, whether written below or written above. This idea would equally apply to Numbers 7–8. The offerings of the tribal leaders are a coherent ritual imagined on its own terms, so too is the seven-day ordination ritual, but attempting to read them together as a single ritual complex introduces all sorts of practical problems.

These different significances of the metaphor of the palimpsest provide a useful standpoint from which to view the relationship between the ritual by which Aaron and his sons are ordained for priestly service, and the ritual by which the Levites are purified for their service. As we have already seen, the purification of the Levites appropriates textual material from Num 3:11–13 in Num 8:14–18, and from Leviticus 1–7 in Num 8:5–13. Interestingly, there is very little textual overlap between the ordination of the priests in Leviticus 8 and the purification of the Levites. First, the expression "from the midst of the sons of Israel" (מתוך בני ישראל) is found in Exod 28:1 and Num 8:6. This precise expression is only found in Exodus 28 and of the Levites in Numbers 3, 8, and 18. It seems more likely though that the use in Num 8:6 is derived from Num 3:12 where the Levites are also said to have been "taken from the midst of the sons of Israel." Secondly, both sets of instructions begin with something like "this is what you shall do to them," but the precise expressions are different in each case. Numbers 8:7 reads וכה תעשה להם while Exod 29:1 reads וזה הדבר אשר תעשה להם. Thirdly, in both rituals a bull is offered as a sin offering, though one or other ritual may reflect the instructions of Leviticus 4 that require a bull to be offered by the congregation. Both rituals share references to the laying of hands upon the sacrifice, but this is a feature of many pieces of sacrificial legislation. Fourthly, in both rituals Moses is required to bring those being ordained or purified to the same location at the entrance of the tent of meeting. In both cases the hiphil of קרב is used. The description of the location is not quite identical. Numbers 8:9 speaks of "before the tent of meeting" (לפני אהל מועד), while Exod 29:4 speaks of the entrance of the tent of meeting (אל פתח אהל מועד).

In sum, the connections between the content of the ritual texts are not substantive, instead they rely on the chronological deformation that would place the two rituals at roughly the same time during the inauguration of the Tabernacle.[30] As a result, many have interpreted the ritual of ordination and the

---

30. The purification of the Levites does not present the same chronological challenges as those that circle around the offerings of the tribal leaders. Numbers 8 lacks any precise

ritual of purification in relation to one another. Baruch Levine, for example, opens his observations on the purification of the Levites with "a comparison of the present description of the dedication of the Levites with the consecration of the Aaronide priests, recounted in Leviticus 8–9, may serve to pinpoint significant differences between the two groups."[31] As Levine's words show the purpose of these connections, the reason why they are not substantive is that the ordination of the priests and the purification of the Levites are to be understood according to their differences rather than their similarities.

The first difference is the intended effect of the ritual. The purpose of the ritual for the priests is to "consecrate them" (לקדש אתם; Exod 29:1). In this way they are able to act in the sanctuary by offering sacrifices. In contrast the Levites are only "purified" (לטהרם; Num 8:7). This key difference is expressed most directly by the sprinkling rites. The priests together with their vestments are sprinkled (נזה) with the blood of the burnt offering and the anointing oil (Lev 8:30). This oil has also been used to anoint the Tabernacle and the altar and indexes the close relationship the priests have with the Tabernacle and the altar (8:11).[32] The Levites, however, are sprinkled (נזה) with the "water of purification" (מי חטאת; Num 8:7), an expression found nowhere else in the Hebrew Bible but perhaps related to the "water of impurity" (מי נדה) that results from the red cow ritual in Numbers 19 and is used to remove corpse impurity.[33] The implication seems to be that there is a concern about impurity around the Levites that needs to be treated before they can serve.

The second difference is the intended role within the cult. According to Exod 29:1 the consecration takes place in order that the Aaronides might be YHWH's priests. The priestly role is indexed by the priestly vestments that are given significant levels of instrumental meaning in Exodus 28.[34] In contrast, the Levites are purified in order to "do the service of YHWH" (לעבד את עבדת יהוה; Num 8:11). עבדה is used consistently of Levitical service in Numbers with the exception of 18:7, an unresolved textual crux.[35] The various menial tasks fulfilled by the Levites do not require any change of garments, only their washing.

---

chronological markers, and the purification of the Levites could be imagined to take place after the twelve days during which the tribal leaders make their offerings and the celebration of the Passover on the fourteenth day of the month. This would place the purification of the Levites almost a week after the seven-day ritual of ordination.

31. Levine, *Numbers 1–20*, 273; Davies, *Numbers*, 76; Philip J. Budd, *Numbers* (WBC 5; Waco, TX: Word Books, 1984), 92; Milgrom, *Numbers*, 61.

32. William K. Gilders, *Blood Ritual in the Hebrew Bible* (Baltimore, MD: John Hopkins University Press, 2004), 103.

33. Gray identifies the two (*Numbers*, 79), while Levine regards it as "improbable" (*Numbers*, 274, 464). Davies is cautious about an equation of the two (Davies, *Numbers*, 77).

34. Nathan MacDonald, "The Priestly Vestments," in *Nudity and Clothing in the Hebrew Bible*, ed. Christoph Berner et al. (London: Bloomsbury T&T Clark, 2019), 435–48.

35. Milgrom observes that the offending clause is missing in the parallel text of 3:10 (*Numbers*, 315n. 17).

Finally, the Levites are described in sacrificial terms, rather than as those who offer sacrifices. The people lay their hands on the Levites as they would a bovine or caprovine, and the Levites are given as a presentation (תנופה) to the Lord. As we have seen, the application of תנופה to the Levites indexes the presentation of the brisket in Leviticus 7. After the ritual of תנופה is performed, the brisket belongs to the priesthood as a whole. The Levites are given to the priesthood from the entirety of the people of Israel just as the brisket was given to the priesthood from the entirety of the sacrifice.[36] The use of the rite of תנופה in the purification of the Levites only makes sense as a literary conceit. As critical interpreters have long observed, the idea that the Levites could be presented as a sacrificial portion through elevation is difficult to understand as a ritual instruction. How could it have been performed? As Baruch Levine notes, "usage here is more figurative than literal."[37] The centrality of the figurative must call into question proposals for discerning a practiced ritual behind Numbers 8. These include Philip Budd's suggestion that we have a Palestinian ordination tradition that contrasted with the Babylonian ordination tradition of Exodus 29 and Leviticus 8.[38] His proposal is highly speculative and relies on Paul Hanson's highly problematic attempt to reconstruct the history of the priests and Levites.[39] They also include Jonathan Stökl's recent analysis of Numbers 8.[40] In Stökl's view a purificatory rite similar to Numbers 8 would have been needed for all priests and temple personnel. I am not convinced this is true. While some physical examination must have been conducted by a priest to ensure that priests and Levites entering cultic service were without blemish, the priestly literature does not lack purificatory procedures such as laundering clothes, bathing and waiting until sundown. In contrast to Stökl I see the purification ritual in Numbers 8 is an artificial conceit, an example of ritual bricolage, which could not have been practiced but was constructed in order to make theological points about the respective status of priests and Levites. Within the Pentateuch distinguishing two levels of clergy is novel and almost entirely restricted to the book of Numbers.

The idea of the palimpsest is again quite a productive one for thinking about the purification of the Levites and how it relates to the priestly ordination in Leviticus. As we have seen with the offerings by the secular tribes, the appearance of this ritual text presents difficulties in seeking to envisage how the ordination of the priests and the purification of the Levites are to be enacted in relation to one another. The conceptual logic is that both ordination and purification mirror one another. As we read the ritual of Levitical purification, the palimpsestuous text of the priestly

---

36. For this reason מאת בני ישראל in Num 8:11 should probably be translated as "from the Israelites" and not as "on behalf of the Israelites" (contra Levine, *Numbers*, 270).

37. Levine, *Numbers*, 276.

38. Budd, *Numbers*, 92.

39. Paul D. Hanson, *The Dawn of Apocalyptic: The Historical and Sociological Roots of Jewish Apocalyptic Eschatology* (Philadelphia, PA: Fortress Press, 1979).

40. Stökl, "Innovating Ordination."

ordination bleeds through, providing the Levitical purification with contrastive meaning. The underlying text disrupts the overwriting text, identifying the ritual of purification as parodic: less an honor and more a humiliation. The underlying text of the priestly ordination is both *not* there and *always* there. On the other hand, the conceptual simultaneity presents a challenge for realizing the ritual practically. How might this ritual be realized at the same time as the ordination ritual? Like the palimpsest, we can only read one text—or rather we can only enact one ritual—if we mentally exclude the other.

A further implication of the imagery of the palimpsest is also relevant here and that is the fact that the original text is never the same once it has been written over, even if we are capable of reading it. We can—and should—use our scholarly tools like chemical detergents or different spectrums of light to read the text in its original context, but there is also a way in which for readers the underlying text is changed by the overwriting. As biblical scholars we rarely attend to the effect palimpsestuousness has on the overwritten text. We are content merely to examine the text that is chronologically later without considering the potential effect a scribe may have produced on the original text. Usually, only if there is a subsequent intervention by a scribe into the original text do we consider the possible implications of a subsequent interpretation. In this respect ritual and ritual texts prove good to think with. It is not possible to think about how to affect the ordination of the priests ritually without also thinking about how it is to be coordinated with the offerings by the secular tribes and the purification of the Levites.

Chapter 12

MONUMENTALIZING SLAUGHTER: "CUTTING A COVENANT" IN THE HEBREW BIBLE AND LEVANTINE INSCRIPTIONS

Melissa Ramos

1. Introduction

The ratification of an oath by ritual enactment is captured in the expression "to cut a covenant" (לכרות ברית) found throughout the Hebrew Bible.[1] This West Semitic expression encapsulates the ritual practice of slaughtering animals as an integral part of the ratification of treaties and covenants in the Levant. Thus, the phrase reflects the intertwining of ritual practice with linguistic technical terminology for oath-making. In the ancient Near East, oaths and treaties were enacted by ritual performances; their textualization was formulated according to a set layout that included a preamble, a list of divine witnesses, a pronouncement of the stipulations of the terms of the agreement, and curses that were typically performed orally. These stock elements were frequently accompanied by a dramatization of the effects of the curses using food products or figurines. The effect of this physical enactment was to illustrate the terrors of violating the oath agreement; thus, the oath or treaty performance served as a form of ritual rhetoric intended to inculcate fear of the curses and to ensure obedience to the oath stipulations.[2] The ritual enactment frequently included the crafting of a visual display of the oath performance, a monumental symbol that captured this ritual and textual rhetoric and made it accessible to all who might encounter the monument.

This study explores the origin of the term "cut a covenant" in the ritual practices of the northern Levant during the Late Bronze and Iron Ages and also examines its

---

1. As early as 1885 H. Clay Trumbull observed the importance of the blood covenant as an important "ancient Semitic rite" that shaped covenantal narratives in the Hebrew Bible, a rite that he claims was still in practice in Syria in his own day and time. H. Clay Trumbull, *The Blood Covenant: A Primitive Rite and Its Bearings on Scripture* (New York: Charles Scribner's Sons, 1885), 4–12.

2. Melissa Ramos, *Ritual in Deuteronomy: The Performance of Doom* (New York: Routledge, 2021), 47–66.

connection with monumentality. The phrase "cut a covenant" is found both in the Hebrew Bible and in other West Semitic texts from the Late Bronze and Iron Ages.³ While the practice of animal slaughter that is reflected in the phrase has long been recognized as a feature of Levantine oath enactment, far less attention has been given to the connection between "cutting a covenant" and monumentality. Iron Age Levantine inscriptions such as the Sefire and Tel Dan stelae, and the Arslan Tash amulets demonstrate the connection between "cutting a covenant" and the crafting of visual media as an important component of the ritual enactment of oaths. Like the Iron Age inscriptions, the Hebrew Bible emphasizes the crafting of monuments as symbols of the performance of a covenant oath.

This study (1) contextualizes the expression "cut a covenant" in the Late Bronze and Iron Age covenant ceremonies and their textualization, thus adding a more robust comparative analysis; (2) argues for the importance of context in the study of the diverse terms and ritual practices connected to this expression; (3) highlights an important change in the Iron Age epigraphic materials, specifically a shift in emphasis away from slaughter as the primary focus of enacting a covenant and toward monumentality and textualization; (4) concludes that the Hebrew Bible, like the Iron Age Levantine inscriptions, frequently transposes the ritual of cutting an animal to the cutting of stone as the primary event of enacting a covenant. While the origins of the phrase "to cut a covenant" are in the Amorite practice of animal slaughter as a means of demonstrating a curse, in the Hebrew Bible and most especially in Deuteronomy and the Deuteronomistic History the phrase takes on a new meaning and a new ritual practice, namely, the erection of a monument. While the Hebrew Bible retains the phrase "cut a covenant" and vestiges of the ancient practice of cutting an animal, narratives of covenant performances more frequently emphasize cutting stone and erecting a monument.

2. *"Cutting a Covenant": Examining Ritual Origins in Northwest Semitic Inscriptions*

While the phrase "cut a covenant" is ubiquitous in the Hebrew Bible, it is not a common phrase in the wider ancient Near East. Neo-Assyrian oath texts employ somewhat different terminology for ratifying oaths and do not use verbs meaning "to cut" to refer to the conclusion of an oath or a treaty. For example, the Succession Treaty of Esarhaddon (STE) uses more prosaic verbs to refer to its loyalty oath, typically *šakānu* ("to make or establish") paired with *adê* ("oath" or "pact").⁴

---

3. William Foxwell Albright, "The Hebrew Expression for 'Making a Covenant' in Pre-Israelite Documents," *BASOR* 121 (1951): 21–2; J. Alberto Soggin, "Akkadisch TAR BERÎTI und Hebraïsch כרת ברית," *VT* 18 (1968): 210–15.

4. The verb *danānu* is also sometimes used in conjunction with *šakānu*, yet no verbs meaning "cut" are employed in language of ratification of the treaty. See the STE, e.g.: Simo Parpola and Kazuko Watanabe, *Neo-Assyrian Treaties and Loyalty Oaths* (SAA 2; Helsinki: Helsinki University Press, 1988), lines 41–2, 65, 96, 104, 283–7.

While the STE does include animal slaughter as a demonstration of a curse, the offering of sacrifices does not seem to be the main featured ritual element of the treaty's ratification. In the entire STE the slaughter of an animal is only mentioned in the ceremonial curse segment in two short curse sequences. The treaty does not mention animal sacrifice in the preamble portion, nor does it mention the instructions or the colophon.[5] An important exception to this characterization of Neo-Assyrian treaties is found in the treaty of Aššur-nerari V with Mati-ilu, the Levantine ruler of Arpad, which seems to present a parallel Akkadian version of the Sefire treaty. The presentation of a lamb is a central feature; however, the treaty specifies that the lamb presented "is not for slaughter."[6] The inclusion of the lamb and emphasis that it will not be slaughtered further also suggest that slaughter was perceived as a Levantine practice rather than an Assyrian one.

Like Neo-Assyrian treaties, Hittite oaths do not use the phrase "cut a covenant" and animal slaughter is not a central feature of oath enactment. As Ada Taggar-Cohen observes, Hittite treaties do not include the element of sacrifice as a means of ratifying the terms of the agreement in the way that biblical covenants do.[7] Hittite uses the unique word *išhiul* ("oath") to refer to treaties themselves and uses more ordinary verbs to refer to the performative enactment.[8] Hittite oath texts include performative ritual actions such as the manipulation of food products or objects but do not include ritual slaughter in concluding a treaty or an oath.

The specific phrase "to cut a covenant" also appears in Levantine inscriptions dating to the Late Bronze and Iron Ages.[9] The specific use of a verb meaning "to cut" in conjunction with a word meaning "oath" or "covenant" occurs in the following texts: economic texts from Mari and Qatna from the Late Bronze Age; stelae from Sefire and Tel Dan; and amulets from Arslan Tash from the Iron Age.[10] While the phraseology for "cut a covenant" is not identical in these texts, each

---

5. Parpola and Watanabe, *Neo-Assyrian Treaties*, 52 (lines 547–54).

6. Ibid., 8–9.

7. Ada Taggar-Cohen, "Biblical Covenant and Hittite išhiul Reexamined," VT 61 (2011): 461–88, here 486.

8. Ibid., 461–88.

9. A similar phrase for oath-making, *horkia tamnein*, is also found in Homer, in some archaic Ionian inscriptions and in Herodotus' description of Scythian oath-making practices. One could perhaps speculate about the spread of Northern Levantine oath-making rituals via the Phoenician maritime trade industry in the Mediterranean world. François Hartog, *The Mirror of Herodotus: The Representation of the Other in the Writing of History*, trans. by Janet Lloyd (New Historicism; Berkeley: University of California Press, 2009), 114.

10. The idea of an underlying West Semitic term is strengthened by a possible occurrence of *brt* in the literature of Ugarit in RS 15.134. *UDB* (1.82:5) renders this line as *hm tgrm lmt brpk*. However, the final letters of the last word are not entirely clear and are inscribed at the rounded edge of a tablet. The word could plausibly also be *brtk* since the difference between a *k* and a *t* in the Ugaritic script is in a single incised line stroke. Gregorio del Olmo Lete,

uses a version of the phrase pairing a verb meaning "cut" with a noun for "oath" or "covenant." Thus, the phrase "to cut a covenant" seems to be unique to West Semitic language and a distinctive feature of oath rituals from the Levant.

The texts from the Late Bronze Age demonstrate that, as early as the fifteenth century BCE, verbs for "cutting" were used in the Northern Levant as technical terminology for covenant-making, and that some of these were used in conjunction with a word phonetically similar to ברית. While several studies have analyzed the biblical phrase ברית and its possible origins, these studies have focused primarily on the origins of the Hebrew word ברית rather than on the combination of a verb meaning "to cut" used together with a word meaning "oath" or "contractual agreement."[11] The combination of "cut" with "oath" or "agreement" forms the ritual terminology and served as a marker of Amorite identity and cultural practice initially but became more broadly Levantine. Along with the ritual technology of slaughter, the specific phraseology כרת ברית most likely spread to ancient Israel by means of enacted treaties between the northern Kingdom of Israel and Aram.[12]

The ritual practice of erecting a monument to memorialize the ritual performance of an oath or a treaty is also seen specifically in the Iron Age Northwest Semitic inscriptions with an emphasis on the visual display of a treaty oath. The phrase appears in different types of media in the Late Bronze versus the Iron Ages: while the Late Bronze Age inscriptions are tablets recording economic transactions, the Iron Age inscriptions are royal monumental inscriptions crafted for display. Although the Sefire treaty includes animal slaughter in the text of its inscription, the emphasis in the Iron Age texts seems to shift toward the crafting of monuments as the primary ritual enactment of oaths. These monuments serve as permanent visual symbols of the oath ratification event, rendering the event of the enactment itself more permanent and more accessible by those who encounter the monument.

This first segment of the study explores the phrase "cut a covenant" from a *longue durée* perspective, surveying the Late Bronze and Iron Age inscriptions of the northern Levant. Late Bronze inscriptions from Mari, Qatna, and Alalah will be explored first, and Iron Age inscriptions from Sefire, Tel Dan, and Arslan Tash second.

Joaquín Sanmartín, and W. G. E. Watson read the text in this manner. See *A Dictionary of the Ugaritic Language in the Alphabetic Tradition*, vol. 1, trans. and ed. W. G. E. Watson; 3rd ed. (HdO 112; Boston: Brill, 2015), 238.

11. Albright, "The Hebrew Expression for 'Making a Covenant,'" 21–2; Cross, *Canaanite Myth and Hebrew Epic: Essays in the History of the Religion of Israel* (Boston: Harvard University Press, 1973), 265–73; Moshe Held, "Philological Notes on the Mari Covenant Rituals," *BASOR* 20 (1970): 32–40; Martin Noth, *The Laws in the Pentateuch, and Other Studies* (Minneapolis, MN: Fortress Press, 1967), 108–17; J. Alberto Soggin, "Akkadisch TAR BERÎTI und Hebraïsch כרת ברית," *VT* 18/2 1968): 210–15.

12. E.g., in 1 Kgs 20:31–35 Ahab of Israel makes a treaty (כרת ברית) with Ben Hadad of Damascus.

2.1. Cutting a Covenant at Mari

Two texts from the Late Bronze Age city of Mari make reference to killing an animal as part of the ritual activity of concluding a treaty. The text of one letter, in particular, uses terminology for making an oath that is remarkably similar to that of the Hebrew Bible and includes the term *birīt*. The text of this letter includes this excerpt:

hayarim qatālim birīt ḫanê u Idamaraṣ

to kill a donkey foal (= to conclude a treaty) between the Hane and Idamaraṣ.[13]

In this line of the Mari text, the phrase "to kill a donkey foal" is used as a technical term for concluding a covenant or treaty. This is made clear further down in the letter:

hayaram mār atānim anāku ušaqtil salīmam birīt ḫanê u Idamaraṣ aškun

a donkey foal, the offspring of a she-donkey, I killed, (which) established an agreement between Hane and Idamaraṣ.[14]

The phrase *hayarim qatālum* ("to kill a donkey foal") in this line of the letter is used as a technical ritual term that is rendered into Akkadian as *salīmam sakānum* ("to establish/conclude an agreement/reconciliation").[15] The two terms are presented in parallel, with the native West Semitic phrase given first and its Akkadian equivalent given second in an explanatory clause. This example from Mari demonstrates that the slaughter of an animal was an integral component to the ritual enactment of covenants in Late Bronze Age Amorite culture, so integral that the phrase "to kill a donkey" served as a technical shorthand to refer to the establishment of an oath agreement.

2.2. Cutting a Covenant at Qatna

Two texts from Qatna in Syria also give clues about the early use of the phrase "to cut a covenant" during the Late Bronze Age.[16] An excavation in 1927 unearthed fifteen cuneiform tablets dating to approximately 1400 BCE.[17] The expression "to

---

13. Held, "Philological Notes," 33.
14. Ibid.
15. Cross, *Canaanite Myth and Hebrew Epic*, 265–6.
16. Albright, "The Hebrew Expression for 'Making a Covenant,'" 21.
17. Hatti destroyed and burned Qatna including its royal palace in the fourteenth century BCE, thus giving a *terminus ad quem* for these texts. Jean Bottéro, "Les Inventaires de Qatna," *Revue d'Assyriologie et d'Archaéologie Orientale* 1–2 (1949): 1–40, here 1; Gernot Wilhelm, "Suppiluliuma and the Decline of the Mittanian Kingdom," in *Qaṭna and the Networks of Bronze Age Globalism: Proceedings of an International Conference in Stuttgart and Tübingen in October 2009*, ed. Peter Pfälzner and Michel Al-Maqdissi, vol. 2 of *Qaṭna Studien Supplementa* (Wiesbaden: Harrassowitz Verlag, 2015), 69–70, 75–7.

cut a covenant" appears in two separate tablets that appear to be economic texts. The first tablet begins with the phrase TAR *be-ri-ti* followed by two lists of names. The second tablet begins with the same phrase followed by a list of goods that likely refer to rations provided as part of the oath or agreement.

The Akkadian construction bears remarkable similarity to the Hebrew Bible's phraseology כרת ברית. The verb written with the logogram TAR is rendered by the verb *parāsu* meaning "to cut, sever, or apportioning something."[18] However, the logogram's usage and history are more complex. As Alberto Soggin observes, TAR appears in New Sumerian legal documents with the meaning "swear" or "take an oath" or even "conjure."[19] The Akkadian word *be-ri-ti* and its relationship to the Hebrew ברית is also fraught with difficulty, especially since, in both of the Qatna texts, the phrase appears in a single opening line before a list of persons or goods, and thus the inscription does not provide much in the way of a contextual framework for discerning whether the word is functioning as the preposition *birīt* meaning "between, among" or the noun *birītu* meaning "link, clasp, or fetter," which could refer to an oath in a metaphorical way.[20] If the word is a preposition, this would fit better with its use in the Mari text discussed below. Yet, if this word is understood as a preposition, there is no direct object for TAR, and some element of the meaning must be implied by the logogram TAR alone.

In the first tablet from Qatna, one could make the argument that the meaning of TAR *be-ri-ti* should be rendered "is/was cut with/between/among" followed by a list of names. No specified object whether real or metaphorical is supplied, but perhaps an economic text such as this might employ this phrase as a shorthand to refer to a covenant that was enacted by a ritual slaughter of some sort. However, this rendering of the phrase is quite problematic and likely impossible for the second tablet that furnishes a list of goods rather than a list of names. If the preposition *birīt* is assumed, then the tablet would read "is/was cut with/between/among" followed by a list of rations. One might arrive at a roundabout meaning of a list of rations shared among a group as part of an oath agreement, yet this understanding of *be-ri-ti* seems to force meaning out of a ration list. The context of the second tablet thus suggests that *be-ri-ti* in both tablets more likely functions more as a noun. Perhaps, as Cross suggests, this is the noun *birītu* meaning "clasp, fetter" intended as a metaphor for the covenant.[21] However, *birītu* might also be a calque for a local West Semitic term for an oath agreement employed as an

---

18. Martha T. Roth, "Parāsu," *CAD* 12: 165–78.
19. Soggin, "TAR BERÎTI und 213."
20. Albright, e.g., argued that the term referred to the Akkadian *birītu* meaning "bond, fetter." However, Moshe Held rejects any etymological connection with the Akkadian preposition. Albright, "The Hebrew Expression for 'Making a Covenant,'" 22n. 6; A. Leo Oppenheim, "Birītu," *AD* 2: 252–4; Held, "Philological Notes," 33–4n. 10.
21. Cross, *Canaanite Myth and Hebrew Epic*, 267.

Akkadian equivalent with a similar sound. Thus, it seems possible that a noun like ברית in West Semitic may underlie the use of an Akkadian term with an approximate sound.

The Qatna inscriptions are especially compelling for exploring a relationship between the Hebrew phrase כרת ברית and the peripheral Akkadian TAR *birīti*. The rare pairing of a verb meaning "to cut" with a phrase that sounds so similar to the Hebrew one is unlikely to be coincidental. Furthermore, the fact that two distinct tablets from this site in the Levant employ this phrase TAR (*parāsu*) *be-ri-ti* suggests that influence from the local West Semitic language may account for this unusual phrasing. Bottéro observed that the Qatna texts contain features similar to the Akkadian of El-Amarna, Bogazkoy, and Nuzi including West Semitic loan words, glosses, and names.[22] Plausibly *birītu* is another example of a West Semitic loan word influencing the choice of an Akkadian word with a similar sound.[23] This same West Semitic phraseology plausibly spread in the Levant through ritual practices of oath-making that flourished into the Iron Age and eventually to the authors of the Hebrew Bible.

2.3. Cutting a Covenant at Alalah

Further evidence for ritual slaughter as an essential component of Levantine oath practice can be seen in a treaty text written in Akkadian cuneiform found at Alalah. This treaty tablet from the eighteenth century BCE details the change in ownership of the city of Alalah between two rulers.[24] The final portion of the treaty includes the typical elements of conditional self-cursing and features the slaughter of a sheep:

> Abban swore an oath (*ni-iš ilāni.MEŠ za-ki-ir*) to Iarimlim and had the neck of a sheep cut (saying these words): "(may I die) if I take back what I gave you!"[25]

While this treaty tablet does not include the terminology "to cut a covenant" found in other oath texts, it demonstrates the importance of animal slaughter in Levantine culture as an element that was perceived as necessary for an oath to have binding authority.

---

22. Bottéro, "Les Inventaires de Qatna," 6–7. Bottéro writes, "il faudrait peut-être penser à un barbarism, dû à l'influence d'une langue étrangère à l'akkadien, voire au sémitique: hurrite? hittite?" (6).

23. For a more complete list of translation possibilities, see the entry *brt* in del Olmo Lete, Sanmartín, and Watson, *A Dictionary of the Ugaritic Language in the Alphabetic Tradition*, 238.

24. Donald J. Wiseman, "Abban and Alalah," *JCS* 12 (1958): 124–9, here 124.

25. Transcription from Wiseman, "Abban and Alalah," 126.

2.4. Cutting a Covenant in the Sefire Treaty[26]

The distinctive phraseology "to cut a covenant" appears in one of the three stelae from Sefire. These stelae preserve treaties of the kings of Arpad, the capital of a small Aramean province in northern Syria near Aleppo.[27] Stele I preserves a political treaty between Bir-Ga'yah, king of a land called KTK (כתך), and Matî'el, king of Arpad.[28] The treaty's content and named parties indicate a date for the inscription between 754 and 740 BCE, prior to the annexation of Arpad by the Neo-Assyrian Empire.[29] The inscription on Stele I is comprised of a preamble, a list of divine witnesses, curses, prohibitions against changing or defacing the treaty inscription, stipulations of mutual political support, and a final blessing for the descendants of the treaty-makers.

Stele I includes two references to "cutting" within its inscription: "cutting a covenant" and also "cutting a calf" into two halves in the ceremonial curse segment. These two uses of the verb גזר are interrelated. The use and manipulation of objects or animals served as part of the ritual enactment of the treaty and dramatically illustrated the destruction to be meted out upon those who would violate the terms of the treaty and, thus, bring its curses upon themselves. The idea of "cutting" in the enactment of the covenant directly references this essential Levantine treaty element of cutting animals in sacrificial slaughter. An excerpt from Sefire I demonstrates this type of curse that seems to function as a script for ritual experts to follow in the performance of the covenant oath enactment:

יזגר עגלא זנה כן יזגר מתעאל ויזגרן רבוה

Just as *this* calf is cut (in two), so may Matî'el be cut (in two) and may his lords be cut (in two)

(Sefire A: 40)[30]

---

26. I am using this phrase "cut a covenant" for the sake of tying together the West Semitic inscriptions that employ this phrase and for its alliterative value. The Sefire inscriptions more properly represent political treaties rather than covenants with deities as in the Arslan Tash Amulet 1 and in Deuteronomy.

27. Arpad is also mentioned in the Hebrew Bible (2 Kgs 18:34; 19:13; Isa 10:9; 36:19; 37:13; Jer 49:23). Joseph Fitzmyer, *The Aramaic Inscriptions of Sefire* (Biblica et Orientalia 19; Rome: Pontifical Biblical Institute, 1967), 2–3, 26–7.

28. For a thorough summary of possible translations of the term KTK and its geographical identification see Fitzmyer, *The Aramaic Inscriptions of Sefire*, 127–35.

29. The Akkadian treaty between Matî'el and Aššur-nirari V demonstrates that Matî'el was king of Arpad in 754 BCE. Furthermore, Arpad was annexed by Tiglath-Pileser III in 740 BCE. Thus, the treaty was written prior to 740 BCE. See, e.g., Amélie Kuhrt, *The Ancient Near East c. 3000-330 BC*, vol. II (New York: Routledge, 1995), 496–7.

30. Text and line number from Herbert Donner and Wolfgang Röllig, eds., *Kanaanäische und aramäische Inschriften*, vol. 1 (Wiesbaden: Harrassowitz Verlag, 2002), 53.

The same verb "cut" (גזר) appears with the word for "oath" (עדי) to reference the general idea of enactment of the treaty:

ונצבא עם ספרא זנה שמו עדיא אלן ועדיא אלן זי גזר ברגאיה

The stele with this inscription he has set up, as well as this treaty. Now this treaty which Bir-Gaʾyah has made (cut)

(Sefire A: 6-7)[31]

The use of the verb גזר ("to cut") in the ratifying of the covenant corresponds to the line from the ceremonial curse segment in which a calf is cut in two. Furthermore, both excerpts from the treaty use demonstrative pronouns to refer to physical objects and animals that formed part of the ritual enactment of the treaty. In line 40 from the ceremonial curse segment, the demonstrative pronoun זנה refers to the calf that was cut in two during the performance of the covenant enactment. The demonstrative pronouns אלן and זנה refer directly to physical objects also: the inscription on the stele (זנה) and perhaps the stelae themselves (אלן) that served as a memorialization of the treaty's performance. The Sefire stele also makes direct reference to the crafting of its own monumental inscription in its epilogue.

Thus, we have spoken and thus we have written. What I, Matîʾel, have written (is) a memorial (לזכרן) for my son and grandson who will follow me.[32]

The crafting of the visual symbol and textualization of the covenant form an integral part of the oath performance.

2.5. Cutting a Covenant at Tel Dan

The Tel Dan stelae is another exemplar of a royal monumental stelae from the northern Levant that employs the phrase "cut a covenant." Three fragments of a single stele that date to the Iron II period were discovered during excavations at Tel Dan in 1994.[33] This stele, plausibly erected by Hazael of Damascus, contains references to political events from the late ninth century BCE.[34] While the opening lines of the Tel Dan inscription are fragmentary, the text makes clear reference to the concluding of a treaty using the verb "to cut" (גזר) in its opening line(s) in the same way that the Sefire does. The first few words of the Tel Dan

---

31. Ibid.
32. KAI 222: C1.
33. Avraham Biran and Joseph Naveh, "An Aramaic Stela from Tel Dan," *IEJ* 43 (1993): 81–98; Avraham Biran and Joseph Naveh, "The Tel Dan Inscription: A New Fragment," *IEJ* 45 (1995): 1–18.
34. William M. Schniedewind, "Tel Dan Stela: New Light on Aramaic and Jehu's Revolt," *BASOR* 302 (1996): 75–90, here 75.

stele are not preserved in their entirety, but these do include a word that begins with the letter *ayin*, which could be the word *adê* (עדי) that is also found in the Sefire treaty; however, there are other possibilities. The location of the stele fragments near a gate also suggests a connection with oath-making practices since gate complexes were frequently the sites of oath performances in the ancient Near East.³⁵

2.5. Cutting a Covenant in the Arslan Tash Amulets

The Arslan Tash amulets present evidence for the use of the phrase "cut a covenant" in popular craftwork from the Northern Levant during the Iron Age. Like the Sefire and Tel Dan stelae, these objects were meant for display; however, their small size suggests that they were placed in a domestic rather than public context. The amulets were purchased in 1933 at the site of Arslan Tash in northern Syria.³⁶ The amulets most likely were unearthed during the excavation of the seventh-century Assyrian town of Ḥadattu, since the purchase took place a few years after the excavation.³⁷ Carved from limestone, the amulets are 3 1/3 inches by 2 2/3 inches each in size, which is large enough to make it impractical for them to be worn. They have a hole at the top with some traces of a cord, indicating that they hung suspended on a door frame. The content and accompanying iconography suggest that these amulets were apotropaic and crafted for the purpose of protection against supernatural malefactors.³⁸ The script and syntax of the amulets most

---

35. Ramos, *Ritual in Deuteronomy*, 88–93.

36. P. Amiet, "Observations sur les 'Tablettes magiques' d'Arslan Tash," *Aula Orientalis* 1 (1983): 109; J. Teixidor, "Les tablettes d'Arslan Tash au Musée d'Alep," *Aula Orientalis* 1 (1983): 105–8; Frank Moore Cross, Jr. and Richard J. Saley, "Phoenician Incantations on a Plaque of the Seventh Century B.C. from Arslan Tash in Upper Syria," *BASOR* 197 (1970): 42–9; Jacobus van Dijk, "The Authenticity of the Arslan Tash Amulets," *Iraq* 54 (1992): 65–8. Due to the nature of their discovery, the authenticity of the amulets was brought into question during the early 1980s by two scholars. Teixidor regarded the limestone material as suspicious, and Amiet contended that the amulets were forgeries. However, the arguments of Amiet seem primarily to be based on the iconography of the male deity figure characteristic of storm-god iconography. This deity is carved with an axe in his right hand, as is typical. Amiet observed that a thunderbolt was missing from the right hand, and this seems to be the strongest argument against the amulet's authenticity. Publications both prior to and following those of Teixidor and Amiet—including Dennis Pardee's thorough analysis—favor the authenticity of the tablets.

37. Robert du Mesnil du Buisson, "Une tablette magique de la région du Moyen Euphrate," in *Mélanges syriens offerts A M. René Dussaud* (Bibliothèque archéologique et historique 30; Paris: Paul Geuthner, 1939), 421–34; van Dijk, "Authenticity," 65.

38. William Foxwell Albright, "An Aramaean Magical Text in Hebrew from the Seventh Century B.C.," *BASOR* 76 (1939): 5–11, here 5.

closely resemble Aramaic from Mesopotamia and the Levant in the Late Iron Age but with a mix of archaic and later forms.[39] The syntax, however, contains many Phoenician elements, and so the language of the amulets is typically characterized as mixed in dialect.

The Arslan Tash amulets highlight the diversity in object typology that can be seen in visual media depicting oath ratification events in the northern Levant and in the wider ancient Near East. These amulets are distinctive from the Sefire and Tel Dan stelae in two important ways. First, the amulets are pieces of popular craftwork and the content of their inscription does not suggest a royal context or purpose. Rather, these are intended for domestic use by a family or individual with an apotropaic intent to their display. The fact that there are two amulets might also suggest that they were produced in a workshop and that this type of popular craftwork might have been more widely distributed than monumental stelae. Secondly, these amulets are accompanied by iconography depicting divine beings, and some of the text is carved directly on top of the images. The Sefire and Tel Dan stelae do not contain iconography; however, the tablets of the *adê* from the Neo-Assyrian period, especially the STE, pair text with images of divine beings. Thus, the amulets seem to be crafted using a mix of elements found in various types of visual media depicting covenants.

The terminology used in the Arslan Tash amulets for the ratification of a covenant has striking similarity to the text of Deuteronomy. The primary content of Amulet 1 centers around the enactment of a covenant made with the god Assur. For example, lines 8–10 from Arslan Tash bear strong resemblance to Deuteronomy 5:2.

כרת לנו אלת עלם אשר

Assur has made an eternal covenant with us

(AT1 lines 8-10)

יהוה אלהינו כרת עמנו ברית

The Lord our God has made a covenant with us

(Deut 5:2)

Both texts use the same verb "to cut" (לכרות) and parallel terms for "covenant." The Arslan Tash amulet uses the term אלת for covenant, while Deuteronomy, and the Hebrew Bible generally, uses the term ברית. However, Deuteronomy also uses this same word אלה for covenant in 29:13, a line that positions אלה and ברית in parallel with one another as the direct objects of the verb לכרות "to cut."

---

39. Dennis Pardee, "Les Documents d'Arslan Tash: Authentiques ou Faux?" *Syria* 75 (1988): 39–40.

ולא אתכם לבדכם אנכי כרת את־הברית הזאת ואת־האלה הזאת

Not only with you alone am I making this covenant, this oath.

In both Deuteronomy and in Arslan Tash Amulet 1, we find parallel usage of distinctive phraseology for "cutting a covenant": כרת ברית/אלת/אלה.[40]

There are also important differences between the Arslan Tash inscriptions and those of Sefire and Tel Dan. The Arslan Tash amulets make no mention of animal slaughter or any other ritual practice involved in making the covenant referred to in line 8. This might be due to the genre of the inscription as an incantation or to the relatively small size of the object, or it could be the case that the crafting of the object itself was understood as the ritual performance element required to enact the covenant.

This survey of the phrase "cut a covenant" in Levantine inscriptions reveals three findings. First, the phrase had a West Semitic origin and its use extended into the Iron Age, flourishing especially in the oath and treaty genres. Secondly, the phrase was used in a diverse array of object types and genres of text including economic texts, royal monuments on stelae, and personal objects, which also suggest that the phrase was used in a variety of social contexts. Thirdly, an important difference can be observed between the inscriptions from the Late Bronze and Iron Ages, namely, emphasis on the ritual element of animal slaughter versus the crafting of visual media as the primary ritual action of ratifying a covenant. The Late Bronze Age texts discussed above emphasize animal slaughter as the primary element of ritual ratification of the oath. These Late Bronze inscriptions are not incised onto monumental objects and they make no mention of visual media to commemorate the oath. However, the texts from the Iron Age that employ the phrase "cut a covenant" are inscriptions on royal monumental stelae and on personal objects. Moreover, the Arslan Tash amulet does not mention animal slaughter as part of covenant-making practice. This difference suggests that, in the northern Levant, the tradition of erecting a monument as part of "cutting a covenant" was a later development from the Iron Age and perhaps became the focal point of ritual enactment of oaths.

3. Cutting a Covenant in the Hebrew Bible

The phrase "cut a covenant" is also common in the literature of the Hebrew Bible where it is associated both with the ritual animal slaughter and the crafting of a monument of the covenant. However, the evidence from the Hebrew Bible is distinct because it derives from textualized and narrativized material depicting

---

40. The pairing of כרת with אלה (and not only with ברית) continued to serve as technical ritual language for concluding a covenant into the late Second Temple period, as seen in one of the sectarian texts of the Qumran community that parallels Deuteronomy 27–30 (1QS 2:16).

covenant ritual practices rather than from material objects themselves. While most of the occurrences of this phrase in the Hebrew Bible simply make passing reference to a covenant or a treaty, some narratives also include details of ritual practices associated with covenant-cutting. Here I address those passages that furnish insight into the kind of ritual actions included in ratifying an oath or a covenant in the literature of the Hebrew Bible. However, the aim of this survey is not to discover historical ritual practices from ancient Israel or Judah but to explore how narratives present and frame covenant-making practices.[41]

This survey of biblical passages that employ the phrase "cut a covenant" reveals three broad categories: (1) ritual enactments that include animal slaughter but make no mention of a monument; (2) ritual enactments that include animal slaughter and the erecting of a monument to symbolize the covenant; (3) ritual enactments that do not include slaughter and only include the crafting of a material object.[42] Far more passages fall into the third category than the first or second. Thus, the most common ritual action performed to conclude a covenant in the Hebrew Bible is the crafting of a visual symbol of the covenant, such as the tablets of the covenant in Exodus and the stones bearing inscriptions with the covenant in Deuteronomy 27.

3.1. "Cutting a Covenant" by Animal Slaughter in the Hebrew Bible

Two passages from the Hebrew Bible exemplify the first category presented above. Genesis 15 and Jeremiah 34 describe oaths ratified by the slaughter of an animal and a performative element in which the parties of the covenant walk between the animal pieces. In the narrative of Gen 15:7–21, Abram has a vision and hears the voice of the divine instructing him to bring a heifer, a female goat, a ram, and various birds. Abram cuts the animals in two except for the birds and waits for the sun to set. Once the sun has set and darkness has descended, two mysterious objects pass between the pieces of the animals: a smoking fire pot and a flaming torch. These objects have traditionally been understood as representations of the divine presence passing through the pieces and enacting the performative ritual action that ratified the treaty.[43]

---

41. See Liane M. Feldman's work in this volume for a thorough discussion of the inherent complexities with attempts to reconstruct ancient Israelite ritual practice by examining descriptions and proscriptions within the biblical text and sparse evidence from the material record.

42. A fourth category of passages worth mentioning are those that employ the term "cut a covenant" in a narrative that refers to a covenant but include no details about ritual actions that accompanied the oath agreement. Since the focus of this article is on the ritual enactment of covenant, I have chosen to focus on passages that include ritual and performative elements.

43. One could, however, view this passage in parallel with Jeremiah 34 discussed below and conclude that YHWH passing through the pieces in the Genesis 15 ritual enactment

Jeremiah 34:18–21 also centers on ritual slaughter and a performative ritual involving a procession of persons between the slaughtered animal pieces. Jeremiah 34 is framed as an oracle delivered directly to Zedekiah at the time of the Babylonian invasion of Jerusalem. In this passage, YHWH brings charges against Israel of breaking a covenant oath to grant liberty to Hebrew slaves. According to this prophetic pronouncement, the abrogation of the covenant has released the conditional self-curses that were part of the oath agreement. The oracle presumes that a covenant enactment was completed at an earlier moment and makes reference to the dramatic performances of curses that were part of this ratification ceremony.

Furthermore, the oracle mentions the enactment of these curses in language strongly reminiscent of Late Bronze and Iron Age treaty texts from the Levant that include similar curses. Jeremiah, speaking on behalf of YHWH, warns, "I will make like the calf when they cut it in two and passed between its parts" (34:18) and lists groups of people who were part of the oath performance and, thus, who are subject to the curse. As was discussed above, this type of curse was a traditional component of the ritual segments of treaty oaths. Although Jer 34:18 presents a narrative of the curse rather than the words spoken while enacting the curse during the ritual performance, the general syntax and ritual actions have a similar pattern to the curses in the Sefire treaty:

לא הקימו את דברי הברית אשר כרתו לפני העגל אשר כרתו לשנים ועברו בין בתריו

You did not uphold the words of the covenant which they cut before me, (and so it shall be to you like) the calf which they cut into two pieces and in between whose pieces they crossed

יגזר עגלא זנה כן יגזר מתעאל ויגזרן

just as this calf is cut in two, so may Matîʔel be cut in two

(Sefire A:40)[44]

Not only is the syntax preserved but also the very same animal (עגל) is mentioned in the texts of Genesis, Jeremiah, and the Sefire treaty. Both Genesis 15 and Jeremiah 34 employ the phrase "cut a covenant" referring to the ritual action of cutting an animal into two pieces with no mention of objects erected or pieces of visual media crafted as a memorial to the covenant.

3.2. "Cutting a Covenant" by Slaughter and Commemoration through Visual Media in the Hebrew Bible

The second category of texts that mention "cutting a covenant" are those that include both the slaughter of an animal *and* the crafting or erecting of some

---

might imply that it is YHWH who faces the doom of the curses if the terms of the covenant are broken.

44. KAI 222.

type of visual media. In the Hebrew Bible and in the wider ancient Near East, the inclusion of a physical artifact served as a permanent visual representation of "cutting the covenant."[45] In the case of oath tablets and stelae, the public display of the artifact in a place of religious worship perhaps reinforced the connection between the self-curses and the divine power that enforced the terms of the oath.[46] As Kathryn Slanski observes of the Hammurabi stele, "the Stele is more than just the vehicle for its inscription: its text and imagery were designed to incorporate elements of performativity and memorialization that would have resonated in its cultural setting."[47] In the same way, the torah stones memorialize the covenant enactment and yet the monument crafted is housed within a narrative, which adds another layer of nuance to the nature of its symbolism.[48] As Lisa Cleath observes, "a literary monument's mutability is a mechanism that enables its endurance."[49] The textual depiction of a monumental object endures longer than the object itself.[50] According to Timothy Hogue, "as communities encounter monuments and imagine through them, they participate in the formation of collective memory, ideology, and identity."[51] These texts memorialize the covenant by narrating the crafting of the torah stones—iconic symbols that are reproduced within the imagination of the audience with each encounter of the text. Just as ancient Near

---

45. Lauinger observes that tablets used in the display of the STE, the *ṭuppi adê*, had a distinctive design: a rotation along the vertical axis and three royal seals representing chronological stages of the empire of Aššur. Thus, the iconography of the tablets also evoked particular historiographic moments. Jacob Lauinger, "The Neo-Assyrian *Adê*: Treaty, Oath, or Something Else?" *ZAR* 19 (2013): 99–116, here 108.

46. Not only were oath tablets displayed in temples but also the Stele of Hammurapi and *kudurrus*. Kathryn Slanski, "The Law of Hammurabi and Its Audience," *Yale Journal of Law & the Humanities* 24 (2012): 102–3; Kathryn Slanski, "Classification, Historiography and Monumental Authority: The Babylonian Entitlement 'narûs (kudurrus)'," *JCS* 52 (2000): 96–8.

47. Kathryn Slanski, "The Law of Hammurabi and Its Audience," *Yale Journal of Law & the Humanities* 24 (2012): 97.

48. Jeremy D. Smoak explores the idea that some biblical texts might serve as a means of preserving cultural memory of ritual performances and ritual objects, a "discursive mapping of temple space" in "From Temple to Text: Text as Ritual Space and the Composition of Numbers 6: 24-26," *JHS* 17.2 (2017): 9, 16–23.

49. Lisa J. Cleath, "Divine Enthronement in a Conquered Land: Constructing a Landscape Monument in Joshua 8:30-35," in *Inscribing Monumentality in the Ancient Levant in the Hebrew Bible and Ancient Israel*, ed. Lisa J. Cleath, Alice Mandell, and Jeremy Smoak HeBAI 10/3 (2021), 12.

50. Timothy Hogue, "The Monumentality of the Sinaitic Decalogue: Reading Exodus 20 in Light of Northwest Semitic Monument-Making Practices," *JBL* 138 (2019): 79–99, here 81.

51. Ibid., 81.

Eastern oath stelae and tablets were placed in temples, the textual narratives also become metaphorical structures where these monuments are housed.

Three passages exemplify this type of oath ratification tradition: Genesis 31, Deuteronomy 27, and Joshua 8. In these passages, a stele is erected that serves to memorialize the covenant oath and the performance of its ratification. In Gen 31:44–54, Jacob and Laban "cut a covenant" together; the ritual actions that ratify the covenant are the erection of a standing stone as a pillar, spoken conditional self-cursing, and the offering of sacrifice. The language employed in this narrative strongly parallels terminology for oath-making in the wider ancient Near East including the Sefire treaty and the STE. The covenant (ברית) that is cut between Jacob and Laban is also called an *eid* (עד), which could mean a witness but likely is the term *adê* used frequently in the epigraphic record of the Iron Age for an oath.[52] Furthermore, the narrative includes a naming of the place where the oath was sworn as Gal-Eid or Gilead, or the valley of the oath. The crafting of a piece of visual media to memorialize the oath parallels the use of a stele or a tablet to represent the oath in Sefire, the STE, and the Arslan Tash amulets. However, in the case of Genesis 31, no inscription is made on the oath stone.

Similarly, Deuteronomy 27 and Joshua 8 prioritize the ritual action of erecting a stone to memorialize the oath performance and slaughter. I include these two passages together since Deuteronomy 27 is written as a set of instructions for the Israelites to fulfill once they enter the promised land and Joshua 8 narrates the fulfillment of these instructions. In these two passages, "cutting a covenant" involves conditional self-cursing just as Genesis 31 does, although a far more elaborate presentation of these curses is given in Deuteronomy 27–28. In Deuteronomy 27–28 and in Joshua 8, the crafting of the visual media piece involves an additional element: inscribing the stone with the words of the covenant oath. This parallels the practice of oath-making seen in the material record of the ancient Near East during the Iron II period: memorializing the oath with an inscription that provides details of the oath that was sworn. Both Deuteronomy 27 and Joshua 8 place narrative emphasis on the crafting and inscribing of stones and give these ritual actions a more detailed description, while the burnt offerings and well-being offerings are only briefly mentioned. Literary elements of repetition, framing devices, and elaborate descriptions of the torah stones in these two texts serve to highlight and prioritize the stones bearing an inscription of the covenant.[53]

3.3. "Cutting a Covenant" by Erecting a Monument in the Hebrew Bible

A third category of passages that feature the phrase "cut a covenant" in the Hebrew Bible are those that narrate the crafting and monumental display of a piece of visual media as the primary ritual action of covenant enactment with *no mention*

---

52. Ramos, *Ritual in Deuteronomy*, 74–7.
53. Ibid., 115–18.

of ritual sacrifice at all. The passages within this category are found primarily within the Exodus Ritual Decalogue, Deuteronomy, and the Deuteronomistic History: Exod 34:27–29, Deut 5:3; 9:9–11; Josh 24:25–26; 1 Kgs 8:21; and 2 Kgs 23:3. In these passages, the ritual enactment of "cutting a covenant" refers to cutting and inscribing stones, and the covenant (ברית) is portrayed as a physical object that visually and symbolically represents the enactment event. The medium of stone is emphasized in various texts of the Hebrew Bible and communicates the permanence of the covenant transaction that is presented in historiographic events. As Slanski observes of Mesopotamian stelae, "we should not underestimate the impact of the medium of stone—even today, texts written in stone, reserved for monuments and memorials, are considered lasting and not subject to change."[54] These stone monuments communicate the inviolability of the covenant and serve as iconic symbols of key historiographic moments in the life of the religious community.

In Exod 34:1–4, Moses is instructed by YHWH to "cut two tablets of stone" (פסל לך שני לחת אבנים).[55] The cutting of the tablets of stone is perhaps analogous to the cutting of animals in ritual slaughter. Further along in the same chapter, these stone tablets are again featured and YHWH commands Moses to inscribe the stone tablets.

כתב לך את הדברים האלה כי על פי הדברים האלה כרתי אתך ברית ואת ישראל
ויכתב על הלחת את דברי הברית עשרת הדברים

Inscribe (for yourself) these words because on the basis of these words I have cut a covenant
with you and with Israel ... and he (Moses) cut/inscribed upon the tablets the words of the covenant, ten words.

(Exod 34:27–28)

In this passage, ritual slaughter is not mentioned at all, and, in fact, the narrative emphasizes that Moses fasted, eating and drinking nothing for forty days (Exod 34:28). Although no animals are cut, Moses cuts the covenant by inscribing the stone tablets with the commandments.

Deuteronomy 5 and 9 repurpose the narrative material from Exodus 34 and incorporate the events of the cutting of the stone tablets within a literary framework of a first-person speech by Moses. Deuteronomy 9:9–11 presents again the Exodus 34 event of the receiving of the tablets of the covenant and also includes the detail that Moses remained on the mountain for 40 days and nights eating and drinking nothing. Deuteronomy 9:10 reads as follows:

---

54. Slanski, "Classification, Historiography and Monumental Authority," 114.

55. The tablets of the covenant are first introduced in Exod 31:18; however, the phrase "cut a covenant" is not mentioned nor are any other ritual actions associated with enacting the covenant.

ויתן יהוה אלי את שני לוחת האבנים כתבים באצבע אלהים

The Lord gave me the two tablets of stone cut/inscribed by the finger of God.

By including the detail that the tablets of stone are the first set inscribed by the finger of God and not by Moses, Deuteronomy 9 draws from both of the narratives of the giving of the first and second sets of stone tablets in Exodus 31 and 34 respectively. In Deut 9:10, as in Exod 34, no animal slaughter is mentioned and "cutting the covenant" is the inscribing of the stone tablets with the commandments. This suggests that the ritual of cutting an animal is transposed to cutting stone tablets in Exodus 34 and Deuteronomy.

Similarly, Deut 5:3 refers to the ritual action of ratifying the covenant and states that YHWH cut *this* covenant (כרת יהוה את הברית הזאת). The use of the demonstrative pronoun "this" suggests that the covenant here was understood to be a material object that could be pointed to in a physical manner.[56] The epigraphic record of the Levant contains many examples of the demonstrative pronouns *zt* or *zy* in Phoenician, Aramaic, and Samalian inscriptions that make reference to the erection of their stelae within the text itself. The Mesha inscription (KAI 181:3), for example, refers to the crafting of its stone inscription in a syntax similar to that of Deut 5:3 with the exception of the verb:

ואעש הבמת זאת

I erected this stone (stele)

Other examples include the opening lines of the Sefire (KAI 222:A:6–7), Zakur (KAI 202:1), and Kutamuwa inscriptions. Like Exodus 34, Deuteronomy 5 and 9 construe the stone tablets as a physical symbol of the event that transpired while Moses was on Mount Sinai/Horeb. Both Exodus 34 and Deuteronomy 9 present the ratification of the covenant as accomplished by the ritual action of cutting or inscribing the stone tablets.[57] The stone seems to take the place of the animal and the ritual action is transposed from cutting as slaughter to cutting as crafting a lapidary inscription.

The book of Joshua also includes two ritual enactments of the covenant oath in which the main ritual action of ratification is erecting stones. Like Exodus 34 and Deuteronomy 9, the focus of the ritual enactment of the covenant in Joshua is on the erection of visual symbols—large stones with an inscription bearing the words of the commandments. Joshua 8 and 24 narrate the fulfillment of the instructions for the covenant enactment that Moses gave to the Israelites in Deuteronomy 27. Joshua 8:30–35 presents a more detailed version of the covenant enactment while

---

56. Dennis Pardee, "A New Aramaic Inscription from Zincirli," *BASOR* 356 (2009): 51–71.

57. In 1 Kgs 8:21 (and 2 Chr 6:11) the *berit* is also presented as a ritual object that is placed inside the ark of the covenant. The procession of the ark into the Jerusalem temple is part of its dedication ceremony.

Josh 24:19–28 presents an abbreviated version. While Josh 8:30–35 does not use the phrase "to cut a covenant," this phrase is found in the reprisal of the enactment in Josh 24:25. However, Joshua 8 includes the ritual actions of sacrificing burnt offerings and well-being offerings while Joshua 24 makes no mention of sacrifices of any kind.[58]

As a part of the covenant enactment in Joshua 8, Joshua erects an altar on Mount Ebal made of unhewn stones (אבנים שלמות). The inclusion of the motif of the stones forms a deliberate textual reference to the instructions in Deut 27:6 that employ this same phrase for unworked field stones. Joshua 8:32 then states that Joshua inscribed a copy of the law of Moses on the stones of the altar. Since Deut 27:5 requires unworked field stones that are untouched by an iron tool (Deut 27:5), what is most likely envisioned in Joshua 8 and 24 is a plaster inscription in accordance with the instructions given in Deuteronomy 27. The ritual actions emphasized in Joshua 24 are the writing of the words of the law and the placement of a large stone as a witness to the covenant in the sanctuary.

ויכרת יהושע ברית לעם ביום ההוא ...
ויכתב יהושע את הדברים האלה בספר תורת אלהים ויקח אבן גדולה ויקימה שם תחת האלה אשר במקדש יהוה.

On that day Joshua cut a covenant on behalf of the people …
And Joshua wrote these words on an inscription of the law of God and he took a large stone and he erected it there, underneath the tree which was in the sanctuary of the Lord.

(Josh 24:25–26)

These two verses include the phrase "cut a covenant" but, like Exodus 34 and Deuteronomy 9, the ritual action of the oath is not cutting an animal but incising stones with an inscription.

The narratives of both Joshua 24 and Deuteronomy 27 use repetition to indicate the importance of the crafting and erection of a monument as a symbol of the covenant. The repetition is readily evident in Deut 27:1–8 where the command to erect and inscribe the torah stones occurs three times.[59] This literary emphasis on the monuments does not necessarily imply a diachronic change in covenant-making ritual practice in ancient Israel and Judah. It seems likely that the ritual

---

58. There may be a diachronic element to this development within Hebrew Bible texts. It seems possible that this shift in emphasis may be due to changing social and historical circumstances, especially around temple sacrifices in the Second Temple period. However, this question is beyond the scope of this initial survey. This is the argument John Day makes regarding language for "establishing" a covenant in P. "Why Does God 'Establish' Rather than 'Cut' Covenants in the Priestly Source?" in *Covenant as Context: Essays in Honour of E. W. Nicholson*, ed. Andrew D. H. Mayes and R. B. Salters (Oxford: Oxford University Press, 2003), 91–106.

59. Ramos, *Ritual in Deuteronomy*, 114–18.

action of cutting an animal remained part of the ritual life of ancient Israel and the wider Levant. The inscriptional record from the Iron Age presented above demonstrates that slaughter was at least in practice into the Iron Age in the northern Levant. A more plausible explanation for the disappearance of animal slaughter from the ritual repertoire of covenant ceremonies in certain biblical texts is one of literary emphasis.

Another example of this literary emphasis can be seen in Josh 24:26 where the action of writing an inscription is presented as the central ritual component of concluding the covenant. The vocabulary and syntax found in Josh 24:26 are similar to the way in which the Sefire stele narrates the crafting of its inscription. The Sefire stele commemorates its stele in this way:

נצבא עם ספרא זנה שמו עדיא אלן ... זי גזר ברגאיה

they erected the stele with this inscription—these treaties ... which Bar-Gaya cut

(Sefire A:6–7)

Similarly, Josh 24:26 states, "Joshua wrote these words in an inscription/scroll (ספר) of the torah of God and he took a large stone and he erected it there." Both Sefire and Josh 24:26 employ the same word to refer to the text that is inscribed (ספר). This word in Joshua 24 is typically translated as a "scroll." However, in the Sefire treaty it is thought to refer to the text of the inscription itself. It seems plausible that Josh 24:26 is also referring to an inscription made on a large stone rather than as a separate object such as scroll or a book. In both Sefire and Josh 24:26, the ritual enactment of the covenant is textualized, meaning that the commemoration event is captured in the inscribing of the stone stele. This act of textualization and display becomes part of the oath-making ritual performance.

The language used for the crafting and erection of the torah stones in Joshua 24 deliberately links this text with the stones in Deuteronomy 27 *and with the curses.* As noted above, the significance of the torah stones in Deut 27:1–9 is evident in the threefold repetition to erect them. The importance of these pieces of visual media is also repeated in the curse segment in Deut 27:11–26. The final imprecation in this collection levies a curse on anyone who does not display or uphold the words of the law:

ארור אשר לא יקים את דברי התורה הזאת

Cursed is the one who does not erect/display the words of this torah

(Deut 27:26)

While this verse is traditionally understood to be a curse against those who do not follow the substance of the law, it could be understood as a curse against those who do not display the contents of the law.[60] The idea of displaying the covenant

60. See n. 50.

and/or the commandments is an important theme in Deuteronomy, which is also connected with the Deuteronomy 6 command to craft household displays of the covenant and with the Arslan Tash amulets. This curse plausibly implies that one who does not display the covenant—whether a public display for the entire community or private displays in domestic contexts—is one who metaphorically fails to display the substance of the covenant in religious practice.

2 Kings 22–23 provides another example of the use of the phrase "cut a covenant" as a ritual action performed by inscribing a monument rather than by cutting an animal. 2 Kings 22–23 narrate the discovery of an inscriptional record (ספר התורה) of the covenant in the temple and a covenant renewal ceremony that includes the erection of a piece of visual media (ספר הברית). While these references might be to the same document, it also seems possible that the "inscription of the covenant" is a second inscription made for display purposes to commemorate the covenant renewal in 2 Kings 23. Like the other covenant enactment narratives already discussed, the narrative of the ritual performance of the covenant in 2 Kings 23 does not mention sacrifice. The ritual enactment is completed when the king "cuts the covenant" in a gathered assembly of the people by making an oral pledge to keep the commandments. The pledge made by the king is typically translated as "to carry out/uphold the terms of the covenant."[61] However, given the narrative's intertextual references to the covenant enactment ceremonies in Exodus 34, Deuteronomy 27, and Joshua 8 and 24, this phrase could also be interpreted as a ritual action of erecting a monument to the covenant:

להקים את דברי הברית הזאת

to erect (a stele/monument) the words of this covenant (2 Kgs 23:33)

The syntax of this phrase follows the general pattern seen in the Northwest Semitic inscriptions mentioned above for the erection of a stele bearing an inscription. In the Sefire, Zakur, and Kutamuwa stelae, various verbs are employed in the inscriptions to narrate the placement or crafting of the monument (עשה, שם, קנה) and the verb is followed directly by a mention of the physical object and the demonstrative pronoun z.[62] Given these inscriptional parallels, the word typically translated as scroll (ספר) in 2 Kgs 23:3 likely refers instead to an inscription on a lapidary stone in the same way that the Sefire treaty and Joshua 24:26 refer to the material display of their stelae. This may involve a more deliberate display of a stele or other inscription discovered in 2 Kgs 22, or it could also involve the crafting of

---

61. This use of the verb קום in the Hiphil paired with words that refer to the statutes of the covenant is common in the Hebrew Bible. However, I have argued above that its use in Deuteronomy 27 suggests a link between a metaphorical interpretation of "adhering to" or "upholding" the statutes of the law and the crafting and display of physical symbols of the covenant.

62. See n. 48 above for exemplars of this formula in the inscriptional record of the Levant.

a second inscription, much like the "copy" that Moses made of the original stone tablets and like the copy (משנה) made in Joshua 8.

A translation of 2 Kgs 23:3 as "to erect the words of this covenant stele" is also supported by the use of the same verb for the torah stones in Deuteronomy 27. The use of the verb "to set up" (קום) in the Hiphil found in 2 Kgs 23:3 is likely a direct reference to Deut 27:2, which begins the script for the ritual enactment of the covenant:

והקמת לך אבנים גדלות ושדת אתם בשיד

You shall erect large stones and cover them with plaster

Not only is the same verb (קום) employed in both 2 Kgs 23:3 and Deut 27:2, but in the same verbal stem. The use of the Hiphil form of קום in 2 Kgs 23:3 follows in the same tradition of erecting the words of the covenant oath or treaty for public display. This suggests that, in addition to the writing of the words of the covenant on a scroll, the narrative also makes reference to the erecting of a monumental display bearing the words of the covenant or a public display of the scroll itself in place of a lapidary inscription.

This third category of texts discussed above both emphasize the crafting of a monument in order to "cut a covenant" and exclude any mention of animal slaughter. The textual emphasis on the crafting of a monument seems especially prominent in covenant ratification traditions in Deuteronomy (D) and the Deuteronomistic History (DtrH). The texts discussed above that command or narrativize the inscribing and erecting of royal monumental stelae in public locations to commemorate ritual covenant performances comport well with the typology of material objects from the Iron Age. This prioritization of the crafting of a visual medium might also explain the frequent use of the term covenant (עדות/ברית) as an object rather than as a verbal or intellectual agreement in D and DtrH. The use of the term oath or covenant to refer to an object also parallels treaty and oath texts from the Iron II epigraphic record including the STE, the Sefire treaty, and possibly also in the Arslan Tash amulets. The ritual practices of "cutting a covenant" in D with emphasis on monumentality versus animal slaughter, thus, aligns more closely with the Iron Age inscriptions than with those from the Late Bronze.

While it is possible that the transposition of cutting stone versus cutting an animal to enact a covenant reflects a diachronic change in ritual covenant-making practice in ancient Israel and Judah, more likely this is the result of literary emphasis on the iconic stones of the covenant. Alice Mandell and Jeremy D. Smoak argue that ancient monumental inscriptions of the Levant were embedded into "architectonic spaces" that gave the stelae a context and connection with historiographic moments important to their social meanings.[63] Like the lapidary

---

63. Alice Mandell and Jeremy Smoak, D. "Reading beyond Literacy, Writing Beyond Epigraphy: Multimodality and the Monumental Inscriptions at Ekron and Tel Dan," *Maarav* 22:1–2 (2018): 83–94.

inscriptions of the wider ancient Near East, the biblical torah stones were erected in public spaces and served as a "visual display that could be accessed by people passing through these structures" where they were housed.[64] One could plausibly consider the texts of the Hebrew Bible themselves as "architectonic spaces" encountered by the ancient audience hearing or reading them and imagining the scenes and events described. This may explain the repeated narration in the Hebrew Bible of events that highlight the crafting of tablets, the erecting of stones, or the travels of the ark that housed the tablets of the covenant.

The significance of covenant symbols is reflected in the text's prioritization and repetition of such narratives at significant historiographic moments within the overarching biblical narrative. While killing an animal is a one-time act during a ritual performance, the textualization of this event in a monument or personal object enables the viewer who encounters the object to experience the enactment and its significance in everyday life. The textualizing and monumentalizing of covenant performance traditions renders them more accessible since objects with inscriptions can be read, heard, or viewed at any moment, thus giving unrestricted access to ancient audiences. The prioritization of the stone symbols of the covenant in the Hebrew Bible reflects their significance within the religious imagination of the community as symbols of key historiographic moments that shaped religious and cultural identity.

4. Conclusion

The use of the phrase "cut a covenant" in Levantine inscriptions surveyed suggests that the phrase's origins are Amorite but that its use continued into the Iron Age and beyond. The inclusion of the ritual action of animal slaughter in oath and treaty texts also demonstrates the flourishing of this practice in the northern Levant during the Late Bronze and the Iron Ages. However, a new component of oath-making appeared in the northern Levant in the Iron Age: the crafting of a piece of visual media as a monument to the oath performance. In the Hebrew Bible, the phrase "cut a covenant" retains its connection with animal slaughter as a ritual component of covenant enactment. The survey of the biblical literature presented above reveals that far more biblical passages feature the crafting of a monument as the primary focus of ritual ratification while fewer passages highlight animal slaughter. This may reflect a diachronic change in the meaning of the phrase "cut a covenant" over time to refer to cutting or inscribing of stones rather than cutting animals. Or, the emphasis on monumentality in biblical texts may reflect a literary prioritization of monumentality due to the importance of these symbols in the religious imagination of the authors.

64. Ibid., 94.

Chapter 13

SILVER SCRIPTS: THE RITUAL FUNCTION OF
PURIFIED METAL IN ANCIENT JUDAH

Jeremy D. Smoak

1. *Introduction*

When the Ketef Hinnom amulets were discovered, they were rolled up like miniature scrolls resting in a level of fill on the floor of a tomb repository.[1] In this setting, the objects spoke to their audiences in much the same way that they had before they were buried in the tomb: through their materiality and design. Both amulets had been manufactured from thin sheets of silver foil and rolled several times to give them their cylindrical shapes. Interpreting the function of the objects was limited to a consideration of their silver, size, and exterior design features. Even before they were unrolled and their inscriptions rediscovered, human eyes could not read their words.[2] This is the irony of the Ketef Hinnom scrolls. For most of their life cycles, these scrolls were not read. It was only with twentieth-century imaging technology that their words were made visible to human eyes. However, once scholars were able to access the words of these scrolls, their materiality and design faded into the background. The fact that both amulets were discovered to contain blessings with close parallels to the priestly blessing of Num 6:24–26 also meant that the majority of studies focused upon their relationship to the composition of the biblical texts.[3] As a result, very few studies asked how

---

1. For a description of the context in which the amulets were discovered, see Gabriel Barkay, "The Priestly Benediction on Silver Plaques from Ketef Hinnom in Jerusalem," *TA* 19 (1992): 148–51.
2. On the difficulties involved in reading the inscriptions, see Gabriel Barkay, Marilyn J. Lundberg, Andrew G. Vaughn, Bruce Zuckerman and Kenneth Zuckerman, "The Challenges of Ketef Hinnom: Using Advanced Technologies to Reclaim the Earliest Biblical Texts and Their Contexts," *NEA* 66 (2003): 162–71.
3. For a detailed discussion of the paleography of the inscriptions, see Gabriel Barkay, Marilyn J. Lundberg, Andrew G. Vaughn and Bruce Zuckerman, "The Amulets from Ketef Hinnom: A New Edition and Evaluation," *BASOR* 334 (2004): 41–71. On the relationship

their manufacture from silver and their design as tiny scrolls communicated meaning.[4]

The present study attempts to fill this lacuna in scholarship by emphasizing two aspects of the amulets' materiality: their properties as purified silver and their design qualities as tiny scrolls.[5] In the *editio princeps* of the amulets, Gabriel Barkay highlighted that the chemical composition of the objects was 99 percent silver and 1 percent copper.[6] Pointing to several allusions to the religious significance of purified silver, Barkay commented that the use of such highly refined silver undoubtedly had a deliberate function.[7] Since Barkay's study, however, scholars have directed little attention to their silver. In what follows, I adopt a material religions approach and evaluate the ways in which silver—and the bundled meaning connected to both its purification and craftsmanship—conveyed ritual meaning. While past works have emphasized how silver was a signifier of the economic and social status of the amulets' owners, I argue that the affordances of silver were central to their *ritual* logic. The amulets from Ketef Hinnom join several other ancient Near Eastern texts that reflect the value that silver held in ritual contexts.[8]

---

between the biblical priestly blessing and the inscriptions, see Ada Yardeni, "Remarks on the Priestly Blessing on Two Amulets from Jerusalem," VT 41 (1991): 176-85; Angelika Berlejung, "Der gesegnete Mensch: Text und Kontext von Num 6, 22-27 und den Silberamuletten von Ketef Hinnom," in *Mensch und König: Studien zur Anthropologie des Alten Testaments: Rüdiger Lux zum 60. Geburtstag*, ed. Angelika Berlejung and Raik Heckl (Freiburg: Herder, 2008), 37-62; Jeremy D. Smoak, *The Priestly Blessing in Inscription and Scripture: The Early History of Numbers 6:24-26* (Oxford: Oxford University Press, 2015).

4. In the *editio princeps* of the inscriptions, Gabriel Barkay emphasized certain material aspects of the objects including their silver materiality and their manufactured characteristics as thin sheets of precious metal (see Barkay "The Priestly Benediction," 174-6; see also Jeremy D. Smoak, "Wearing Divine Words: In Life and Death," *Material Religion* 15 (2019): 433-55).

5. By property, I refer to the "natural" or "inherent" ability of silver to produce a shine, whereas I use the terminology of quality to refer to their manufactured features as highly purified metal sheets that were rolled up into scrolls. I borrow the terminology of property vs. quality from Kim Benzel, "'What Goes in Is What Comes Out': But What Was Already There? Divine Materials and Materiality in Ancient Mesopotamia," in *The Materiality of Divine Agency*, ed. Beata Pongratz-Leisten and Karen Sonik (Berlin: de Gruyter, 2015), 89-118; see also Nicholas Postgate, "Mesopotamian Petrology: Stages in the Classification of the Material World," *Cambridge Archaeological Journal* 7 (1997): 205-24.

6. Barkay, "The Priestly Benediction," 174-6.

7. Ibid., 174.

8. Klaas R. Veenhof, "Silver in Old Assyrian Trade: Shapes, Qualities and Purification," in *Studies in Economic and Social History of the Ancient Near East in Memory of Péter Vargyas*, ed. Z. Csabai L'Harmattan (Budapest: Department of Ancient History, The University of Péc, 2014), 393-422; Jack Ogden, "Metals," in *Ancient Egyptian Materials and Technology*, ed. P. T. Nicholson and I. Shaw (Cambridge: Cambridge University Press, 2000), 170-1;

In particular, I engage with studies that emphasize the important roles that silver and gold contributed to notions of the divine presence, the decoration of temples and cult statues, and rituals of purification.[9]

2. Silver's Materiality in the Mediterranean and Near East

In the 2011 article "Text, Image and Medium," Christopher Faraone drew attention to the role that the medium of Graeco-Roman gemstones played in their perceived magical function.[10] He stressed that while studies tend to focus upon the text or image inscribed on such stones, the ancient sources often draw explicit attention to their medium and color. For example, Faraone cites the example of the use of a yellow jasper gemstone inscribed with an image of an eight-legged scorpion.[11] He argued that the yellow-colored stone came to be associated with the "yellow Palestinian scorpion" through the principle of "like-banning-like." The yellow Palestinian scorpion was a more lethal type of scorpion in the eastern Mediterranean both because it was more easily camouflaged by the soil and because its venom was especially lethal. Faraone contended that it was the medium of the stone—particularly its yellowish color—that guided a magician's decision to associate it with the yellowish-brown scorpion and deploy it against

---

Noël H. Gale and Zofia A. Stos-Gale, "Ancient Egyptian Silver," *JEA* 67 (1981): 103–15; Noël H. Gale and Zofia A. Stos-Gale, "Lead and Silver in the Ancient Aegean," *Scientific American* 244 (1981): 176–92, 202; Victor A. Hurowitz, "What Goes in Is What Comes Out: Materials for Creating Cult Statues," in *Text, Artifact, and Image: Revealing Ancient Israelite Religion*, ed. Gary M. Beckman and Theodore J. Lewis (Providence: Brown Judaic Studies, 2006), 3–23; Karl H. Singer, *Gold, Silber, Bronze, Kupfer und Eisen im Alten Testament und ihre Symbolik* (Würzburg: Echter, 1980); Thomas Raff, *Die Sprache der Materialien: Anleitung zu einer Ikonologie der Werkstoffe* (Munich: Deutscher Kunstverlag, 1994).

9. See Leo A. Oppenheim, "The Golden Garments of the Gods," *JNES* 8 (1949): 172–93; Tallay Ornan, "The Role of Gold in Royal Representation: The Case of a Bronze Statue from Hazor," in *Proceedings of the 7th International Congress on the Archaeology of the Ancient Near East, 12 April–16 April 2020, the British Museum and UCL, London. Volume 2*, ed. R. Matthews and J. Curtis (Wiesbaden: Harrossowitz Verlag, 2012), 448–9; Theodore L. Lewis, "Syro-Palestinian Iconography and Divine Images," in *Cult Image and Divine Representation in the Ancient Near East*, ed. N. H. Walls (Boston: American Schools of Oriental Research, 2005), 69–107; Irene Winter, "Gold! Light and Lustre in Ancient Mesopotamia," in *Proceedings of the 7th International Congress on the Archaeology of the Ancient Near East*, ed. R. Matthews and J. Curtis (Wiesbaden: Harrossowitz Verlag, 2012), 153–71.

10. Christopher Faraone, "Text, Image, and Medium: The Evolution of Graeco-Roman Magical Gemstones," in *"Gems of Heaven": Recent Research on Engraved Gemstones in Late Antiquity, AD 200–600*, ed. C. Entwistle and N. Adams (London: British Museum Press, 2011), 50–61.

11. Ibid., 55.

the bites of this type of danger.¹² In this way, he prioritizes the various media of the gemstones, which were seen to hold inherent protective or healing powers. Rather than starting with the text or the image on such objects, Faraone demonstrates the value of studying the relationship between the properties of ritual objects and their ritual function.¹³

Faraone's work is an important reminder that scholars have tended to ignore the role that a gemstone's physical properties played in defining its specific application in apotropaic or curing rituals. The importance of his arguments rests not only in the way that it redirects the focus of study toward the materiality of the amulets but also to the way that it draws attention to the possibility that the medium of such amulets may have in certain cases influenced or guided decisions about what was inscribed on such objects.¹⁴ As Frankfurter emphasizes, "the stones were not decorative backdrops or vehicles for the complex iconographies with which they were inscribed. Rather, the images, phrases, and signs that craftsmen carved into them served as interpretations—even strategies to guide—the powers in the stones themselves."¹⁵ The physical characteristics of gemstones signaled to their manufacturers what was innate within the material that needed to be extracted and harnessed verbally or pictorially. This understanding underscores the importance of prioritizing the materiality of amulets and other ritual objects.

When we consider the use or popularity of silver and gold as the media of cultic objects in the ancient Near East, it becomes clear that their chemical properties were perceived to harbor ritual power. As alluded to in the introduction of this study, silver and gold metals may have been perceived to possess inherent divine properties in ancient Near East cultures. In a recent article, Kim Benzel draws a helpful distinction between the inherent agency of silver and gold in Mesopotamia and the value that was assigned to them when they were shaped or crafted into objects for ritual use.¹⁶ Borrowing from David Freeberg's study *The Power of Images*, she defines inherency "as the degree of life or divinity believed to *inhere* in an image or object."¹⁷ Benzel emphasizes that the words for silver in Sumerian (KU₃.BABBAR, *kaspum*) and Akkadian (*ellu*) also possess the meaning "(to be) pure, bright, shiny."¹⁸ Building on the work of Irene Winter and Beate Pongratz-Leisten, she details the ways in which Mesopotamian texts held the metal to hold intrinsic or inherent divine properties, sacredness, and radiance.¹⁹ Benzel

---

12. Ibid.
13. Ibid.
14. David Frankfurter, "Magic and the Forces of Materiality," in *Guide to the Study of Ancient Magic* (Religions in the Graeco-Roman World; Leiden: Brill, 2019), 659–77, here 662.
15. Ibid., 662.
16. Benzel, "'What Goes in Is What Comes Out,'" 97–8.
17. Ibid.
18. Ibid., 100.
19. Ibid., 102. See Beate Pongratz-Leisten, "Reflections on the Translatability of the Notion of Holiness," in *Of God(s), Trees, Kings, and Scholars: Neo-Assyrian and Related*

argues that because silver and gold possess an ability to maintain their lustrous appearance, they came to hold a special place in religious discourse about divinity and in the aesthetics of temples in Mesopotamia.[20] Stressing the inherent purity or divinity of these metals, she concludes, "Nowhere is there mention of these precious materials needing their own purification or consecration; they simply 'exist' in the text as materials ready to consecrate the not-so-ready materials needed for the ritual."[21]

Benzel also emphasizes the distinction between gold and silver in terms of each metal's levels of purity.[22] Whereas gold occurs more frequently in a pure state, silver often requires a much more thorough refining process to remove unwanted impurities.[23] This meant that silver came to hold a different mythology that was associated with the process of purifying it so that it could be worked and so that its luster could be brought out more fully and maintained through polishing. Mesopotamian texts appear to have distinguished between lower metals because their shine could wear off without human polishing, whereas silver's luminous properties endured longer apart from human care.[24] Silver in particular came to be associated with purification rites and in certain cases the process of refining human behavior through social and legal action. For instance, a Sumerian hymn from the third millennium equates prison's ability to rehabilitate human character with silver's ability to take a polish and shine: "When [the prison?] has appeased the heart of his god for him; when it has polished him clean like silver of good

---

Studies in Honour of Simo Parpola, ed. M. Luukko et al. (Helsinki: Finnish Oriental Society, 2009), 409–27; Irene Winter, "Radiance as an Aesthetic Value in the Art of Ancient Mesopotamia (and Some Indian Parallels)," in *Art: The Integral Vision*, ed. B. N. Saraswati et al. (New Delhi: D. K. Printworld, 1994), 123–32. See also Michaël Guichard and Lionel Marti, "Purity in Ancient Mesopotamia: The Paleo-Babylonian and Neo Assyrian Periods," in *Purity and the Forming of Religious Traditions in the Ancient Mediterranean and Ancient Judaism*, ed. Christian Frevel and Christophe Nihan (Leiden: Brill, 2013), 51–62.

20. Benzel, "'What Goes in Is What Comes Out,'" 98.

21. Ibid., 107. For further discussion of the purifying powers of gold and silver, see Stefan M. Maul, *Zukunftsbewältigung: Eine Untersuchung altorientalischen Denkens anhand der babylonisch-assyrischen Löserituale* (Mainz am Rhein: Verlag Philipp von Zabern, 1994), 95; Christopher Walker and Michael B. Dick, "The Induction of the Cult Image in Ancient Mesopotamia: The Mesopotamian mîs pî Ritual," in *Born in Heaven, Made on Earth*, ed. M. B. Dick (Winona Lake, IN: Eisenbrauns, 1999), 102.

22. Walker and Dick, "The Induction of the Cult Image in Ancient Mesopotamia," 104.

23. Peter R. S. Moorey, *Ancient Mesopotamian Materials and Industries: The Archaeological Evidence* (Oxford: Clarendon Press, 1994), 234; Amir Golani, *Jewelry from the Iron Age II Levant* (Göttingen: Vandenhoeck & Ruprecht, 2013), 16–18.

24. For discussion of precious metals in Mesopotamian traditions, see William W. Hallo, "Lexical Notes on the Neo-Sumerian Metal Industry," *BibOr* 20 (1963): 136–41; Marc van de Mieroop, "Gold Offerings of Šugli," *Or* 55 (1986): 131–51.

quality; when it has made him shine forth through the dust; when it has cleansed him of dirt like silver of best quality."[25]

While Benzel's study focused upon the chemical properties of silver and gold and how such properties influenced the qualities assigned to them, several other recent studies have drawn attention to the significance of silver's color or aesthetic visual qualities. In her article "Radiant Things for God and Mean," Shiyanthi Thavapalan emphasizes that most of the words for color in Akkadian "describe the behavior of light as it interacts with various surfaces and when it reaches the eye."[26] She notes that whereas some cultures conceive of color through the category of hues, Mesopotamians developed notions of color through a spectrum of lightness and darkness.[27] She argues that in Akkadian texts "brightness" is conceived of in different categories or "colors" based upon its perceived interaction with materials. Whereas some colors are conceived of as wholly abstract or "pure-brightness" like "dazzling" (*namru*) and "shiny" (*ebbu*), silver and gold are "brightness-dominated" colors because they evoke different hues *and* denote qualities of brightness.[28] As a result, silver was associated with the color white and denoted notions of radiance, shine, and brightness.[29]

One way to interpret this distinction is to recognize its ritual application in ancient Mesopotamia. Whereas terms that denoted "pure-brightness" were associated with divinity, "brightness-dominated" colors that took their names from precious metals and other stones evoked notions of divine *manifestation*. By divine *manifestation*, I mean the effect that the metal had upon persons in the realm of visual experience. The shining of the metal denoted the availability of the divine presence to manifest in the human realm. The distinction here is decidedly material: the "brightness-dominated" properties of silver and gold signaled an inherent divinity and ritual purity that could be employed in the cult. As a result, Thavapalan's observations follow closely upon Irene Winter's study of the aesthetics of radiance in the Mesopotamian cult traditions. In several studies, Winter emphasized the importance that the aesthetic of precious metals had in terms of its ritual appropriateness in the temple cult.[30] The shiny or shimmering

---

25. Jeremy Black et al., *The Literature of Ancient Sumer* (Oxford: Oxford University Press, 2004), 342.

26. Shiyanthi Thavapalan, "Radiant Things for Gods and Men: Lightness and Darkness in Mesopotamian Language and Thought," *ColourTurn* 7 (2018): 1–36; Shiyanthi Thavapalan, *The Meaning of Color in Ancient Mesopotamia* (Leiden: Brill, 2020), 221–3.

27. Thavapalan, *The Meaning of Color in Ancient Mesopotamia*, 8.

28. Ibid.

29. For discussion of silver as a color in ancient Egypt, see Wolfgang Schenkel, "Color Terms in Ancient Egyptian and Coptic," in *Anthropology of Color: Interdisciplinary Multilevel Modeling*, ed. R. E. MacLaury et al. (Amsterdam: John Benjamins, 2007), 211–28; John Baines, "Color Terminology and Color Classification: Ancient Egyptian Color Terminology and Polychromy," *American Anthropologist* 87 (1985): 282–97.

30. Winter, "Radiance as an Aesthetic Value," 128–9; Winter, "Defining 'Aesthetics' for Non-Western Studies: The Case of Ancient Mesopotamia," in *Art History, Aesthetics, Visual*

properties of silver and gold in particular were held to signal to their users that the two metals had an intrinsic radiance that made them suitable for evoking notions of divine presence. As Irene Winter argued, "Radiant light was a positively affective visual attribute—one of the primary means by which the sacred was made manifest."[31]

Benzel and Thavapalan's studies provide new insights into the motivations behind the use of silver in rituals of purification in the ancient Near East. Because silver was a metal that required a more extensive purification process by removing other metal impurities, it was perceived to hold particular value in purification rituals. Silver's inherent properties *and* its ability to be refined to produce a higher chemical quality (and brighter shine) made the metal especially meaningful as a ritual analogue. For instance, Hittite ritual texts invoke silver's purity and other characteristics as analogues in human purification. One such text contains the following statement: "Like silver, may you be pure before the gods, the male gods and the female gods!"[32] A similar statement about silver's ritual efficacy is preserved in *CTH* 777: "As silver is pure, shining, strong and eternal."[33] Significantly, the text refers to not only silver's natural purity but also its shining appearance, its strength as a precious metal, and its ability to endure.[34]

A similar understanding of silver's efficacy in ritual is found in the Mesopotamian *Šurpu* incantations. In several of such incantations, silver and gold along with other metals are invoked as part of rituals aimed at the removal of impurities.[35] The invoking of such precious metals is especially apparent in the incantations preserved on tablets VIII and IX.[36] I cite the relevant parts *Šurpu* VIII: 83–90 here to highlight the role that silver and gold play as part of the text's conception of purification:

[83]He is purified, cleansed, bathed, washed, cleaned,
[84]with the water of the pure Tigris and Euphrates, the water of the sea (and) [vast] ocean,
[85]pure water, silver, gold, copper, tin, lead, carnelian, lapis lazuli, chalcedony, "pure"—stone,

Studies, ed. M. A. Holly and K. Moxley (Williamstown: Sterling and Francine Clark Art Institute, 2002), 123–32.

31. Winter, "Radiance as an Aesthetic Value," 129.

32. *CTH* 471: IV, 61–2.

33. *CTH* 477: IV, 27–8.

34. For discussion of these texts, see Rita Strauss, *Reinigungsrituale aus Kizzuwatna: Ein Beitrag zur Erforschung hethitischer Ritualtradition und Kulturgeschichte* (Berlin: de Gruyter, 2006), 232.

35. Erica Reiner, *Šurpu: A Collection of Sumerian and Akkadian Incantations* (Graz: Weidner, 1958).

36. Ibid., 39–49.

⁸⁶*pappardilû*-stone, *papparminu*-stone, *abašmu*-stone, *engiša*-stone, lamassu=stone, breccia

⁸⁷*ajartu*-stone ... tamarisk, *ēdu*-plant, *maštakal*, palm-shoot, *šalālu*-reed, pure plant ...

⁸⁸upon the command of Marduk, exorcist among the gods, the wisest (apkal) among the gods, lord of life,

⁸⁹may (all this), with the waters from your body and the washwater from your hands, be

⁹⁰discarded so that the earth take it away; may the curved mace release your sin.³⁷

In this text, silver is listed along with several other stones and other materials as ingredients that have purifying powers that may be transferred to the body.³⁸ The citation of the precious metals and other purifying agents in this text appear alongside a reference to the command of Marduk, whom the text identifies as the exorcist among the gods. Here we are reminded of Benzel's argument that Mesopotamian texts appear to indicate that silver and gold do not need to be purified like other materials used in ritual performance; they possess an innate purity that makes their effectiveness in purification rituals evident.³⁹

3. Yahweh as Divine Metallurgist and Israelite Mythologies of Silver's Purity

Several biblical texts reflect the value that silver and other precious metals held in ancient Israelite and Judean cultures. Such texts attest to a tradition of mythologizing the process of refining silver and deploying it as a metaphor for

---

37. Ibid., 43–4.

38. For further discussion of the roles that silver and gold play in these incantations, see Fritz Stolz, "Dimensions and Transformations of Purification Ideas," in *Transformations of the Inner Self in Ancient Religions*, ed. H. G. Kippenberg and E. T. Lawson (Leiden: Brill, 1999), 211–29.

39. Eduardo Escobar's study of this *Šurpu* text offers insight into the motivations behind the use of silver and gold in the ritual ("Technology as Knowledge: Cuneiform Technical Recipes and the Material World" [PhD dissertation, University of California, Berkeley, 2017], 84–5). Following the study by Alasdair Livingstone, he emphasizes that the list of stones and other materials invoked in this *Šurpu* incantation also appear in lexical lists from Nippur and Nineveh (Escobar, "Technology as Knowledge," 85; see also Alasdair Livingstone, *Mystical and Mythological Explanatory Works of Assyrian and Babylonian Scholars* [Winona Lake, IN: Eisenbrauns 2007], 180). In the lexical lists, stones such as silver and gold (and several others) are attributed divine properties and associated with specific gods. For instance, in *CBS* 6060, silver (ᵈkù.babbar) and gold (ᵈguškin) are identified with Anu (ᵈ*a-nu-[um]*) and Enlil (ᵈ*en-líl*), respectively.

Yahweh's purification of his people.⁴⁰ Especially striking is the image of Yahweh as a divine metallurgist who employs pyrometallurgy to extract or remove human impurities.⁴¹ Such imagery is especially evocative for an understanding of the ritual significance of Ketef Hinnom's silver. As I describe below, such texts offer a way to better appreciate the logic of the words and phrases employed in the inscriptions. Indeed, we would do well to ask whether their inscriptions would have been as efficacious had they been inscribed on wood or other medium. Returning to the point I made at the beginning of this study, we might ask how the silver properties of the amulets guided the content of the inscriptions. It may well be that the inscribing of allusions to covenant loyalty and blessings that invoke the shining face of Yahweh on the amulets was an act that was perceived to complement the shining properties of silver and the chemical purity of the metal.

That ancient Israel and Judah had their own mythologies of the ritual meaning of silver and gold is evidenced in several biblical texts. We might begin here with the role that the term טהר, "purity," plays in descriptions of the appearance of precious metals and stones. As Yitzhaq Feder has demonstrated, the term's origins can be traced to the luster or brilliance of precious metals and stones.⁴² Hebrew טהר is semantically parallel to Akkadian *ellu*, which often refers to the high chemical quality of silver and gold and their shiny appearances.⁴³ That there is a connection between the quality טהר and ritual objects and spaces is also evident in several textual sources. In several biblical texts (as well as Ugaritic texts), the word טהר denotes the radiance or shiny appearance that is produced by the precious metals or stones used to decorate divine dwellings.⁴⁴

A particularly striking instance of this meaning is preserved in the description of the revelation of Yahweh at Mount Sinai (Exod 24:9–10): "Then Moses and Aaron, Nadab, and Abihu, and seventy of the elders of Israel went up, and they saw the God of Israel. Under his feet there was something like a pavement of sapphire stone, like the very heaven for clearness (לטהר)." In this passage, the use of the term טהר is used to describe the glow or shine of the pavement under Yahweh's feet (v. 10). In this context, the term's meaning is relatively clear: it denotes the appearance of materials found in Yahweh's abode. William Propp's comment on the expression

---

40. For summary, see Nissim Amzallag, "The Material Nature of the Radiance of YHWH and its Theological Implications," *SJOT* 29 (2015): 80–96; Nissim Amzallag, "The Identity of the Emissary of YHWH," *SJOT* 26 (2012): 123–44; Nissim Amzallag, "Copper Metallurgy: A Hidden Fundament of the Theology of Ancient Israel?" *SJOT* 27 (2013): 151–69.

41. See Amzallag, "Copper Metallurgy," 162–4; Dan Levene and Beno Rothenberg, "Word-Smithing: Some Metallurgical Terms in Hebrew and Aramaic," *AramSt* 2 (2004): 193–206.

42. Yitzak Feder, "The Semantics of Purity in the Ancient Near East: Lexical Meaning as a Projection of Embodied Experience," *JANER* 14 (2014): 87–113, here 91–2.

43. Ibid., 95. See also CAD_E, 105–6.

44. Ibid., 91. See also James N. Ford, "The Ugaritic Letter RS 18.038 (KTU² 2.39) and the Meaning of the Term *spr* 'lapis lazuli' (=BH *sappīr* 'lapis lazuli')," *UF* 40 (2008): 302–4.

is helpful here—the term "here refers both to a gemstone's pure color ... but its most frequent meaning is also apposite: the ritual *purity* of Heaven."[45]

Israelite and Judean texts not only dwell upon silver's luminosity, but they also direct specific attention to the technology of purifying and manufacturing the metal. Several biblical texts envision Yahweh as a divine craftsman who fashions elements of the cosmos by hammering, beating, or spreading out metals.[46] Yahweh is imagined as creating the earth or the heavenly expanse by hammering metal or other materials into solid plates. The verb that is used to convey this divine action is רקע, commonly translated as "hammer out" or "spread out."[47] In poetic texts, the verb conveys the act of Yahweh hammering out the expanse (Ps 19:2; Isa 42:5; 44:24) or spreading out the earth (Ps 136:6). Genesis 1:7 envisions God as a divine metallurgist who fashioned a plate of metal to separate the waters below from the waters above.[48]

The priestly literature also employs the verb רקע to describe the priesthood's crafting of the cultic furniture for the tabernacle. In the description of the tabernacle in Exodus, the term is used to convey the action of hammering gold leaves for priestly garments (39:3): "And they beat out (וירקעו) the gold plates and cut threads to work amid the blue and amid the purple and amid the worm-crimson, and amid the linen, in skilled design."[49] The fact that the references to the manufacture of such metal are concerned not only with the value of the metal but also with its skilled design is indicated by the very last clause in this passage. The description of the technology of hammering the gold leaves for the priestly garments is concluded by a note that qualifies the golden materials as the product of "skilled design." According to the book of Numbers, the covering for the tabernacle altar was made from hammered copper (17:2, 4). The description of the use of precious metal plating in these contexts is reminiscent of the references to the use of silver and gold in Mesopotamian and Ugaritic descriptions of the gods and divine sanctuaries. The function of the use of such precious metals in temples and similar contexts was to produce notions of divine manifestation in such settings. As Kiersten Neumann argues, "Stemming from these visual phenomena

---

45. William Propp, *Exodus 19–40: A New Translation with Introduction and Commentary* (Garden City, NY: Doubleday, 2006), 297.

46. Paula McNutt, *The Forging of Israel—Iron Technology, Symbolism and Tradition in Ancient Society* (Sheffield: Almond Press, 1990), 265. For a description of the process of manufacture, see Golani, *Jewelry from the Iron Age II Levant*, 26.

47. Amzallag, "Copper Metallurgy," 162–4. See also Ellen van Wolde, "Why the Verb ברא Does Not Mean Create in Genesis 1.1–2.4," *JSOT* 34 (2009): 3–23.

48. Amzallag, "Copper Metallurgy," 163.

49. See Propp, *Exodus 19–40*, 669. For further discussion, see Nissim Amzallag, "Beyond Prestige and Magnificence: The Theological Significance of Gold in the Israelite Tabernacle," *HTR* 112 (2019): 296–318.

would have been a sense of the otherworldly, of the *melammû*, 'divine radiance,' that was presenced through the image's brilliance."[50]

As noted above, silver differs from gold in the amount of refining that is required to purify the metal of undesired alloys. The process that would have been used to produce highly refined silver is known as cupellation.[51] Cupellation involves the use of a porous cup or dish (i.e., *cupel*) to separate base metals (i.e., lead) from more precious metals (i.e., gold and silver). When the metals are heated the base metals are oxidized and then a blast of hot air is blown into the cup or dish in order to draw out or remove the impure metals from the silver or gold.[52] For silver the process of cupellation requires temperatures of 900–1000 degrees centigrade to separate the metal from the lead sulfide.[53] When the base metals were separated and removed the molten silver and gold would come to have a shining or glowing appearance. Hans E. Wulff's description of the process is especially helpful here:

> Crucibles are used that are lined with a mixture of wood ash, sand and ground potsherds. Lead is melted into the precious metal, and the dross that forms on the surface and contains all the base metal impurities is continually removed by scraping it over the edge of the crucible until the molten precious metal shows a *brightly shining surface*.[54]

Israelite literature alludes to this metallurgical process in a variety of ways, though most often through the verb צרף, "refine, purify." Nearly half of the uses of this verb connect it specifically to the process of refining silver.[55] The biblical poetic texts often pair this word with the term טהר "purify, refine," which, as we saw, captures the visual quality of metals. In such texts, we might think about צרף as conveying

---

50. Kiersten Neumann, "Gods among Men: Fashioning the Divine Image in Assyria," in *What Shall I Say of Clothes? Theoretical and Methodological Approaches to the Study of Dress in Antiquity*, ed. M. Cifarelli and L. Gawlinski (Boston: Archaeological Institute of America, 2017), 3–23, here 10–11.

51. See Vincent C. Pigott, "Near Eastern Archaeometallurgy: Modern Research and Future Directions," in *The Study of the Ancient Near East in the Twenty-First Century*, ed. J. S. Cooper and G. M. Schwartz (Winona Lake, IN: Eisenbrauns, 1996), 139–76; James D. Muhly, "Mining and Metalwork in Ancient Western Asia," in *Civilizations of the Ancient Near East*, ed. J. M. Sasson (New York: Macmillan, 1995), 3: 1501–21.

52. Jerome O. Nriagu, "Cupellation: The Oldest Quantitative Chemical Process," *Journal of Chemical Education* 62 (1985): 668–74; Karin Reiter, *Die Metalle im Alten Orient unter besonderer Berücksichtigung altbabylonischer Quellen* (AOAT 249; Münster: Ugarit-Verlag, 1999), 412–15.

53. Kay Prag, "Silver in the Levant in the Fourth Millennium B.C.," in *Archaeology in the Levant*, ed. P. R. Moorey and P. J. Parr (Warminster: Aris & Phillips, 1978), 36–45.

54. Cited in Levene and Rothenberg, "Word-smithing," 197. Italics mine.

55. Isa 48:10; Jer 6:29; Zech 13:9; Mal 3:2, 3; Pss 12:7; 66:10; Dan 11:35; 12:10.

something about the chemical property of the metal whereas טהר refers to the physical appearance that is produced by refining the metal.

The relationship between silver's purity and its shiny appearance is emphasized in the language of Ps 12:7–9.[56] The passage compares the power of Yahweh's utterances to the shine of silver that has been purified seven times. I cite the passage here:

> The utterances of Yahweh are pure words (אמרות טהרות),
> Silver refined (כסף צרוף) in a furnace in the ground,
> Purified seven times (מזקק שבעתים).
> You, O Yahweh, will guard them,
> You will protect us from this generation forever.
> Over every side the wicked prowl,
> As vileness is exalted among the sons of men.

The passage uses three terms that evoke metallurgical activity and the results that it has upon silver's appearance: טהר "pure," צרף "refine," and זקק "purify." While most translations convey the adjective טהר in v. 7a as "pure," the term may also be interpreted to denote visual aesthetics. Indeed, in a passage where the focus is upon silver's materiality it is likely that the term and its connection to Yahweh's utterances evoked the metal's shiny aesthetics and hence their ritual suitability. This is not to suggest that the sense of pure, that is, highly refined metal, is not in the purview of the verse but to emphasize that טהר here may connote the properties and qualities of silver.

The verb צרף in 7b is found frequently in the biblical texts to describe the process of refining silver. It is the primary verb that the biblical texts use to describe the cupellation of precious metals. The verb found in the third clause of v. 7—זקק "purify"—appears rather infrequently in the biblical literature.[57] In this context, the verb is employed to describe the high chemical quality of the silver: it has been purified "seven times." The use of such a rare verb in this context may serve to elevate further the picture of the ritual efficacy of Yahweh's utterances. Taken together, the verbs convey that the degree of purity achieved in refining the metal was connected to its perceived value in protective rituals. Silver that had been *highly* purified of impurities was perceived to be especially effective in guarding or protecting against various ills.

A particularly rich illustration of the way in which the refining of precious metals was mythologized in ancient Judah is found in Jer 6:27–30.[58] The passage

---

56. Jeremy D. Smoak, "Amuletic Inscriptions and the Background of YHWH as Guardian and Protector in Psalm 12," *VT* 60 (2010): 1–12.

57. For discussion, see Carola G. Merlini, "The Lexical Field of 'Purity' Verbs in Ancient Hebrew," *Revue Européenne des Études Hébraïques* 5 (2001): 145–52.

58. For a thorough discussion of the metallurgical imagery in this text, see William L. Holladay, *Jeremiah: A Commentary on the Book of the Prophet Jeremiah (Chapters 1–25)* (Hermeneia; Philadelphia, PA: Fortress Press, 1986), 228–33. For further discussion of this

follows several oracles of judgment, in which Yahweh describes the Babylonian's destruction of Judah and Jerusalem (6:1–26). In vv. 27–30, the text uses the imagery of cupellation to describe Yahweh's call of Jeremiah. The passage envisions the people of Judah and Jerusalem as silver that the prophet attempts to purify or refine.[59] Especially noteworthy is the imagery found in v. 29, which likens the רעים of Judah to metal impurities that are not removed in the process of cupellation. Given the relevance of the passage for the present study, I cite it in full here:

> [27]I have made you an assayer and a refiner among my people
> so that you may know and test their ways.
> [28]They are stubbornly rebellious,
> going about with slanders;
> They are bronze and iron,
> all of them act corruptly.
> [29]The bellows blow fiercely,
> the lead is consumed by the fire;
> In vain the refining goes on,
> for the wicked (רעים) are not removed
> [30]They are called "rejected silver,"
> for Yahweh has rejected them.

The first clause in v. 29 opens with a reference to the use of bellows to blast air into the furnace to achieve a desired temperature and remove unwanted alloys. A reference to the fire consuming the undesired alloys (i.e., lead) follows in the next clause of v. 29. The following verse, however, captures the larger purpose of the oracle, namely, a comparison of the failed process of removing the impurities from the silver and Jeremiah's failure to remove the wickedness from Judah.

While studies tend to focus upon the imagery of cupellation found in this passage, I would draw attention to the significance of the term רעים "evil, wicked" in this context. The use of the imagery of cupellation in the passage results in an analogy between human wickedness and the metallic impurities that are not separated from the silver. In this way, the passage might be interpreted to reflect the role that the process of cupellation played as an analogue in ritual purification in ancient Judah.[60] Jeremiah is identified as an assayer who has been appointed by

---

passage, see also Godfrey Driver, "Two Misunderstood Passages of the Old Testament," *JTS* 6 (1955): 82–7.

59. For discussion, see Amzallag, "Copper Metallurgy," 160–1. For similar imagery of Yahweh as a divine metallurgist attempting to purify Israel, see also Ezek 22:17–18: "The word of Yahweh came to me: Mortal, the house of Israel has become dross to me; all of them, silver, bronze, tin, iron and lead. In the crucible they have become dross."

60. For further on the connection between human wickedness and metallic impurities, see the discussion in Y. Feder, "Defilement, Disgust, and Disease: The Experiential Basis of Hittite and Akkadian Terms for Impurity," *JAOS* 136 (2016): 99–116.

Yahweh to use cupellation to remove the רעים from the people of Judah. The passage envisions Judah as "rejected silver," which has been tossed aside because of its lack of purity. When we look back to the Šurpu ritual, Jeremiah, perhaps, also acts as a ritual specialist who performatively purifies Jerusalem of undesired impurities through expert knowledge of metal working.

4. The Shine of Yahweh's Face at Ketef Hinnom

In the present study, I have argued that the materiality and design of the amulets spoke as forcefully as the inscriptions found on the objects' interiors. In doing so, I have attempted to provide a more robust understanding of the variety of means by which Ketef Hinnom's amulets communicated meaning. This involves a consideration of not only the texts on their surfaces but also the manufacture and design of the objects. My foray into the study of material religion has added a new dimension to my work on these amulets by challenging my own assumptions about their meaning as inscriptions connected to the history of the biblical texts. Indeed, while we may be tempted to think of the inscriptions as the main ingredient in the making of the objects we would do well to remind ourselves that their words were perhaps one of the last elements added to their design. And, due to their small size and form these words were all but illegible to human eyes until the twentieth century when scholars used imaging technology to magnify them.

With this in mind, we might begin by observing that Ketef Hinnom's amulets were designed and shaped into tiny scrolls.[61] This aspect of their design located them within the tradition of Egyptian, Phoenician, and Punic *lamellae* (gold and silver sheet metal) that were inscribed with incantations and worn upon the body.[62] Particularly noteworthy here is the tradition preserved in the so-called amuletic decrees of Egypt of wearing small strips of rolled papyrus that contained divine words of protection upon the body. The small rolls of papyrus are relevant here because they bore in written form the utterances of temple gods in Egypt and in certain cases were placed inside tubular cases made of precious metals. Such amuletic decrees inspired later Phoenician and Punic silver and gold *lamellae*, which also often bore inscriptions of protection and blessing.[63] One particularly relevant example of such *lamellae* is a silver amulet that contains an inscription that reads, "Protect, guard, and bless ʿšy."[64] This design aspect has obvious overtones to

---

61. For a summary and description of such silver and gold sheet metal (*lamellae*), see Roy Kotansky, "Textual Amulets and Writing Traditions in the Ancient World," in *Guide to the Study of Ancient Magic*, ed. D. Frankfurter (Religions in the Graeco-Roman World; Leiden: Brill, 2019), 507–54; Carolina López-Ruiz, "Near Eastern Precedents of the 'Orphic' Gold Tablets: The Phoenician Missing Link," *JANER* 15 (2015): 52–91.

62. Barkay, "The Priestly Benediction," 181–2; Smoak, *The Priestly Blessing in Inscription and Scripture*, 43–52.

63. Smoak, "Amuletic Inscriptions," 1–12.

64. Kotansky, "Textual Amulets," 532.

the later practice of using *mezzuzot* and *tefillin* to protect one's house and body, as several studies have noted.[65]

The content of Ketef Hinnom's silver scrolls, however, extends beyond short invocations of blessing and protection. Although both amulets contain language reminiscent of the Phoenician and Punic *lamellae* mentioned above (i.e., "bless" and "guard"), they also include blessings that invoke the shining face of Yahweh.[66] In the biblical texts, the blessing of the shining face of Yahweh plays an important role as part of the instructions given to the priesthood for use in the tabernacle.[67] Numbers 6:22-27 introduces the blessing as revelation that Yahweh gave to Moses to give to the sons of Aaron.[68] The description of the blessing in this context establishes its liturgical function in relation to the tabernacle and the priesthood. In the context of silver, however, allusions to the shining face of the Judean god might be interpreted as the verbal complement to the shining surface of the metal. The writing of allusions to the radiant face of Yahweh gave verbal expression to what the shining properties of the silver already conveyed—the manifestation of the divine presence upon the body. The expression "may Yahweh make his face shine" echoed the metallurgical process of purifying the metal to give it its shining appearance. The shiny qualities of Ketef Hinnom's silver produced a visual aesthetic of what the motif of Yahweh's face turned in the direction of a person conveyed: divine blessing and favor.

Beyond the allusions to Yahweh's shining face and the references to evil, the amulets also invoke language related to notions of covenant loyalty. Lines 4-7 invoke Yahweh's protection and blessing for "those who love him and those who keep his commandments." As several studies have noted, the language is reminiscent of covenant language in Deut 7:9, Neh 1:5, and Dan 9:4.[69] In these biblical texts, the meaning of such language connects it to the wider discourse over the covenant between Yahweh and Israel. In a context of silver, however, we

---

65. André Lemaire, "Amulettes personelles et domestiques en phénicien et en hébreu (Ier millénaire av. N. É.) et la tradition juive des *tefillin* et *mezuzot*," in *Croyances popularizes. Rites et representations en Méditerranée orientale* (Athens: Université nationale et capodistrienne d'Athènes, 2008), 85-98; Yehuda B. Cohn, *Tangled Up In Text: Tefillin and the Ancient World* (Providence: Brown Judaic Studies, 2008).

66. For discussion, see Jeremy D. Smoak, "From Temple to Text: Text as Ritual Space and the Composition of Numbers 6:24-26," *JHS* 17 (2017): 1-26.

67. For a discussion of the imagery of the shining face in the blessing, see Simeon Chavel, "The Face of God and the Etiquette of Eye-Contact: Visitation, Pilgrimage, and Prophetic Vision in Ancient Israelite and Early Jewish Imagination," *JSQ* 19 (2012): 13-19; Michael Fishbane, "Form and Reformulation of the Biblical Priestly Blessing," *JAOS* 103 (1983): 115-21; Chaim Cohen, "The Biblical Priestly Blessing (Num. 6:24-26) in the Light of Akkadian Parallels," *TA* 20 (1993): 228-38.

68. Jacob Milgrom, *Numbers: The Traditional Hebrew Text with the New JPS Translation* (JPS Torah Commentary; Philadelphia, PA: Jewish Publication Society, 1990), 362-7.

69. Barkay et al., "The Amulets from Ketef Hinnom," 61-2.

gain an opportunity to consider how such language functioned in daily life and in a very material way. The appearance of covenant language on the amulets might be viewed in this case to take on specific meaning against the background of the imagery of Yahweh's purifying acts in Jer 6:27–30. While the text connects failed cupellation with Israel's violation of the covenant, the inscriptions seem to allude to the practice of wearing refined silver on the body as an expression of covenant obedience. One likely possibility is that Ketef Hinnom's silver communicated statements about the religious devotion of their wearers. As William Holladay emphasizes about the language of the passage, "silver is a metaphor for the people who are devoted to Yahweh's covenant (see v. 30)."[70] In the context of the amulet, however, we do not have a metaphorical equation between silver and covenant loyalty but rather a very material application of silver's ritual power.

Finally, we might conclude this section by emphasizing again that Ketef Hinnom's silver became "shiny" by the removal of impurities from the precious metal. According to Jer 6:27–30, this pyrometallurgical process served as an analogue for the removal of human impurity. This observation draws attention to the significance of the references to רע, "evil," in the inscriptions on both amulets. Amulet 1 contains an affirmation that Yahweh's blessing is more (powerful) than Evil (ה[ברכה מכל ח[פ] ומהרע]).[71] This statement occurs in the inscription just before the invocation of blessings alluding to the shining face of Yahweh. The inscription on Amulet 2 includes appellatives for Yahweh that include "the one who expels evil" (והגער ב[ר[ע]).[72]

The discussion of metallurgical imagery offered in this study provides a new way to think about the significance of these expressions in the context of purified silver. This is especially the case when considering the oracle in Jer 6:27–30, which connects Yahweh's attempt to remove human רעים, "impurities," with the process of purifying silver through the removal of base metals. Read in a context of highly purified silver, we might interpret the statement that Yahweh's blessing is more powerful than evil as playing upon the metallurgical process of removing רעים, "impurities," in order to produce such highly purified silver. The objects—as silver that had been purified of רעים, "impurities"—served as particularly apt ritual analogues for bodily purification, healing, and protection.

---

70. Holladay, *Jeremiah*, 232.

71. For discussion of the phrase, see Barkay et al., "The Amulets from Ketef Hinnom," 59–60.

72. For recent discussion of this expression on the amulets, see Theodore J. Lewis, "'Athtartu's Incantations and the Use of Divine Names as Weapons," *JNES* 70 (2011): 207–27, here 211; Theodore J. Lewis, "Job 19 in the Light of the Ketef Hinnom Inscriptions," in *Puzzling out the Past: Studies in the Northwest Semitic Languages and Literatures in Honor of Bruce Zuckerman*, ed. S. Fine et al. (Leiden: Brill, 2012), 99–113. See also the discussion of the term in Barkay et al., "The Amulets from Ketef Hinnom," 65.

5. Conclusion

The present study has attempted to offer a different approach by prioritizing the materiality and design of the amulets. In doing so, I have asked how both the chemical properties and the design qualities of the amulets contributed to their ritual function. I argued that by prioritizing the materiality and design of the amulets we arrive at a clearer understanding of the meaning of the inscriptions scratched on their interiors. Such an approach blurs the tendency in scholarship to define and categorize the objects as inscriptions and prioritize their linguistic content. Specifically, I have also asked how silver as a precious metal exerted agency in ancient Near Eastern amulets. Such an approach fronts not the history of the biblical texts but instead the perspective of the body and the role that the body plays in shaping meaning. I have argued that the amulets *were* Yahweh's blessings for their wearers. The chemical, visual, and tactile elements of the amulets were experienced as the manifestation of Yahweh's presence. The benefit of these objects was located in their handheld function—they could be made to interact with or reflect the sun's rays in order to produce notions of the divine presence for the wearer.

When we look back at the properties of the Ketef Hinnom amulets, it becomes clear that the use of silver was not just a statement about the economic status of their owners. The silver was an integral ingredient in their ritual logic. Beyond the use of silver, the biblical texts described above suggest that silver's value in ritual also derived from purifying the metal of impurities to enhance the visual shine. Refining the silver produced a radiance on the surface of the metal. In the Israelite texts, process and result were explicitly connected: both the act of purifying the metal to make it shine (i.e., radiance, glow) and the resulting chemical purity (elimination of impurities) were ritualized. As a result, their imagery offers new insight into the variety of meanings that Ketef Hinnom's silver may have held in the realm of personal religion.

Contributors

Lindsey A. Askin, Lecturer in Jewish Studies, University of Bristol

Isabel Cranz, Assistant Professor of Hebrew Bible, University of Pennsylvania

Liane M. Feldman, Assistant Professor of Hebrew and Judaic Studies, New York University

Timothy Hogue, Assistant Professor of Ancient West Asian History, University of Tsukuba

Ekaterina E. Kozlova, Lecturer of Old Testament, London School of Theology

Nathan MacDonald, Professor of the Interpretation of the Old Testament, University of Cambridge

Alice Mandell, William Foxwell Albright Chair in Biblical and Ancient Near Eastern Studies; Assistant Professor, Johns Hopkins University

Laura Quick, Associate Professor of Hebrew Bible/Old Testament, University of Oxford

Cat Quine, Assistant Professor of Hebrew Bible, University of Nottingham

Melissa Ramos, Assistant Professor of Biblical Studies, George Fox University

Nicole J. Ruane, Senior Lecturer, University of New Hampshire

Jeremy D. Smoak, Senior Lecturer of Near Eastern Languages and Cultures, University of California, Los Angeles

Kerry M. Sonia, Visiting Assistant Professor, Colby College

INDEX OF SCRIPTURE

OLD TESTAMENT

Genesis

1	195, 200	47:29	19, 25, 26
1:7	246	47:30	25
2:7	181	48:16	134 n.103
2:18	128, 136	49:24	73 n.6
2:20	128, 136	49:25	70
3:14	65 n.53		
4:10	188 n.11	**Exodus**	
9:3-4	79	1:5	19 n.31
9:4	62	2:24	142 n.13
9:15	142 n.13	3	187 n.10
9:16	142 n.13	4:24-26	19
9:22	16	5:17	76 n.15
15:7-21	225	6:14-25	203 n.16
15:17	124 n.40	6:25	203 n.16
16:4-9	38 n.35	10:9	81
17:12	66	12	204
18:1	187 n.10	12:6	204 n.19
18:8	55 n.9, 70	12:8	63 n.46
19:30-38	15	12:10	204 n.19
21:4	66	12:14	81
21:6	81	12:43	204 n.19
21:7	65 n.53	12:46	204 n.19
21:8	54 n.5	12:48-49	204 n.19
24	9–25, 19 n.33, 23 n.50	13:2	65
		13:3	142–3, 142 n.16
24:2-9	18–20, 26	13:6	81
24:3	19–20, 23	19:15	69
24:41	20, 23	19:18	124
31	228	20:4	145
31:42,	20 n.34	20:5	145
31:44-54	228	20:7	145
31:53	20 n.34	20:8	139–56, 142 n.16
35:22-26	164 n.23	20:9	144
38	15	20:9-10	143–4
38:28	127 n.59	20:10	145
39:12	17 n.21	20:11	144–5
39:14	81	20:18	124 n.40
39:17	81	20:23	143 n.21
41:42	83	20:24	81
42:24	127 n.59	21:5	65 n.53
46:26	19 n.31, 76 n.17	22:23	65 n.53
47	19, 24, 25	22:28-29	58
		22:29-30	65–9, 67 n.55
		22:30	66
		23	54, 65 n.52

23:12	144	34:1-4	229
23:13	143 n.21	34:13-16	81
23:14-19	63-4	34:23	81
23:14	79, 81	34:26	55, 58, 60-5
23:15	81	34:27-29	229
23:16	55 n.8, 81	37	202
23:17	60, 79, 81	38:21	203 n.16
23:18	55	38:22-23	168
23:19	55, 58, 60-5	39	159-181
24:9-10	245	39:3	246
25-40	208	39:6-7	160
25	202	39:6	160, 164, 168
25:1-7	163	39:10-14	160
25:16	159 n.3	39:14	160, 164, 168
25:21	159 n.3	39:18	202 n.13
25:22	201	39:19	202 n.13
25:31-40	202	39:30-31	160
25:37	202 n.13	39:30`	160, 164, 168
26:9	202 n.13	40	201-2, 206
28	82 n.44, 159-81, 209	40:1	200
28:1	208	40:17	200
28:9-38	159-60	40:20-21	159 n.3
28:9	101	40:29	187 n.9
28:11	160, 164	40:33	200
28:9-12	160	40:34-35	201
28:17-21	160		
28:21	101, 160, 164	**Leviticus**	
28:25-26	202 n.13	1-16	3 n.6
28:29	160	1-7	3 n.6, 184 n.1, 191,
28:36-38	160		192, 194, 208
28:36	101, 160, 164	1:1	202
28:37	202 n.13	1:2	194 n.36
28:38	101-2, 163	1:3-9	192-3
29	99, 184 n.1, 210	1:4	192 n.27
29:1	208-9	1:5	192 n.28
29:4	208	1:10	192 n.26
29:38-46	190-1	1:11	192 n.28
29:38-42	189	1:15	192 n.26
29:40-41	56 n.20	2	54
30:7-8	132	2:1	132
31	144 n.26, 230	2:2	192 n.26
31:13	141 n.9	2:11	5, 56 n.20
31:12-17	144	2:14-16	55 n.8
31:18	229 n.55	2:14	192 n.26
32	71-85	3:1	192 n.26
32:1-2	71	3:2	192 nn.27, 28
32:2	82 n.44	3:6	192 n.26
32:4	71 n.2, 72 n.3	3:8	192 nn.27, 28
32:5	72 n.3, 80-1	3:13	192 nn.27, 28
32:6	71, 80-1	3:12	192 n.26
32:8	72 n.3	3:17	65 n.52
32:20	72, 80-4	4	208
32:25-28	203 n.16	4:2	194 n.36
34	54, 65 n.52, 230-3	4:3-21	195 n.37

Index of Scripture

4:3	192 n.26	20:6	106, 114
4:4	192 nn.27, 28	20:27	114
4:14	192 n.26	22:4	69
4:15	192 nn.27, 28	22:27-28	58, 65-9, 67 n.55
4:23	192 n.26	23:3	144
4:24	192 nn.27, 28	23:13	56 n.20
4:28	192 n.26	23:17	56 n.20
4:29	192 nn.27, 28	23:24	204
4:33	192 nn.27, 28	24	202
5:6	192 n.26	24:7	140
5:11-12	54	25:9	204
6-7	195	25:32-33	203 n.16
6:2	194 n.36	26:2	141 n.9
6:17	56 n.20	26:42	142 n.13
7	210		
7:13	56 n.20	**Numbers**	
7:19-21	52	1-4	200-1, 205-6
7:19-20	194 n.33	1-2	203-4
7:23-25	65 n.52	1:1	201-2
7:28-36	204	3-4	203
8	99, 208, 210	3	199, 204, 208
8-10	202 n.15	3:5-13	204
8-9	209	3:11-13	208
8:10	207	3:12	208
8:30	209	3:16	202 n.14
9	202 n.15	3:39	202 n.14
9:24	186 n.1, 191 n.21	3:51	202 n.14
10	203 n.15, 205 n.23	4:37	202 n.14
10:2	186 n.1	4:41	202 n.14
10:9	56 n.20	4:45	202 n.14
11-17	184 n.1	4:49	202 n.14
11-16	194	5-6	184 n.1
11-15	191	5	23 n.50, 24
11	64, 79	5:1-4	204
11:2	194 n.36	5:11-31	23
12	52-4	5:17-24	75-7
12:2	52, 194 n.36	5:21	19 n.31
12:3	66	5:22	19 n.31
12:4	194	5:27	19 n.31
14:4-7	78 n.27	6:3-4	56 n.20
14:49-53	78 n.27	6:20	56 n.20
15:2	194 n.36	6:22-27	251
15:16-18	69	6:24-26	237
15:19-24	52	7:1-88	199
16	99, 195	7-10	201-7
16:1-28	195 n.39	7-8	208
16:39-34	195 n.39	7	199-211
16:21-22	78 n.27	7:1	200
17:11-14	62	7:3-9	202
18	16	7:10	207
19:3	141 n.9	7:10-88	202
19:30	141 n.9	7:89	201-2
19:31	106	8	184 n.1, 199-200, 208, 208 n.30, 210
20:2-6	106		

8:1-4	202, 202 n.13	6	233
8:5-13	208	6:8	175 n.66
8:5-22	200, 204	7:9	251
8:6	208	7:18	143
8:7	208, 209	8:18	143 n.20
8:9	208	9	83-5, 231
8:11	209, 210 n.36	9:7	143
8:14-18	208	9:9-11	229
9:1-14	200, 204	9:10	229-30
9:1	201	9:16	73 n.8
9:2-14	204	9:21	73 n.9, 83-4
9:15-23	202	12:2-3	73 n.9
10:1-10	204	12:12	54 n.7, 65
10:13	202 n.14	12:18	54 n.7, 65
11:8	84	12:23-27	62
11:22	122 n.27	14	79
13:3	202 n.14	14:1-2	64
14:45	84 n.48	14:21	55
15:1-16	54	15:15	143
15:5-10	56 n.20	14:3-20	60, 64
15:39-40	143 n.22	14:21	58-65, 64 n.50
16:1-35	109	16:3	143
16:7	132	16:5-8	73 n.9
17:2	246	16:11	54 n.7, 65
17:4	246	16:12	143
17:17-25	159 n.3	16:13	142
17:23	160 n.5	16:14	54 n.7, 65
18	194 n.35, 208	16:16	64, 79, 81
18:1-7	196 n.42	17:3	73 n.9
18:7	209	18	114-15
18:13	55 n.8	18:4-5	55 n.8
19	184 n.1, 209	18:8	73 n.9
19:1-22	204	18:9-12	114
20:6	191 n.21	18:9-11	110
22	187 n.10	18:10-12	114
22:22	95	18:10-11	106, 115
22:32	95	18:11	113-14
23:22	73 n.6	18:20-12	106
24:8	73 n.6	18:22	103
25:1-5	15	22	65 n.52, 67
28:2	204	22:6-7	58, 59-60
28:26	55 n.8	23:10-11	69
33:38	202 n.14	23:14	98
36:5	202 n.14	24:9	143
		24:18	143
Deuteronomy		24:22	143
1:44	84 n.48	25:17	143
4:24	186 n.7	27-30	224 n.40
5-11	141	27-28	228
5:2	223	27	225, 228, 230-3
5:3	229-30	27:1-9	232
5:12	141-4	27:1-8	231
5:13-14	143	27:2	234
5:15	143-5	27:5	231

Index of Scripture

27:6	231	3:9-13	25
27:11-26	232	3:9	18, 26
28:22	129 n.71	3:10-13	15
29:13	223–4	3:10-11	26
32:17	125	3:11	25, 27
32:18	70	3:12-13	16
33:17	73 n.6	3:13	17–18, 26
34	195, 200	4:7-8	25
		4:11-12	24
Joshua		4:13	16
1:13	143 n.22		
6	204	**1 Samuel**	
8	228, 230–1, 233–4	1:20-25	53–4
8:30-35	230–1	4-6	183
8:32	231	4:18	143 n.23
10:13	74 n.11	6	70
23:7	143 n.21	9:6-9	109
24	230–3	9:20	103
24:19-28	231	10:1	34, 103
24:19	108 n.12	10:24	103
24:25-26	229, 231	13:8-14	36 n.26
24:25	231	14:24-45	36 n.26
24:26	232–3	15:2-34	36 n.26
		16:13	33 n.12, 34
Judges		17:17-18	55
4:4	46 n.67	21:4-5	69
4:19	55	25:23-24	18 n.24
5:25	55	28	103–16
6:21	186 n.7	28:3-19	36 n.26
8:26	82 n.44	28:3	107
8:27	82 n.44	28:13	107, 108, 111 n.19
8:30	19 n.31, 76 n.17	29:4	95 n.21
8:34	143 n.20	31	35
13:20	191 n.21		
15:10	127 n.59	**2 Samuel**	
15:12	127 n.59	1:8	74 n.11
16:29	16–17	2	35
17:10	109	12:13	100 n.41
		12:16	18 n.24
Ruth		14:11	143 n.20
1:17	18, 23–5, 27	18-19	35
1:13	23 n.49	18:18	143 n.21
1:19-20	23 n.49	19:23	95 n.21
2:10	25	22:9	186 n.7
2:12	26	24:10	100 n.41
2:13	25		
2:20	25	**1 Kings**	
3	13–27	1	36 n.26
3:3	15–16	1:13	34
3:4	15–16, 26	1:32-48	33 n.12
3:5-6	25	1:39	34
3:6	16	1:50-53	36
3:7	26	2:13-25	36
3:8	15–18, 21, 26	5:18	95 n.21

7:15	71 n.2	4:8-38	47
7:21	17 n.21	4:23	152
8:21	220, 230 n.57	4:32-35	107 n.10
11:14	95 n.21	6:20	189 n.16
11:23	95 n.21	9:6	33 n.12, 34
11:25	95 n.21	9:12-13	33 n.12
11:29	46 n.67	9:27-28	34
12	72–5, 84	9:30-37	43–5
12:28-33	153	9:36	44
12:28	72 n.3	10:11	45
12:32-33	72 n.3	10:13-14	38 n.35
13:1	46 n.67	10:18-28	42 n.48, 43
14	46	10:29	73 n.8
14:1-18	46	11	32–8, 47–8
14:22-24	39	11:1	35 n.22
15	38–45, 48	11:2	34
15:2	38	11:12-19	33
15:3	39	12:2	34 n.19
15:8	38 n.34	12:20-21	35
15:10	38	12:23	35
15:12	38, 39	13:21	107 n.10
15:13	38	14:19	35
15:14	38–9	16:15	189
16:31-32	41, 43	17:16	73 n.8
17-19	185	18:4	40 n.42, 84 n.48
17:1-7	41 n.46	18:34	220 n.27
17:1	46 n.67	19:2	46 n.67
17:17-24	46	19:13	220 n.27
18	42, 42 n.51, 43 n.54, 185–91	21:6	106
	190 n.20	21:23	35
18:1		22-23	48, 233–4
18:4	41, 43	22	45–8
18:13	43	23	75, 78, 85
18:19-40	109	23:3	229, 233–4
18:19	41	23:4	47, 73 n.9
18:27	189 n.14	23:4-8	40
18:29	189 n.14	23:5	39
18:37	191	23:6	74–5
19:2-3	42	23:7	82 n.44
19:19	46 n.67	23:8-23	73 n.9
20:7	121 n.24	23:12	74–5
20:24	41		
20:31-35	216 n.12	**1 Chronicles**	
21	43, 46	10:13-14	104, 106, 110, 115
22	90 n.2, 94		
22:8	46 n.67	16:4	143 n.20
22:24	46 n.67	16:15	142 n.13
22:52-53	42	21	95
		21:8	100 n.41
2 Kings			
1:10	186 n.7	**2 Chronicles**	
3:2	42 n.48	6:11	230 n.57
3:2-3	36 n.26	13:8	73 n.8
4:1-7	46	11:15	73 n.8

Index of Scripture

15:6	84 n.48	111:5	142 n.13
15:16-17	38 n.34	119:49	143 n.22
15:16	40 n.42	112:10	130 n.77
33:6	106	118:7	108 n.12
34:7	84 n.48	132:2	38 n.35, 73 n.6
		136:6	246

Ezra
8:35	68	**Proverbs**	
		26:23	181
Nehemiah		30:12	98
1:5	251	30:23	38 n.35
1:8	143 n.22		
4:8	143 n.20	**Ecclesiastes**	
9:16-18	84	12:1	143 n.20
9:18	73 n.8		
		Song of Songs	
Esther		7:2	76 n.17
9:8	142	8:1	57

Job

Isaiah

1-2	94–5	1:24	73 n.6
4:20	84 n.48	1:13	152
6:18	16–17	2:4	84 n.48
16:9	130 n.77	4:4	98, 98–9 n.35
16:18	188 n.11	6	90, 94
20:16-17	56 n.20	7:4	124 n.40
35:10	108 n.12	7:15	57
		7:15-16	56 n.20
Psalms		8:18-20	110–12, 115
2:9	181	8:19	104–5, 107, 110,
12:7-9	248		111 n.18, 112
12:7	247 n.55	10:9	220 n.27
19:2	246	10:14	111 n.18
20:4	143 n.23	13:21	125 n.47
20:8	143 n.21	17:10	145 n.20
22:28	143 n.20	24:2	38 n.35
31:13	181	26:13	145 n.21
35:16	130 n.77	28:7-22	113
37:12	130 n.77	28:8	98
42:8	143 n.20	28:9	57, 113
63:7	143 n.20	29:4	111 n.18, 112–13
77:4	143 n.20	30:14	84
81:4	152	30:22	71 n.2
89:23	84 n.48	30:27	186 n.7
95:5	125 n.47	34:14	125 n.47
103:18	143 n.22	36:12	98
105:8	142 n.13	36:19	220 n.27
105:53	143 n.22	37:13	220 n.27
106:7-9	97	38:14	111 n.18
106:19	73 n.8	38:21	130
106:19-23	84	42:3	124 n.40
106:37	125	42:5	246
106:45	142 n.13	44:24	246
109:6	95 n.21, 96	47:2	84

47:5	38 n.35	22:17-18	249 n.59
47:7	38 n.35	23:32	81
48:1	145 n.20	37:17	127
48:10	247 n.55	42:13	186 n.7
49:1	145 n.21		
49:26	73 n.6	**Daniel**	
50:2	97	9:4	251
55:1	55	11:35	247 n.55
56:2	141 n.9		
56:4	141 n.9	**Hosea**	
56:6	141 n.9	2:13	152
57:11	145 n.20	2:19	143 n.21
60:16	73 n.6	8:5-6	73 n.8
62:6	145 n.20	10:5	73 n.8
64:4	145 n.20	9:1	15, 23
65:2-5	81	9:11	23
66:3	143	9:12-13	23
66:13	70	9:14	24
Jeremiah		**Joel**	
3:16	143 n.23	3:10	84 n.48
4:30	123, 136		
6:20	132	**Amos**	
6:27-30	248–50, 252	1:9	142 n.13
6:29	247 n.55, 249–50	4:11	96–7
10:9	82 n.44	6:10	140, 143 n.21
11:19	143 n.21	7:8	100 n.41
13:18	38 n.35	7:12-15	109
16:5-8	81	8:2	100 n.41
19:11	181	8:5	152, 153
20:9	143 n.20		
22:24	168 n.38	**Jonah**	
22:28	181	2:1	122 n.27
28:9	104	2:8	143 n.20
29:2	38 n.35	2:11	122 n.27
34	225–6, 225 n.43		
34:18-21	226	**Micah**	
34:18	226	1:7	84 n.48
46:5	84 n.48	3:11	109
48:38	181	4:3	84 n.48
49:23	220 n.27	7:18	100 n.41
51:34	181		
		Nah	
Lamentations		1:4	97
2:16	130 n.77		
		Haggai	
Ezekiel		2:21	168 n.38
2:8-3:4	79 n.32		
3:23	192 n.21	**Zechariah**	
4:12	98	1:17	96 n.29
6:9	143 n.20	2:12	96 n.29
16:8	26	3	89–102
16:18	83 n.44	3:1-2	94–8
16:60	142 n.13	3:2	96

Index of Scripture

3:3-5	98–101	**NEW TESTAMENT**	
3:8-10	101–2		
3:9	101 n.44, 102	**Matthew**	
4:6-10	101	2:22	126 n.52
10:9	143 n.20	12:42	126 n.53
11:6	84 n.48	15:21	126 n.52
13:2	143 n.21	16:13	126 n.52
13:9	247 n.55	26:57-68	106 n.8
Malachi		**Mark**	
3:2	247 n.55	8:10	126 n.52
3:3	247 n.55	14:53-65	106 n.8
4:4	143 n.22		
		Luke	
APOCRYPHA		11:24	126 n.52
		22:64	106 n.8
Tobit		10:32	121 n.24
3:7	128		
3:17	127, 128	**John**	
5:17	129	19:23	126 n.52
6:2	128	21:6	126 n.52
6:3-7	122 n.26		
6:4-9	118, 122–3	**Acts**	
6:5	122	2:10	126 n.52
6:8	123, 132 n.91	19:1	126 n.52
6:9	123	20:1	126 n.52
6:17	118, 122 n.26, 123–6		
8:1-9	118, 126–8	**Romans**	
8:2	122 n.26, 131	7:13	126 n.50
8:3	126		
8:4	127–8	**1 Corinthians**	
8:5-8	132	3:2	57
8:6	128, 136		
11:4	118, 122 n.26, 128–31	**Ephesians**	
		4:9	126 n.52
11:7-15	118, 128–31		
11:7	122 n.26	**Revelation**	
11:8	129–30	3:18	123, 136
11:9	128	16:19	126 n.52
11:11	129–30	18:2	126 n.53
11:12	130	18:23	126 n.50
12:3	122 n.26		

AUTHOR INDEX

Aberbach, Moses 73 n.4
Abraham, Kathleen 24 n.54
Abrahams, Israel 128, 128 n.63
Abusch, Tzvi 81 n.39, 91 n.8
Achenbach, Reinhard 202 n.13, 202 n.15, 203 n.16, 204 n.17, 205 n.23
Ackerman, Susan 40, 40 nn.39, 40, 43, 41 n.46
Ackroyd, Peter R. 30 n.2
Adams, Carol 56 n.19, 57, 57 nn.20, 24
Adams, Francis 125 n.41
Agostini, Camilla 180 n.81
Ahituv, Shmuel 174 n.61, 176, 176 n.71, 177, 177 n.72
Aitken, James K. 118 n.3
Albertz, Rainer 107 n.9, 142 n.15
Albright, William Foxwell 214 n.3, 216 n.11, 217 n.16, 218 n.20, 222 n.38
Alexander, Philip S. 206 n.25
Altmann, Peter 79 n.29
Ames, Frank Ritchel 2 n.4
Amiet, P. 222 n.36
Amzallag, Nissim 76 n.18, 245 nn.40, 41, 246 nn.47, 48, 49, 249 n.59
Andersen, Burton R. 132 n.89
Anderson, Gary A. 203 n.15
Artemov, Nikita 125 n.48
Aschkenasy, Nehama 44 n.56
Askin, Lindsey A. 7
Aslanoff, Grégoire 130 n.76
Attia, Annie 117 n.1, 121 n.23, 133, 133 n.95
Avigad, Nahman 169 nn.44, 45
Avrahami, Yael 13 n.1
Ayali-Darshan, Noga 153 n.70

Bachi, G. 179
Baentsch, Bruno 195 n.39
Bahrani, Zainab 146, 146 nn.34, 35, 36, 147, 147 nn.38, 41
Baines, John 242 n.29
Balentine, Samuel E. 3 n.5
Barkay, Gabriel 237 nn.1, 2, 3, 238, 238 nn.4, 6, 7, 250 n.62, 251 n.69, 252 nn.71, 72
Barker, Margaret 121 n.20
Bartlett, Matt 126 n.54
Barré, Lloyd M. 36 nn.23, 27, 37 n.30

Baukal, Charles E., Jr., 185 n.5, 189 n.17
Baum, Robert M. 42 n.50
Baumgarten, Joseph M. 69 n.60
Beattie, Derek R.G. 15 n.8, 17 n.18
Beck, John A. 185 n.5
Becking, Bob 25 n.57
Beckman, Gary 134 n.102
Begg, Christopher T. 78, 78 n.26, 108 n.13
Beit Arieh, I. 173
Bell, Catherine 10, 10 n.9, 26 n.64, 49 n.76, 139 n.2
Ben-Barak, Zafira 38 n.35
Bench, Clayton 33 n.14, 34 n.18
Ben-Dov, Jonathan 45 n.62
Benjamin, Seymour 196 n.40
Ben-Marzouk, Nadia 168 n.42
Bennett, Jane 149, 149 n.50
Benoît, Gideon 131 n.78
Ben-Tor, D. 163 n.17, 167 n.36, 178
Benzel, Kim 238 n.5, 240–4, 240 nn.16, 17, 18, 19, 241 nn.20, 21
Bergen, Wesley J. 3 n.6, 29 n.2, 48 n.74
Berlejung, Angelika 238 n.3
Bernstein, Moshe J. 15 n.11
Bewer, Julius A. 96 n.27
Beyer, Klaus 120 n.17, 128
Bhayro, Siam 119 n.12, 126 n.54, 132 n.88
Bibb, Bryan D. 3 n.6, 30 nn.2, 4, 184, 184 nn.3, 4
Bič, Miloš 95 n.20, 99 n.36
Binger, Tilde 40 n.39
Biran, Avraham 221 n.33
Black, J. Sutherland 20 n.33
Black, Jeremy A. 122 n.25, 242 n.25
Blackledge, Catherine 19 n.28
Blenkinsopp, Joseph 111 n.16
Bloch-Smith, Elizabeth 115 n.28
Blum, Erhard 141 n.8, 143, 143 n.24, 144 n.29, 145 n.31, 154, 154 n.72
Boda, Mark J. 90, 90 n.3, 100 n.43
Bodenheimer, F.S. 55, 55 n.12, 56 n.18
Bohak, Gideon 131 n.79, 131 n.82
Bosman, Hendrik 143 n.18
Bottéro, Jean 217 n.17, 219, 219 n.22
Bourghouts, J.F. 131 n.86
Bourguignon, Erika 105 n.5

Bovati, Pietro 18 n.24
Bowen, Nancy 38 n.35, 41, 41 n.45
Brenner-Idan, Athalya 42, 42 nn.47, 52, 43 n.53
Brettler, Marc Zvi 150 n.56
Brewer-Boydston, Ginny 35 n.22, 38 n.34, 39 n.37, 41 n.45, 42 nn.51, 52
Breyfogle, Caroline M. 54 n.7
Breytenbach, Cilliers 95 nn.21, 22, 23
Briggs, Richards S. 76 n.18
Brim, Charles J. 76 n.18
Brück, Joanna 180 n.81
Brumberg-Kraus, Jonathan 79 n.29
Bryan, Cyril P. 134 n.104
Buc, Philippe 49 n.76
Budd, Philip J. 209 n.31, 210, 210 n.38
Bush, Frederic 17, 17 n.20

Cahill, Jane M. 164 nn.21, 22, 172 n.58
Campbell, Edward F. 14 n.5, 15 n.12, 17 n.19
Cansdale, George 55 n.14
Caquot, André 55 n.11, 56, 56 nn.17, 18, 57 n.20, 96 n.28, 97 nn.32, 33
Carasik, Michael 207 n.26
Carmichael, Calum M. 15 n.10, 25 n.57, 62 n.41
Carr, David 143 n.17
Carroll, Robert P. 111 n.16
Cassuto, Umberto 174 n.62
Chapman, Cynthia R. 21 n.41, 57 n.23
Chavel, Simeon 188 n.11, 204 n.19, 205, 205 n.22, 251 n.67
Cheyne, Thomas K. 19 n.33
Childs, Brevard S. 61 n.36, 139 n.1, 140 n.6, 144 n.27
Chrysovergi, Maria 117 n.2, 121 n.22
Cleath, Lisa J. 227, 227 n.49
Cogan, Mordechai 74 n.13, 185 n.6
Cohen, Chaim 251 n.67
Cohn, Yehuda B. 251 n.65
Collon, Dominique 164 n.32, 167 n.36
Cook, Edward M. 119 n.13
Cook, Stephen L. 107 n.9
Cooper, Alan M. 63 n.46
Cox, Collett 44 n.60
Craigie, Peter C. 60 n.31
Cranz, Isabel 6, 90 n.3
Cross, Frank Moore 31 n.5, 74 n.11, 177 n.73, 216 n.11, 217 n.15, 218, 218 n.21, 222 n.36
Curtis, Anthony 26 n.64

Daiches, Samuel 113 n.23
Daniélou, Alain 19 n.28
Darby, Erin 22 n.41
Daube, David 55–6, 55 n.15

Davies, Eryl W. 200 n.3, 201, 201 nn.8, 9, 209 nn.31, 33
Davis, Kipp 118 n.6
Day, John 40 n.39, 231 n.58
Day, Peggy L. 90 n.2, 95 nn.21, 22, 23
Dayagi-Mendels, Michal 165 n.25
Delkurt, Holger 89 n.1, 96 n.24, 99 nn.35, 36, 100 n.41, 101 n.45, 102 n.48
De Pury, Albert 30 n.5
Deselaers, Paul 120 n.13
Dewrell, Heath 22 n.46
Dick, Michael B. 241 nn.21, 22
Dieter Betz, Hans 127 n.57
Dijk, Jacobus, van 222 nn.36, 37
Dillon, Sarah 207 n.29
Doak, Brian 13 n.1
Donner, Herbert 220 n.30
Douglas, Mary 79 n.29
Driver, G. R. 76 n.18, 249 n.58
Driver, S. R. 203 n.16
Durham, John I. 139 n.1
Dutcher-Walls, Patricia 33 nn.14, 15, 16, 36 nn.24, 25, 27, 43 nn.54, 55, 44 n.58

Ebbell, B. 134 n.104
Eberhart, Christian A. 2 n.4
Ego, Beate 121 n.21
Eilberg-Schwartz, Howard 57 n.21, 62 n.43
Eising, Hermann 139, 140 n.3
Ekroth, Gunnel 59 n.28
Elgvin, Torleif 119 n.6
Ellen, Roy 149, 149 n.49
Elliger, Karl 195 n.39, 202 n.11
Emerton, J.A. 40 n.39
Escobar, Eduardo 244 n.39
Eshel, Esther 118, 118 n.5, 120 n.17, 176, 176 n.71
Eynikel, Erik 30 n.2, 31 n.5

Fabry, Heinz-Josef 95 n.21
Faraone, Christopher 239–40, 239 n.10
Fauconnier, Gilles 150 n.55, 151 nn.58, 59
Feder, Yitzhaq 194 n.34, 245, 245 n.42
Feldman, Ines 118 n.6
Feldman, Liane M. 8, 192 nn.25, 38, 39, 225 n.41
Firmage, Edwin 61 n.35
Fishbane, Michael 251 n.67
Fitzmyer, Joseph A. 119 n.10, 120 nn.14, 15, 17, 126 nn.51, 53, 128, 128 n.64, 132 n.91, 137 n.112, 220 nn.27, 28

Fleming, Daniel E. 73 n.7, 146 n.37, 147, 147 nn.39, 43, 148, 152, 152 nn.65, 66, 153 nn.67, 69, 154, 154 n.73
Ford, James Nathan 132 n.88, 245 n.44
Förstel, Christian 130 n.76
Frankel, David 77 n.21
Frankfurter, David 5 n.7, 6 n.8, 240, 240 nn.14, 15, 16, 17, 18, 19
Frazer, James G. 67 n.56, 82 n.40
Freedman, R. David 18 n.26, 19, 19 n.32
Frevel, Christian 45 n.60, 49 n.76, 161 n.10, 162, 162 nn.11, 12, 13, 165 n.24, 174 n.64, 175 nn.66, 68
Frey-Anthes, Henrike 94 n.19, 95 n.22, 97 n.31, 126 n.53
Fritz, Volkmar 44 n.58
Frymer-Kensky, Tikva 76 n.15

Gale, Noël H. 239 n.8
Gane, Roy E. 43 n.54
Gardthausen, Viktor Emil 128 n.66
Gaspa, Salvatore 164 n.21, 172 n.58
Gaster, T. H. 67 n.56
Gathercole, Simon J. 120 n.18, 122 n.26
Gell, Alfred 150, 150 nn.51, 52, 160 n.7, 161 n.7
Geller, Markham J. 92 n.11, 132 n.89
Genette, Gerard 207, 207 n.29, 208
George, Andrew 122 n.25
Gerbrandt, G.E. 31 n.5
Gerstenberger, Erhard S. 68 n.58
Geva, Sh. 178
Gieselmann, Bernd 31 n.5
Gilders, William K. 2 n.4, 29 n.2, 209 n.32
Goedicke, Hans 66 n.55, 67 n.55
Golani, Amir 241 n.23, 246 n.46
Goldstein, Bernard R. 63 n.46
Golub, Mitka R. 170 n.49
Gorelick, Leonard 166 n.31
Gorman, Francis 66 n.54
Gorman, Frank H., Jr, 29 n.2, 30 n.4, 31 n.7, 32 n.10, 48 n.74, 195 n.39
Grabbe, Lester L. 109, 109 n.14
Gray, George Buchanan 77 n.19, 201, 201 nn.7, 10, 209 n.33
Gray, John 17 n.19
Gray, Louis H. 121 n.21
Greer, Jonathan S. 153 n.71
Grimes, Ronald 2 n.1
Gruber, Mayer 53 n.3, 54 n.7
Gruenwald, Ithamar 3 n.5, 31 n.10, 48 n.74, 49 n.78
Gudme, Anne K. de Hemmer 163 n.16, 175 n.67

Guichard, Michaël 241 n.19
Guillaume, Philippe 77 n.21, 163 n.16, 174 n.63
Gwinnett, A. John 166 n.31, 168 n.37

Hadley, Judith M. 40 n.39, 40 n.42
Hallaschka, Martin 89 n.1, 96 nn.25, 29, 101 n.44
Hallermayer, Michaela 119 n.6, 120 n.17
Hallo, William W. 153 n.70, 165 n.28, 168 nn.39, 41, 241 n.24
Halpern, Baruch 90 n.3, 101 n.44, 113 n.23
Halton, Charles 17 n.21, 25 n.60
Hamilton, Mark W. 13 n.1
Hamilton, Victor 20 n.34, 23 n.47
Hamori, Esther J. 45, 45 nn.63, 64, 46, 46 nn.66, 69, 70, 104, 104 n.2, 104 n.4, 106, 106 n.7
Handy, Lowell K. 46 n.62
Hanhart, Robert 96 nn.25, 28, 98 n.34, 99 nn.35, 36, 101 n.45, 102 n.48, 120 n.18, 122 n.27, 123 n.34, 129 n.68
Hanson, Paul D. 210, 210 n.39
Hanson, R. S. 172 n.57
Haran, Menachem 58, 58 n.25, 61 nn.38, 39, 63 n.44, 65 n.52, 159 n.1
Harris, Rivka 18 n.27
Hartley, John 193 n.31
Hartog, François 215 n.9
Hauser-Schäublin, Brigitta 37 n.28
Hauspie, Katrin 130 n.75
Hayes, Christine E. 75 n.14, 84 n.47
Hays, Christopher B. 19 n.29, 105 n.5, 111 n.17
Held, Moshe 216 n.11, 217 nn.13, 14, 218 n.20
Hendel, Ronald S. 30 n.2
Herr, Larry G. 169 n.45
Hestrin, Ruth 165 n.25
Hillers, Delbert 100 n.42
Hogan, Larry P. 117 n.2, 121 n.22
Hogue, Timothy 7, 142 n.16, 145 n.32, 149 nn.47, 48, 154 n.76, 155 n.77, 227, 227 nn.50, 51
Holladay, William L. 248 n.58, 252, 252 n.70
Holt, Else K. 185 nn.5, 6
Horst, Pieter W., van der 117 n.2, 121 n.22
Hossfeld, Frank-Lothar 139 n.1, 140 n.6, 142 n.14
Hout, Theo P.J., van den 32 n.9
Houtman, Cornelius 159 n.2, 164 n.23, 165 n.24, 174 nn.62, 64, 180 n.77
Hubbard, Robert 14 n.5, 17 n.19, 23 n.49, 24 n.55, 25 n.58, 26 n.61
Hurowitz, Victor Avigdor 30 n.2, 239 n.8
Hüsken, Ute 48 n.74
Hutton, Jeremy M. 73, 73 n.8

Ilan, Tal 45, 46 nn.65, 68
Imes, Carmen Joy 162 n.11

Jacobs, Naomi S. S. 132 n.91, 133, 133 nn.92, 96, 137 n.112
Jacobsen, Thorkild 20, 20 nn.35, 36, 21 nn.37, 39
Jaffee, Martin S. 44 n.60
Janzen, David 3 n.4, 29 n.1, 37 n.31, 48 n.74, 49 nn.76, 77
Janzen, J. Gerald 73 n.6
Jay, Nancy 51–2, 52 n.1, 69, 70
Jean, Cynthia 92 n.11
Jeffers, Ann 76 n.15, 105 n.5
Jensen, Hans J. Lundager 117 n.1, 121 nn.23, 24
Jenson, Philip Peter 29 n.2, 195 n.38
Jeremias, Christian 89 n.1, 90 n.2, 95 n.20, 99 n.38
Jewitt, Carey 161 n.8
Johnson, Mark 180 n.78
Johnstone, William 139 n.1
Joüon, Paul 17 n.19

Kaiser, Walter C., Jr., 80, 80 n.35
Kalimi, Isaac 33 n.14
Kaltner, John 15 n.7, 16 nn.13, 15
Keel, Othmar 58, 58 n.27, 69, 163 n.15, 171 n.53
Kelle, Brad E. 2 n.4
Kellermann, Diether 202 n.13
Kertzer, David I. 32 n.10, 34 n.17
Keulen, P. S. F., van 31 n.5
Kienast, Burkhart 21 n.40
Kilpatrick, Joel 15 n.7
Kitz, AnneMarie 23, 23 nn.51, 52
Klawans, Jonathan 68 n.59, 194 n.32
Klingbeil, Gerald A. 4 n.5, 31 n.6, 32 n.10, 37 n.29, 48 n.74
Knauf, Axel 63 n.49
Knohl, Israel 195 n.39
Knoppers, Gary N. 110 n.15
Koch, Ido 164 n.22, 172 nn.58, 59, 173
Köcher, Franz 21 n.41
Kollmann, Bernd 117 n.1, 121 n.23, 131, 131 n.83, 133 n.95, 134 n.99
König, E. 113 n.23
Kotansky, Roy 250 nn.61, 64
Kozlova, Ekaterina E. 4, 76 n.17
Knierim, Rolf 2 n.3
Kraŝovec, Jože 77 n.22
Kress, Gunther 161 n.8
Kruger, Paul A. 26 nn.63, 65
Krutzsch, Myriam 118 n.6
Kuenen, Abraham 199, 199 nn.1, 2

Kuhrt, Amélie 220 n.29
Kuloba, Wabayanga Robert 35 n.22
Kunin, Seth 79 n.29

Laato, Antti 89 n.1
Labuschagne, C. J. 62 nn.40, 42
LaCocque, André 15 n.12
Lakoff, George 180 n.78
Lambert, W. G. 186 n.7
Lang, Bernhard 143, 144 n.25
Laskaratos, J. 117 n.1, 133 n.95
Lauinger, Jacob 227 n.45
Lawrence, Jonathan David 3 n.4
Leach, Edmund R. 91 n.6
Lebram, J. C. H. 119 n.9
Lee, John A. L. 118 n.3
Leeuwen, Theo, van 161 n.8
Leick, Gwendolyn 20 n.36
Lemaire, André 171 n.52, 251 n.65
LeMon, Joel M. 111 n.17
Lernau, Omri 170 n.48
Leuchter, Mark 48 n.75
Levene, Dan 245 n.41, 247 n.54
Levenson, Jon D. 155 n.78
Levin, Christoph 31 n.5, 145 n.31
Levine, Baruch A. 68 n.58, 187, 187 n.8, 193 n.29, 201, 201 n.5, 209, 209 nn.31, 33, 210, 210 nn.36, 37
Levine, Dan 132 n.88
Levinson, Bernard M. 45 n.60, 144 n.28
Lewis, Theodore J. 97 n.32, 112 n.20, 239 nn.8, 9, 252 n.72
Lipka, Hilary 35 n.21
Lipschits, Oded 164 n.22, 170 n.47, 171 n.52, 172 n.58, 173
Liverani, Mario 38 n.33
Livingstone, Alasdair 244 n.39
Loewenstamm, Samuel E. 77, 77 n.23
Long, Burke O. 44 n.58
López-Ruiz, Carolina 250 n.61
Loretz, Oswald 17, 17 n.19
Lowry, Rich 30 n.2
Lukács, Ottilia 144 nn.27, 30
Lundberg, Marilyn J. 237 nn.2, 3
Lundbom, Jack R. 141 n.11
Lux, Rüdiger 90 n.5, 95 n.21, 96 n.25, 97 n.31, 99 n.38

MacDonald, Nathan 2 n.4, 8–9, 30 n.3, 72 n.3, 79 n.30, 81, 81 n.37, 205 n.21, 209 n.34
MacRae, George W. 153 n.70
Macwilliam, Stuart 35 n.21, 36 n.24
Maeir, Walter A. 40 n.39
Malafouris, Lambros 149, 149 n.49

Malul, Meir 17 n.21, 20 n.34, 21 n.40, 22, 22, 22 nn.42, 44, 25, 25 n.59
Mandell, Alice 8, 76 n.15, 83 n.45, 166 n.29, 176 n.70, 234, 234 n.63
Marketos, S. 118 n.1, 133 n.95
Marti, Lionel 241 n.19
Maul, Stefan M. 91 nn.9, 10, 92 nn.12, 14, 15, 96 n.26, 100 nn.39, 40, 241 n.21
McCarter, P. Kyle, Jr., 53 n.2
McCutcheon, Russell T. 114 n.27
McKane, William 76 n.18
McKay, John 30 n.2
McKenzie, Steven L. 15 n.7
McNutt, Paula 246 n.46
Meinhold, Johannes 140 n.8, 141 n.8, 152, 152 n.64, 153 n.71
Merlini, Carola G. 248 n.57
Meshel, Naphtali S. 2 n.4, 192 n.23
Meshel, Ze'ev 176, 176 n.71, 177
Mesnil du Buisson, Robert, du 222 n.37
Mettinger, Tryggve N.D. 153 n.70
Meyers, Carol L. 53 n.4, 54 n.6, 97 nn.30, 31, 99 nn.36, 37, 101 n.44
Meyers, Eric M. 97 nn.30, 31, 99 nn.36, 37, 101 n.44
Michalowski, Piotr 125 n.48
Mieroop, Marc, van de 241 n.24
Milgrom, Jacob 56 nn.18, 20, 58, 58 n.26, 59 n.29, 62, 63 n.47, 66 n.54, 67 n.57, 68 n.58, 186 n.7, 193 nn.31, 32, 194 nn.34, 35, 195 n.39, 196 nn.41, 42, 201, 201 n.6, 202 n.12, 204 n.21, 207, 207 n.27, 209 nn.31, 35, 251 n.68
Miller, Daniel 76 n.15
Mitchell, Hinckley G. T. 96 n.27, 101 nn.44, 45
Monroe, Lauren A. S. 29 n.1, 40, 40 n.41, 141, 141 n.10, 154 n.75
Moore, Carey A. 123 n.37, 130, 130 n.73, 132 n.91, 135 n.109
Moore, Johannes C., de 153 n.70
Moorey, Peter R. S. 241 n.23
Morgan, David 14, 14 n.4
Mouton, Alice 134 n.101
Mowinckel, Sigmund 153 n.70
Muhly, James D. 247 n.51
Mundhenk, Norman A. 15 n.9
Muñoa, Phillip 121 n.20
Muraoka, T. 122 n.27, 125 n.47

Na'aman, Nadav 45 nn.61, 62
Naveh, Joseph 132 n.88, 172 n.57, 221 n.33
Neumann, Kiersten 246-7, 247 n.50
Nielsen, Harald 134 n.105

Nielsen, Kirsten 15 n.12, 16
Nielsen, Kjeld 132 n.87
Nihan, Christophe 105 n.5, 162 nn.11, 12, 14, 165 nn.24, 28, 171 n.53, 195 n.39, 202 n.15, 203 n.16
Nissinen, Martti 13-14, 13 n.2, 26 n.62
Noth, Martin 61 n.36, 74 n.11, 193 n.29, 195 n.39, 221 n.33
Nriagu, Jerome O. 247 n.52
Núñez, Rafael E. 151 n.57

Oettinger, Norbert 23 n.52
Ogden, Jack 238 n.8
Olmo Lete, Gregorio, del 215 n.10, 219 n.23
Olyan, Saul M. 2 n.4, 3 n.4, 30 n.2, 40 n.39, 80-1, 81 n.42, 109 n.13, 141 n.9, 144 n.26
Oppenheim, A. Leo 21 n.41, 164 n.21, 172 n.58, 218 n.20, 239 n.9
Ornan, Tallay 239 n.9
Orwell, George 166, 166 n.30
Otto, Eckart 142 n.15

Pakkala, Juha 30 n.2
Papayannopoulos, I. 117 n.1, 133 n.95
Pardee, Dennis 183 n.1, 222 n.36, 223 n.39, 230 n.56
Park, Song-Mi Suzie 35 n.22, 42 n.52, 43 n.55, 44 n.57
Park, Sung Jin 40 n.39
Parpola, Simo 21 n.41, 32 n.11, 44 n.59, 214 n.4, 215 nn.5, 6
Patai, Raphael 40 n.39, 42 n.48
Peritz, Ismar J. 54 n.6
Perrin, Andrew B. 118 n.4, 121 n.19
Petersen, David L. 90 n.2, 96 n.25, 96 n.27, 97 n.31, 98 nn.34, 35, 100 n.43, 101 n.45
Pietsche, Michael 73 n.9
Pigott, Vincent C. 247 n.51
Pippin, Tina 44 n.57
Pittman, Holly 165 n.25, 165 n.26
Pola, Thomas 89 n.1
Polinger, Karen 180, 180 nn.79, 82
Pongratz-Leisten, Beate 240 n.19
Porada, Edith 167 n.34
Post, Paul 2 n.2
Postgate, Nicholas 122 n.25, 238 n.5
Powis Smith, J.M. 96 n.27
Prag, Kay 247 n.53
Preisendanz, Karl 127 n.57
Press, Richard 77 n.19
Pressler, Carolyn 15 n.11
Propp, William H.C. 56 n.20, 60 nn.33, 34, 61, 61 n.37, 65 n.52, 139 n.1, 143, 143 n.19,

162 n.12, 174 nn.62, 64, 186 n.7, 245–6, 246 nn.45, 49

Quick, Laura 5, 24 n.53, 26 n.63, 31 n.8, 82 n.42, 83 n.46
Quine, Cat 4, 29 n.1, 35 n.21, 39 n.35, 44 n.60, 47 n.71, 48 n.74, 78 n.28

Rabenau, Marten 120 n.13
Rabin, Ira 118 n.6
Rad, Gerhard, von 59 n.30
Radner, Karen 167 n.33
Raff, Thomas 239 n.8
Rahlfs, Alfred 120 n.18, 122 n.27, 123 n.34, 129 n.68
Rainey, Anson F. 176 n.69
Ramos, Melissa 3 n.4, 9, 24 n.53, 213 n.2, 222 n.35, 228 nn.52, 53, 231 n.59
Rappaport, Roy 91 n.6
Ratner, Robert 61 n.38
Reich, Ronny 170 n.48
Reiner, Erica 243 nn.35, 36
Reiter, Karin 247 n.52
Rendsburg, Gary A. 114 n.26, 189 n.19
Rhyder, Julia 162 nn.11, 13, 14, 165 n.28
Rofé, Alexander 153 n.70
Röllig, Wolfgang 220 n.30
Rollston, Christopher A. 169 n.45
Römer, Thomas C. 30 n.5, 74 n.11
Rosner, Fred 133 n.97
Roth, Martha T. 24 n.54, 218 n.18
Rothenberg, Beno 245 n.41, 247 n.54
Rothenbuhler, Eric W. 91 n.6
Ruane, Nicole J. 4–5
Ruwe, Andreas 203 n.15

Samuel, Harald 203 n.16, 204 n.20
Saley, Richard J. 222 n.36
Sanders, Seth 149 n.47
Sanmartín, Joaquín 216 n.10, 219 n.23
Sarna, Nahum M. 19 n.33, 61 n.39, 63 n.44, 139 n.1, 150, 150 n.53, 151 n.61
Sass, Benjamin 169 n.44, 170 n.50
Sasson, Jack M. 16 n.17, 17 n.19, 60 n.31, 64 n.50, 65 n.52
Schearing, K. S. 35 n.22, 37 n.30
Schenkel, Wolfgang 242 n.29
Schipper, Jeremy 16 n.14
Schmidt, Brian 105 n.5, 108 n.12, 109 n.13, 111 nn.16, 19
Schmitt, Rüdiger 107 n.9
Schniedewind, William M. 170 n.48, 172 n.57, 221 n.34

Schorch, Stefan 64 n.51
Schwartz, Baruch J. 2 n.4
Schwemer, Daniel 81 nn.39, 41
Scurlock, JoAnn 126 n.49, 132 n.89
Searle, John 151 n.62
Seeman, Don 44 n.57
Sefati, Yitschak 21, 21 n.38
Sergi, Omer 35 n.22
Seybold, Klaus 89 n.1
Shafer-Ellior, Cynthia 79 n.30
Shaked, Shaul 132 n.88
Sharifi, Amir 171 n.54
Sharp, Carolyn K. 14, 14 nn.5, 6, 15, 15 n.10, 27, 27 n.67
Shukron, Eli 170 n.48
Silverman, Jason M. 90, 90 n.4
Singer, Karl H. 239 n.8
Ska, Jean-Louis 140 n.6, 144 n.28
Skemp, Vincent T.M. 119 n.13
Slanski, Kathryn 227, 227 nn.46, 47, 229, 229 n.54
Smelik, Karen 104, 104 n.1
Smith, Andrew C. 30 n.2
Smith, Joanna S. 167 nn.32, 33, 168 n.43
Smith, Mark 22, 22 n.45
Smith, Mark S. 23 n.48, 25 n.56, 77 n.24, 115 n.28, 186 n.7, 189 n.18
Smith, W. Robertson 55, 55 nn.10, 11, 56 n.18, 57, 57 n.22, 77 n.19
Smoak, Jeremy D. 9, 163 n.19, 164 n.20, 177, 177 n.72, 178, 178 nn.74, 75, 76, 179, 227 n.48, 234, 234 n.63, 238 nn.3, 4, 248 n.56, 250 nn.62, 63, 251 n.66
Smolar, Leivy 73 n.4
Soden, Wolfram, von 117 n.1, 121 n.23, 133 n.95, 134 n.99
Soggin, J. Alberto 214 n.3, 216 n.11, 218, 218 n.19
Soler, Jean 62 n.43
Sommers, Benjamin D. 13 n.1, 141 n.9
Sonia, Kerry M. 6–7, 107 n.11
Souza, M. A. Torres de 180 n.81
Speiser, Ephraim 19 n.32
Spitzmüller, Jürgen 166 n.29
Stackert, Jeffrey 2 n.4, 142 n.12, 144 nn.26, 27, 188 n.12
Staubli, Thomas 91 n.7
Stavrakopoulou, Francesca 13–14, 13 n.2, 14 n.4, 19 n.30, 26 n.62, 76 n.15
Stavrianopoulou, Eftychia 90 n.6
Stead, Michael R. 97 n.30, 101 n.45
Stern, Ephraim 172 n.60
Stevenson, Jill 150 n.54, 151, 151 n.60
Stokes, Ryan 95 n.23

Stökl, Jonathan 200 n.4, 210, 210 n.40
Stol, Marten 20 n.35, 21 nn.38, 41, 23 n.52, 56 n.18
Stolz, Fritz 244 n.38
Stos-Gale, Zofia A. 239 n.8
Stott, Katherine M. 45 n.61, 73 n.10
Strauss, Rita 243 n.34
Stuckenbruck, Loren T. 119 nn.7, 8, 120, 120 nn.16, 18, 122 n.26, 128 n.65, 136, 136 nn.110, 111
Sturdy, John 201 n.9
Sütterlin, Christa 19 n.28
Svärd, Saana 38 n.35
Sweeney, Marvin A. 33 n.13, 41 n.46, 43 n.56
Sweetser, Eve 146, 146 n.33, 151, 151 n.59, 152 n.63
Swete, H. B. 121 n.18, 123 n.34

Tadmor, Hayim 74 n.13
Taggar-Cohen, Ada 215 n.7
Tammuz, Oded 140 n.7, 154, 154 n.74
Tawil, Hayim 17 n.21
Taylor, Joan E. 13 n.1
Teissier, Beatrice 167 n.35, 168 n.39
Teixidor, J. 222 n.36
Thavapalan, Shiyanthi 242, 242 nn.26, 27, 28, 243
Tidwell, N. L. A. 90 n.2, 98 n.34
Tiemeyer, Lena-Sofia 96 n.29, 97 n.30, 98 n.35, 99 nn.36, 37, 38, 101 nn.44, 45, 102 n.46
Tigay, Jeffrey 162 n.12, 165 nn.24, 27, 174 n.62
Toorn, Karel, van der 111 n.16, 113 n.23
Touwaide, Alian 130 n.76
Trevaskis, Leigh M. 3 n.6
Trible, Phyllis 24 n.55
Tropper, Josef 105 n.6, 111 n.17
Trumbull, H. Clay 213 n.1
Turner, Mark 150 n.55, 151 nn.58, 59
Turner, Victor 2 n.3, 57, 57 n.21

Uehlinger, Christoph 170 n.49
Unseth, Peter 166 n.29

Van Der Toorn, Karel 153 nn.68, 70
Van Hecke, Pierre 80 n.33
Van Straten, F. T. 69 n.60
Vanderhooft, David S. 170 n.47, 171 n.52
Vanderkam, James C. 99 n.37, 102 nn.46, 47
Vaughn, Andrew G. 170 n.45, 237 nn.2, 3
Vaux, Roland, de 82 n.44, 131 n.78

Veenhof, Klaas R. 238 n.8
Virolleaud, Charles 61 n.38
Waard, Jan, de 15 n.9
Wade, G. W. 113 n.23
Wagner, Andreas 13 n.1
Wagner, Christian J. 120 n.18
Walker, Christopher 241 nn.21, 22
Waldman, Marilyn Robinson 42 n.50
Warren, Meredith J. C. 79–80, 79 nn.30, 31, 32, 83, 84
Watanabe, Kazuko 21 n.41, 214 n.4, 215 nn.5, 6
Waters, Jaime L. 3 n.4
Watson, Paul L. 78 n.25
Watson, W. G. E. 216 n.10, 219 n.23
Watts, James W. 3 n.6, 29 n.2, 48 n.74, 161 n.10, 184, 184 n.2
Weeks, Stuart 119 nn.7, 8, 13, 120, 120 nn.15, 16, 18, 122 n.26, 124 n.39, 128 n.65, 136 n.111
Wegner, Judith 163 n.17, 167 nn.33, 36
Weippert, Helga 31 n.5
Wellhausen, Julius 199, 199 n.2
Welton, Rebekah 79 n.30, 80, 80 n.34, 81 n.38
Wenham, Gordon J. 206 n.24
Wetter, Anne-Mareike 25 n.57
Wilhelm, Gernot 217 n.17
Williams, Michael A. 44 n.60
Willi-Plein, Ina 96 n.28
Winderbaum, Ariel 170 n.49
Winter, Irene 239 n.9, 240, 240 n.19, 242–3, 242 n.30, 243 n.31
Winton Thomas, Dale 99 n.37
Wiseman, Donald J. 219 nn.24, 25
Wolde, Ellen, van 246 n.47
Wolff, Hans Walter 140, 140 n.5
Wolters, Albert M. 95 n.20, 96 n.28, 97 n.30, 33, 98 n.34, 100 n.42
Wright, David P. 2 n.4, 29 n.1, 49 n.76, 78 n.27, 92 n.13, 192 nn.24, 27
Wright, Jacob L. 2 n.4

Xeravits, Géza G. 119 n.13, 121 n.20

Yadin, Yigael 176 n.69, 178
Yardeni, Ada 238 n.3
Yona, Shamir 76 n.18

Zahn, Molly M. 142 n.17, 206 n.25
Zannoni, Arthur E. 185 n.5
Zenger, Erich 30 n.2

Zevit, Ziony 73 n.5, 106 n.8
Zhakevich, Phillip 170 n.45
Ziegler, Yael 18 n.26, 19 n.32
Zsengellér, József 119 n.13

Zuckerman, Bruce 61 n.38, 237 nn.2, 3
Zuckerman, Kenneth 237 n.2
Zwickel, Wolgang 159 n.2, 160 n.4, 162 n.14, 171 n.53, 172 n.55

www.ingramcontent.com/pod-product-compliance
Lightning Source LLC
Chambersburg PA
CBHW052216300426
44115CB00011B/1710